HOW TO EVALUATE AND NEGOTIATE GOVERNMENT CONTRACTS

HOW TO EVALUATE AND NEGOTIATE GOVERNMENT CONTRACTS

Peter S. Cole, CPCM

MANAGEMENTCONCEPTS
Vienna, Virginia

Management Concepts, Inc.
8230 Leesburg Pike, Suite 800
Vienna, Virginia 22182
Phone: (703) 790-9595
Fax: (703) 790-1371
Web: www.managementconcepts.com

Printed in the United States of America

Library of Congress Cataloging-in-Publication Data

Cole, Peter S.
How to evaluate and negotiate government contracts / Peter S. Cole.
p. cm.
Includes bibliographical references and index.
IBSN 1-56726-094-2
1. Public contracts—United States. 2. Government purchasing—United States. 3. Letting of contracts—United States—Decision making. 4. Proposal writing in public contracting—United States. 5. Negotiation in business—United States. 6. Government purchasing—Law and legislation—United States. 7. United States. General Services Administration. FAR Secretariat. Federal acquisition regulation. I. Title.

HD3861.U6 C65 2000
658.7'23—dc21

00-045071

About the Author

Peter S. Cole has more than 34 years of experience in the field of acquisition and contracts management. During his military service he spent 4½ years as a contracting officer in the Navy laboratory system; 4 years teaching basic and advanced procurement at ALMC, Fort Lee; and 4 years at the headquarters staff level working on procurement policy matters. Since his retirement from the Navy in 1979, Mr. Cole has researched and developed textbooks and presented training programs in cost-plus-award fee contracting, competitive negotiation, implementation of OMB Circular A-76, FAR implementation, and contract management for technical personnel (COTR training). He has provided consulting services to both government and commercial clients and has written 15 manuals and handbooks for individual government agencies, including the Departments of Agriculture, Interior, Labor, and Treasury, and the Central Intelligence Agency. Mr. Cole's most recent book on contracting is *Technical Evaluations,* also published by Management Concepts, Inc.

Mr. Cole is currently a sole proprietorship in the state of Maryland, providing consulting and training services in the area of government contracting for government and commercial clients.

Table of Contents

Preface

The evaluation, negotiation, and award of government contracts is often considered to be a complicated process, made more so by the Federal Acquisition Regulation (FAR) 15 rewrite, which deliberately left a number of areas only loosely defined "to give the contracting officer more flexibility." What this did, in effect, was leave the definition of these areas up to the Comptroller General and the U.S. Court of Federal Claims as they decide protests related to how contracting officers exercise their "flexibility." Unfortunately, such definitions will take years to complete. So what to do?

This book addresses the process of evaluating, negotiating, and awarding government contracts after the FAR 15 rewrite using a generic approach that suggests ways to avoid problems in those ill-defined areas and still "get the job done." It provides both technical and contracting personnel with a detailed examination of how the process works and what "rules" are to be followed. The purpose of this book is to assist both government and contractor personnel in the successful execution of the evaluation, negotiation, and award process.

The specific procedures for the procurement process vary from agency to agency. Therefore, this book uses a generic approach. The process is addressed from the standpoint of a single individual rather than a team being responsible for the various activities to stress the fact that each person involved in a procurement should be knowledgeable of the entire process in order to do his or her job properly. Readers will note some redundancy in coverage as points are repeated in the context of the particular chapters. This redundancy is intended to reinforce important points and to provide continuity in the subject matter.

WHAT THIS BOOK OFFERS

This book offers both government and contractor personnel guidance in the evaluation, negotiation, and award process.

For Government Personnel

This book addresses each step in the evaluation, negotiation, and award process and suggests what to do, and not do, to conduct an effective and efficient procurement successfully. It specifically addresses the FAR 15 rewrite changes and how to cope with those areas not fully defined. While primarily addressing competitive procurements, it also covers certain related aspects of the negotiation of sole source procurements and procurements using the simplified acquisition process.

Technical personnel (as opposed to contracting personnel) are responsible for significant portions of the competitive procurement process. In addition to developing the statement of work (SOW), they are responsible for developing the evaluation criteria and conducting the technical evaluations. One of the problems in the government procurement process is that the involvement of individual technical personnel is often sporadic and these individuals do not get involved often enough to know all of the necessary details. It is incumbent, therefore, on the contracting personnel to know these details so they may appropriately oversee those areas for which the technical personnel are responsible and provide the proper advice and training to ensure an effective and efficient procurement.

If you want to conduct an efficient and effective procurement, your first goal should be to keep it simple. You must minimize the number of evaluation factors, define the factors and their relative importance clearly, and relate them to the requirements of the SOW. A scoring plan and evaluation process should be established that is easy to understand and apply. A competitive range that maximizes competition within the concept of "the most highly rated proposals" should also be established, and you should ensure that the discussions address all of an offeror's deficiencies and significant weaknesses. Above all, you must document all actions taken and why. Strict adherence to documentation requirements will significantly enhance your ability to get the job done right. The evaluation and negotiation process is no more difficult than you make it.

For Contractor Personnel

This book is also useful for those contractor personnel who develop proposals and negotiate government contracts. Primarily, it shows contractor personnel what the government personnel are supposed to do and why. This provides important insights into how best to respond to government solicitations. Knowing how the government will evaluate a proposal, develop the competitive range, and conduct negotiations gives a contractor an advantage over its competitors who may not be as knowledgeable on government procedures.

As a contractor, if you want to compete effectively you need to know how to respond to government solicitations. One of the more common problems is a failure to provide sufficient detail in proposals. You must respond to all RFP requirements and provide all of the information requested. You must check the evaluation factors in Section M of the RFP and the proposal preparation instructions in Section L and match them to the SOW requirements. If something is not clear, you should ask the contracting officer for clarification. Keep in mind that you must ask such questions before the time set for the receipt of proposals.

Other common problems are the failure to adequately respond to discussion questions regarding deficiencies and significant weaknesses, and the introduction of new information (staffing changes, changes in methodology or techniques, pricing changes, etc.) in the final proposal revision without sufficient supporting information to account for the validity of the change.

This book addresses these issues and, although directed at government personnel, it should not be difficult to translate this information into actions to be taken when writing proposals and negotiating for a government contract (and developing grounds for a protest if need be).

In addition, this book provides numerous examples, citing excerpts from Comptroller General procurement decisions, to address the procurement issues being discussed. These examples provide invaluable information on what contractors should or should not do when submitting proposals in the competitive environment.

ADVICE FROM THE COMPTROLLER GENERAL

The "rules" governing the evaluation, negotiation, and award of government contracts are based on laws and regulations largely derived from procurement decisions rendered by the Comptroller General. The Comptroller General has, for years, reviewed protests and ruled on the propriety of government actions during the preaward procurement process. Comptroller General decisions, in effect, constitute rules that government personnel would be well advised to follow. Unfortunately, there is often a considerable time lag between Comptroller General decisions and their implementation in procurement regulations. This leads to a repetition of similar problems, until finally either the regulations are changed or the word gets around about the problem and it is fixed locally. This book relies extensively on excerpts from Comptroller General decisions to provide examples of problems in the evaluation, negotiation, and award process and how to avoid them.

Government and contractor personnel would be well advised to read these decisions closely. These excerpts provide insight into how the Comptroller General looks at the procurement process and resolves problems. They also show how the Comptroller General treats precedents. This is important because, while the Comptroller General will change its position when warranted, most decisions rest on decisions made in the past. For the next few years, the Comptroller General will be writing the rules with respect to the implementation of the FAR 15 rewrite. Government and contractor personnel involved in the government procurement process should review current Comptroller General decisions closely to see what the rules will be (these decisions are available on the Internet at several locations).

Those who wish to research the full text of the decisions referenced in this book should note the following information:

- Decisions referenced as "65 Comp. Gen. 510 (1986)" refer to *Decisions of the Comptroller General of the United States,* volume number 65, page number 510, rendered in the year 1986.
- Decisions referenced as "86-1 CPD ¶398" refer to *Comptroller General's Procurement Decisions* (CPD) published by Federal Publications; 86-1 indicates the year and volume number and ¶398 is the case number. The more recent references will also indicate page numbers.
- Decisions referenced as "GCR 107,849" refer to *Government Contracts Reporter* published by the Commerce Clearing House (CCH); and 107,849 is the applicable paragraph number.

AVOIDING PROTESTS

Protests are losing propositions for the government. Regardless of the final results, much time is spent analyzing the protest and developing a rebuttal, and the award may be delayed or performance suspended while the protest is pending. If the protest is sustained because of government error, the problem must be corrected and everything done all over again. In addition, the government may have to pay the successful protester's costs of filing and pursuing its protest, including attorney's fees.

The best way to avoid protests is to know how to properly conduct and document the evaluation, negotiation, and award process, to ensure that it is done properly, and then to provide debriefings to unsuccessful offerors that demonstrate that the process was conducted fairly. Following this procedure will not eliminate protests, but it will minimize their occurrence.

Technical personnel often complain that after spending a lot of time evaluating proposals and developing an award recommendation, their recommendation is ignored and award is made to the lowest priced offeror. When this happens, the underlying problem is often simply a lack of documentation to adequately support the evaluators' recommendations. If evaluators do not provide contracting officers with sufficiently documented support for award to other than the lowest priced offeror, the contracting officers may feel that they have no other choice but to award on the basis of the lowest price. Contracting officers do have other choices. This book explains what they are.

Protests are also often losing propositions for the protesters. Submitting a protest is expensive in time and effort and usually involves significant legal expenses, particularly if the issues are complicated. The odds that a protest will be sustained are not good; the majority of protests are decided in the government's favor. The primary reason for this appears to be a lack of understanding of how the procurement process works on the part of contractor management. This book addresses the issues leading to contractor protests, provides suggestions that will help contractor management decide whether to protest, and cites examples of both successful and unsuccessful protests.

CONSULT AGENCY PROCEDURES

Government readers are cautioned to become familiar with their own agency's procedures. Guidance in this book may differ from a particular agency's regulations or procedures. This is not unusual; there are many ways to get the job done in government procurement. This book addresses how the evaluation, negotiation, and award process can be conducted. It identifies problems and offers solutions but does not purport to be the final word. With respect to the details, *be sure to follow your agency regulations and procedures.*

Peter S. Cole, CPCM
October 2000

CHAPTER 1

Developing an Evaluation Plan

Evaluation plans may be developed as part of the source selection plan or as a separate document. In either case, the purpose and elements of the evaluation plan are the same. This book treats the evaluation plan as a separate document.

OVERVIEW OF THE EVALUATION, NEGOTIATION, AND AWARD PROCESS

Before getting into the details of the evaluation, negotiation, and award process, it would be beneficial to get a broad overview of how the overall process fits together. The process begins before submission of the procurement request (PR) package to the contracting officer and continues through contract award and the debriefing of unsuccessful offerors. It includes the:

- Evaluation process
- Negotiation process
- Award process.

The Evaluation Process

The evaluation process involves: (1) development of the evaluation plan, (2) initial evaluation, and (3) final evaluation.

Development of the Evaluation Plan

The development of an evaluation plan (generally not applicable for a sole source procurement) initiates the evaluation process. Development of the evaluation plan usually follows completion of the statement of work (SOW) and sufficient market research to establish the probability of competition. The evaluation plan identifies the evaluation factors and their relative importance, a scoring plan, the proposal preparation instructions, and a description of how the evaluation process will be conducted. The contracting officer receives the evaluation plan as part of the PR package and uses it to develop the request for proposals (RFP).

Initial Evaluation

The initial evaluation begins after issuance of the RFP and receipt of offerors' proposals. All proposals received on time must receive an initial evaluation. The initial evaluation is based on the information provided in the proposals, which are evaluated using the evaluation factors set forth in the RFP. Exchanges may occur between the contracting officer and individual offerors during the initial evaluation, but these are limited as to content and cannot be used to revise an offeror's proposal. The initial evaluation establishes which proposals will be included in the competitive range and which will be eliminated from the competition. The initial evaluation ends with the establishment of the competitive range (unless it is determined to make the award without conducting discussions, in which case the negotiation process is aborted and the award process gets under way). The competitive range is limited to the most highly rated proposals, and discussions are conducted with only those offerors in the competitive range.

Final Evaluation

After completion of discussions and receipt of the final proposal revisions, a final evaluation determines the otherwise successful offeror. This evaluation is based on the evaluation factors set forth in the solicitation and applied to the offeror's initial proposal as revised in its final proposal revision. Depending on its complexity, this evaluation is conducted by all or only some of the same evaluators who conducted the initial evaluation. The final evaluation ends when the final evaluation results and award recommendations (when requested) are submitted to the source selection official who will make the source selection decision. The source selection official (or source selection authority—SSA) is generally the contracting officer, but may be some other official if specifically designated.

The Negotiation (Discussions) Process

The negotiation (discussions) process begins after the initial evaluation and establishment of the competitive range. Discussions are conducted with each offeror in the competitive range based on the information developed in the initial evaluation. The purpose of the discussions is to advise offerors of any problems (deficiencies, weaknesses, excesses, etc.) with their proposals and afford them an opportunity to revise their proposals and improve their chances for award. An offeror may be rejected from the competitive range if the discussions reveal that its proposal is no longer in contention for award. Once the discussions are completed, all offerors still in the competitive range are requested to submit their final proposal revisions by a common date. Generally, this marks the end of the negotiation process; however, negotiations may be reopened under certain circumstances.

The Award Process

The award process begins after completion of the final evaluation and submission of the evaluation results and award recommendations to the source selection official. The source selection official is generally the contracting officer, but another individual may be assigned these responsibilities by an agency head or designee (usually only for major acquisitions). The award process consists of two different activities:

1. In the *source selection decision,* the source selection official examines the results of the final evaluation and the evaluators' award recommendations, makes any necessary tradeoffs to determine the best value, and inde-

pendently makes the decision as to which offeror will receive the award. Once the source selection official makes the award decision, the unsuccessful offerors are notified of the award decision and afforded an opportunity to request a debriefing.

2. The *debriefing of unsuccessful offerors* is the final step in the evaluation, negotiation, and award process. The contracting officer conducts debriefings based on information developed during the evaluation process as to why the offeror was not successful. Debriefings are conducted only upon specific request by an unsuccessful offeror.

EVALUATION PRINCIPLES

Development of a sound evaluation plan is predicated on the following principles:

- *Knowledge*—To formulate an intelligent and responsive proposal, offerors must know how proposals will be evaluated.
- *Equality*—Offerors must compete on an equal basis. Consequently, evaluation factors must be equally applicable, and equally applied, to all offerors.
- *Consistency*—The application of evaluation factors must be consistent. Do not make any changes in the factors or their relative importance unless the changes made are applicable to all offerors' proposals and all offerors are afforded an opportunity to revise their proposals accordingly.
- *Method*—Those parts of the evaluation plan that are published in the RFP must describe how each offeror's proposal is to be evaluated and, through the proposal preparation instructions, what information is to be provided.

The evaluation plan is normally developed as a part of the PR package. The PR package consists of those documents that agency procedures require to be presented to the contracting officer before a procurement action can be initiated.

Early development of the evaluation plan is necessary because certain parts of the plan must be published in the RFP. This helps to ensure that all prospective offerors are fully and equally informed as to how their proposals will be evaluated. In addition, early development of the complete evaluation plan, before any sources are solicited and proposals received, helps avoid allegations that the evaluation plan was structured to favor a particular offeror.

CONTENTS OF THE EVALUATION PLAN

The evaluation plan consists of the following:

- The evaluation factors and significant subfactors (see Chapters 2–4)
- An expression of the relative importance of each published evaluation factor and subfactor (see Chapter 5)
- A scoring plan (see Chapter 6)
- The proposal preparation instructions (see Chapter 7).

The evaluation factors and subfactors, their relative importance, and the proposal preparation instructions are published in the RFP. Once published, *they cannot be changed,* except by issuance of a formal amendment to the solicitation. This measure ensures an equitable evaluation and avoids the appearance that the agency engineered the evaluation to favor a particular offeror or group of offerors.

The scoring plan, evaluation organization and procedures, and the source selection plan are not published in the RFP and may be changed, but only if the changes are reasonable and result in rational evaluation results. These parts of the evaluation plan are internal agency instructions. As such, they do not give outside parties any legal rights as to how they are developed or used, as the Comptroller General notes in Example 1.1.

Example 1.1—Internal agency instructions do not give rights to outside parties[1]

Preliminarily, we note that to the extent LSI argues that the Navy failed to follow the source selection plan, its argument ignores the distinction between an evaluation scheme included in the RFP, and a source selection plan provided to evaluators as a guideline. As between these two documents, it is the RFP—and the evaluation scheme set forth therein—that forms the compact between the agency and the offerors about how proposals will be evaluated.[2] Source selection plans are internal agency instructions and do not give rights to outside parties.[3]

Making changes, however, is not recommended, particularly after the receipt of proposals. Changes can cause confusion and may generate a protest. Even if you win the protest, you will have needlessly expended a significant amount of time and energy. *A workable evaluation plan should be developed and followed. You should not make any changes unless the changes are necessary to ensure that the evaluation is fair and equitable to all parties.*

EVALUATION METHODS

The Federal Acquisition Regulations (FAR) recognizes two different acquisition strategies: (1) best value with tradeoffs, and (2) lowest priced technically acceptable offer. Each strategy requires a different evaluation approach.

Best Value

Best value is the most commonly used approach. While the term *best value* is relatively new, the concept of awarding a contract to the offeror providing the best overall value, price and other factors considered, has been around for some time. The best value approach is appropriate whenever the requirement is not fully defined, development work is required, there is performance risk, or the technical quality or past performance considerations may be more important than the cost or price. The best value approach uses comparative assessments and tradeoffs and permits award to other than the lowest price or other than the highest technically ranked proposal, when appropriate.

Comparative Assessments

Best value procurements are evaluated using comparative assessments. In this method, the evaluation factors and significant subfactors are weighted according to their relative worth with respect to accomplishing the requirement. The proposals are evaluated and scored in accordance with the weighted evaluation factors and ranked in order of their comparative value. This facilitates the assessment of the strengths and weaknesses of the competing proposals and the making of tradeoffs to determine the successful offeror.

Tradeoffs

Once the comparative assessment has been performed, tradeoffs between cost or price and noncost evaluation factors (e.g., technical excellence, management capability, personnel qualifications, corporate experience, past performance, and compliance with solicitation requirements) can be done to determine which proposal provides the best value to the government.

Lowest Priced, Technically Acceptable Offer

This approach is most appropriate for requirements in which there is little or no performance risk and no need for quality beyond satisfactory performance. The government uses this approach for acquisitions that might otherwise be procured by sealed bidding, except for the need to evaluate and perhaps negotiate noncost factors to determine which proposals are technically acceptable. This approach is evaluated using a pass/fail assessment.

To conduct a pass/fail (or go/no-go) assessment, you must first establish minimum acceptability standards in the solicitation. Proposals are evaluated against these minimum standards. The pass/fail assessment does not consider the relative worth of individual proposals; a proposal is evaluated and determined to be either acceptable or unacceptable. An unacceptable proposal—one that does not meet the minimum standards—is rejected immediately. Award is then made to the acceptable proposal offering the lowest price.

Two-step procurements, in which the technical proposals are received and evaluated before the submission of any pricing information, also use this evaluation technique. Those offerors found to have acceptable technical proposals (first step) are then asked to submit a pricing proposal (second step), and award is made to the lowest priced offer.

Combination Assessments

Some agencies use a combination assessment in best value procurements. In this assessment, some evaluation factors are subject to a comparative assessment and others are subject to a pass/fail assessment. This can cause problems, because a failure to meet the cited pass/fail requirements means that the entire proposal must be rejected. A failure to meet a pass/fail standard indicates an uncorrectable deficiency, and an award cannot be made to a deficient offeror.

You do not want to create a situation in which an offeror has met all the requirements except one that is a pass/fail requirement. The Comptroller General may not agree to a proposal rejection under such circumstances. In past cases, the Comptroller General has criticized a strict application of pass/fail evaluation criteria that led to the automatic and final exclusion of a potentially acceptable proposal. These cases have generally involved offerors that have demonstrated compliance with all but one of a number of mandatory requirements and were eliminated from the competition solely for that reason.[4]

If you must use a combination assessment, you must clearly identify those factors subject to a comparative assessment and those subject to pass/fail. Pass/fail criteria should be such that they cannot be corrected through discussions and that a failure clearly demonstrates the entire proposal is unacceptable.

List pass/fail factors separately, with a warning that they will be evaluated first and that offerors must demonstrate that they meet the pass/fail factors to be considered further. Then list those factors subject to comparative assessment, in a descending order of importance, with a description of each factor's relative importance.

Avoid using an evaluation factor as both a pass/fail and a comparative assessment factor as this can confuse offerors. If this cannot be avoided, however, ensure that the RFP indicates that you will first evaluate the pass/fail criteria and that, if passed, it will then be included in the comparative assessment along with the other factors (this happens when an agency wants to first identify the technically acceptable proposals and then rank them by a comparative assessment). In such instances, offerors should be reminded that any factor that fails the pass/fail assessment will cause the entire proposal to be rejected.

When you use a combination assessment, you must ensure that the RFP clearly describes how the factors will be evaluated, and then you should conduct the evaluation as described.

Example 1.2 illustrates the problems that can result if you do not follow these guidelines.

Example 1.2—Using a combination assessment[5]

An agency indicated in the RFP that the combined weight of the technical factors was more important than cost or price and listed the evaluation factors in a descending order of importance. Qualification of Key Personnel (Factor 1) was listed first, making it the most important of the four evaluation factors. The RFP also stated that Factor 1 would be evaluated on a go/no-go basis: if an offeror failed to demonstrate that it had five years of experience, its proposal would be rejected.

The agency evaluated the qualifications of key personnel on a pass/fail basis and calculated each offeror's total technical score by point scoring the other technical factors. The agency did not point score the key personnel factor. It then compared the total technical evaluation score against price in the cost/technical tradeoff and source selection.

An unsuccessful offeror protested that the evaluation was not done properly, and the Comptroller General agreed.

We find, as described below, that the only reasonable reading of the award selection criteria is that the qualifications of key personnel would first be evaluated on a go/no-go basis to determine which offerors would receive further consideration in the agency's technical evaluation. Those offerors that satisfied the go/no-go evaluation requirement would then be evaluated under the stated evaluation factors, listed in descending order of importance, that identified qualifications of key personnel as the most important evaluation criterion.

The RFP provided that the "combined" weight of the technical evaluation factors was more important than price and set forth the technical evaluation factors in descending order of importance, with key personnel qualifications identified as the most important factor. By listing evaluation factors in descending order of importance, the RFP contemplated a comparative technical evaluation balanced against price to determine the most advantageous proposal. In performing this cost/technical tradeoff, the total weight of all technical factors (of which key personnel was identified as most important) is more important than price.

Here, GSA calculated the offerors' total technical score by only point scoring the three lowest rated technical evaluation factors, and comparing that evaluation score against price in its cost/technical tradeoff and award selection. Since the key personnel qualifications factor was not qualitatively evaluated or point-scored, it was not considered in the cost/technical tradeoff and award selection. In other words, this factor effectively had no evaluation weight even though it was said to be the most important evaluation factor.[6] *That is, if the key personnel qualifications factor was only to be evaluated on a go/no-go basis, as GSA argues is provided by the RFP, then this factor cannot be more important than the remaining three factors that were numerically scored and compared to price. In our view, the only interpretation that gives effect to all the RFP provisions is that key personnel qualifications would be evaluated both objectively as a pass/fail mandatory solicitation requirement and qualitatively as a listed evaluation criterion.*

Example 1.2 shows how easy it is to get confused when you try to use a combination assessment. The example also demonstrates the importance of making an early determination as to how you will do the evaluation, the need to accurately describe what you are going to do in the RFP, and the requirement to then do what you said you would do.

The agency lost this protest because it failed to evaluate the proposals in accordance with the stated evaluation scheme. You may not publish one evaluation scheme, such as an award on the basis of a comparative assessment, and then use another scheme, such as award to the lowest priced, technically acceptable proposal.

Evaluation schemes may be changed by an amendment to the solicitation, but if not changed, the published evaluation scheme must be followed. Failure to pay attention at this point can lead to problems, as shown in Examples 1.3 and 1.4.

Example 1.3—Ensure that evaluation procedures used are consistent with published procedures[7]

An RFP stated that the technical factor scores would be considered more important than price and listed four evaluation factors, some of which were to be evaluated on a pass/fail basis, and the others on a comparative assessment basis.

The source selection plan (SSP) instructed the evaluators to use a color rating scheme. Green was to be assigned if the proposal met or exceeded requirements, amber if the proposal might meet requirements, and red if the proposal did not meet requirements. After assignment of the color ratings, the ratings were to be converted to numerical scores. Green received 100 points, amber received 30 points, and red received 0 points.

After evaluating the best and final offers (BAFO), the contracting officer found all the proposals technically equal. Awards were made to the three lowest priced offerors. An offeror protested the award on the grounds that the agency had abandoned the RFP evaluation scheme by using a scoring method that essentially converted a comparative evaluation scheme to one favoring the lowest-priced, technically acceptable offer. The Comptroller General sustained the protest.

...the SSP stipulated the award of a green rating for every facet of a proposal that met or exceeded the stated evaluation elements. In addition, after rating the technical elements of the proposals, the SSP prescribed the subsequent conversion of ratings to numerical scores. Since every green rating received 100 percent of all available points for that element (a perfect score), a technically superior proposal received the same score as one that was merely acceptable. Once all acceptable proposals were assigned perfect scores, as was preordained by the SSP, the contracting officer determined that the proposals must be technically equal, and made award to the three lowest cost proposals. Thus, in our view, the evaluation scheme in the RFP was converted to one resulting in selection of the low-priced, technically acceptable proposal.

... While procuring agencies must have broad discretion in determining the evaluation plan they use, they do not have the discretion to announce in the solicitation that one plan will be used, and then follow another in the actual evaluation.[8] *Once offerors are informed of the criteria against which their proposals will be evaluated, the agency must adhere to those criteria or inform all offerors of any significant changes made in the evaluation scheme.*[9]

In this example, the evaluation scheme was based on a combination of comparative assessment and pass/fail factors, but the emphasis was placed on the comparative assessment by stating that technical superiority was considered to be more important than price. The agency might have been able to successfully evaluate the proposals if not for the scoring procedures required by the source selection plan, which essentially required that every acceptable proposal be rated as perfect. The scoring procedures were clearly out of step with the evaluation scheme and once applied, improperly changed the evaluation scheme.

Example 1.4—Evaluation scheme published in RFP takes precedence over internal agency evaluation plan[10]

An agency's internal technical evaluation plan indicated that award would be made to the "lowest technically acceptable offeror." The RFP, however, stated that award would be based on a best value evaluation scheme that would consider five specified technical evaluation factors as well as price. The protest ensued when award was made to the lowest priced, technically acceptable proposal without weighing the awardee's low price against the potential benefits associated with the protester's higher-rated proposal. The Comptroller General sustained the protest.

Even though DCA reports that it always intended to select the lowest-priced technically acceptable proposal and, in fact, expressly included such an evaluation scheme in its internal (and undisclosed) technical evaluation plan, DCA was not free to disregard the RFP's stated evaluation scheme.[11]

As noted earlier, evaluation plans are internal agency instructions and as such do not give contractors any legal rights as to how they are developed or used. However, while offerors cannot successfully protest that an agency didn't follow its evaluation plan, they can, and do, successfully protest when an agency does not follow the evaluation scheme published in the RFP. In the case presented in Example 1.4, the contracting officer failed to review the RFP to ensure that the evaluation scheme published in the RFP complied with the agency's internal evaluation plan. The contracting officer compounded the mistake by choosing to award based on the internal evaluation plan rather than what was published in the RFP.

PROVIDING EVALUATION INFORMATION IN THE RFP

FAR 15.304 requires that all evaluation factors and significant subfactors and their relative importance be identified in the RFP. This includes cost or price factors, and noncost evaluation factors such as past performance, technical excellence, management capability, personnel qualifications, corporate experience, and compliance with solicitation requirements. This information must explicitly be set forth in the RFP (see Figure 1.1, the Table of Contents for an RFP).

FAR 15.204-1 requires that all solicitations and resulting contracts be prepared using the uniform contract format depicted in Figure 1.1. Although there are some exceptions, such as for construction and architect-engineer contracts, the majority of contractual actions use the uniform contract format.

The uniform contract format presents both the contract (Parts I–III) and the solicitation (Part IV) in a single document. Upon award, Part IV is physically detached. Section K is incorporated into the contract by reference. Sections L and M are not included in the contract, but are retained in the contract file.

The evaluation process is involved primarily with the proposal preparation instructions in Section L (see Chapter 7) and the evaluation factors in Section M. With the exception of Section C, which contains the SOW, most of the rest of the RFP consists of contract clauses and solicitation provisions selected by the contracting officer according to the type of contract used.

Figure 1.1 TABLE OF CONTENTS FOR AN RFP

PART I - THE SCHEDULE
A Solicitation/contract form
B Supplies or services and prices/costs
C Description/specifications/work statement
D Packaging and marking
E Inspection and acceptance
F Deliveries or performance
G Contract administration data
H Special contract requirements

PART II - CONTRACT CLAUSES
I Contract clauses

PART III - LIST OF DOCUMENTS, EXHIBITS, AND OTHER ATTACHMENTS
J List of attachments

PART IV - REPRESENTATION AND INSTRUCTIONS
K Representations, certifications, and other statements of offerors or respondents

L Instructions, conditions, and notices to offerors or respondents
M Evaluation factors for award

The purpose of Section M is to inform offerors how their proposals will be evaluated. At a minimum, Section M must identify the evaluation factors and significant subfactors and their relative importance. If the evaluation will be complicated, however, this may not be enough. For example, as noted earlier, if you are going to use a combination assessment, you must indicate that the pass/fail factors will be evaluated first. Those proposals that pass will then be evaluated by comparative assessment. If you are going to evaluate cost realism (see Chapter 4), you should explain in general terms how this will be done. If you are going to use cost as an unweighted evaluation factor (see Chapter 5), you must explain the circumstances under which cost may become the discriminating factor.

You are not, however, required to reveal every detail of your evaluation plan in Section M. For example, do not include the scoring plan in Section M. Publication of this information is of little real value to offerors and may cause enough confusion to result in a protest. You are not required to reveal the precise numerical weights to be used, but if you don't, you must otherwise indicate the relative importance of the evaluation factors and significant subfactors (see Chapter 5), as shown in Example 1.5.

Example 1.5—You must show the relative importance of evaluation factors, but not all of the details[12]

While a solicitation must advise offerors of the broad method of scoring to be employed and give reasonably definite information concerning the relative importance of the evaluation factors, the precise numerical weight and scoring method to be used need not be disclosed.

Carefully review the information to be placed in Section M to ensure that it is clearly stated. In addition, review the proposal preparation instructions to ensure that they are consistent with the information in Section M. Section M should contain all of the information about the evaluation factors and significant subfactors, their relative importance, and how the evaluation will be conducted. If the information in Section M is not consistent, problems are likely to develop. Inconsistent wording or other ambiguities can lead to unnecessary protests that will cost the government time and money to resolve. You must review your work carefully (this is discussed in more detail in Chapter 8).

The proposal preparation instructions, which are found in Section L, are also important to the evaluation. They contain instructions related to the format and contents of the proposals, such as information to be provided by the offerors in relation to each of the evaluation factors (see Chapter 7).

OTHER GENERAL REQUIREMENTS

There are other general requirements that should be considered and placed in the evaluation plan as appropriate.

Starting Time

One of the more common problems in the evaluation process is not getting the evaluation completed in an efficient and expeditious manner. To this end, the evaluation plan should indicate that the initial evaluation is to begin as soon as practicable after the date set for receipt of proposals, preferably the following day. This information should be placed in the evaluation plan to give the government personnel who will be involved in the evaluation ample planning time. It also provides the contracting officer the authority to require the individual evaluators to be present when the evaluation is scheduled to begin.

Dedicated Personnel Assignments

In addition to indicating the starting time, the evaluation plan should indicate who will conduct the evaluation. Individual evaluators need not be named, but the organizations to provide evaluators should be identified so plans can be made to provide the appropriate personnel.

Technical evaluation is most effective when the evaluation effort is assigned as primary duty for the individual evaluators. Most evaluations can be completed within a week, if pursued aggressively. Depending on the priority and complexity of the evaluation effort, evaluators may not have to be assigned to work on the evaluation full-time, but the establishment of a specific time for work on the technical evaluation, freed from all other duties, will produce the best results. Putting this in writing in the evaluation plan *with the concurrence of the components providing the evaluation personnel,* will enhance the evaluation team leader's ability to obtain the dedicated services of the evaluators, when the time comes to conduct the evaluation.

Dedicated Space for the Evaluation

To conduct an efficient and timely evaluation, evaluators need an environment conducive to the work to be performed. A specific area should be reserved for the evaluation team to conduct the evaluation. This space should be large enough for the evaluation team to work comfortably without interruption and, if possible, away from the immediate working areas of the evaluators. To the extent possible, designate the space for use only by the evaluators and limit access to the space to only those participating in the evaluation.

Because space is at a premium at most agencies, you may not be able to obtain dedicated space for the evaluation. However, you should make every effort to do so because the use of a dedicated space will enhance the efficiency of the evaluation. If dedicated space is not available at your agency, look into obtaining space at another agency or even renting space, if funds are available.

Evaluating proposals is not an easy task. It requires concentration and freedom from interruptions and the pressures of other work. This is not usually possible when the evaluator is working at his or her own desk.

Use of Outside Consultants

Outside (nongovernment) consultants may be used to assist in the evaluation if the government lacks the necessary expertise. If outside consultants are used, you must ensure that they do not have a conflict of interest with respect to the evaluation (i.e., you cannot allow them access to the proposals of their competitors). Require the consultants to sign nondisclosure statements to the effect that any information obtained during the evaluation will be used only for evaluation purposes and not released to anyone outside of the evaluation process. Allow consultants access to only those parts of the technical proposals that are pertinent to the particular consultant's specific expertise. Inform prospective offerors that nongovernment personnel will be involved in the evaluation and provide offerors the opportunity to obtain nondisclosure certifications from such individuals, if they so desire.

The use of outside consultants in the evaluation process can be controversial. This procedure should be used sparingly and only when it can be established that no qualified government resources are available.

References

1. Lear Siegler Services, Inc., B-280834; B-280834.2, 11/25/98, GCR 110,471.
2. Loral Aeronutronic, B-259857.2; B-259858.2, 7/5/95, 95-2 CPD ¶213 at 9. 3Id at 9-10.

4. The Computer Company, B-198876, 10/3/80, 80-2 CPD ¶240; Aydin Corp., B-224354, 9/8/86, 86-2 CPD ¶274.
5. Lithos Restoration, Ltd., B-247003, 4/22/92, 92-1 CPD ¶379, GCR 106,564.
6. Trijicon Inc. 71 Comp. Gen. 41 (1991), 91-2 CPD ¶375.
7. Trijicon Inc., B-244546, 10/25/91, 71 Comp. Gen. 41 (1991), 91-2 CPD ¶375, GCR 105,981. In this case a reevaluation was directed. The proposals were reevaluated, with the same award results. Trijicon protested again and the protest was again sustained, primarily because the agency substituted a legal opinion for the opinion of the technical evaluators to make sure that Trijicon did not receive the award. See Trijicon, Inc., B-244546.3, 6/22/92, 92-1 CPD ¶537, GCR 106, 724.
8. Cenci Powder Prods., Inc., B-234030, 4/17/89, 89-1 CPD ¶381, GCR 103,101.
9. Greenbaum and Rose, B-227807, 8/31/87, 87-2 CPD 212, GCR 101,059.
10. Technical Support Services, Inc., B-279665; B-279665.2, 7/8/98, GCR 110,370.
11. Trijicon Inc., B-244546, 10/25/91, 91-2 CPD ¶375 at 6-7; Hattal & Assocs., B-243357; B-243357.2, 7/25/91, 91-2 CPD ¶90 at 7.
12. Ebasco Constructors, Inc. et al., B-244406 et al., 10/16/91, 91-2 CPD 341, GCR 105,940. See also Chadwick-Helmuth Co., Inc., B-238645.2, 11/19/90, 90-2 CPD 400, GCR 104,895.

CHAPTER 2

Establishing Evaluation Factors

Evaluation factors are the criteria used for judging the relative worth or value of competing proposals. They provide the basis for measuring an offeror's ability, as expressed in its proposal, to meet the government's needs as stated in the RFP. Evaluation factors are established by analyzing the SOW to determine those aspects of the requirement most important to successfully accomplishing the project. When establishing the evaluation factors, ask yourself the following questions: (1) What are the critical areas of the SOW I need to evaluate to determine if the offeror can do the work? and (2) What information do I need from the offeror to fully evaluate its proposal?

The answers to these questions form the basis of the evaluation criteria, which are communicated to the offerors through publication in the RFP. Publication of the evaluation criteria helps offerors understand what aspects of the requirement are important to the government and how the proposals will be evaluated. Publication also benefits the government because it helps ensure that offerors will address those issues considered most important and that there will be a degree of uniformity in the content of the proposals.

SELECTING EVALUATION FACTORS

You must maintain a clear relationship between the evaluation factors and the SOW. Any minimum essential or threshold requirements must be spelled out and, to the extent possible, all evaluation information should be cross-referenced to the appropriate sections of the SOW.

The individual contracting agencies select the evaluation factors. The buyer (the contracting agency) is in the best position to decide what is important in the evaluation of proposals, and the selection of evaluation factors is not normally questioned.

Tailor the Factors to the Procurement

Evaluation factors must be tailored to the requirement being procured. The evaluation scheme should include only those evaluation factors and significant subfactors that represent the key areas of importance and emphasis to be considered in the source selection decision and that can be applied equitably to all offerors. When selecting evaluation factors:

- Examine the SOW to determine if unique efforts or contractor qualifications are required. Stress these in the evaluation.
- Ensure that you maintain a clear relationship between the SOW and the evaluation factors.
- To the extent possible, cross-reference the evaluation factors to the appropriate SOW paragraphs.

Make Sure the Factors Discriminate Between Offerors

Evaluation factors and significant subfactors must support meaningful comparison and discrimination between and among the competing proposals. The technical evaluation factors must reflect that which is most important in determining which offeror can perform the contract successfully and, when considering the cost or price, offers the best value. Select evaluation factors and significant subfactors that point out the differences rather than the similarities between the proposals. This may be difficult to do, and it is often easier to fall back on using the standard evaluation factors (discussed later in this chapter). However, you must exercise discipline to ensure that the result of the evaluation is the selection of the proposal offering the best value to the government. Putting in the necessary up-front time and effort to select discriminating technical evaluation factors helps minimize the problem of having all proposals evaluated as being relatively equal, leaving cost or price as the only discriminating evaluation factor.

Limit the Number of Evaluation Factors

Keep the number of different evaluation factors and subfactors to a minimum. Scoring often becomes diluted if the evaluation uses a large number of factors. The total scores tend to level off and become roughly equal. This makes it difficult to distinguish between and rank the relative worth of the competing proposals. Limit the evaluation factors and significant subfactors to only those *most* important to the success of the program. Normally, the use of more than three or four primary factors and a similar number of subfactors will have a leveling effect.

Always Include Cost or Price and Quality

All procurements must include cost or price as an evaluation factor. Cost or price need not be the most important factor. It does not even need to be weighted or scored, but it must be considered in the source selection. An evaluation scheme in which cost or price is not considered in some fashion can be successfully protested.

Quality must also be addressed. As an evaluation factor, quality may be expressed in terms of past performance, technical excellence, management capability, personnel qualifications, prior experience, and compliance with solicitation requirements. Cost realism and other relevant noncost factors, specific to your requirement, may also be included as quality factors. Past performance is now a required evaluation factor in acquisitions expected to exceed $100,000, although the contracting officer can document that it is not appropriate for use in a particular procurement (see Chapter

3 for detailed coverage on the use of past performance as an evaluation factor).

Consider Best Value

When appropriate, award may be based on the best value to the government rather than the lowest cost or price. This is often the case where the requirement bears some risk to successful performance, such as research and development, professional or technical services, or in a cost-reimbursement contract. When the award will be based on best value, it is particularly important to select evaluation factors that will discriminate between the proposals and to keep these factors to a minimum. In most instances, award will be determined by a cost/technical tradeoff (see Chapter 18). The validity of a cost/technical tradeoff often depends on the ability to distinguish the differences between proposals and determine their relative worth.

Other Considerations

Other considerations may come into play as you select evaluation factors.

Standard Evaluation Factors

You should avoid the *automatic* use of standard evaluation factors such as Technical, Management, Past Performance, and Corporate Experience—first evaluate your requirement to determine if the use of other specifically tailored factors is appropriate. Often, however, you will find yourself using the standard evaluation factors as the primary factors and tailoring the subfactors to more clearly define what you are evaluating—but this should be done only after a review of your requirement indicates that such tailoring is appropriate.

Cost Reimbursement, Time-and-Materials, and Labor-Hour Contracts

Low cost should not be the controlling factor in the award of *cost-reimbursement contracts*. Cost estimates are not valid indicators of what the actually incurred costs will be and what the government will be obligated to reimburse. To award on the basis of the lowest cost estimate may encourage the submission of unrealistically low estimates, which, in turn, increases the probability of a cost overrun. Evaluation of cost-reimbursement contracts is based on evaluated costs (proposed costs as adjusted by the use of cost analysis and the assessment of cost realism) and a cost/technical tradeoff.

Low price should not be the controlling factor in the award of time-and-materials and labor hour contracts either. These are *fixed-rate contracts* and the final price to be paid is a function of the number of hours worked. Overemphasizing price could lead to award of a contract to the offeror who has most underestimated the work requirements.

The primary consideration for award of cost reimbursement, time-and-materials, and labor-hour contracts should be the selection of an offeror who can perform the contract in a manner most advantageous to the government and offers the best value. This is based on a technical evaluation, an analysis of each proposal's cost realism, and a cost/technical tradeoff that properly assesses and balances the value of the technical and pricing differences between the proposals. This increases the importance of carefully selecting technical evaluation factors and significant subfactors that will help discriminate between the proposals.

Base Evaluation on the Factors Specified in the RFP

When selecting the appropriate evaluation factors, keep in mind that FAR 15.305(a) requires that proposals be evaluated solely on the factors specified in the solicitation, as shown in Example 2.1.

Example 2.1—Evaluate only what you identify as an evaluation factor in the RFP[1]

The Comptroller General has consistently ruled that you cannot evaluate something that was not identified as an evaluation factor in the RFP.

As part of the technical evaluation, an agency may assess the reasonableness of a low price to evaluate an offeror's understanding of the solicitation requirements, so long as the RFP provides for evaluation of offeror understanding.[2] *In this case, there was no technical evaluation criterion or proposal requirement addressing the offeror's understanding of requirements. The solicitation did not provide for a relative ranking of technical merit: all technically acceptable proposals were to be further considered only with respect to price and past performance. Under the announced technical evaluation criteria, Envirosol's proposal was technically acceptable.*

The example cited above was a little more complicated than the excerpt indicates (it involved the difference between responsibility factors and evaluation factors, which is addressed in Chapter 4), but it serves to illustrate the point that only factors listed may be evaluated. For this reason, evaluation factors should be carefully selected and the requirement examined to determine if there are any special factors to consider.

DESCRIBING EVALUATION FACTORS

FAR 15.204-5(c) requires you to identify, in Section M of the RFP, all evaluation factors and significant subfactors, their relative importance, and any other information relevant to how the evaluation will be conducted.

Do not simply list the evaluation factors in your RFP. Describe what each evaluation factor and significant subfactor means and how it will be evaluated. This includes identifying any minimum requirements that apply to particular factors and subfactors.

Describe Evaluation Factors and Significant Subfactors Clearly

It is particularly important to describe evaluation factors and significant subfactors clearly. This is your first and best chance to ensure that the evaluation process will lead to the selection of an offeror who can and will perform the contract successfully. Consider the evaluation factors as problems that you want the offerors to resolve in their proposals. Describe the problem, not the solution. If, however, you have certain preconceived preferences, they should be described to ensure that the offerors' proposals are responsive to your needs. Offerors design their proposals around the evaluation factors in Section M and the proposal preparation instructions in Section L. The quality of your selection and description of the evaluation factors and subfactors, therefore, will directly affect the quality of the proposals.

Describe each primary evaluation factor with a title and a short narrative illustrating the salient characteristics of the factor in a manner that explains how the proposals will be evaluated. Use subfactors to support the primary factors and pinpoint the specific areas that are the most important. Describe subfactors in the same manner as the primary factors. For example, a primary evaluation factor and related subfactors for a study could be expressed as follows.

Technical (Primary Factor)

Proposals shall be evaluated on the basis of the soundness and workability of the proposed technical approach, the demonstrated understanding of the requirement, and the validity of the technical plan and proposed methodology.

Technical Approach/Understanding the Requirement (Subfactor)

The offeror shall demonstrate a sound and workable technical approach that ensures a high probability of successful performance. The offeror shall demonstrate its understanding of the requirement through the degree of thoroughness, soundness, and comprehension of the requirement as demonstrated by the proposed technical approach.

Technical Plan/Methodology (Subfactor)

The offeror's technical plan, schedule, and the methodology to be employed to identify, obtain, and research appropriate articles and reports will be evaluated for its appropriateness for this study and the extent of the effort proposed.

Subfactors May Be Used in Two Ways

Subfactors may be used to help define the primary factor or they may be used to identify specific areas of the requirement that are to be evaluated. For example:

A	*B*
Technical Adequacy	*Technical Adequacy*
1. Understanding the requirement	1. CATV Towers
2. Feasibility of approach	2. Transmitters
3. Technical plan and schedule	3. Receivers

In *column A*, the subfactors amplify what is to be evaluated under the primary evaluation factor (technical adequacy). When describing these subfactors, you must explain what you are looking for or what you will evaluate under each subfactor.

In *column B*, the subfactors indicate which specific areas of the requirement will be evaluated under the primary evaluation factor (i.e., the technical adequacy of the proposal will be evaluated in the three areas listed). When describing the primary factor, indicate, for instance, that the offeror's understanding the requirement, the feasibility of its technical approach, and the proposed technical plan and schedule will be evaluated in each of the three areas listed as subfactors. When describing these subfactors, you must explain what you are looking for or what you will evaluate under each subfactor.

Do not mix the subfactors in columns A and B. All of the subfactors should be used in the same way. Mixing the subfactors, with some amplifying the primary factor and some indicating specific areas of interest, leads to confusion and degrades the quality of the proposals. If it becomes necessary to mix the subfactors, use a narrative to explain that the offeror's proposal should separately address the specific areas (column B) and that they will be evaluated against the amplifying subfactors (column A). You are going to have problems, however, if your explanation is not clearly stated.

Use the Proposal Preparation Instructions for Amplification

Use the proposal preparation instructions in Section L of the RFP to further amplify the evaluation factors. There is a direct link between the listing of the evaluation criteria and their relative importance in Section M and the proposal preparation instructions in Section L. Proposal preparation instructions are used to expand the description of the evaluation factors, establish the format and contents of the offerors' proposals, and to require the submission of relevant information needed to evaluate each factor. (Proposal preparation instructions are discussed in detail in Chapter 7.)

Why a Full Description Is Needed

The purpose of identifying the evaluation factors and significant subfactors with both a title and a narrative description in the RFP is twofold. First, offerors must be told how and against what criteria their proposals will be evaluated. Second, you want the offerors to respond with the information needed to fairly evaluate their proposals. This cannot be done effectively if only a title is used. You cannot be sure that the offerors will interpret the title the same way you do.

Keep in mind that you control the evaluation process. You determine which evaluation factors are important. You will maintain control only if you effectively communicate what is to be evaluated. The most effective way to do this is to describe exactly what information is needed. It is in your best interest to help ensure that offerors submit their best proposals because this helps ensure that you select the offeror most likely to succeed in contract performance.

Requiring an offeror to second-guess the type and detail of the information to be provided in its proposal is counterproductive. In effect, this practice amounts to evaluating the offeror's ability to guess what information is needed. If the offeror guesses wrong, its proposal may not address the issues considered most important or provide the detail commensurate with the evaluation factor's relative importance.

This may adversely affect the competitive aspects of the procurement and result in the loss of an otherwise fully qualified contractor.

PROBLEMS WITH THE USE OF UNSTATED SUBFACTORS

FAR 15.304(b) requires that each solicitation clearly state the evaluation factors and significant subfactors as well as their relative importance. The FAR also says these factors must represent the key areas of importance and emphasis to be considered in source selection and must support meaningful comparison and discrimination between and among competing proposals. However, by referring to "significant" subfactors rather than "all" subfactors, the FAR introduced an element of uncertainty with respect to exactly what subfactors must be listed.

Need to Reveal Significant Subfactors

What is a "significant" subfactor? A significant subfactor represents an important element of the primary evaluation factor and is needed to explain what the primary factor is all about and to provide an appropriate emphasis (i.e., weighting) to the evaluation of the primary factor. In other words, a significant subfactor is one that could make a difference as a discriminator in the overall evaluation. Significant subfactors must be listed in the solicitation, as shown in Example 2.2.

Example 2.2—Include all significant subfactors in the RFP[3]

An RFP listed six evaluation factors in descending order of importance. No subfactors were listed. The first and most important factor was "Experience in multidisciplinary natural resource planning involving cooperative interagency teams." This factor was evaluated against four undisclosed subfactors, the first of which, "River Basin Experience," was worth 60 of the

100 points available. An unsuccessful offeror protested that this subfactor was significant and should have been disclosed in the RFP. The Comptroller General agreed.

Experience in the River Basin program was by far the most important subfactor under the general experience factor. Specifically, the program experience was worth 60 of 100 points under the experience factor, which itself was worth 42 percent of the total score; as a result, the program experience subfactor was worth approximately 25 percent of the total score. None of the other subfactors approached the importance of the River Basin subfactor; in fact, of the other five general *evaluation factors listed in the RFP, the next closest in weight to the River Basin experience subfactor ("knowledge and experience in conducting natural resource economic evaluations") was worth only 21 percent of the total score. Accordingly, experience in the River Basin program was not only the single most important subfactor, but was worth more by itself than five of the six general evaluation factors.*

Contracting agencies are required by statute to include in solicitations all significant evaluation factors and their relative importance.[4] *Further, the Federal Acquisition Regulation (FAR),*[5] *requires that solicitations disclose "any significant subfactors" to be considered in the award decision. Here, the River Basin subfactor clearly constituted a significant subfactor within the meaning of the FAR in light of its relative weight in the evaluation scheme. ... Accordingly, we find that SCS was required under the FAR to disclose in the RFP that experience in the USDA River Basin program would be the most significant factor in the evaluation.*

The use of percentages in this example is for illustrative purposes only; the unstated River Basin subfactor was significant because it was a discriminator. Not only was it the most important subfactor of the most important primary factor, but it also clearly limited the competitive field to contractors that had specific River Basin experience.

The agency could have avoided this if it had listed River Basin experience as the most important primary evaluation factor and then listed "other related experience" as the second most important primary evaluation factor.

Need Not Reveal Subfactors Clearly Related to the Primary Factor

FAR 15.306(a) states that agencies shall evaluate competitive proposals and then assess their relative qualities solely on the factors and subfactors specified in the solicitation. Does this mean that forgetting to list a subfactor precludes its use in the evaluation? Not necessarily. You are not required to reveal subfactors that are so clearly related to the primary factor that offerors should reasonably expect them to be included in the evaluation, as shown in Example 2.3.

Example 2.3—Unstated subfactors clearly related to primary factor need not be revealed[6]

An RFP listed five evaluation factors and their weights. The most important factor was "Personnel Qualifications," weighted at 45 percent. Three of the other factors were weighted at 10 percent and one at 5 percent. The technical factors were weighted at 80 percent and cost at 20 percent. The RFP did not identify any subfactors. One of the unsuccessful offerors protested when it learned that unstated subfactors were used in the evaluation of Personnel Qualifications, arguing that these subfactors should have been disclosed. The Comptroller General disagreed.

We find that the subfactors, "Compliance with Stated Minimum Requirements," "Additional Experience/Qualifications of Key Personnel," and "Experience in the Topical Area" are clearly related to the factor "Personnel Qualifications" under which they were evaluated. In fact, it is difficult to imagine what alternative items ITAC believed would be evaluated under an evaluation factor entitled "Personnel Qualifications." We further find that the evaluation subfactors are not "significant," so that they were not required by FAR 15.605(e) to be separately listed....Here, each of the three subfactors was equally weighted, worth 15 percent of available evaluation points. We find nothing unusual or unexpected in the agency's judgment that meeting minimum qualifications, experience in excess of the minimum required, and experience in the specific area being procured would be major elements of an evaluation of personnel qualifications, which the

RFP stated would be worth 45 percent of available points. Accordingly, the agency was not required to disclose the subfactors in the solicitation.

In this example, just looking at the numbers could be confusing. Each of the unstated subfactors was worth 15 percent of the total available points, and each was worth more than any other prime factor by at least 5 percent. The total of the unstated subfactors was worth 45 percent of the total available points. Does this make these factors significant? Not in this instance. Here the subfactors were so clearly related to the primary factor that an offeror could reasonably be expected to anticipate that these areas would be evaluated. While the primary factor was important, and so listed, the subfactors were not discriminators and not, in and of themselves, significant enough to merit listing.

Over the years, the Comptroller General has consistently ruled that two things should be considered with respect to unstated evaluation subfactors:

1. A subfactor, significant in terms of its relative importance in the evaluation, must be identified in the RFP. A significant subfactor is a discriminator, in that its assessment could make a difference in the evaluation results.
2. A subfactor inherently related to the prime factor, to the extent that offerors could reasonably be expected to anticipate that the subfactor would be evaluated, need not be specifically identified in the RFP.

In general, *not revealing the subfactors is poor practice.* It should be noted, however, that the Comptroller General has only ruled that you are not *required* to reveal such subfactors, not that you are prohibited from doing so. Failing to list subfactors leaves the description of the primary evaluation factor incomplete.

Proper evaluation planning requires that you consider how you are going to conduct the evaluation at the time you are making up the evaluation plan. Subfactors identify how you are going to evaluate the primary factor. If you do not identify the subfactors, you risk confusing the contractors and perhaps losing what is otherwise a good contender for award. In addition, failing to list subfactors may cause misunderstandings that could lead to unnecessary protests that consume excessive amounts of time and money—even if you win.

USING STANDARD (TYPICAL) EVALUATION FACTORS

As noted earlier in this chapter, *do not automatically use the standard evaluation factors*. First examine the SOW to determine which evaluation factors should be tailored to the particular requirement, determine what procurement-unique evaluation factors are required, and then combine them with any applicable standard factors.

The standard evaluation factors are technical, management, corporate experience, past performance, and cost/price. Cost/price is a mandatory evaluation factor and must be used in all evaluations. Past performance is mandatory for procurements in excess of $100,000 (past performance is covered in detail in Chapter 3). The other standard factors may be applicable in one form or another, but often bear differing titles to more clearly express the intent of the evaluation.

Technical Factors

The following are examples of technical evaluation factors that could be used as primary factors or as subfactors under a primary technical evaluation factor:

Technical Approach

Evaluate the offeror's technical approach with respect to the successful completion of the technical requirement. The merit of the technical approach is demonstrated by its soundness and workability; the use of a standard or innovative approach, depending on which is preferred; and the probability of success or risk associated with the proposed approach.

Technical Understanding

Evaluate the offeror's understanding of all the elements of the technical requirement as demonstrated by the thoroughness, soundness, and comprehensiveness of the proposed technical approach. Consider the offeror's analysis of the requirement, the identification of problem areas and suggested solutions, the use of innovative approaches and state-of-the-art advances (if such are desired), technical approach and its feasibility, and probability of success.

Technical Plan

Evaluate the proposed technical plan for the completeness of detail, the validity of the techniques to be used, scheduling and sequencing, the use of contingency planning, and other details as appropriate, such as the extent of subcontracting. Your considerations should include both the probability of technical success and the probability of meeting the required contractual time frames.

Management Factors

The following are examples of management evaluation factors that could be used as primary factors, or as subfactors under a primary management evaluation factor:

Management Plan

Evaluate the degree to which the proposed management plan establishes well-defined lines of authority, responsibility, and communication and how well proposed management techniques will facilitate the early identification and resolution of problems and allow the offeror to respond to changes. Assess the offeror's commitment to the success of the program as demonstrated by corporate level of the proposed project manager, that individual's access to upper management, and the degree to which upper management is committed to providing assistance in the event of problems.

Staffing Plan

Evaluate the degree to which the proposed staffing level and labor mix reflect the technical input and ability for successful and timely contract performance and, as appropriate, the offeror's ability to react to workload fluctuations. The stated purpose of staffing as an evaluation factor is to determine if the offeror is proposing adequate staffing. Staffing, however, is also inherent to assessing the offeror's understanding of the requirement.

Staffing levels are usually evaluated against a government estimate of the number and types of personnel required to perform the requirement. You must ensure that the government estimate has a valid basis. Your staffing estimate should be based on the performance work statement, historical staffing levels, and staffing levels at other agencies with similar requirements. It should also consider events that might affect the staffing levels, such as an anticipated increase or decrease in the work requirement.

Although you are not required to reveal your staffing estimates in the RFP, you are not prohibited from doing so, as shown in Example 2.4.

Example 2.4—Government is not required to reveal its staffing estimates in RFP[7]

...we do not agree with the protester that the agency was required to disclose in the RFP the manning model or estimates. Generally, an agency is not required to disclose in the solicitation a manning level developed by the agency's evaluators and technical personnel to assess whether proposed personnel were adequate.[8]

There is no standard approach to revealing staffing estimates. A decision to reveal minimum staffing requirements depends on the particular procurement. Your objective is to ensure that the offerors have sufficient information upon which to base an intelligent, workable, and competitive proposal.

Be prepared to carefully assess the offeror's proposed organization and method of performance and its impact on the staffing requirements. Also consider that contractors often operate with lower staffing levels than the government. To maintain peak workloads, civilian contractors adopt cross-utilization (i.e., workers trained for more than one task and moved around depending on the workload). Cross-utilization occurs in the private sector to a much greater extent than in the government. However, if an offeror's proposed staffing does not match the government estimate, do not automatically assume that the offeror is wrong. The offeror may simply have a better way of getting the job done.

Use the proposal preparation instructions to require offerors to provide the level of detail necessary to fully evaluate their proposed staffing. Require offerors (whether government estimates are revealed or not) to explain how their proposed staffing will ensure that all requirements are met. Mere promises to cover all work areas are not sufficient. Offerors must show exactly how they plan to manage their proposed staffing under both normal and peak workloads.

For example, if an offeror proposes reduced staffing and cross-utilization, it must show where the workers will come from, when, and why. The offeror must also show how it will handle the workload in the areas from which the workers moved. The offeror must demonstrate that shifting workers to meet workload requirements will not compromise overall performance.

You may also want to consider personnel turnover and its effect on contract performance. If your requirement involves work effort that typically experiences high turnover rates (such as janitorial and guard services) or if personnel fluctuations may jeopardize effective contract performance (as with technical support services or R&D), use the proposal preparation instructions to require offerors to address this issue in their proposals. Require offerors to explain their recruitment, compensation, and training plans so you can assess their ability to maintain a stable staff and cope with turnover.

Corporate Experience

Corporate experience is usually used as a primary evaluation factor.

Assessing Corporate Experience

Corporate experience is typically evaluated on the basis of the offeror's experience with the same or similar work and is related to whether the offeror has done such work in the past. It is *not* evaluated on how well the offeror performed the work. You should be aware of this distinction because corporate experience can also be viewed as a measure of a firm's capability as demonstrated by its past performance. One must be distinguished from the other to avoid confusion in the evaluation (see Chapter 3 for further details on the distinction between corporate experience and past performance).

The importance of corporate experience in the evaluation depends on the complexity of the work. Corporate experience is valuable for evaluating an offeror's ability to complete a complex effort that involves many personnel and multiple work units and requires interfacing both inside and outside the corporate structure. In large efforts, corporate experience can often provide some assurance that corporate memory will be retained.

Corporate experience is less important on smaller efforts that involve only a few personnel because retention of corporate experience cannot be assured if only a few personnel are involved in the contract. Corporate experience is, after all, little more than the corporate memory of the individuals currently working for the offeror.

Describing Corporate Experience

Before using corporate experience as an evaluation factor, determine what you are looking for and how it should be described.

The first step is to decide what you are looking for in corporate experience. Is it comparable experience in general; comparable specific experience, such as use of a specific method or technique; or just having been in business long enough to demonstrate an ability to perform? It is important to document what you are looking for and why. In the event of a protest, you must be able to demonstrate that your assessment of corporate experience was reasonable.

Once you have decided what you want to evaluate, develop a description for use in the RFP. Corporate experience may be described as years of general or specialized experience or numbers of comparable contracts. You may want to use another description. In that case, you must clearly explain what you mean by corporate experience and how you intend to evaluate it. You must ensure that you have a reasonable basis for what you say, as shown in Example 2.5.

Example 2.5—Explain in the RFP what you mean by corporate experience[9]

Two RFPs from the same agency required that offerors have an established asbestos abatement business for five years and have conducted five asbestos abatement projects within the last three years. Three of those projects must have been of comparable complexity and dollar value to the work under the RFP. Protests were submitted regarding the five-year business requirement. The Comptroller General agreed with the protesters.

As indicated, the agency provides no explanation as to why, in seeking to protect people in and around its medical centers, the determining factor regarding an offeror's experience is whether the offeror has existed in its present form and has an established asbestos abatement business for at least 5 years. While a reasonable offeror experience requirement will be upheld[10] we have no basis on this record for concluding that the requirement here is reasonable. For example, although we do not dispute the VA's belief that offeror experience is a relevant consideration in connection with health and safety concerns in the hospital environment, the solicitations require that offerors have "conducted within the last 3 years 5 asbestos abatement projects 3 of which are of comparable complexity and dollar value with this project." The agency has failed to provide any rational explanation as to why offerors who have successfully performed the requisite number of similar projects and who employ individuals with appropriate experience (the experience of the individuals actually involved in performing the work obviously also can affect the health and safety of hospital inhabitants) are nonetheless, incapable of meeting the government's needs simply because they do not have an additional 2 years of experience in their current corporate or other business status. Since the agency has offered no rational support for this restriction, we find it unduly restrictive.[11]

In this example, the only explanation the agency provided was that the requirements were imposed for health and safety reasons and that the provision used was required by the agency for this type of work. In a protest situation, the Comptroller General requires rational reasons for questioned actions, not bureaucratic responses. It therefore sustained the protest.

The problem in this example was that the agency required five years of corporate experience, but only three years of related experience. This does not make sense, which was probably why only a bureaucratic response was provided. A claim that "my agency made me do it" is not a proper response when replying to a protest.

When defining corporate experience, keep in mind that corporate experience can be defined in terms of the firm's past experience and in terms of the experience of its senior technical and management personnel. This can be an important distinction when evaluating the corporate experience of small or newly formed firms, as shown in Example 2.6.

Example 2.6—Definition of corporate experience particularly important for evaluating small or new firms[12]

Our review of the evaluation documents shows that the evaluators were aware that Seaward does not have the extensive test range support experience that GOC has. However, the evaluators also recognized that the firm has broad experience in the performance of tasks comparable to those required here, including deep water range operations, facilities planning, and ocean engineering. Our review of Seaward's proposal supports this conclusion. More importantly, the evaluators noted that Seaward's president was GOC's project manager for the test range support contract from 1980 through 1987. While GOC is correct that it generally is improper to consider personnel experience under a corporate experience factor where there are separate evaluation factors for each,[13] *we think the agency's consideration of the experience of Seaward's president under the institutional experience subfactor of the corporate experience factor was consistent with the RFP. In this regard, the RFP designated two subfactors under the personnel qualifications factor, engineering and technical/skilled labor. The evaluation of these subfactors was to address the education, experience, and capabilities of "key engineering personnel" and "technical/skilled personnel." Since the personnel evaluation was thus limited to consideration of these personnel, there was no way for the agency to evaluate the extensive experience of Seaward's president under this factor. Moreover, we specifically have held that in evaluating the experience of a new business, such as this one, an agency may consider the experience of supervisory personnel.*[14] *We conclude that the agency properly considered the extensive experience of Seaward's president in awarding the firm a relatively high score for its institutional experience under the corporate experience and test support factors.*

This case illustrates the flexibility available to evaluators as long as they make rational decisions and document them well. The evaluation factors were set up in a manner that precluded evaluating the experience of the awardee's president under the personnel qualifications factor. Rather than ignoring this experience, the evaluators considered the president's experience under the corporate experience factor. This was a sensible thing to do since the president's experience would have a significant impact on contract performance.

Corporate experience requirements must make sense in relation to what is being procured. Do not develop a corporate experience requirement that precludes the participation of small, newly established firms. It is not unusual for highly qualified personnel to leave large firms to form their own businesses, particularly in high technology areas. Excessive corporate experience requirements might preclude the participation of new firms with highly qualified personnel. Since corporate experience is largely the experience of the personnel involved, it is appropriate to consider the experience of the key personnel in a newly formed firm when assessing its corporate experience. The RFP should indicate that newly established firms may establish their experience and qualifications through the experience of their key personnel. Along similar lines, you should evaluate the experience of joint ventures on the basis of experience the individual members bring to the joint venture.

Corporate experience must be evaluated on the basis of objective evidence. In addition to describing what corporate experience means, describe how you want the offeror to demonstrate that it has the requisite corporate experience. Use the proposal preparation instructions to require offerors to identify current and past contracts for the same or similar work and to provide the contract number, dollar value, dates, a brief description of the work effort, the name of the contracting agency, and a contact telephone number at that agency. Offerors should also be required to demonstrate how the referenced contract relates to the proposed effort. Instructions must be as specific as possible.

Cost or Price

FAR 15.304(c)(i) requires the use of cost or price as an evaluation factor. Cost or price need not be the most significant evaluation factor, but it *must* be included in the evaluation process. Cost or price is evaluated through cost analysis, price analysis, and when appropriate, an analysis of cost realism. The purpose of both cost and price analysis is to determine the probable cost to the government for each proposal within the competitive range. The purpose of a cost realism analysis is to determine if the proposed costs are realistic with respect to the proposed technical approach.

Cost Analysis

Cost analysis is the review and evaluation of the separate cost elements and proposed profit in an offeror's proposal (including cost or pricing data or information other than cost or pricing data), and the application of judgment to determine how well the proposed costs represent what the cost of the contract should be, assuming reasonable economy and efficiency.

While cost analysis is primarily concerned with the evaluation of the cost elements, a certain amount of technical analysis is also required. FAR 15.404-1(e) defines technical analysis as the use of personnel having specialized knowledge, skills, experience, or capability in engineering, science, or management to perform a technical analysis of the proposed types and quantities of materials, labor, processes, special tooling, facilities, the reasonableness of scrap and spoilage, and other associated factors set forth in a proposal in order to determine the need for and reasonableness of the proposed resources assuming reasonable economy and efficiency.

Cost analysis is normally conducted separately from the technical evaluation by a separate evaluation team. When a technical analysis is conducted in conjunction with the cost analysis, it can be accomplished either by adding technical personnel to the team doing the cost analysis or by using the personnel who conducted the technical evaluation. You would be well advised to use personnel from the technical evaluation team to support the cost analysis team. This ensures continuity between the technical evaluation and the technical analysis. The evaluation process is at best a subjective assessment. A cost analysis supported by different technical personnel might yield results based on technical conclusions at odds with those arrived at by the technical evaluation team.

Price Analysis

Price analysis is the process of examining and evaluating a proposed price without evaluating its separate cost elements and proposed profit. This is usually done by price comparisons with other current prices, historical prices, and with the government estimate. Price analysis *must* be conducted if cost analysis is not used and *may* be conducted in conjunction with cost analysis.

The price analysis is normally conducted separately from the technical evaluation by a separate evaluation team. Since price analysis does not involve the submission of detailed cost or pricing data, technical analysis is usually not required. When circumstances warrant, however, limited cost or pricing information may be requested to support a technical analysis of specific areas of an offeror's proposal.

Cost Realism

Cost realism is the process of independently reviewing and evaluating specific elements of each offeror's proposed cost estimate to determine whether the estimated proposed cost elements are realistic for the work to be performed; reflect a clear understanding of the requirements; and are consistent with the unique methods of performance and materials described in the offeror's technical proposal. In short, a cost realism analysis matches the proposed costs against both the proposed technical approach and the government requirement. If the costs do not match these elements and the differences are not satisfactorily explained, they are not realistic.

The purpose of the cost realism evaluation is to assess the degree to which the proposed costs accurately represent the proposed work effort included in the technical proposal. Cost realism analysis is also used to verify the offeror's understanding of the requirement. In addition, it is used to assess the degree to which the cost proposal reflects the approaches and risk assessments made in the technical proposal as well as the risk that the offeror will be able to complete the requirement. This is discussed in greater detail in Chapter 4.

THINK ABOUT WHAT YOU ARE DOING

The standard technical evaluation factors are often used without much critical analysis of their real value in the evaluation process. When selecting an evaluation factor you should know what it is that you expect to find in an offeror's proposal, that is, you should have a listing of the key items the evaluators are to look for in the proposal. These key items should be in the form of an evaluator's worksheet (an internal document not published in the RFP). If the evaluators are not told what to look for, their evaluations will be haphazard and may be based more on how well the offeror writes than how well the offeror has addressed the evaluation factor.

The language used in the RFP to describe an evaluation factor is broad by nature—to give the offeror leeway in how it approaches the evaluation factor. The evaluators, however, should have some sort of guide or standard to use in their evaluation. This guide should not be mandatory—evaluators must be permitted to be flexible—but the lack of a guide can result in widely disparate evaluations.

The process of trying to develop an evaluator's guide will help determine the validity of the evaluation factors initially selected. An examination of the SOW will help determine what is important in discerning an offeror's capability to successfully perform the contract and to distinguishing the capability differences between the offerors.

When examining the SOW's technical requirements, identify those areas the offerors must address for you to determine the offeror's technical capabilities and understanding of the requirement. For example, if there are a number of different ways to accomplish the work, the offeror's proposed methodology or technical approach might be an important factor for evaluators to examine. The evaluator's guidance should indicate some of the different approaches and the how they might be evaluated. If there is a government preference, this should be stated in the RFP; otherwise the pros and cons of each approach should be indicated.

You may find, for example, that all you need to see is the offeror's technical plan (keep in mind that technical understanding would be an inherent subfactor whether expressed or not). The evaluator's guidance should indicate what should be in the technical plan, the level of detail to expect, and any particular problem areas that should be addressed.

You may also find that, due to the nature of the work effort, the offerors' technical description is not likely to vary significantly among the most probable offerors, in which case a technical description will not be a valid discriminator. If the technical description is not likely to be a discriminator, it should not be used as an evaluation factor.

Examine the SOW closely to determine if an offeror's description of how it would manage the effort is going to contribute significantly to the evaluation. You must decide what, if anything, you really need to know about the offeror's management approach and to what degree this is likely to discriminate among the offerors. The offeror's guidance should indicate what aspects of an offeror's management approach are most important. If the offerors' management approaches are not likely to be significantly different, management need not be an evaluation factor.

Staffing, particularly in a labor-intensive effort, is often a valid discriminator in an evaluation. Evaluators should be told what labor mix to look for, what staffing level was used in the government estimate, and generally what factors might justify a different staffing level. If appropriate to the work effort, evaluators should be told to look for the offeror's explanation as to how workload fluctuations would be handled and how to evaluate staffing shifts to meet peak workloads.

If the proposed effort is not labor intensive, staffing may not be a significant evaluation factor, but this does not preclude the use of the key personnel factor in the evaluation. If key personnel is used as an evaluation factor, evaluators should be provided a copy of the RFP's listing of qualification requirements and any key personnel clause used. The evaluators should be told that proposals are to be evaluated against the published criteria and that exceptions are not permitted except as authorized by the contracting officer.

Corporate experience is a commonly used factor to determine if an offeror has previously done work of the same or similar nature as the proposed work. Generally, the evaluator's guidance should include the Section M and Section L description of this evaluation factor and any specific requirements, as shown in Examples 2.5 and 2.6 earlier in this chapter.

Past performance is a mandatory evaluation factor. While past performance is addressed in detail in Chapter 3, it should be noted here that past performance may be one of the technical evaluation factors or it may be the only technical evaluation factor. Some agencies, for example, have reduced their evaluation factors to just past performance and price where the work effort is of a standard and continuing nature. This makes sense where the primary discriminator between the most probable offerors is how well they have performed this work in the past.

It is not necessary, or even desirable, to use the standard evaluation factors simply because that is how it has been done in the past. This is particularly true when acquiring supplies or services of a standard and continuing nature. Examine the SOW to determine the most important discriminating factor or factors and use only those most important to distinguish which proposal offers the best value. For example, if the only real difference among the most probable offerors is how they will staff the requirement and the qualifications of proposed key personnel, there is nothing wrong with restricting the technical evaluation factors to just those factors (keeping in mind that past performance and pricing are mandatory factors). The selection of evaluation factors should be a reasoned decision, not something done by rote.

References

1. Envirosol, Inc., B-254223, 12/2/93, GCR 107,960.
2. PHP Healthcare Corp., B-251933, 5/13/93, 93-1 CPD ¶381, GCR 107,562; Family Realty B-247772, 7/6/92, 92-2 CPD ¶6, GCR 106,742; Binghamton Simulator Co., Inc., B-244839, 11/5/91, 91-2 CPD ¶429, GCR 106,032.
3. Devres Inc., B-224017, 12/8/86; 86-2 CPD ¶652, GCR 100,119.
4. 41 U.S.C. 253a (b)(1) (Supp. III 1985).
5. 48 C.F.R. 15.605 (e) (1985).
6. Management Systems Designers, Inc.; Information Technology & Applications Corporation; Epoch Engineering Inc, B-244383.4; B-244383.5; B-244383.6, 12/6/91, GCR 106,116.
7. Aerostat Services Partnership, B-244939.2, 1/15/92, 92-1 CPD ¶71, GCR 106,261.
8. Intelcom Support Servs., Inc., B-222547, 8/1/86, 86-2 CPD ¶135.
9. Keeson, Inc.; Ingram Demolition Inc., B-245625; B-245655, 1/24/92, 92-1 CPD ¶108, GCR 106,297.
10. Brevco Inc., B-232388, 12/29/88, 88-2 CPD ¶634.
11. See also Wadell Eng'g Corp., 60 Comp. Gen. 11 (1980), 80-2 CPD ¶269; Am. President Lines Ltd., B-236834.3, 7/20/90, 90-2 CPD ¶53, GCR 104,557; Military Servs., Inc. of Georgia, B-221384, 4/30/86, 86-1 CPD ¶423.
12. General Offshore Corp., B-246824, 4/1/92, 92-1 CPD ¶335, GCR 106,523.
13. Washington State Comm'n. for Vocational Educ.,—Recon., 64 Comp. Gen., 681 (1985), 85-2 CPD 59.
14. LD Research Corp., B-230912.3, 9/9/88, 88-2 CPD ¶223, GCR 102,301; Data Flow Corp. *et al.*, B-209444 *et al.*, 7/6/83, 83-2 CPD ¶57.

Chapter 3

Using Past Performance As an Evaluation Factor

Increased emphasis is being placed on past performance as an evaluation factor. In 1995, the Federal Acquisition Streamlining Act required the Office of Federal Procurement Policy (OFPP) to prescribe guidance regarding consideration of past performance in awarding contracts. FAC 90-26, effective May 30, 1995, served to implement the OFPP guidance. After the FAR 15 rewrite, the FAR [at 15.304(c)] states that past performance shall be used as an evaluation factor in all competitive procurements in excess of $100,000 unless the contracting officer documents the reason why it is not an appropriate evaluation factor for the instant procurement.

Prior to the issuance of the OFPP guidance, past performance was primarily evaluated as a responsibility factor. Generally, this involved an examination of an offeror's past performance to determine if its performance was so seriously deficient as to jeopardize successful performance of the proposed contract. The use of past performance as an evaluation factor was not a common practice.

The emphasis on past performance as an evaluation factor came about as part of the Federal Streamlining Process designed to make federal procurement more efficient. The evaluation of past performance is not a simple process, however. There are a number of factors to consider when planning to use past performance as an evaluation factor:

- Determining the relative importance of past performance
- Distinguishing past performance as a responsibility factor from past performance as an evaluation factor

- Distinguishing past performance (as an evaluation factor) from corporate experience (a commonly used evaluation factor)
- Determining what will be evaluated as past performance
- Determining how past performance will be evaluated
- Determining how past performance information will be obtained.

This chapter will address these points, suggest how this concept might be implemented, and address some of the problems that might be encountered.

RELATIVE IMPORTANCE AS AN EVALUATION FACTOR

In its May 1995 Interim Edition of *A Guide to Best Practices for Past Performance,* the OFPP recommended that past performance be used as a primary (stand-alone) evaluation factor weighted at 25 percent or more or at least equal in significance to any other noncost evaluation factor. That is one approach—the following is another.

Despite the current emphasis on the use of past performance in evaluation, keep in mind that FAR 15.304(c)(iii) leaves the final decision to the contracting officer. It is up to the contracting officer to determine if the use of past performance as an evaluation factor is appropriate, and how it should be used.

Using past performance as an evaluation factor should depend on the significance of past performance as a discriminator in the current procurement. Do not automatically assume that past performance is an important factor without first considering whether you need it to discriminate between offerors. For example, if all potential offerors are good performers, the evaluation of past performance will not enhance the evaluation process.

The relative importance of past performance depends on the circumstances of the procurement. If previous contracts for the same or similar items or services have a history of performance problems, then past performance, as an indicator of performance risk, may be a very important criterion and should be used as a primary evaluation factor.

Past performance may also be significant if strict conformance with the specifications and delivery times is critical to the program the procurement supports. This applies, for example, to the procurement of supplies, if the required items are sensitive and complex devices and the proven ability to successfully produce the items in conformance to the SOW requirements and to make timely delivery is critical to the selection of the successful offeror. This may also apply to technical support services where the proven ability to respond successfully to complex technical requirements is equally critical to source selection.

When used, past performance is usually one of the primary evaluation factors, but not necessarily one of the most important. The technical, management, and corporate experience factors provide insight into how the contractor proposes to perform the current requirement. If this is important, such as in cases where there are a number of ways to accomplish the requirement, how an offeror proposes to do the work could be a critical discriminator in the evaluation. In such instances, past performance would be of lesser importance in the evaluation scheme.

There are times, however, when the technical or management factors might not be significant to the source selection. For example, in the procurement of continuing commercial-like services (particularly when using performance-based service contracting), how a contractor plans to perform or manage the contract might not be as important as its track record in performing the same or similar services. Where the performance of services is standardized, as in commercial or commercial-like services, the competitors will generally be alike in their technical and management approaches. This tends to result in their proposals being rated as roughly equal, and, in effect, makes the evaluation of technical and management as primary evaluation factors ineffective. In such instances, evaluating on the basis of past performance and price might be the most effective approach.

Past performance is not always appropriate as a primary evaluation factor. If past performance is not considered important enough to use as a primary evaluation factor, or if the past performance to be assessed relates more to technical requirements than delivery or administrative requirements, it may be used as a significant subfactor under a technical factor rather than as a primary evaluation factor.

You should also consider the effect of adding another primary evaluation factor on the overall evaluation scheme, because having too many primary evaluation factors will dilute the evaluation results. Using past performance as a significant subfactor rather than as a primary evaluation factor helps avoid this scenario.

The selection and relative importance of evaluation factors should depend on an objective assessment of the value of each factor to the overall evaluation.

RESPONSIBILITY FACTOR VERSUS EVALUATION FACTOR

The use of past performance as a *responsibility* factor must be distinguished from the use of past performance as an *evaluation* factor.

FAR 9.104-3(b) requires the use of past performance in making determinations of responsibility, stating that, "A prospective contractor that is or recently has been seriously deficient in contract performance shall be presumed to be nonresponsible, unless the contracting officer determines that the circumstances were properly beyond the contractor's control, or that the contractor has taken appropriate corrective action. Past failure to apply sufficient tenacity and perseverance to perform acceptably is strong evidence of nonresponsibility. Failure to meet the quality requirements of the contract is a significant factor to consider in determining satisfactory performance."

FAR 15.304(c) requires that past performance be used as an evaluation factor in all competitive procurements in excess of $100,000 *unless* the contracting officer documents the reason why it is not an appropriate evaluation factor for the instant procurement.

Distinguishing between past performance as a responsibility factor and past performance as an evaluation factor is necessary because the determination of responsibility and the evaluation of proposals are two distinct and separate functions, performed at different times by different people during the procurement process, as follows:

- Technical evaluation factors are assessed by the application of specified evaluation standards through a comparative assessment that establishes the relative value of each proposal and the relative ranking of each offeror. A technical evaluation team performs this evaluation during the evaluation process.
- Responsibility factors are assessed by the application of established responsibility standards on a pass/fail basis, to determine if the proposed contractor is a responsible business able to perform the contract. The contracting officer performs this assessment after completion of the final evaluation and just prior to award.

Past performance is evaluated by a comparative assessment in the technical evaluation and by a pass/fail criterion in the responsibility determination. These actions differ in that a failure to meet the minimum requirements of an evaluation factor does not in and of itself require an automatic rejection of the proposal. It simply results in a lower assessment or score. A failure to meet the minimum requirements of a responsibility factor, however, *requires* the rejection of the proposal. A contractor is either responsible or not responsible; there is no middle ground.

Evaluating past performance as an evaluation factor is not a substitute for assessing past performance in the responsibility determination. Past performance is an established responsibility factor and *must* be considered in a determination of responsibility. Therefore, if past performance is used as an evaluation factor, it could be evaluated twice—first, as part of the assessment of the value of an offeror's proposal in comparison to the proposals of other offerors, and second, to determine if an offeror's past performance meets the minimum standards of responsibility.

Generally, however, an offeror whose past performance is such that it would be considered nonresponsible would not remain in the competition long enough for a responsibility determination. An offeror with a significantly deficient performance record usually has other technical problems and the combination of problems will, in most cases, lower the offeror's score enough to result in proposal rejection during the initial proposal evaluation. Only the most highly rated offerors are included in the competitive range. A responsibility determination usually focuses on the otherwise successful offeror since it is the last action taken before contract award.

PAST PERFORMANCE VERSUS CORPORATE EXPERIENCE

Evaluators must also distinguish between *past performance* and *corporate experience,* another commonly used evaluation factor. The evaluation of past performance and corporate experience uses the same database—previous contracts for the same or similar effort—but each is evaluated differently. When both are used in an evaluation, consider what each factor evaluates and how each should be used. *Corporate experience* is used to assess an offeror's technical expertise and is typically evaluated on the basis of the offeror's experience with the same or similar work. It is related to whether the offeror has done such work in the past, not how well it performed. *Past performance* is used to assess the quality of an offeror's performance and is typically evaluated on the basis of how well the offeror performed the same or similar effort in the past and how that past performance is likely to affect the current effort.

When both past performance and corporate experience are used as evaluation factors, each should be specifically defined in the RFP. Define past performance as an indicator of how well the offeror is likely to perform on the current contract, as demonstrated by how well the offeror performed on comparable prior contracts. Define corporate experience as an indicator of the offeror's expertise, as demonstrated by its work on past and current contracts of the same or similar nature.

Another way to look at the difference between the two factors is to consider corporate experience to be personnel-oriented (i.e., it demonstrates the corporate memory of the personnel involved). Past performance is results-oriented (i.e., it demonstrates how well the offeror performed).

WHAT IS EVALUATED UNDER PAST PERFORMANCE

A number of areas can be evaluated under past performance, depending on the needs of your particular procurement. The following are some of the more common areas considered; however, you should tailor the evaluation to your current requirement.

Conformance to Specifications and Standards of Good Workmanship

This area includes the assessment of the quality of the products or services delivered under past or other current contracts and the extent to which the end products or results conformed to the contractual requirements. The assessment includes the examination of past performance problems, particularly with respect to rejections and high rates of rework. The number of changes made during performance is also examined to see if any were made to accommodate the contractor's inability to meet the stated requirements, and why these accommodations were made.

Adherence to Delivery and Administrative Schedules

This area has to do with how well the contractor met contractual milestones and delivery dates for interim and end products as well as administrative deliverables, such as progress reports. Examine any schedule failures to determine why the schedule was not met and the extent to which government actions may have contributed to the schedule problems. Determine if contractual modifications were made to accommodate schedule failures and the circumstances under which they were made.

Record of Forecasting and Containing Costs

This area involves cost reimbursement, time and materials, and labor-hour contracts used where the government requirements are not defined sufficiently to use a firm-fixed price. This lack of definition often creates cost or hour problems as the contractor reacts to performance realities. As the contract progresses and the work requirements become better defined, the cost or hour requirements may well increase. Examine such increases to determine if contractor inefficiency or matters beyond the contractor's control caused them. The extent to which government actions may have contributed to the problems should also be determined. This area also includes an assessment of the accuracy of contractor estimates and how contract changes are priced.

History of Reasonable and Cooperative Behavior and Commitment to Customer Satisfaction

This area includes assessing contractor response to problems and changes that affect the delivery of a quality product or create administrative problems. A contractor concerned with customer satisfaction will respond quickly and cooperatively to problems and changes and demonstrate an interest in delivering a quality product. Be alert, however, to situations in which a contractor's reported problems represent an assertion of the contractor's rights under the contract as opposed to situations in which the contractor has simply failed to respond properly. For example, the fact that an offeror has submitted a number of contract claims in the past cannot be used to downgrade the offeror' past performance on the basis of a lack of reasonable and cooperative behavior. A contractor has a right to submit contract claims even if doing so irks the government. Because of its subjective nature, this area is difficult to evaluate.

Areas of Specific Concern

In addition to the considerations noted in the preceding paragraphs, there may be specific areas of concern particular to your requirement, such as staffing, quality control, or subcontracts—particularly if subcontractors will be doing a significant portion of the work. When evaluating at the subcontractor level, ensure that you explain exactly what will be evaluated and what documentation is required, because the offeror must pass this information down to its proposed subcontractors.

It should be noted that the evaluation of past performance is used as an indicator of how the offerors will perform under the current requirement. Tailor the description of past performance as necessary to ensure that you get only the information you need (i.e., do not use any of the evaluation areas noted above if they will not be important in discriminating between offerors). Ensure that the information to be obtained is relevant, meaningful, and related to the key performance criteria in the SOW.

EXPLAINING HOW PAST PERFORMANCE WILL BE EVALUATED

Assessing past performance is no easy matter; contractors are sensitive to allegations that they do not perform well. Ensure that offerors understand the term "past performance" and how it will be evaluated.

Define Past Performance

Define past performance in Section M of the RFP in terms of the kinds of information that will be evaluated. The OFPP definition below is a good starting point, but you should tailor it to your requirement. The definition should not include anything that will not be evaluated.

Past performance information is relevant information regarding a contractor's actions under previously awarded contracts. It includes the contractor's record of conforming to specifications and to standards of good workmanship; the contractor's record of containing and forecasting costs on any previously performed cost reimbursement contracts; the contractor's adherence to contract schedules, including the administrative aspects of performance; the contractor's history for reasonable and cooperative behavior and commitment to customer satisfaction; and generally, the contractor's business-like concern for the interests of the customer.[1]

Indicate How Past Performance Will Be Evaluated

In RFP Section M, state that past performance will be evaluated to assess the relative merits of the offeror's prior performance as compared to that of competing offerors. Indicate that the evaluation will be based on present and past performance information furnished by the offeror and other available sources such as other government agencies, suppliers, subcontractors, or customers of the offeror.

Indicate the Documentation Required

In the proposal preparation instructions (RFP Section L), identify the information that the offeror should submit as past performance information. Require offerors to identify current and past contracts for the same or similar work and include the contract number, dollar value, dates, name of the contracting agency, a contact telephone number, and a brief description of the work effort that demonstrates how the referenced contract relates to the proposed effort.

In addition, it is important to require offerors to identify contracts in which they experienced performance difficulties and to discuss the corrective action taken. Indicate that the offeror must provide evidence that it was able to identify the cause of the problems and demonstrate that the problems were resolved. Tell the offerors that if past problems are not fully addressed, it will be assumed that they still exist. If deemed appropriate, you should identify specific areas of concern, such as late deliveries, cost overruns, or product deficiencies, but do not limit the information to just those areas.

OBTAINING PAST PERFORMANCE INFORMATION

The primary source for past performance information is *the offeror*. Require each offeror to provide a reference listing of past or current contracts in the same manner as you require such information to support the evaluation of corporate experience. In most cases, a single listing will serve both purposes.

Checking Sources

Generally, the referenced contracts should be limited to those performed within the past three years, or another appropriate time frame. You should also consider limiting the number of references to whatever number you are prepared to check to verify the offeror's performance. While you are not required to check all of the referenced contracts, you risk a protest where you only check some, but not all, of the references. Generally such protests are unsuccessful, but they are disruptive to the procurement process regardless of the outcome.

Checking only the sources provided by the offeror is usually not sufficient, particularly since the offeror may not identify past contracts that had serious performance deficiencies. Other sources, such as the *Federal Procurement Data System* or the procurement data systems at the agency level, can help identify an offeror's past and current contracts. Private sector sources such as subcontractors, suppliers, financial institutions, and commercial customers may also be used. When using these sources you must ensure that written documents support any comments used in the evaluation.

Before contacting any sources, either within your agency or in other agencies, you should identify the personnel to be contacted. Your primary contact should be the individual responsible for monitoring the contract (the contracting officer's technical representative (COTR) or equivalent). This individual can address the contractor's technical performance. You should also contact the contracting officer, who can comment on the contractor's compliance with contractual requirements. The contracting officer has access to the official contract file, which may contain performance reports and assessments made during contract performance or upon contract completion.

FAR 42.1503 calls for an evaluation report to be done on a contractor's performance for each contract upon contract completion, with interim evaluations, as appropriate, for contracts over one year. These reports are to be provided to the contractor for comment and are retained on file as "source selection information." This information can only be released to other contracting officers or the contractor whose performance is being evaluated when needed for past performance evaluations. When checking an offeror's past performance, you should check the availability of these reports.

When requesting information from other agencies or sources, your biggest challenge will be getting someone to respond to your queries with usable information. Getting a negative response (and this is of greater interest) may be more of a problem than getting a positive response because the responder must expend more time and effort to explain why the offeror's past performance was deficient. You cannot accept "yes" or "no" responses to your questions when the response is negative. Explanations are required.

An agency's allegation of poor past performance, particularly when in conflict with reports of other agencies, should be examined closely, first to determine the accuracy of the allegation and then to determine if the reported poor past performance is likely to affect performance under the current contract.

It is not difficult to get a positive response, but you must remember to ask for identification of the contractor's strong points, too. These may prove to be important when trying to distinguish the quality of one offeror's past performance over that of another offeror.

Asking the Right Questions

Before examining your files or contacting other agencies for past performance information, you should develop a list of the questions you will ask. Questions should be tailored to your particular requirement and should reflect the SOW requirements, in terms of the work effort, as well as how the responses will be evaluated and scored. Design the questionnaire as though you were going to have to respond to it (i.e., keep it short and simple). You may have difficulty getting responses to long, convoluted questionnaires. Initially, you should ask general questions such as the following:

- If you had a choice, would you contract with this contractor again? If no, why not? If yes, does the contractor have any particular performance strong points?
- Did the end product or services meet contractual requirements, particularly with respect to the quality provided?
- Did the contractor complete the effort within the budget? If not, was the cost growth due to contractor inefficiency or lack of expertise?
- Did the contractor make contractual and administrative deliveries on time? If not, why not, and what specific delivery dates were not met?
- Were contract changes made because of the manner of the contractor's performance, particularly with respect to delivery times and contract specifications?
- Was the contractor cooperative and responsive to your needs?
- If there were problems, did the contractor act promptly to resolve them?

Responses to these questions will help you to properly assess past performance.

Since past performance is evaluated by a comparative assessment, you are looking for points that distinguish one proposal from another—either strong points that enhance an offeror's standing or weak points that indicate potential performance problems. With respect to *past performance problems*, you need to know, at a minimum, answers to the following questions, which can either be part of the questionnaire or used as follow-up questions:

- *What went wrong and why?* An allegation of problems in past performance must be specific and supported by a written explanation.
- *Who (government or contractor) was at fault?* Did the government contribute, directly or indirectly, to the problem?
- *Was the problem a local problem?* Was the problem related only to a particular contract, or the result of a higher-level corporate decision or policy? Corporate-level problems are often much more difficult to resolve and are more likely to affect the current contract than are local contract-related problems.
- *What corrective action was taken to resolve the problem?* This includes assessing whether the corrective action was responsive and timely, and corrected the problem. Past performance problems that have been corrected or will be corrected before performance of your contract begins should not be considered problems.
- *Have any past performance problems been inadequately corrected or otherwise remain unresolved?* Unless there is a strong showing that such problems will not reoccur, the presumption should be that unresolved problems are likely to reoccur.
- *Will contractor personnel involved with past performance problems be employed on the current contract?* This is particularly important with respect to unresolved problems. You cannot use blacklisting techniques, but the use of such personnel on your contract should be a matter for discussions. Do not assume that contractor personnel involved with problem contracts are responsible for the problems without discussing this with the contractor.

Getting Answers

Getting a timely response to your questions may be difficult. If you simply send out a questionnaire, with no advance notice, it may end up perpetually at the bottom of someone's in-basket. You should make an initial contact by telephone, speak to the personnel involved, explain what you are doing, and then send the questionnaire.

The following problems and potential solutions should be considered when planning your approach to contacting other agencies:

- *The contact person identified in the offeror's proposal may no longer be at the agency or may have transferred to other duties.* If the person cannot be located, ask if another COTR is involved with the contract, or ask the contracting officer for an analysis of the contract file.
- *The contract file may not be readily available.* If the file has been retired or for some other reason is not readily available in the contracting office, you are not likely to get a timely response. An initial telephone call will help to ascertain the availability of the file.
- *The contract file may not have been adequately documented.* There is no federal standard for documenting contractor performance. Some agencies document performance well; others do not document it at all. Even where documenting procedures exist, there is no guarantee that the documentation will have been done properly or, even if done properly, will provide the answers you seek.
- *The contact person may be too busy to respond in the detail required.* This is a particular problem with contracting personnel at the end of the fiscal year. An advance telephone call may help to get the cooperation of busy personnel.
- *The contact person may be reluctant to be candid if the agency bears some responsibility for the problem.* Agencies tend to frown on personnel who tell other agencies of their mistakes. You may have to read between the lines to properly assess negative reports.

- *Past problems may be more related to personality conflicts than a failure to meet requirements.* This is particularly true in "soft" areas such as a contractor's responsiveness to problems. A telephone conversation can often help assess if personality conflicts are part of the problem.
- *The problems may have resulted from honest differences of opinion, such as the interpretation of specifications or other requirements.* The validity of responses in such instances often depends on the candor of the responding individual, which underlines the importance of making an initial telephone call to establish rapport with the contact individual.

RATING PAST PERFORMANCE

When establishing the evaluation plan, consideration should be given to how past performance will be rated or scored. In the initial evaluation, past performance is assessed to develop an initial rating and ranking of offerors' proposals. This is done to establish a competitive range. In the final evaluation, past performance, and the other evaluation factors, are assessed on a comparative basis with the other proposals to determine the otherwise successful proposal.

Generally, there are two ways to rate past performance. You can rate past performance with respect to the degree of risk in the same manner proposal risk is evaluated (i.e., by a broad scoring range such as "low risk," "moderate risk," and "high risk," or you can rate it in the same manner as the other noncost evaluation factors using a numeric system, color codes, or some other method.

The evaluation of past performance is essentially an assessment of the risk of successful performance based on an offeror's past performance history. Risk assessment is usually rated using broad ranges, as noted above, primarily because it is not realistic to try to rate it more closely. A quote cited in a Comptroller General decision amplifies this point.[2]

Past performance instills confidence that a company will probably do well but does not, in and of itself, guarantee that a company will do well, whereas, poor performance is a good indicator of performance risk.

When assessing risk, however, it is necessary to fully document the risk assessment. Thus while two proposals might be rated as moderate risk, the documentation should identify the differences, if any, between the two proposals relative to performance risk. The documented detail of the differences between two equally rated offerors may be sufficient to support a preference of one over the other, such as strong points in one proposal that are not found in the other proposal.

Past performance may also be rated numerically, by color code, or whatever other method is used to rate the noncost evaluation factors. The OFPP *Guide to Best Practices for Past Performance* provides an example of how past performance could be rated numerically. There is a potential problem, however, when trying to measure past performance too closely.

Trying to score past performance on a numerical basis can be an exercise in futility. What is the difference between a past performance score of 90 and a score of 85 in terms of the likelihood of successful performance? Numerical scoring, in effect, tries to measure how good is good and how bad is bad. This is probably more information than you really want, and may not be that accurate. The effective use of a numerical system, or any system with a lot of ratings, depends to a large degree on the information base being used. The other noncost evaluation factors (other than corporate experience) are evaluated based on the information provided in the offeror's proposal, using the offeror's own words. Past performance, however, uses a larger information base, including information provided from government records and other sources. This information is very subjective and its validity may be questionable.

Scoring by color codes, however, uses broader ranges and is similar to risk assessments in that it does not imply the preciseness of numerical scoring. Color coding is more appropriate in the evaluation of past performance than numerical scoring, but evaluating it separately as performance risk is probably the most appropriate evaluation technique.

The evaluation of past performance is worthwhile with respect to identifying poor performers, but trying to distinguish the best performer from among the good performers is a "coin toss." Using a broad scoring range that does not attempt to distinguish the best of the best helps avoid this scenario.

Past performance may also be used as an unweighted, unscored evaluation factor as is often done with cost or price. The importance of past performance in the evaluation would then depend on the evaluation of the other technical evaluation factors. If the other factors are evaluated as essentially equal, past performance increases in importance and could become the primary discriminating factor in the award decision. This might be appropriate where past performance is not considered to be a major discriminator, but you do not want to ignore it completely.

When evaluating a best value procurement you are always subject to unintended consequences. The least important evaluation factor may become the deciding factor because all of the other factors are rated as essentially equal. The best way to deal with this potential problem is to ensure that the evaluation results are fully documented, particularly with respect to the assessment of the differences between the proposals. This documentation will help if you must make a tradeoff determination between past performance and cost or price, or other technical factors.

References

1. OFPP Policy Letter 92-5, Past Performance Information, dated 1/11/93.
2. Keane Federal Systems, Inc., B-280595, 10/23/98, GCR 110,440.

CHAPTER 4

Other Considerations in Selecting Evaluation Factors

Chapter 2 addressed the selection of evaluation factors and the use of the standard evaluation factors. Chapter 3 discussed the use of past performance as an evaluation factor. Other considerations in the selection of evaluation factors need to be addressed, however, including cost realism, responsibility factors, key personnel, facility use, proposal risk, and security requirements.

COST REALISM

As noted at the end of Chapter 2, the evaluation of cost realism involves an assessment of the degree to which proposed costs accurately represent the proposed work effort. Cost realism may be used as a stated or unstated evaluation factor, but it is best used as a stated factor to help ensure that offerors price their proposals realistically.

Relationship to Technical Understanding and Risk Assessment

Cost realism is inherent to evaluating an offeror's understanding of the requirement. Proposed costs that do not accurately represent the proposed technical effort indicate a lack of technical understanding. Cost realism is also inherent to evaluating risk in that unrealistic pricing increases the likelihood that contract performance will not be successful at the costs proposed.

Relationship to Cost Analysis

Cost realism was not well defined until the FAR 15 rewrite and was often confused with cost analysis, despite the fact that they are different activities.

FAR 15.404-1(c) defines cost analysis as the review and evaluation of the separate cost elements and profit in an offeror's proposal (including cost or pricing data or information other than cost or pricing data), and the application of judgment to determine how well the proposed costs represent what the cost of the contract should be, assuming reasonable economy and efficiency.

FAR 15.404-1(d) defines cost realism as the process of independently reviewing and evaluating specific elements of each offeror's proposed cost estimate to determine whether the estimated proposed cost elements are realistic for the work to be performed; reflect a clear understanding of the requirement; and are consistent with the unique methods of performance and materials described in the offeror's technical proposal.

Cost realism analysis and detailed cost analysis are different and can produce different results. A cost analysis could produce a determination that the proposed costs are reasonable for what the offeror proposes to do, while a cost realism analysis could indicate that the same offeror's proposed costs are not realistic because they do not match with the proposed technical approach and the government requirement.

Cost analysis addresses an offeror's cost proposal on the basis of what the costs should be and whether they are reasonable for what the offeror proposes to do. For example, in a cost analysis, the detailed labor rates are examined to see if the rates are reasonable for the labor categories proposed and if the projected rates reflect reasonable judgment with respect to such factors as inflation. The results would be a determination that either the rates were reasonable or they were not reasonable and the probable costs should be a certain amount. *The results of the cost analysis are used when negotiating the contract cost or price.*

Cost realism addresses the same costs, but in a different way. For example, in a cost realism analysis, the labor rates are examined to determine the level (senior, junior, journeyman, etc.) of labor proposed. The level of proposed labor is matched against what the offeror promised in its technical proposal and what is necessary to meet the government requirement. If a high-level, state-of-the-art technical approach was proposed but the proposed labor rates indicated that most of the personnel were inexperienced personnel in junior (lower paid) positions, it would appear that the proposed costs are not realistic for the proposed technical approach. *The results of a cost realism analysis may be used in a technical evaluation and in the discussions that follow to measure an offeror's understanding of the requirement. The results may also be used in the negotiation of the proposed cost or price as a backup for the results of the cost analysis.*

Cost analysis and cost realism analysis also differ with respect to the personnel and data required to conduct the analysis. Auditors and cost/price analysts who are experienced in deciphering contractor's cost proposals perform cost analysis and may be supported by technical personnel. Cost realism analysis requires technical personnel who can make the connection between the technical approach and the proposed costs with the support of cost/price analysts as appropriate. Cost realism analysis requires less data than cost analysis, as it examines specific areas such as labor costs, engineering costs, labor and overhead rates, and make or buy plans.

Cost analysis and cost realism do not reflect differing functions but differing perspectives. Cost analysis is centered on the pricing perspective, to determine if the price is fair and reasonable. Cost realism is viewed from both the pricing perspective and the technical perspective.

From the pricing perspective, cost realism plays an important part in deciding if additions or subtractions are appropriate in determining the probable or evaluated cost or performance of each offeror. Keep in mind that the source selection decision is made based on evaluated costs, not the dollars set forth in the proposals.

From the technical perspective, cost realism is important as a means of assessing the offeror's understanding of the requirement and the viability of its proposed technical approach. If the costs are not realistic, there is a good chance the proposed technical approach is also flawed.

Both perspectives can be applied in the evaluation of the same procurement. It is not "double-counting" to use cost analysis to determine the reasonableness of the proposed costs and cost realism as the basis for adding to or subtracting from the proposed costs to develop an evaluated price and for upgrading or downgrading a proposal on the basis of technical understanding as demonstrated by the proposal's cost realism.

Consideration of Contract Type

The use of cost realism in the evaluation depends to an extent on the contract type.

Cost Reimbursement

A cost realism analysis is required when evaluating a cost reimbursement proposal. In the cost-reimbursement environment, the government is obligated to pay actually incurred contract costs. An offeror's estimated costs, however, may not provide valid indications of these costs. The proposals, therefore, must be evaluated for cost realism and the proposed costs adjusted, for evaluation purposes, so source selection decisions may be made based on evaluated costs that more closely represent what the costs are likely to be.

Time-and-Material and Labor Hours

You should consider using cost realism analysis to evaluate time-and-materials and labor-hour proposals. These are labor intensive efforts; therefore, evaluating the realism of proposed labor costs (i.e., proposed staffing, labor mix, and technical approach) is important to assessing both the offeror's understanding of the requirement and the offeror's proposed price.

Fixed-Price

With respect to fixed price proposals, however, the Comptroller General discourages the use of a cost/price realism analysis except when used as a measure of the offeror's understanding of the requirement, as shown in Example 4.1.

Example 4.1—Use cost/price realism analysis on a fixed-price proposal only when necessary as a measure of the offeror's understanding of the requirement[1]

Generally, cost realism (a measure of the likely cost of performance in a cost-reimbursement contract) is not a factor in the evaluation of proposals when a fixed-price contract is to be awarded, since the government liability is fixed, and the risk of cost escalation is borne by the contractor.[2] However, since the risk of poor performance when a contractor is forced to provide services at little or no profit is a legitimate concern in evaluating proposals, an agency in its discretion may, as it did here, provide for a price realism analysis in the solicitation of fixed price proposals.[3] The depth of an agency's price realism analysis is a matter within the sound exercise of the agency's discretion.[4]

In general, you should consider using cost/price realism analysis in the evaluation of a fixed-price contract if your requirement is technically complex or labor intensive, where doing so will assist in the evaluation of the offeror's understanding of the requirement.

Notification to Offerors

When planning to perform a cost realism evaluation, whether as part of the cost analysis or separately in the technical evaluation, indicate in Section M of the RFP that a cost realism analysis will be done, generally how it will be done, and how the offeror should document its proposal with respect to cost realism.

Section M should also include a notice that the proposed costs will be assessed for cost realism and that the proposed costs may be adjusted, for the purposes of evaluation, based on the results of the cost realism evaluation. In addition, warn offerors that if they do not substantiate all proposed costs and fully explain cost inconsistencies, particularly in their final proposal revisions, their proposals may be downgraded.

RESPONSIBILITY FACTORS

The evaluation of proposals is essentially an assessment of an offeror's overall technical approach and related pricing as expressed in its proposal. Basically, this assessment is restricted to the contents of the proposal itself.

Responsibility, on the other hand, relates to evaluating a prospective contractor's ability to perform a contract from a business standpoint. Responsibility is assessed based on information provided in the offeror's proposal and information obtained from other sources.

Traditional responsibility factors such as corporate experience and past performance, however, are often used in the evaluation process. It is important to understand the relationship between responsibility and evaluation factors to avoid problems when using responsibility factors as evaluation factors.

Responsibility Standards

FAR 9.103(c) requires that contract award be made only to responsible contractors.

... award of a contract to a supplier based on lowest evaluated price alone can be false economy if there is subsequent default, late deliveries, or other unsatisfactory performance resulting in additional contractual or administrative costs. While it is important that government purchases be made at the lowest price, this does not require an award to a supplier solely because that supplier submits the lowest offer. A prospective contractor must affirmatively demonstrate its responsibility, including, when necessary, the responsibility of its proposed subcontractors.

In addition, FAR 9.104-1 and 9.104-2 established the following standards for determining responsibility. It should be noted that some of the circumstances can change between the time of evaluation and award. This will affect when a responsibility determination is made because a final determination of responsibility must be made just prior to award.

Credit

The contractor must have adequate financial resources or the ability to obtain them. The contractor's ability to meet this standard can change between the time of evaluation and the time of award.

Capacity

The contractor must be able to comply with the required or proposed delivery or performance schedule, considering all existing business commitments, both government and commercial. The contractor's ability to meet this standard can change between the time of evaluation and the time of award.

Past Performance

The contractor must have a satisfactory record of past performance, which includes having sufficient tenacity and perseverance. The contractor either meets this standard or doesn't; compliance is historical in nature and cannot be changed between the time of evaluation and the time of award. This can be mitigated, however. Before finding a contractor nonresponsible because of poor past performance, the contracting officer should determine if the circumstances were beyond the contractor's control or if the contractor has taken appropriate corrective action. If the problems were beyond the contractor's control or the problems have been fixed, the contractor can be determined to be responsible.

Integrity

The contractor must have a satisfactory record of integrity and business ethics. The contractor either meets this standard or doesn't; compliance is historical in nature and cannot be changed between the time of evaluation and the time of award. This can be mitigated, however, if the contractor has taken action to fix the problem, such as firing the employees that caused the problem and demonstrates that it has established internal procedures that will prevent the problem from recurring.

Competency

The contractor must possess the necessary organization, experience, accounting and operational controls, and technical skills or demonstrate the ability to obtain them. This includes production control procedures, property control procedures, quality assurance measures, and safety programs applicable to the materials to be produced or services to be performed. This standard applies to both the prime contractor and subcontractors. The contractor's ability to meet this standard can change between the time of evaluation and the time of award.

Capability

The contractor must possess the necessary production, construction, and technical equipment and facilities or demonstrate the ability to obtain them. The contractor's ability to meet this standard can change between the time of evaluation and the time of award.

Be Otherwise Qualified and Eligible

The contractor must be otherwise qualified and eligible under applicable laws and regulations. There are laws and regulations, primarily in the labor and environmental areas, which, if violated, make a contractor ineligible for award of a government contract.

Some procurements are limited to contractors who are on qualified bidders lists (QBL), qualified manufacturers lists (QML), and qualified products lists (QPL). To be listed, a contractor must have met certain qualification requirements prior to award.

Contractors debarred, suspended, or proposed for debarment are excluded from receiving government contracts.

The names of such contractors are listed in the "Parties Excluded from Procurement Programs" maintained by the General Services Administration (GSA).

Generally the circumstances that made a contractor unqualified or ineligible to receive an award are historical in nature and as such cannot be changed.

Special Standards

Special standards of responsibility may be used when experience has demonstrated that unusual expertise or specialized facilities are needed for adequate contract performance. A contractor's ability to meet these standards varies depending on the specific requirements.

A requirement for specialized experience is usually considered to be historical in nature because the offeror either has the experience or doesn't; however, in some instances a contractor can hire an individual with the requisite experience before the time of award.

A requirement for specialized facilities is usually considered to be changeable because an offeror may be able to obtain the facilities required during the evaluation and negotiation process.

Ability to Obtain Resources

With respect to the credit, competency, capability, and special standards, a contractor must either possess the resources or be able to obtain them by the time of contract award. A contractor demonstrates possession by showing sufficient internal resources to meet the standards or by proposing to subcontract in those areas in which it does not meet the standards. Offerors demonstrate the ability to obtain the necessary resources by evidence of a commitment or explicit arrangement at the time of award to rent, purchase, or otherwise acquire the necessary resources.

Meeting the Standards

A prospective contractor must meet *all* of the standards above to be eligible for contract award.

Using Responsibility Factors in the Evaluation

Lately, it has become common practice for government agencies to use responsibility factors as evaluation factors. This can create problems, however, because responsibility is a pass/fail factor. A contractor is either responsible or not responsible, and award cannot be made to a nonresponsible contractor, even if it is nonresponsible with respect to only one of the responsibility factors. Two basic problems arise when responsibility factors are used as pass/fail evaluation factors: the timing of the determination and the need to refer nonresponsibility determinations that involve a small business to the Small Business Administration (SBA).

Timing

Responsibility is finally determined just prior to award, although it may be assessed earlier in the process. FAR 9.105-1(b)(3) states that information on financial resources and performance capability shall be obtained or updated on as current a basis as is feasible up to the date of award. This includes five of the eight standards noted above: credit, capacity, competency, capability, and special standards. These responsibility factors are subject to change during the evaluation and negotiation process. There is often a period of time, sometimes months, between the evaluation and the award of a contract. A rejection based on the failure to meet one of the standards noted above made during the initial evaluation could be seen as premature if the contractor fixes the problem prior to contract award. Contractors usually win protests based on such actions.

When necessary, however, it is permissible to delay contract award to permit an otherwise successful offeror to cure problems concerning its responsibility, as illustrated by Example 4.2.

Example 4.2—Government may allow bidder time to cure responsibility problems #1[5]

Here the contract start date was revised twice in order to comply with the FAR 19.809 requirement that SBA determine whether Classico was competent and responsible to perform as SBA's subcontractor. Since the SBA was unwilling to approve the award because Classico's responsibility was in question, the Coast Guard's decision to revise the start date in order to permit the SBA the opportunity to consider the matter was proper. That is, the delay in award to January 1 to allow Classico the opportunity to obtain adequate financing was mutually agreed to by the Coast Guard and SBA as contemplated by applicable regulations. See also Base-Operation-Mgmt.-Serv. Inc.,[6] (agency may delay award for a reasonable period of time to permit a low bidder to cure problems concerning its responsibility). Moreover, the contract start date was not fixed at October 1, as contended by New Life, but could be extended for reasonable periods of time for such reasons as permitting a low bidder an opportunity to obtain the ability to perform the contract.[7]

New Life argues that the Coast Guard's actions with respect to the start date resulted in the misapplication of definitive responsibility criteria. We disagree. A definitive responsibility criterion is an objective standard, such as a specific number of years of particular specified experience, established by the agency to measure an offeror's ability to perform the contract.[8] Here, the contract start date was not an objective standard for measuring performance under the contract, but rather was a material provision of the contract, which by its own terms was flexible.

The case in Example 4.2 is only one of many in which the Comptroller General has indicated that the government may allow the otherwise successful offeror or bidder time to cure responsibility problems. The ruling in Example 4.3 more clearly explains why.

Example 4.3—Government may allow bidder time to cure responsibility problems #2[9]

Whether a proposed contractor's production facilities are adequate for contract performance involves a question of responsibility, that is, a bidder's performance capability.[10] An agency may allow a prospective awardee a reasonable period of time after bid opening within which to cure a problem related to its responsibility since contract award and not bid opening is the critical time for determining the responsibility of a firm.[11]

It is important to note that responsibility is determined just prior to contract award and not at the time of bid opening or the receipt and evaluation of proposals in a negotiated procurement. Despite the wording of the FAR, which in a number of places indicates that responsibility may be determined early in the evaluation process, you must guard against a premature determination that an offeror is nonresponsible and therefore should be rejected immediately.

Past performance, integrity, and otherwise qualified and eligible standards, however, are historical in nature in that they deal with events that happened in the past. As such they cannot be changed and could be the basis for a nonresponsibility determination during the initial evaluation. Your most prudent action, however, would be to wait until discussions are concluded and the final proposal revisions received and evaluated before making a responsibility determination. You should address any questions about responsibility during the discussions. If the offeror cannot satisfactorily account for the problems, you then have a better basis for your decision.

Small Business

FAR 9.104-3(d) requires that nonresponsibility determinations regarding small businesses be referred to the SBA. You cannot reject a proposal from a small business on the basis of responsibility factors without referring the matter to the SBA, because such a rejection is tantamount to a nonresponsibility determination. The SBA has the final word as to the responsibility of small business firms. The SBA reviews all small business nonresponsibility determinations, and if it does not agree with the agency, the SBA will issue a certificate of competency (COC). The COC is a determination that the firm is responsible. It is binding on all government agencies.

The Comptroller General's position on the use of responsibility factors in evaluations and the involvement of the SBA and the Small Business Act is illustrated in Example 4.4.

Example 4.4—Findings of nonresponsibility must be reviewed by the SBA[12]

The Act provides that when a procuring agency believes a small business concern will be unable to satisfactorily perform a given contract due to questions regarding the qualities or characteristics listed, the procuring agency must refer the matter to the SBA for a final determination in that regard.[13] On the other hand, under the procurement statutes and regulations, contracting agencies are responsible for awarding contracts on the basis of proposals that are "most advantageous to the United States"[14] and to sources "whose performance is expected to best meet stated government requirements."[15] Procuring agencies are responsible for including in solicitations the evaluation factors necessary to determine which proposals are most advantageous to the government;[16] these evaluation factors often include offeror experience, management, and other matters that traditionally have been regarded as bearing on responsibility. 10 USC 2305(a)(3)(Supp II 1990) added that evaluation factors must include the quality of the product or services to be provided, including technical capability, management capability, and prior experience of the offeror.[17]

In light of the obvious overlap between the Small Business Act and the procurement statutes, we have recognized that, while procuring agencies may use responsibility-type factors for the technical evaluation of proposals, they may do so only if the agency's needs warrant a relative assessment comparing offerors in those areas. This means that an agency may not avoid the requirements of the Small Business Act by determining offeror responsibility in the guise of a technical evaluation that finds offerors acceptable or unacceptable with regard to traditional responsibility criteria.[18] Here, the record establishes that DLA is reasonably assessing offeror's relative production capability (including personnel, machinery, and a production plan), experience, and quality control. Accordingly we do not view the RFP evaluation scheme as inconsistent with the Small Business Act.

The gist of this ruling is that where an agency uses responsibility-type factors for evaluation, on a pass/fail basis, it must still refer nonresponsibility determinations to the SBA, if a small business is involved.

A responsibility factor is, by its very nature, a pass/fail factor. An offeror is either responsible or not responsible. You cannot change a responsibility factor into an evaluation factor by simply labeling it as such. A responsibility factor evaluated on a pass/fail basis is still a responsibility factor, subject to the SBA COC process. To avoid SBA involvement, you must transform the responsibility factor into an evaluation factor.

Transforming Responsibility Factors to Evaluation Factors

Responsibility is a determination of an offeror's capability to successfully perform the proposed contract as measured by the responsibility standards. A determination of responsibility is not a qualitative assessment; an offeror is either responsible or not responsible, and there are no comparisons with other offerors. To transform a responsibility factor to an evaluation factor, you must change both the manner of assessment and the standard of evaluation.

This is not as difficult as it sounds. To transform a responsibility factor, change the manner of assessment from pass/fail to a comparative assessment and the standards from the fixed responsibility standards to evaluation criteria that measure the quality of performance rather than adherence to particular standards.

You can transform traditional responsibility factors such as past performance by assessing the factor qualitatively, that is, determining how bad or good the past performance was and how this reflects on the prospective performance. The "how bad" or "how good" assessment is then matched (comparative assessment) against the performance of the competing offerors to assess the relative value of the offeror's past performance with respect to the other offerors' past performance and how this reflects on the prospective performance.

You can use responsibility-type factors as technical evaluation factors only if the evaluation is done by a comparative assessment in which each factor and subfactor is scored and ranked in accordance with its expressed relative importance.

Technical evaluation factors are not subject to SBA review because, in a comparative assessment, failure to meet the requirements of a technical evaluation factor does not mandate automatic rejection, merely a lowering of the assigned score or ranking. The Comptroller General ruling in Example 4.5 illustrates this point.

Example 4.5—Responsibility factors evaluated on a pass/fail basis rather than by comparative assessment are subject to SBA review[19]

The technical subfactor on which MSSC's proposal was judged technically unacceptable—corporate experience—traditionally is considered a responsibility factor, that is, a matter relating to MSSC's ability to perform the contract.[20] While traditional responsibility factors may be used as technical evaluation criteria in negotiated procurement,[21] the factors may be used only if circumstances warrant a comparative evaluation of those areas.[22] Otherwise, in effect, an agency, under the guise of making a technical evaluation of proposals, actually would be determining the responsibility of the offeror. Under the Small Business Act, agencies may not find that a small business is nonresponsible without referring the matter to the SBA. Thus a small business may not be found technically unacceptable under an evaluation criterion that measures a traditional responsibility factor unless the agency has performed a proper comparative evaluation/relative assessment of competing proposals under that criterion, or unless the matter is ultimately referred to the SBA for a final determination.

Here the record shows that the Coast Guard did not use the responsibility-type technical evaluation criterion for the purpose of a comparative evaluation of the merits of the proposals received. Rather, proposals were found technically acceptable on a go/no-go basis with award to be made to the lowest cost, technically acceptable offeror. MSSC's proposal was rejected solely because of the firm's insufficient corporate experience, without regard to how the rest of its proposal was judged. In this regard we note that MSSC otherwise received a score above the minimum qualifying score set for inclusion in the competitive range (The establishment of such predetermined cut-off scores is not in accord with sound procurement practice).[23] *Under these circumstances, the determination that MSSC was technically unacceptable was, in effect, a determination by the contracting agency that MSSC was not a responsible contractor. Therefore MSSC's elimination from the competitive range without referral to SBA was improper.*

In Example 4.5, the agency may have intended to use a comparative assessment, but when it established and applied an automatic cut-off score for rejection, it converted the corporate experience factor to a pass/fail factor. This made the rejection of the protester subject to SBA referral because corporate experience is a responsibility factor when evaluated on a pass/fail basis.

Problems such as those in Example 4.5 can easily be avoided by not combining pass/fail factors and comparative assessment factors in the same evaluation. If a particular factor is so important that it can only be evaluated on a pass/fail basis, it should be identified as a responsibility factor to be evaluated just prior to award. You *must* make a determination of responsibility just prior to contract award.

Obtaining Responsibility Information

Where you intend to use a responsibility-type factor as an evaluation factor you must obtain the information needed for evaluation from the offeror's proposal. To ensure that you get this information, determine what is needed, such as information on past performance or corporate experience, and then require submission of the information through the proposal preparation instructions. Require only that information related to the evaluation factor as it is defined in the RFP.

FAR 9.105-1(b)(1) indicates that responsibility information, including preaward surveys, should be obtained promptly after receipt of proposals, and in some cases before issuing the RFP. This requirement should be interpreted loosely. Collecting responsibility information on all potential sources can involve a considerable, but unjustified effort. Most procurements are time-sensitive, and your efforts must be devoted to executing a prompt award. Collecting responsibility information on offerors not in line for award is not likely to help in making a prompt award. In addition, this effort could lead to making a premature determination of nonresponsibility, based on information that is outdated by the time of award.

If you intend to collect responsibility information, it might be more practical to wait until either the final proposal revisions have been received and evaluated or the otherwise successful offeror has been selected. This limits the information-collecting activity, focuses it on those offerors actually in line for award, and assures that the information collected is timely. It also eliminates the need to compile information about offerors who are not going to be awarded a contract. As noted in FAR 9.105-1(c), the following are the primary sources of responsibility information:

- *The list entitled Parties Excluded from Procurement Programs, maintained by the GSA.* This lists contractors who are debarred, suspended, proposed for debarment, or otherwise declared ineligible. You should reject listed offerors on receipt of their proposals because they are not eligible for the award of government contracts unless the acquiring agency head or designee determines, in writing, that there is a compelling reason to make them eligible (see FAR 9.405).
- *Pertinent information from your records and experience,* including verifiable knowledge of personnel within the contracting office, audit offices, contract administration offices, and other contracting offices. You can collect this information any time after the offerors are identified. Generally, however, it is only pertinent to offerors in line for award: either those offerors who have submitted final proposal revisions or the otherwise successful offeror.
- *Information from the prospective contractor,* including proposal information, questionnaire replies, financial data, information on facilities, production equipment, and

personnel information. This information should be required, as appropriate, in the proposal preparation instructions. When requesting this information, be careful to clearly distinguish between information required for evaluation purposes and information required to determine an offeror's responsibility. If you confuse offerors on this point, you are likely to generate a protest.

- *Information from preaward survey reports*. Preaward surveys are normally required when the information on hand or readily available is not sufficient to make a responsibility determination. Preaward surveys are pertinent only to offerors who are in line for award: either those offerors who have submitted final proposal revisions, or the otherwise successful offeror.
- *Information from other sources* such as publications; suppliers, subcontractors, and customers of the prospective contractor; financial institutions; other government agencies; and business and trade associations. Generally, this information is only pertinent to offerors who are in line for award: either those offerors who have submitted final proposal revisions, or the otherwise successful offeror.

KEY PERSONNEL

The identification of key personnel and their qualifications is often important in the evaluation of proposals for research and development, information technology services, technical and other support services, and other requirements in which the quality of the key personnel is vital to the success of contract performance. The purpose of this evaluation factor is to assess the availability, competency, pertinent education, and related experience of the offeror's key technical, management, and administrative personnel, as appropriate, with respect to their potential contribution to successful contract performance.

Key personnel is often used as a primary evaluation factor where the qualifications of the key personnel are critical to the success of the contract. Where the key personnel factor is important, but not critical, it is usually used as a subfactor under the management factor. It may also be appropriate to use it in conjunction with the staffing evaluation factor.

Using Key Personnel in Proposal Evaluation

There are two basic steps to the use of key personnel in proposal evaluation:

- Identify the key positions so the offerors can provide specific names and resumes
- Identify the qualifications required of the personnel proposed to fill these positions so the offeror can provide the appropriate qualification information.

Identify the Key Personnel Positions

If you are going to evaluate the qualifications of those who will fill key positions, you must first identify those key positions. The proposal preparation instructions should require offerors to submit resumes for each key person. The instructions should also indicate the information offerors must include in the resumes.

Depending on the requirement, key personnel can include technical, management, operational, and administrative personnel. Identify the key personnel positions (such as project manager, assistant project manager, senior engineer, and principal investigator) you consider most important to the success of the contract. Describe the positions in general terms; specific titles vary significantly throughout the industry.

You must exercise care in the number of positions you identify; you must evaluate the qualifications for each. In a fairly complicated R&D support services solicitation, one agency identified more than 200 positions as key personnel.

The positions ranged from project manager to ship's cook. Most of these positions were not vital to program success, but once identified, each had to be evaluated. This was a waste of time and effort, because the results did not help to discriminate between the offerors.

In most instances, only the primary management and technical positions, such as the project manager and leading technical or scientific personnel are critical, for evaluation purposes, to the success of the program. It is important to determine which positions are important and keep the number manageable.

Identify the Minimum Qualifications Required

If you are going to evaluate key personnel, you must tell the offerors the minimum qualifications required. If you do not identify the qualification requirements in the RFP, it will be difficult to determine that an offeror failed to propose qualified personnel.

Key personnel qualifications are usually expressed in terms of a minimum number of years of experience and educational level. This should be done carefully. Key personnel requirements should be expressed in terms of the experience and educational level you would want if you were going to hire for that position on your staff.

With respect to experience, you should consider what experience would be required to perform the proposed effort. There should be a direct relationship between the past experience and the proposed requirements. Consider the extent to which the experience really qualifies an individual for the proposed effort. Managing a number of small contracts, for example, may not be qualifying experience if the requirement is to manage a single large and complex contract. Identify experience levels that relate to the proposed effort, but only if such experience is significant to that effort.

Key personnel qualifications may be stated generally or specifically depending on your requirement. Generally, the greater the relative importance of this factor, the greater the specificity of the qualifications. Greater specificity is needed because the more important evaluation factors should serve as discriminators between the proposals. Otherwise, all the proposals will be technically equal, price will become the discriminating factor, and you will have expended a considerable amount of evaluation time with little to show for your effort.

The minimum qualifications may also be combined, citing both general and specific requirements. For example, for a training requirement you might require four years of experience in a general area, such as adult education, to include two years of experience in a specialized part of the general area, such as procurement training.

The minimum key personnel qualifications are usually established in the SOW, but they could be set forth in a contract clause if the clause is appropriately referenced in Section M of the RFP. The minimum qualifications are part of the contractual requirement. While they are applicable to the solicitation for proposal preparation purposes, they are also applicable during contract performance, for the evaluation of proposed substitute personnel.

Once your minimum personnel requirements are set forth in the RFP, you must evaluate and award in accordance with the stated requirements. The requirements cannot be waived or changed, except by amending the RFP and allowing all offerors to submit revised proposals.

You may, however, introduce some flexibility by wording the qualification requirements so that the offeror may submit other, equivalent qualifications. This provides a degree of protection in the event there is equivalent qualifying experience or education of which you are unaware. The requirements should state that the offeror may submit equivalent experience, other than that specified, but the government is not obligated to accept such experience unless the government agrees that the equivalent experience meets the minimum qualification requirements.

Example 4.6, while not involving listed educational qualifications, illustrates what could happen if educational requirements are listed, and no flexibility is provided.

Example 4.6—Offer flexibility when listing experience or educational requirements[24]

In this case, the protester argued that the awardee's proposed material technologist did not meet the minimum qualification requirements, in that his resume showed that he did not have a degree in material technology or specialized work in the field (the RFP did not cite any educational requirements). The Comptroller General did not agree.

The record of the evaluation indicates that the TEB determined that the technologist has pioneered the testing of high-load bearing materials at earthquake velocities and their use in seismic isolators and possessed considerable experience in testing PTFE materials, particularly relating to the friction pendulum bearing. He had served as the material technologist for EPS for the seismic isolation retrofit of the water tank and apartment building projects, and has tested a variety of formulation of PTFE materials for use in bearings. The technologist is the inventor of the friction pendulum system and the TEB believed that the technologist exhibited more practical experience under this criterion than the technologist of any other offeror. The TEB determined that the technologist, although lacking in formal training in the field, demonstrated sufficient technical and practical experience in the field of PTFE material testing.

Based on our review of the qualifications of the EPS/VSL technologist, as set forth in the proposal, we find that GSA had a reasonable basis for its rating and determination that the technologist was acceptable. In this regard, we agree that no specific education requirements were imposed and that the considerable practical experience of the EPS/VSL technologist who invented the friction pendulum system could be considered under the evaluation scheme.

The protester's complaint about the material technologist's lack of schooling was denied because the RFP requirement did not cite any educational requirements and, therefore, there was no requirement for any particular educational background. If educational requirements had been listed, however, and no provision for substitute qualifications provided, the inventor of one of the only three acceptable systems would have been disqualified. As noted earlier, you can avoid such problems by permitting offerors to provide substitute qualifications that you can consider, or not, as the circumstances warrant.

Be sure that you can justify your selection of the minimum qualifications necessary to effectively perform the duties of the key personnel. Do not write your requirements around a particular individual unless you are prepared to defend the required qualifications against allegations that they are unduly restrictive. You may face the additional problem that the particular individual is not available because of work on other contracts, illness, or death, in which case you would be stuck with restrictive requirements that few can meet. It would be beneficial to document your rationale for the file, particularly when your requirements appear to be restrictive.

In addition to identifying the minimum qualifications, you may, if appropriate, indicate the percentage of time you expect the key personnel to devote to the contract. This should be done, for example, when you want to ensure that a specific key individual, rather then a subordinate, does the work, or when it is likely that the key individual will not be working full time on your project. This issue is of particular concern when dealing with academics who use research assistants for much of their work, or corporate divisions whose senior personnel oversee a number of contracts.

If you do not want to dictate the degree of participation but want a commitment, use the proposal preparation instructions to require offerors to propose the degree of participation by key personnel. You should also indicate how you will evaluate the degree of participation, usually by indicating an acceptable minimal participation or by indicating that you will favor the highest the degree of participation.

Using a Key Personnel Clause

Use a key personnel clause in conjunction with listing the qualifications of key personnel. This makes use of the key personnel contractually binding and gives you control over substitutions made during contract performance.

Depending on your agency, you may have to develop your own clause locally. The FAR does not provide a standard key personnel clause. Some agencies have developed agency-wide clauses, but most, including DOD, have not.[25] A key personnel clause should do the following:

- Require the contractor to identify the specific key personnel by position and name (the clause should have blanks for this purpose).
- Require the contractor to provide resumes that demonstrate the appropriate education and experience of the named key personnel.
- State that the contractor may not change key personnel without advance notification and must submit the substitute's name and qualifications for review by the contracting officer. Do not word the clause so that the substitute must have the same or better qualifications. If the original individual was the world's leading expert on the subject matter, no one else could match the qualifications. Require only that the substitutes must meet the minimum qualifications set forth in the SOW.
- Indicate that review and approval of the substitute may be done after the fact, by ratification. This should be worded so that it applies only in unusual instances such as death, sickness, or other events that would preclude advance submission. Otherwise, you will lose control over substitutions.

Availability of Key Personnel

Before using key personnel as an evaluation factor, you must understand its limitations. The key personnel clause and the use of key personnel qualifications as an evaluation factor does not require the contractor to use a specific individual. The contractor must provide personnel who meet the qualification standards established in the contract and, when applicable, possess the requisite security clearances. Because of the time period between proposal writing and contract award, the availability of specific personnel may change.

Example 4.7 summarizes the Comptroller General's position on the availability of key personnel.

Example 4.7—Offeror must propose key personnel who can reasonably be expected to perform the work[26]

Proposing to employ specific personnel that the offeror does not expect to actually use during the contract performance has an adverse effect on the integrity of the competitive procurement system and generally provides a basis for proposal rejection.[27] This does not mean that an offeror must use the personnel it proposed or risk losing the contract for which it is competing in every case. For example, where the offeror provides firm letters of commitment and the names are submitted in good faith with the consent of the respective individuals (that is, the offeror is not proposing personnel it has no intention of providing), the fact that the offeror, after award, provides substitute personnel does not in itself make the award improper.[28]

Conversely, however, an offeror may not be awarded a contract where it does not have the individuals' permission to use their names for key positions for which they are proposed and cannot provide a satisfactory explanation for use of the names.[29] Similarly, where an offeror knows prior to submission of its BAFO that proposed key employees are no longer available, the offeror should withdraw the individuals and, in its BAFO, propose substitutes who will be available.[30] To do otherwise is, in effect, to misrepresent the availability of proposed personnel which, in turn, compromises the validity of the technical evaluation, regardless of whether post-award substitutions of key personnel may later be made and approved by the agency pursuant to a clause in the awardee's contract.[31]

We are not unmindful of the difficulty faced by a non-incumbent contractor of securing a qualified work force sufficient to secure an award. Nevertheless, we believe that an offeror has a responsibility to propose persons who it reasonably may expect will be available for contract performance without the RFP having to provide that the offeror must do so. This is particularly so where the solicitation expressly states that a proposal should include only those persons the contractor intends to use for performance and that the proposal will be evaluated based upon the qualifications of those persons. Otherwise, there is no assurance to the government that it will receive what was offered.[32]

Here, the record showed that, at the time it submitted its BAFO, Telesec could not reasonably have expected that two of the four individuals it proposed as key personnel would be available to perform the contract.

While Telesec had a two point advantage in technical score as well as a significant price advantage, the evaluators thought highly of the two key individuals Telesec proposed who in fact were not available and considered these positions to be important to successful performance of the contract. We conclude that it is possible that the selection would have been different but for Telesec's failure to assure the availability of the personnel it proposed. We sustain the protest for this reason.

When using key personnel as an evaluation factor, you must be aware of the problems you might encounter in the evaluation, and try to avoid them by carefully describing the key personnel factor and how you will evaluate it. Consider the following:

- Indicate in the RFP that the proposal should include only those persons the offeror intends to use for contract performance and that the proposal will be evaluated based on the qualifications of those persons.
- Require the offeror to propose personnel currently employed by the offeror and to submit letters of commitment from each person not currently employed by the offeror or employed only part time. These letters must authorize the offeror to use the individual's resume and state that the individual agrees to work under the contract in the event of award.
- Advise offerors that they are responsible for ensuring that proposed personnel are available for contract per-

formance and for indicating any changes to proposed personnel in their final proposal revision. In addition, point out that the resumes of personnel first identified in the final proposal revision must be complete. There will be no opportunity to correct any deficiencies in these resumes because no discussions will be conducted after receipt of the final proposal revisions.

Even though the offeror must provide firm letters of commitment and submit the names in good faith with the consent of the respective individuals, the offeror's substitution of personnel after award does not make the award improper. No offeror can guarantee that proposed personnel will actually work on the contract. An offeror is only required to make its best efforts to propose persons that will be available for performance under the contract. Generally, current employment by the offeror or letters of commitment from the proposed individuals determine availability.

FACILITY USE

Availability of facilities—the contractor's possession of adequate facilities and sufficient resources and plant capacity to do the work—is a responsibility factor. If it is used as an evaluation factor, it must be evaluated by comparative assessment.

You can avoid the responsibility connotations by evaluating facility use rather than facility availability. Define facility use as the offeror's ability to demonstrate its expertise and understanding of the requirement through a description of how the offeror proposes to use existing facilities or facilities to be acquired in contract performance. Consider the quantity and quality of the proposed facilities, facilities layout and use, and the accuracy and capacity of the proposed equipment with respect to the offeror's proposed technical approach, the offeror's technical expertise, and the probability that the proposed facility use will produce the required technical results within the required time frame.

When facility use is evaluated as just described, the offeror's possession of adequate facilities is not germane. Simply evaluate whether the offeror knows what facilities are required and how to use them. Evaluate the offeror's understanding of facility use (technical evaluation) and only later, if the offeror is in contention for award, determine if the offeror possesses or can obtain the requisite facilities (responsibility determination). This technique is appropriate if you plan to conduct a discrete responsibility evaluation after the technical evaluation and the possession of adequate facilities is important to successful contract performance.

PROPOSAL RISK

Technical evaluation factors are assessed in terms of how well the offeror's approach or expertise meets or exceeds the SOW requirements. Proposal risk is an assessment of the likelihood the proposed approach will be successful. It indicates the extent of the risk of failure or disruptive problems during contract performance *as evidenced by the proposed technical approach.* Assessment of proposal risk usually takes into account the potential risk of schedule disruption, increased costs, or degradation of performance.

Do not confuse proposal risk with performance risk. Performance risk pertains to the assessment of an offeror's *past performance and how this might affect the proposed contract.* You assess performance risk based on reports of how well the offeror performed on other contracts. Proposal risk, however, assesses the risk represented by the proposed technical approach and is based on the offeror's technical proposal. Unfortunately, these terms are often used interchangeably; therefore, if you are going to evaluate proposal risk, you should ensure that the RFP fully defines what is to be evaluated.

The Air Force provides a good definition of proposal risks:[33]

> "The risks which must be assessed are those associated with cost, schedule, and performance or technical as-

pects of the program. Risks may be inherent in a program by virtue of the program objectives relative to the state of the art. Risks may occur as a result of a particular technical approach, manufacturing plan, the selection of certain materials, processes, equipment, etc., or as a result of the cost, schedule, and economic impacts associated with these approaches. Risk may also occur from the impact that these will have on the offeror's ability to perform."

Proposal risk is usually evaluated separately from the other evaluation factors and may be evaluated by a separate evaluation group, depending on the complexity of the requirement. Splitting the evaluation in this manner permits the evaluators to more effectively focus their attention on what they are evaluating.

Whether proposal risk is evaluated separately or not, you should require offerors to provide a risk analysis in complex procurements such as R&D. Risk analysis identifies risk areas and indicates how the offeror plans to minimize the impact of the risks on the overall success of the program. This not only provides information helpful in assessing the risks, but also indicates how well the offeror understands the requirement.

The evaluation of proposal risk does not necessarily require that it be stated as an explicit evaluation factor. Sometimes the manner in which the offeror proposes to do the work represents a proposal risk and this can be evaluated as an unstated technical evaluation factor, as shown in Example 4.8.

Example 4.8—Proposal risk can be evaluated even if not stated as an evaluation factor #1[34]

An offeror's proposed use of uncompensated overtime was considered to be an unacceptable proposal risk because the contracting agency determined that it would adversely affect the offeror's retention of skilled personnel and be a risk with respect to the quality of work. The Comptroller General agreed:

We find that the Army reasonably concluded that QRI's substantial reliance on employees working 2,600 hours per year created a risk with regard to QRI's ability to double the size of its work force and to retain new and existing employees. Consideration of risk created by an offeror's approach to performing required tasks is properly considered in the evaluation of technical proposals.[35] *We also find reasonable the Army's determination that the product QRI offered, that is, manhours performed by employees working 50 hours per week, was less advantageous than it would have been had QRI chosen not to propose this level of extended work week.*[36]

Do not assume that all uncompensated overtime represents an unacceptable proposal risk. The use of uncompensated overtime can be a valid approach and its attendant risk must be evaluated and assessed in each instance it is used.

The risk of successful performance as represented by the offeror's proposal is inherent in any evaluation and does not need to be set forth as a specific evaluation factor to be evaluated, as shown in Example 4.9.

Example 4.9—Proposal risk can be evaluated even if not stated as an evaluation factor #2[37]

Agencies have broad discretion in determining the manner and extent to which they will make use of technical and price evaluation results. In reaching an award decision, an agency may make price/technical tradeoffs, subject only to the test of rationality and consistency with established evaluation factors.[38] *In this connection, it is well established that consideration of the risk involved in an offeror's approach is inherent in the evaluation of technical proposals.*[39] *This is because the degree of risk present is clearly related to the technical approach proposed and the ability of the firm to perform the contract.*[40] *Thus an agency properly may find one technical proposal superior to another based on their relative levels of risk, and make a price/technical tradeoff decision in favor of that technically superior proposal. That is what the Navy did here. Given that technical factors were considered as important as cost in the evaluation, moreover, we think the agency reasonably concluded that the relative strength of Symetric's proposal—based on its low risk—under the most important evaluation factor and two other factors warranted paying Symetric's 2.56 percent higher price.*

You should consider using proposal risk as an explicit evaluation factor where the requirement is complex, unusual, or otherwise considered to be difficult to perform successfully. You must keep in mind, however, that should the manner in which the offeror proposes to accomplish the work represent a proposal risk, this risk may be evaluated even if proposal risk is not a stated evaluation factor.

SECURITY REQUIREMENTS

Do not overlook the evaluation of security requirements in solicitations involving classified material or restricted access. Some contracts can only be performed by contractors who possess or can obtain the appropriate facility and personnel clearances.

Facility clearances are necessary where contract performance requires that the contractor possess and store classified material at the contractor's facility. Normally, the possession of or the ability to obtain facility clearances is not used as an evaluation factor. Obtaining a facility clearance is primarily a matter of establishing the appropriate security procedures and acquiring the appropriate security containers. This should be an SOW requirement. Adherence to this requirement thus is a matter of contract administration, and failure in this area is a breach of contract.

Personnel clearances are required when contractor personnel will have access to classified government material. Security, as related to having appropriately cleared personnel or being able to obtain the required clearances, may be used as an evaluation factor, as shown in the Comptroller Generals decision in Example 4.10.

Example 4.10—Security clearance requirements may be an evaluation factor[41]

We find no legal basis on which to object to the security clearance requirement. The solicitations state that orders placed under the contemplated contracts will be classified up to and including "CONFIDENTIAL-RESTRICTED DATA, FORMALLY RE-

STRICTED DATA, and NATIONAL SECURITY INFORMATION." The solicitations also state that the information contained in publications so classified affects the national defense, and notify the contractor that the transmission of such material or the revelation of its contents in any manner to an unauthorized person is prohibited and punishable by laws. The solicitations indicated that the security clearance is required of the successful bidder prior to award because all deliveries and/or pickups of classified materials must be handled only by employees of the contractor who have security clearance in accordance with DOE security regulations.

It thus is apparent from the solicitations that a security clearance is required to meet the agency's minimum needs. Neither in its protest nor in its comments on the agency report does Link show that the requirement is not needed to perform the contract. Instead, Link essentially complains that the requirement unduly restricts competition because clearance action will not be initiated by DOE until a contractor has received notice of contract award, and that, anyway, the process takes much too long for it to be practicable for a bidder that is not already cleared to compete. However, the fact that a requirement may be burdensome or even impossible for a particular firm to meet does not make it objectionable if it properly reflects the agency's minimum needs.[42] *This part of the protest is denied.*

The key here is that contractual performance could not even begin without the presence of appropriately cleared contractor personnel. If work could have begun with uncleared personnel and there was sufficient time for those personnel requiring clearances to obtain them, the Comptroller General's response might have been different.

Do not assume that a requirement for personnel with security clearances automatically requires the personnel to have the clearances before contract award. Examine your requirement carefully to determine when (in terms of contract performance) the presence of cleared personnel is required, and establish the solicitation requirements accordingly.

If your minimum needs can only be met by a contractor who can provide appropriately cleared personnel at the time of award, you should use security as a primary evaluation factor. In some instances, however, a contractor can obtain interim clearances while being processed for a full clearance. You must provide for this, if it applies.

If your requirement does not require cleared personnel immediately, but does require that they be cleared eventually, use security as an evaluation factor in which you evaluate the offeror's recruiting and pre-clearance screening plans (as a measure of the offeror's ability to obtain personnel who can be cleared) by a comparative assessment. In such instances, security should probably be evaluated as a subfactor under the management factor.

References

1. RMS Information Systems Inc., B-280521.3, 10/21/98, GCR 110,447.
2. PHP Healthcare Corp.; Sisters of Charity of the Incarnate Word, B-251799 et al., 5/4/93, 93-1 CPD ¶366 at 5.
3. Id.
4. Family Realty, B-247772, 7/6/92, 92-2 CPD ¶6 at 4.
5. New Life Group, Inc., B-247080.2, 5/22/92, 92-1 CPD 463, GCR 106,650.
6. Base-Operation-Mgmt.-Serv. Inc., B-218223, 2/26/1985, 85-1 CPD 242.
7. FAR 12.102(a) and 12.103.
8. Action Serv Corp., B-246413, B-246413.2, 3/9/92, 92-1 CPD ¶267, GCR 106,455.
9. Base-Operation-Management-Service Inc., B-218223, 2/26/85, 85-1 CPD ¶242.
10. U.S. Jet Aviation, B-214093, 5/25/84, 84-1 CPD ¶575.
11. Ameriko Maintainance Co., B-208485, 8/27/82, 82-2 CPD ¶184.
12. F&H Manufacturing Corp., B-244997, 12/6/91, 91-2 CPD ¶520, GCR 106,118.
13. PHE/Maser, B-238367.5, 8/28/91, 91-2 CPD ¶210, GCR 105,817; Sanford and Sons, 67 CG 612 (1988), 88-2 CPD 266.
14. 10 USC 2305 (b)(4)(B).

15. FAR 15.603(d).
16. 10 USC 2305(a)(2) (Supp II 1990).
17. See 41 USC 404(7) (1988); FAR 9-104-1; SBD Computer Servs; B-186950, 12/21/76, 76-2 CPD ¶511; Design Concepts, B-184754, 12/24/75, 75-2 CPD ¶410.
18. See Flight International Group, B-238953, 9/28/90, 90-2 CPD ¶257, GCR 104,757; Sanford and Sons, 67 CG 612 (1988), 88-2 CPD ¶266.
19. Modern Sanitation Systems, Corp., B-245469, 1/2/92, 92-1 CPD ¶9, GCR 106,205.
20. FAR 9.104-1(c)(e); Clegg Indus., B-242204.3, 8/14/91, 91-2 CPD ¶145, GCR 105,760.
21. Pacific Computer, B-224518.2, 3/17/87, 87-1 CPD ¶292, GCR 100,464.
22. Flight Int'l; 90-2 CPD ¶257, GCR 104,757; Sanford & Sons, 88-2 CPD ¶266.
23. PRC Computer Center Inc., 55 Comp. Gen. 60 (1975), 75-2 CPD ¶35.
24. Dynamic Isolation Systems, Inc., B-247047, 4/28/92, 92-1 CPD ¶399, GCR 106,587.
25. Such as DOT clause 1252.215-71, Key Personnel and Facilities; NASA clause 18-52.237-71, Key Personnel and Facilities; EPA clause 1552.237-12, Key Personnel; and DOE which has two 952.235-70, Key Personnel, for R&D contracts and 970.5204-42, Key Personnel, for management and operations contracts.
26. CBIS Federal Inc., B-245844.2, 3/27/92, 92-1 CPD ¶308, GCR 106,495.
27. Informatics, Inc., 57 Comp. Gen. 217 (1976), 78-1 CPD ¶53.
28. Unisys Corp., B-242897, 6/18/91, 91-1 CPD ¶577, GCR 105,573. See also: Robocom Systems, Inc., B-244974, 12/4/91, GCR 106,114; and Informatics Gen. Corp., B-224182, 2/2/87, 87-1 CPD ¶105, GCR 100,293.
29. Ultra Technology Corp., B-230309.6, 1/18/89, 89-1 CPD ¶42, GCR 102,765.
30. Omni Analysis, 60 Comp. Gen. 300 (1989), 89-1 CPD ¶239.
31. Ultra Technology Corp., supra.
32. Management Serv., Inc., B-184606, 2/5/76, 76-1 CPD ¶74.
33. AFFARS Appendix AA, paragraph 3-5d.

34. Quantum Research, Inc., B-242020, 3/21/91, GCR 105,316.
35. Modern Technologies Corp.; Scientific Sys. Co., B-236961.4; B-236961.5, 3/19/90, 90-1 CPD ¶301, GCR 104,210.
36. Wheeler Indus., B-230972; B-230972.2, 8/16/88, 88-2 CPD ¶150. See also Public Law No. 101-510, 104 Stat. 1613 (1990) (legislation requiring DoD to issue regulations ensuring that proposals are evaluated on a basis that does not encourage mandatory uncompensated overtime).
37. Herley Industries, Inc., B-251792.2, 4/16/93, GCR 107,508.
38. Shirley Constr. Corp., 70 Comp. Gen. 62 (1990), 90-2 CPD ¶380, GCR 104,874.
39. S-TRON, B-244767.2, 5/1/92, 92-1 CPD ¶409, GCR 106,595.
40. Consolidated Group, B-220050, 1/9/86, 86-1 CPD ¶21.
41. G.S. Link and Assoc., B-229604; B-229606, 1/25/88, GCR 101,535.
42. Microwave Radio Corp., B-227962, 9/21/87, 87-1 CPD ¶288, GCR 101,129; Joerns Healthcare Inc., B-227697, 9/18/87, 87-2 CPD ¶276, GCR 101,124.

CHAPTER 5

Expressing the Relative Importance of Evaluation Factors

FAR 15.304(d) states that all evaluation factors and significant subfactors that will affect contract award *and their relative importance* shall be stated clearly in the solicitation. In addition, FAR 15.304(e) requires that the solicitation indicate the relationship of the non-cost (technical) evaluation factors to cost or price (which is a required evaluation factor). This is done by indicating that the combined technical evaluation factors are (1) significantly more important, (2) approximately equal to, or (3) significantly less important than the cost or price factor. The FAR offers no further information as to how the relative importance of the individual technical evaluation factors should be expressed in the solicitation.

Chapters 2 through 4 addressed the problems of deciding what evaluation factors and subfactors to include in the RFP; this chapter discusses how to express the relative importance of those factors and subfactors you decide to use.

TECHNIQUES FOR EXPRESSING RELATIVE IMPORTANCE

The following paragraphs address how to express the relative importance of the technical evaluation factors and significant subfactors. It is important to remember that in order to submit accurate and realistic proposals, offerors must understand the criteria against which their proposals will be evaluated. Therefore, you must identify the evaluation factors and significant subfactors and the degree of importance accorded to each in a manner that clearly expresses the interrelationships of the factors and subfactors. The clarity with which you express the relative importance directly affects the quality of the proposals.

It is in your best interest to express the relative importance as directly and clearly as possible.

The Comptroller General has long ruled that evaluation factors and their relative importance must be identified, as shown in Example 5.1.

Example 5.1—Expressing the relative importance of technical evaluation factors[1]

As a matter of sound procurement policy, the fullest possible disclosure of all of the evaluation factors and their relative importance is to be preferred to reliance on the reasonableness of the offeror's judgment as to the relative significance of the various evaluation factors.

List the Factors in a Descending Order of Importance

The relative importance of evaluation factors and subfactors is first expressed by listing them in the RFP in a descending order of importance. This demonstrates the general order of importance. Simply listing the factors in a descending order of importance, however, is not sufficient when some of the factors are more important than others.

When certain factors or subfactors are significantly more important than others, you should include a more explicit expression of the relative importance. This is done by expressing the relative importance that each factor and subfactor carries in the overall evaluation scheme, either through a narrative explanation or by publishing the specific weights assigned.

Provide a Narrative Explanation of the Relative Importance

You may express the relative importance of the evaluation factors and subfactors through a narrative explanation such as the following:

Factor A is three times as important as factor B. Factor B is twice as important as C. All subfactors are of equal importance.

Subfactor A1 is of significantly greater importance than subfactors A2 and A3, which are of equal importance.

Use a narrative explanation only if the relationships are simple, easy to understand, and there are not very many factors to consider.

Where there are a number of evaluation factors and subfactors and the relationships are complex, the use of a narrative explanation can be a problem. The narrative explanation often becomes extremely complicated and fails to effectively communicate your intentions. The following example, taken from an actual solicitation, illustrates the problem. Avoid using such narratives.

Criteria I and IV are of equal importance and each are of greater weight. Criteria II and III are of less importance and are of equal weight. Individually, Criteria I and IV are 1 1/2 times the weight of Criteria II and III individually. Subcriteria I.A is of greatest weight and is twice as important as Subcriteria I.d, which is of least importance. Subcriteria I.b is of slightly less importance than Subcriteria I.A and Subcriteria I.C is of slightly greater importance than Subcriteria I.D.

A narrative explanation provides a legally sufficient reference to the relative importance of the evaluation factors, may be misunderstood by the offeror. Such misunderstandings can result in a proposal from an otherwise qualified offeror that does not adequately address your concerns even where the relationships are simple. Offerors should not have to guess at the relative importance of the evaluation factors and subfactors. In effect, this makes an offeror's ability to guess well an unstated evaluation factor. In most instances, the most effective way to clearly express relative importance is to publish the specific evaluation weights in the RFP.

Publish the Specific Evaluation Weights in the RFP

If you intend to use more than three primary evaluation factors or there are significant differences in the relative importance among the factors, publish the specific evaluation weights in the RFP. Numerical weights provide the clearest explanation of the relative importance of the factors and help ensure that each offeror will address the issues represented by the evaluation factors and subfactors with appropriate emphasis.

Despite the fact that the use of numerical weights is the most effective way to avoid evaluation problems, some agencies still hesitate to use them. The following are some of the arguments used.

- *By revealing the relative weights, the government will open itself to protests against how the factors and relative weights were derived.* This was never a valid argument. Even in the 1970s, such decisions were within an agency's discretion and were not questioned by the Comptroller General unless they represented an arbitrary abuse of discretion, were made in bad faith, or were in violation of law or regulation. This remains the case, as demonstrated by Example 5.2.

Example 5.2—Protester's disagreement with agency does not establish that evaluation was unreasonable[2]

We will examine an agency's evaluation only to ensure that it was reasonable and consistent with the stated evaluation criteria and applicable statutes and regulations, since determining the relative merit of competing proposals is primarily a matter within the contracting agency's discretion.[3] The protester's mere disagreement with the agency's judgment does not establish that an evaluation was unreasonable.[4]

- *Identifying the evaluation weights in the RFP would commit the government to using those weights and this would limit the government's flexibility in evaluation.* This argument runs counter to one of the basic premises of the competitive process—that the process must "ensure impartial and comprehensive evaluation of offerors' proposals."[5] In the context of this argument, "flexibility" appears to mean the freedom *not* to plan ahead and *not* to reveal how proposals will be evaluated because the government does not want to be held accountable for its actions.

If the competitive process is to work, offerors must be fully informed as to how their proposals will be evaluated. Explicitly stating the evaluation weights to be used achieves this goal. Failing to fully inform offerors provides a basis for misunderstandings and protests. Even if the government wins the protest, the government loses, in terms of the time and effort devoted to defending itself from the protest.

- *Identifying the evaluation weights in the RFP would permit prospective contractors to "game" the evaluation process by stressing those factors carrying the greatest weight, to the detriment of the other factors, and somehow gain an advantage over the government.* To consider this argument, you need to examine the purpose of the technical evaluation of competitive proposals. Initially, the purpose of the evaluation is to provide a basis for the determination of the competitive range—deciding with whom you will negotiate. Finally, the purpose is to identify that proposal that is most advantageous to the government. The evaluation criteria and their relative importance as set forth in the RFP control the evaluation process and these are developed on the basis of what is important to the government. If the offeror responds to your RFP by stressing those factors you have indicated are the most important, who is "gaming" whom? If the offeror does not respond with the appropriate emphasis, it is likely that it will receive a lower evaluation score. It should be noted here that the Comptroller General has ruled in favor of full and timely disclosure of all relevant evaluation criteria (see Example 5.1).

Unless the circumstances clearly indicate otherwise or your agency regulations expressly prohibit publishing of the specific weights, you should express the relative importance of the evaluation factors by listing them in a descending order of importance and indicating the specific weights assigned to each factor and subfactor.

Expressing the Relative Importance of Evaluation Subfactors

If a subfactor is listed in Section M of the RFP, it is a significant subfactor and you should indicate its relative importance. In Chapter 2, Example 2.2 showed that all significant subfactors should be listed in the RFP, and Example 2.3 indicated that unstated subfactors inherently related to a primary evaluation factor need not be revealed. The bottom line is that if a subfactor is significant enough to be listed in the RFP, its relative importance should also be listed. To do otherwise is to risk a misunderstanding and subsequent protest.

ESTABLISHING EVALUATION WEIGHTS FOR TECHNICAL EVALUATION FACTORS

Whether you plan to publish the evaluation weights or not, you must still establish a weighting scheme if you are planning to evaluate by a comparative assessment. If you are planning to evaluate by pass/fail criteria, evaluation weights are not necessary because you are not evaluating relative quality, only whether the proposals are minimally acceptable.

Establish the evaluation weights in conjunction with the development of the evaluation plan and evaluation criteria. A review of the SOW and the selected evaluation criteria will help determine the relative importance of each factor in the evaluation. The weights to be assigned can be developed through a standard approach or an analytic approach.

Using the Standard Approach

The standard approach is the most commonly used method of assigning weights. In this approach, the relative importance of the factors is determined starting with the most important factor and working down to the least important factor. Weights are usually assigned on the basis of 100 percent or 100 points (but other numbers such as 1,000 points can also be used). The standard approach is accomplished as shown in Figure 5.1:

Figure 5.1—Standard Approach

Primary Evaluation Factor		**Assigned Weight**
I	Technical Approach	60 (1)
II	Understanding the Requirement	20 (2)
III	Management Approach	10 (3)
IV	Key Personnel	05 (4)
V	Corporate Experience	05 (04)

(1) The most important factor is usually assigned 40–60 points in order to express its great importance. An assignment of 60 points leaves 40 points to be divided among the rest of the factors.
(2) Normally the second most important factor is assigned the largest part of the remaining points. An assignment of 20 points leaves 20 points to be divided among the remaining factors.
(3) The third most important factor usually receives the bulk of the remaining points, in this case 10 points, half of the remaining points.
(4) The rest of the points are usually divided evenly among the remaining factors. An assignment of 10 points to the Management Approach leaves 10 points to be divided among the remaining factors.

The standard approach has a basic flaw. While the first and most important factor usually receives an appropriate weighting, the weighting of the remaining factors is constricted by the remaining points that can be assigned. Once the most important factor has been weighted, assigning weights to the other factors is more a matter of dividing them up rather than reasonably assessing relative importance.

One way to counter this problem is to go back, after the initial weight assignment, and rearrange the numerical assignments so they more closely reflect the relative importance of the factors.

Rearrangement usually involves inflating the numbers to achieve the appropriate relationships. There is nothing inherently wrong with weightings that total 244 points, or even 2,440 points. There is no rule that says 100 points is the maximum that can be used. Once the total points have been assigned, if you feel that the evaluators would be more comfortable working on the basis of 100 percent, you can normalize the assigned points to 100 percent (see Figure 5.3).

Using the Analytical Approach

The analytical approach to assigning weights is less commonly used, probably because it is perceived as requiring a greater effort. In this approach, the relative importance is assessed starting with the least important factor and analyzing the relative importance of each factor from the bottom up. This technique provides a better balance in weighting because it requires an analysis of the interrelationships of each of the factors and has no artificial limitations such as a maximum number of points. This approach is accomplished as shown in Figure 5.2.

Figure 5.2—Analytical Approach

Primary Evaluation Factor (1)	**Assigned Weight**
1. Technical Approach	60 (4)
2. Management Approach	20 (3)
3. Corporate Experience	10 (2)
Total Points	90

(1) List the primary evaluation factors in descending order of importance.
(2) Assign the least important factor a nominal weight of 10 (10 or 100 are the numbers most often used, but any number will do).
(3) Analyze the relationship between factor 2 (the next higher factor) and factor 3. Assuming factor 2 is twice as important as factor 3, assign 20 points to factor 2.

(4) Now analyze the relationship between Factor 1 (the next higher factor) and Factor 3. This is where the analytic approach may become complicated. Once you establish the relationship between Factors 1 and 3, you must also consider the relationship between Factors 1 and 2. For example, assume the intended overall relationship was that Factor 1 was to be three times as important as Factor 2 and five times as important as Factor 3, and Factor 2 was to be twice as important as Factor 3. This would result in Factor 1 being assigned 60 points to maintain the intended relationship with Factor 2 or 50 points to maintain the intended relationship with Factor 3. Assigning Factor 1 50 points will not work, however, because it changes the relationship between Factor 1 and Factor 2.

If the figures do not work out the first time, re-evaluate the relationships to determine which are the most important to maintain. Normally, the relationships between the top two or three factors are the most important. The relationship between Factors 1 and 2 was more important than the relationship between Factors 1 and 3. Therefore, Factor 1 was assigned 60 points which maintains the relationship between Factors 1 and 2 and generally does not significantly change the relationship between Factors 1 and 3. Generally, you should not assign a factor the same number of points as another factor unless it is determined that the factors are equal in importance.

It is often necessary to change assigned weights during this analysis to ensure that all of the relationships express the intended relative importance, one to another. Be flexible; there is nothing sacred about these numbers. They may be manipulated as necessary to develop an appropriate relationship among all of the factors. This technique is not meant to be an exact mathematical exercise; the analysis determines the *relative* importance, not the mathematically exact relationship.

Using Normalization

In Figure 5.2 the total number of points assigned to the primary evaluation factors is 90. It is not mandatory to go further; however, most evaluators are more comfortable with a 0–100 point system. Conversion to a 0–100 basis is done through a process called "normalization." To normalize individual factor weights to a 0–100 percent basis, divide the points assigned to each factor by the total points and multiply by 100, as shown in Figure 5.3.

Figure 5.3—Normalization

Primary Evaluation Factor	*Assigned Weight*		*Total Points*	×	*100*		*Normalized Weight*
1. Technical Approach	60	÷	90	×	100	=	67
2. Management Approach	20	÷	90	×	100	=	22
3. Corporate Experience	10	÷	90	×	100	=	11
	90						100

Subfactor Weights

Once the evaluation weights have been assigned to the primary evaluation factors, the next step is to determine the relative importance of the subfactors. This is done in the same way as the primary factors. In Figure 5.4, the evaluation subfactors for Factor 1, Technical Approach, are listed in a descending order of importance. The least important subfactor has been assigned a nominal 10 points. The originally intended relationships were as follows:

- Subfactor A is five times more important than Subfactor C, and is roughly equal to Subfactor B.
- Subfactor B is three times more important than Subfactor C.

Figure 5.4—Weighting Of Subfactors

	(1)	(2)
1. TECHNICAL APPROACH		
A. Technical Plan/Methodology	50	**42**
B. Understanding the Requirement	30	**40**
C. Identification of Problems	10	**10**
Total Points	90	**92**

(1) In column (1) the relationships of Subfactor A to Subfactor C, and Subfactor B to Subfactor C, have been maintained, but doing so throws the relationship of Subfactor A to Subfactor B out of line.

(2) It is now necessary to reexamine the interrelationships to determine which are the most important. Assume that maintaining the relationship of A to B is more important than maintaining the original relationships of A to C and B to C. To achieve this relationship, arbitrarily decrease A by 8 points, and increase B by 10 points. This leaves the relationship of A and B roughly equal, and generally maintains the relationship of A to C, but increases the difference between B and C. This is closer to what you wanted than the numbers in column (1). This is only one of a number of possible solutions. The important thing is to manipulate the numbers as necessary to develop integrated relationships that express your needs. Keep in mind that you are not trying to be mathematically precise, all you need to do is find a combination of numbers that generally reflect the intended relationships.

The analytical approach is not as difficult as it looks, it just requires more discipline than the standard approach. The primary difference between these approaches is that the analytical approach forces you to consider all of the evaluation factors and more carefully examine the intended relationships between them.

Normalizing Subfactor Weights

Once weights have been assigned to all the primary evaluation factors and normalized, you must decide how to normalize the subfactors. Subfactors may be normalized to 100 percent in the same manner that the primary factors were normalized, or they can be normalized to the total points assigned to each primary factor. Either method produces satisfactory results. Figure 5.5 demonstrates how this might be done.

Figure 5.5—Normalizing Subfactor Weights

Evaluation Factors/Subfactors	(1)	(2)	Primary Factor Weight Normalized to 100 Percent
I. Technical Approach			67
A. Technical Plan/Methodology	46	31	
B. Understanding the Requirement	43	29	
C. Identification of Problems	11	7	
Total	100%	67	

Column (1) shows the subfactors normalized to 100%.

$42 \div 92^{*} \times 100 = 46\%$ $40 \div 92 \times 100 = 43\%$ $10 \div 92 \times 100 = 11\%$

Column (2) shows the subfactors normalized to the total points assigned to the primary evaluation factor. To do this, multiply the assigned weight of the primary factor (67) by the percentage in column 1. Some creative rounding may be required to make the totals come out right. Do not be concerned, mathematical precision is not required.

$67 \times 46\% = 31$ $67 \times 43\% = 29$ $67 \times 11\% = 7$

The same procedure can be applied to each of the primary evaluation factors and related subfactors.

*See column (2) in Figure 5.4.

ESTABLISHING THE RELATIVE IMPORTANCE OF COST OR PRICE AS AN EVALUATION FACTOR

In negotiated procurement, cost or price need not be the primary basis for award, or even a significant factor, but *must* always be considered to some degree as a part of the final source selection.[6] Therefore the RFP must indicate that cost/price will be evaluated *and* show its relative importance with respect to the technical evaluation factors in the evaluation.[7] If you do not indicate that cost/price will be evaluated, your procurement may be successfully protested. If you do indicate that cost/price will be evaluated but fail to indicate the relative importance, the cost/price factor will be considered to be equal with the technical considerations, as shown in Example 5.3.

Example 5.3—If the relative importance of the cost/price factor is not stated, it is equal to the technical factors[8]

In short, because the solicitation clearly put offerors on notice that a cost/technical tradeoff would be performed, but did not establish that either cost or technical/management factors would be more important, the agency was obligated to give approximately equal weight to technical/management factors and cost in the source selection decision.[9]

The relative importance of the cost/price factor may be expressed as a weighted or unweighted evaluation factor. Generally, cost/price should be used as a weighted factor (expressed in the RFP) when you want this factor to have significant importance. You should use cost/price as an unweighted factor when you want the technical aspects to dominate the evaluation. In any event, the RFP must clearly express your intentions.

Cost/Price as a Weighted Evaluation Factor

When cost/price is used as a weighted evaluation factor it usually is weighted relative to the total of the non-cost (technical) evaluation factors, such as weighting technical at 70 percent and cost/price at 30 percent. Weighting the cost/price factor can have unintended consequences. As discussed in the following paragraphs, using cost/price as a weighted factor may reduce the value (technical difference) of the technical factors and may unreasonably inflate the value of the lowest-priced proposal.

The problem here is that an unusually low-priced proposal may appear to be of greater value than it really is because the low price (after weighting) inflated its score. Even though award decisions should not be based primarily on numerical scores, the scores and resulting rankings do have considerable influence in the decision-making process. Generally, if you want technical factors to predominate, do not weight cost/price at more than 25 to 30 percent. Although this does not guarantee that you will avoid problems with an unusually low-priced proposal, it will minimize its effect. Figure 5.6 and Examples 5.4 through 5.6 illustrate this point. Government agencies commonly use the formula shown in Figure 5.6 to ensure a comparative evaluation of the cost/price factor (see Chapter 6).

Figure 5.6—The Basis for Examples 5.4, 5.5, and 5.6

- Two proposals have been received.
- The evaluated cost of Company A is $387,000. A total of 92 technical points were assigned. Company A is considered to have a significantly superior technical proposal.
- The evaluated cost of Company B is $193,500. A total of 69 technical points were assigned. Company B has the lowest evaluated price, but is considered to have a less acceptable technical proposal.

The Cost/Technical Formula To Be Used

$$\frac{\text{Cost of lowest acceptable offer}}{\text{Cost of acceptable offer being evaluated}} \times \text{Maximum number of cost points} + \text{Weighted technical score for acceptable offer being evaluated} = \text{Total score for offeror being evaluated}$$

EXAMPLE 5.4—Application of cost/technical formula where technical is 70 percent and cost is 30 percent

$$\frac{\$193{,}500}{\$387{,}000} \times 30\ (=15) + 64.4\ (70\%\text{ of }92) = 79.4\ (\text{Company A})$$

$$\frac{\$193{,}500}{\$193{,}500} \times 30\ (=30) + 48.3\ (70\%\text{ of }69) = 78.3\ (\text{Company B})$$

On the basis of the raw technical score, Company A has a 23-point advantage (92 to 69), but this changes when cost is factored in, as shown in the following:

- In the application of the formula, Company B gains 15 points in cost because the lowest cost offeror always gets 100 percent of the cost points.
- Company B also gains 6.9 technical points because converting the raw score technical points to show the relative importance (70 percent) of the technical factors gives Company B less of a reduction (from 69 to 48.3) than Company A (from 92 to 64.4). The technical difference between A and B is reduced from 23 points to 16.1 points.
- The total gain for Company B is 21.9 points through application of the formula, leaving only a 1.1 point difference between the proposals.

A careless contracting officer might assume that this means that the proposals are roughly equal and award can be made on the basis of lowest cost. In fact, a cost/technical tradeoff analysis (see Chapter 13) would now be required to determine the relative value of the technical and cost differences. The question to be addressed is whether the *technical* differences between Company A and B are worth the *price* premium of $193,500 that would be paid if award is made to Company A.

EXAMPLE 5.5—Application of cost/technical formula where technical is 60 percent and cost is 40 percent

$$\frac{\$193{,}500}{\$387{,}000} \times 40\ (= 20) + 55.2\ (60\%\text{ of }92) = 75.2\ (\text{Company A})$$

$$\frac{\$193{,}500}{\$193{,}500} \times 40\ (= 40) + 41.4\ (60\%\text{ of }69) = 81.4\ (\text{Company B})$$

In this example, Company A loses even more ground because of the greater importance of cost in the application of the formula:

- Company B gains 20 points in cost because the lowest-cost offeror always gets 100% of the cost points.
- Company B also gains 9.2 technical points because converting the raw score technical points to show the relative importance (60 percent) of the technical factors

gives Company B less of a reduction (from 69 to 41.1) than Company A (from 92 to 55.2).

- Total gain for Company B is 29.2 points through application of this formula, resulting in Company B receiving an overall score 6.2 points *higher* than Company A.

A careless contracting officer might assume that the higher score warrants award to Company B, however, as in Example 5.4, a cost/technical tradeoff analysis would now be required to determine the relative value of the technical and cost differences.

In both examples, the technical superiority of Company A was reduced by application of the formula. But the real problem is the impact of unusually low prices on the formula results; with the 70/30 split the proposals are scored as nearly equal, and with the 60/40 split the lowest-rated technical proposal receives the greatest number of points. Considering that Company A has a significantly more superior technical proposal, the weighting of the cost/price factor has made award to Company A more difficult.

The weighting of the cost/price factor works better when the lowest price of an acceptable offer is in line with the other prices, as shown in Example 5.6.

Example 5.6—Application of cost/technical formula where prices are generally in line with one another

$$\frac{\$193{,}500}{\$200{,}000} \times 30\ (= 29) + 64.4 = 93.4 \text{ (Company A)}$$

$$\frac{\$193{,}500}{\$193{,}500} \times 30\ (= 30) + 48.3 = 78.3 \text{ (Company B)}$$

In this example, where the pricing differences were more modest, a major pricing difference does not skew the application of the formula. Company B still gains 6.9 technical points because of the application of the 70 percent weighting, but the overall difference is still great enough to serve as a guide to making the award decision.

Using the cost/price factor as a weighted evaluation factor can lead to misleading results, particularly where an offeror is "buying in" or otherwise offering an unusually low price. When deciding whether or not to use the cost/price factor as a weighted factor, consider how the competition or complexity of the requirement might affect the pricing of proposals. Examine the pricing history of similar procurements. If it is likely that some of the offerors might offer unusually low prices, weighting the cost/price factor may not be in your best interest.

If you decide to use cost/price as a weighted factor, you must carefully consider how much weight should be assigned to the cost/price factor, particularly in light of the possible effects, as shown in the examples above. Keep in mind that the purpose of evaluation is to identify the differences in the proposals so the differences can be assessed to determine their relative value. Do not introduce elements, such as a high weight for the cost/price factor, that might blur the differences between the proposals without first considering the possible consequences. The weights assigned to the technical factors and to the cost/price factor must be set forth in the RFP, but you are not required to show the formula, if any, that will be used. In any event, do not use wording that commits you to make an award based on the results of mathematical calculations.

The use of cost/price as a weighted evaluation factor may be appropriate in efforts where it is anticipated that the offerors' estimates will be reasonably accurate and generally within the same pricing range. However, if the pricing is likely to vary considerably, perhaps because of varying techniques for meeting the requirements, the use of cost/price as an unweighted evaluation factor might be more effective.

Cost/Price As an Unweighted Evaluation Factor

Using cost/price as an unweighted evaluation factor does not mean that cost/price is considered in the evaluation process. You must still indicate in the RFP the relative importance of the technical and pricing factors, and the pricing must always be assessed through cost or price analysis and when appropriate, an analysis of the cost realism.

Using cost/price as an unweighted factor is an evaluation technique that separates the pricing considerations from the technical considerations and permits concentration on the technical aspects of the proposals. Once the technical proposals are rated and ranked, the results are matched with each proposal's evaluated pricing, and a cost/technical tradeoff determination (see Chapter 20) is conducted to determine which proposal offers the best value to the government. The use of cost/price as an unweighted evaluation factor is appropriate where technical excellence is a paramount consideration, where there may be a number of different ways (therefore different prices) of doing the work, or where the use of a cost-reimbursement, time-and-materials, or labor-hour contract is otherwise appropriate.

Where cost/price is used as an unweighted evaluation factor, offerors must be made aware of how it will be used. Place a statement in section M of the RFP to the effect that:

- The evaluation of technical factors will provide the primary basis for award.
- Cost/price is not a weighted evaluation factor, and is of minimal importance initially. It will be considered separately from the technical evaluation, except that the analysis of cost realism may affect the evaluation of the offeror's understanding of the requirement.
- Cost/price will be evaluated to determine if it is realistic and reasonable, to judge the offeror's understanding of the requirement, and to assess the likely impact of the proposal's cost realism on performance. For evaluation purposes only, proposed costs may be adjusted as a result of the government's evaluation.
- As the technical proposals approach substantial equality in evaluation, the cost/price factor will increase in importance as a discriminator between proposals and could become the determining factor in contract award.
- Because cost/price could become the determining factor, offerors should ensure that all proposed costs are fully explained and substantiated in the initial pro-

posal, each proposal revision, and particularly in the final proposal revision.

- Award will be made to the responsible offeror whose proposal best meets the needs of the government at a reasonable price and offers the best value.

Once the evaluation factors and their relative importance have been determined, the next step is to develop a scoring plan to be used by the evaluators to rate and rank the proposals.

References

1. BDM Services Co., B-180245, 5/9/74, 74-1 CPD 237.
2. Battelle Memorial Institute, B-278673, 2/27/98, GCR 110,270.
3. Information Sys. & Networks Corp., 69 Comp. Gen. 284, 285 (1990), 90-1 CPD ¶203 at 3, Advanced Tech. and Research Corp., B-257451.2, 12/9/94, 94-2 CPD ¶230 at 3.
4. Medland Controls, Inc., B-255204; B-255204.3, 2/17/94, 94-1 CPD ¶260 at 3.
5. FAR 15.002 (b).
6. FAR 15.304(c)(1).
7. FAR 15.304(e).
8. Logicon RDA, B-252031.4, 9/20/93, GCR 107,854.
9. Johns Hopkins Univ., B-233384, 3/6/89, 89-1 CPD 240, GCR 102,959.

Chapter 6

Scoring Plans

The evaluation factors and their relative importance are published in the RFP to inform offerors about the criteria against which their proposals will be evaluated and how those criteria will be applied. The scoring plan is the other side of the coin; it guides evaluators in applying the criteria for grading, or scoring, the proposals. Scoring plan information constitutes internal agency instructions and generally should not be published in the RFP. Once the scoring plan is established, it should not be changed except for good reasons; however, it should be noted that deviations from internal agency instructions do not provide a basis for protests, as shown in Example 6.1.

Example 6.1—Deviations from internal agency instructions, such as a scoring plan, do not provide a basis for protests[1]

Allegations of deviations from an agency's rating plan do not constitute a basis for questioning the validity of an award selection. Rather, such plans are internal agency instructions and, as such, do not give outside parties any rights.[2] In any event, the evaluation was consistent with both the RFP and the rating plan.

The last sentence of the quote above is important. An offeror may not protest the fact of a deviation from the scoring plan; however, if the scoring is not consistent with the evaluation factors published in the RFP—that could be the basis of a protest.

Develop the scoring plan in conjunction with the development of the evaluation plan. It is easier to maintain continuity among the evaluation factors, weights, and scoring if all are developed at the same time. This will also help protect from charges by an offeror that the scoring plan was developed after the proposals were examined, to favor a particular offeror.

PURPOSE OF SCORING PLANS

A scoring plan brings the discipline to the evaluation process necessary to ensure that proposals are evaluated equitably, that is, the same evaluation criteria are applied to all proposals. Determining the evaluation factors and their relative importance is the first step. But the task is not finished until you develop a scoring plan that requires all evaluators to look at and evaluate the evaluation factors in a similar manner.

If you do not develop and apply scoring plans, the evaluation results may surprise you, as shown in Example 6.2. (This is not based on a Comptroller General decision as there is no protest.)

Example 6.2—Evaluators must use a common scoring plan

In a relatively small R&D procurement, one evaluator (a confirmed pessimist) had rated all of the proposals very low, on the basis that no one was perfect. Another evaluator (a dedicated optimist) had rated all of the proposals very high, on the basis that the offerors were all experienced firms and therefore they should be able to perform well. The third evaluator (who had recently transferred from another agency) had scored the proposals using a system where a (+) means *exceeds requirements*; a (0) means *meets requirements*; and a (-) means *does not meet requirements*. In addition, the evaluators provided no supporting narratives. When the evaluators met to reach a consensus, they found themselves deadlocked.

What went wrong here? The basic problem was that the contracting officer had failed to ensure that the evaluation plan was complete. There was no established scoring plan. The evaluators were experienced technical personnel and the contracting officer assumed that they knew how to evaluate proposals. Although the evaluators had evaluated proposals before, lacking specific direction they followed their own instincts and training. Unfortunately this approach did not work well.

When presented with this evaluation, the contracting officer threw out the evaluation results, instructed the evaluators in how to evaluate proposals, provided a common scoring plan, and directed them to conduct the evaluation again. The evaluators reevaluated the proposals, properly this time, and an award was made. In this case, with the exception of about five lost working days, damage was minimal. But problems of this nature can cause serious delays and even negate an award if not caught early and corrected. It is better to take the time to do it properly the first time, and avoid the problems entirely.

Scoring plans provide a logical basis for ranking proposals and establish a common frame of reference for evaluators to use in scoring the proposals. Sound scoring plans provide an orderly, uniform approach to translating the individual proposal evaluations into the rating and ranking necessary for the comparison of the relative merit of all proposals, one to another.

Do not assume that all evaluators will look at the evaluation process in the same way. If you want an equitable evaluation you must provide the appropriate direction. Put another way, if you want the evaluators to follow the same evaluation script, you had better provide them with it and make sure that they understand it before starting the evaluation process.

It is important to understand that the scoring plan is just a tool used to help display the ranking and rating of the proposals. Scores *must not* be used as the primary justification for an award (e.g., Offeror A wins because it had the highest score). The written technical narrative that identifies proposal weaknesses, deficiencies, and risks, upon which the scores are based, provides the primary award justification (see Chapter 11).

The application of a scoring plan supports decision making, but is not the final word, as noted in the Comptroller General decision set forth in Example 6.3.

Example 6.3—Scoring plans are only guides #1[3]

Although technical point ratings are useful as guides for intelligent decision making in the procurement process, too much reliance should not be placed on them. Whether a given point spread between two competing proposals indicates a significant superiority of one proposal over another depends upon the facts and circumstances of each procurement.[4] *Even when point scores and technical evaluation ratings are indicative of the technical superiority of one proposal over another, selection officials are not bound by recommendations made by a technical evaluation panel.*[5]

The decision above was rendered in 1983 but is still valid, as shown in Example 6.4, a more recent decision.

Example 6.4—Scoring plans are only guides #2[6]

While adjectival ratings and point scores are useful as guides to decision-making, they generally are not controlling, but rather must be supported by documentation of the relative differences between proposals, their weaknesses and risks, and the basis and reasons for the selection decision.[7]

TYPES OF SCORING PLANS

There is no single "best" scoring plan. Agencies score proposals using a variety of methods, which range from numerics or color coding to specially designed plans, depending on direction provided at the agency or local level. In general, however, any plan that makes sense and can be applied equitably to all proposals is acceptable, as shown in Examples 6.5 and 6.6.

Example 6.5—Any sensible scoring plan is acceptable #1[8]

Responding to a protest about the application of a scoring system, the Comptroller General said the following:

This portion of PBI's protest essentially challenges the validity of the Coast Guard's color-based evaluation scheme. In this regard, we note that even numerical point scores, when used for proposal evaluation, are useful only as guides to intelligent decision-making and, generally, such guides do not mandate selection of a particular awardee since they reflect the disparate, subjective judgments of the evaluators.[9] *Our Office has previously examined rating systems other than strict mathematical scoring and has recognized the validity of such systems, provided they give the selection official a clear understanding of the relative merit of the proposals.*[10]

Example 6.6—Any sensible scoring plan is acceptable #2[11]

GSI next contends that the agency improperly used adjectives to rate the proposals. The protester believes that only numerical scoring can properly distinguish among competing proposals. This is not the case. Whatever evaluation method is used must give the selection authority a clear understanding of the relative merits of proposals; the use of adjectival rating schemes, supported as here by narrative assessments of individual proposals can reasonably convey a proper appreciation of the strengths and weaknesses of individual proposals.[12] *We have no basis to conclude that the evaluation scheme used here created any artificial equality of proposals; the record demonstrates that the adjectival scheme, in conjunction with the narrative assessments of individual proposals, provided a reasonable method for discerning the relative strengths and weaknesses perceived by the evaluators and a reasonable method for recognizing the advantages and disadvantages of award to one offeror as opposed to another.*[13]

As shown above, any type of scoring system may be used as long as it gives the source selection authority a clear understanding of the relative merit of the proposals.

Simplicity is the key to a good scoring plan. Complex plans increase the possibility of misunderstandings and errors on the part of evaluators. There is, however, one prohibition. Scoring plans must *never* use predetermined cutpoints or passing grades that automatically cause the rejection of proposals (e.g., scores over 49 are acceptable; scores of 49 or less are unacceptable and automatically rejected). This is demonstrated in Example 6.7.

Example 6.7—Never use predetermined cutoff scores[14]

We also note what we consider to be another deficiency in determining the competitive range. It is stated in the initial evaluation report that Datum is acceptable with a score of 75 percent and that Moxon is unacceptable with a score of 69 percent. Reliance on these scores appears to have been a major factor in determining the competitive range and was based upon a March 30, 1973, memorandum . . . concerning the evaluation criteria, which states that to be acceptable an offeror shall obtain a score of 75 percent or better. We have stated that a determination of competitive range based upon a comparison of an offeror's score with a predetermined score for acceptability is improper.[15] Rather, the competitive range should be determined by examining the array of scores for all proposals submitted,[16] and borderline proposals should not automatically be excluded from consideration if reasonably susceptible of being made acceptable.[17] In view of the closeness of the Datum and Moxon scores (75 to 69), and considering the other matters discussed above, we question the reasonableness of the Air Force position that Moxon was properly excluded from the competitive range because its proposal would require major revision.

The decision in Example 6.7 was rendered before the FAR 15 rewrite, but there is nothing in the rewrite that would change this ruling. The rewrite, however, did change how the competitive range is established (only the most highly rated proposals), so this problem is less likely to occur. Nevertheless, you should make sure that your documentation does not indicate that there is a "passing" score necessary for consideration of a proposal.

As noted earlier, the scores assigned by evaluators serve as guides or support for decisions regarding the establishment of the competitive range and source selection. The evaluation process is necessarily subjective and is never so precise that numerical scores, color codes, or similar ranking indicators can serve as the primary basis for decisions. The primary basis for competitive range and source selection decisions is the narrative technical evaluation written during the evaluation, on which the assignment of scores is based (see Chapters 10 and 11).

Using Numerics

The most common method of scoring uses numerics and adjectival ratings. This method involves the establishment of a set of adjectival ratings, the assignment of a numeric point range to each rating, and the development of a rating description or standard for each rating. The rating description is the most important part of the scoring plan. It establishes what is required to earn points within the point range for each adjectival rating, thus providing the evaluators with a common basis for evaluation. The use of a common standard for assigning points minimizes the possibility of wide variances in scoring because of the personal idiosyncrasies of individual evaluators.

Two evaluations are conducted during the evaluation process, each with a different purpose. The first is the initial evaluation. It is designed to provide the contracting officer with a basis for making the competitive range determination (see Figure 6.1). The second or final evaluation comes after discussions are completed and the final proposal revisions are submitted. It is used to determine which offeror will receive the contract award (see Figure 6.2).

The initial evaluation is designed to evaluate each proposal based on its contents and to rate and rank the proposals as a guide to which proposals are the most highly rated. Comparisons between proposals are not done during the initial evaluation; the scoring of rating is done based on the contents of each proposal, without regard to what other proposals offered. Once the proposals are rated, they are then ranked according to their scores. Then comparisons are made between the proposals to determine which are the most highly rated proposals.

The final evaluation involves an assessment of the final proposal revisions and how they changed the overall proposals and a comparison between the proposals to identify the proposal(s) offering the best value to the government. The differences between the initial and final evaluations are reflected in the rating description/standard used in Figures 6.1 and 6.2.

Figure 6.1—Scoring Plan For Initial Evaluation

ADJECTIVAL RATING/ POINT RANGE	RATING DESCRIPTION/STANDARD
Excellent 90–100	Meets or exceeds all requirements. Proposal demonstrates complete understanding of the requirement and offers a substantial chance of success. No deficiencies or significant weaknesses. Cost realism analysis indicates a close relationship between the technical proposal and related costs.
Very Good 80–89	Meets all requirements. Proposal shows reasonable understanding of the requirement and offers a high chance of success. No significant deficiencies or weaknesses that cannot be corrected through discussions. Cost realism analysis indicates a reasonable relationship between the technical proposal and related costs.
Good 70–79	Meets basic requirements. Proposal indicates basic understanding of the requirement and offers a reasonable chance of success. There are deficiencies and weaknesses, but these should be correctable through discussions. Cost realism analysis is acceptable, but the correction of deficiencies and weaknesses is expected to cause corresponding changes in cost.

Fair 50–69	Barely meets requirements. Proposal indicates only a marginal understanding of the requirement and offers only a minimal chance for success. There are significant deficiencies and weaknesses that must be corrected in order to make the proposal acceptable. The correction of the deficiencies and weaknesses is possible, but uncertain. Cost realism analysis is marginal because of the significant deficiencies and weaknesses. If the deficiencies and weaknesses are corrected, the related costs are expected to change also.
Poor 0–49	Does not meet requirements. Proposal demonstrates a significant lack of understanding of the requirement and does not offer a reasonable chance for success. There are substantial deficiencies and weaknesses that cannot be corrected except by substantial proposal revisions of a nature that would be tantamount to the submission of a new proposal. Meaningful discussions cannot be conducted unless such revisions are made. Cost realism analysis is doubtful, but cannot be fully assessed because of the substantial proposal deficiencies and weaknesses.

When establishing a scoring plan for the initial evaluation, three steps should be followed:

1. The first step is to select a set of adjectival ratings. Use any adjectives except those that connote outright unacceptability. The number of adjectival ratings used depends on the complexity of the evaluation and how definitively you want to distinguish one proposal from another. For example, if you anticipate the technical evaluation will be relatively simple, the adjectives may be as simple as "Excellent," "Good," and "Poor." If you

anticipate the evaluation to be more complex and you want to more clearly distinguish the comparative quality of the technical proposals, adjectives similar to those used in Figure 6.1 are more suitable. Keep in mind, however, that the purpose of the initial evaluation is to determine which offerors will be in the competitive range. A basic rule in determining the competitive range is that the competitive range should consist of only the most highly rated proposals. Do not unnecessarily complicate your evaluation process by using too many adjectival ratings.

2. The second step is to assign a scoring point range to each adjectival rating. Normally, scoring is done on a 0–100 or 0–1000 point basis, but any sensible numeric scheme is acceptable. The points do not have to be equitably distributed among the ratings; any reasonable distribution is acceptable.
3. The final step, and the most important, is to develop a rating description, or standard, for each adjectival rating/point range. You must relate each rating description or standard to the contract requirement, but state it in a general manner that permits the evaluators maximum flexibility. Each standard should indicate the extent to which the proposal meets the requirement, how well the offeror understands the requirement, the extent of deficiencies and weaknesses, and whether they are correctable. Also, if cost realism is to be evaluated, the relationship between the technical proposal and the related costs must be identified and commented upon. The rating description/standards used in Figure 6.1 demonstrate how this may be done. Any standards that are reasonable for a particular procurement are acceptable. The principal purpose of the rating description/standard is to provide evaluators with a common basis for evaluation by predetermining the criteria to be used in assigning scores during evaluation.

The primary difference between the scoring plan for the final evaluation and the scoring plan for the initial evaluation is the rating description. As shown in Figure 6.2, the rating description in the final evaluation reflects the basic purpose of this evaluation, which is to select the offeror to whom award will be made. The only purpose of a second scoring plan is to stress the difference between the initial and final evaluations; therefore, use of a second scoring plan is optional. You may combine the scoring plans into one, but be careful to ensure that the evaluators understand the difference in the purpose of each evaluation.

Figure 6.2—Scoring Plan For Final Evaluation

ADJECTIVAL RATING/ POINT RANGE	RATING DESCRIPTION/STANDARD
Excellent 90–100	Meets or exceeds all requirements. No deficiencies. Offers substantial chance of success. Proposed costs are acceptable.
Very Good 80–89	Meets requirements. No significant deficiencies. Offers high chance of success. Proposed costs acceptable.
Good 70–79	Marginally meets requirements. Some deficiencies remain uncorrected. Proposal acceptable, but offers only moderate chance of success without significant government assistance through close contract administration. Proposed costs are minimally acceptable.
Fair 50–69	Barely meets requirements. Significant deficiencies remain uncorrected. Proposal offers minimal chance of success even with significant government assistance through close contract administration. Proposed costs are uncertain.
Poor 0–49	Normally not applicable. Proposals scoring in this range should have been rejected as a result of the initial evaluation or during the negotiation process.

It should be noted that since the FAR 15 rewrite changed the competitive range to consist of only thse most highly rated proposals, it is not likely that the Fair and Poor ratings would be applicable in the final evaluation. It is possible, however, that changes made in the final proposal revisions might result in a significant reduction of a proposal's score, particularly if significant deficiencies are not corrected or where significant deficiencies result from the changes made.

A numeric system is easy to use and understand, which probably accounts for its popularity. The biggest drawback to its use is the danger that you might believe in it too much. Numbers signal preciseness. One proposal graded 89, a high "Very Good," and another at 81, a low "Very Good," would appear to indicate a significant difference between the two proposals. This is often illusory, because evaluation results are derived from subjective assessments, which may be more reflective of the evaluator's background and predisposition than of his or her objectivity. The numbers are only indicators of relative value and cannot be the basis for decisions. Decisions should be made based on the evaluator's written technical narrative, which details why a particular score was assigned. The scores assigned must fully support the technical narratives. If they do not, the source selection authority will have to require a reevaluation, or ignore the evaluation results and make an independent decision.

Using Color Codes

Many agencies are now using use color coding systems rather than numerics. Figure 6.3 is an example of a color coded scoring plan.

Figure 6.3—Color Coded Scoring Plan

Color	*Rating*	*Definition*
Blue	Exceptional	Exceeds specified performance or capability in a beneficial way; has high probability of satisfying the requirement; and has no significant weaknesses.

Green	Acceptable	Meets evaluation standards; has good probability of satisfying the requirement; and any weaknesses can be readily corrected.
Yellow	Marginal	Fails to meet minimum evaluation standards; has low probability of satisfying the requirement; and has significant, but correctable, deficiencies.
Red	Unacceptable	Fails to meet minimum requirement; and deficiencies require major revisions to the proposal to make it acceptable.

The color coding in Figure 6.3 substitutes colors for numerics, uses one less category than in the numeric example, and defines each category with different words. There is little effective difference between these systems, except that the color codes do not distinguish between offerors scoring in the same category (i.e., there is no difference between a "High Green" and a "Low Green." For practical purposes, however, the value of such distinctions is usually minimal.

It should be noted that the broad ranges of the color coding system are more compatible with the FAR 15 rewrite changes to the competitive range definition than the numerics system. Since the lower rated, but otherwise acceptable proposals are not likely to be included in the competitive range, the seemingly more precise numeric systems may not be needed.

Other Scoring Plans

As noted by the Comptroller General's comments in Examples 6.5 and 6.6, other types of scoring plans can be used. When using a scoring plan other than the numeric or color coded plans, you should make sure the scoring plan will provide the information desired. Your plan must be definitive enough to permit you to discriminate among the proposals—first to determine the competitive range and later to determine the successful offeror. The following are examples of some of the other scoring plans used by government agencies:

Barebones Approach

Some agencies use a barebones approach to scoring plans, reducing them to the minimum essentials, as shown in Figure 6.4:

Figure 6.4—Barebones Approach

Score	*Definition*
4	Proposal meets solicitation requirements and offers great advantage to the government.
3	Proposal meets solicitation requirements and offers considerable advantage to the government.
2	Proposal minimally meets solicitation requirements.
1	Proposal is deficient, but could be corrected through discussions.
0	Proposal is clearly deficient and could not be corrected without substantial changes or complex negotiations.

This plan is a simplified version of the color coded system. The numbers 0–4 have simply been substituted for the colors, and the definitions shortened. This approach may be too simple for a complex requirement. The rating description tends to influence the detail of the evaluator's written technical narratives. If you use simple definitions, you may get simple narratives that do not provide sufficient detail in complex requirements.

Symbols

Probably the most simplified system is one that uses symbols, as shown in Figure 6.5.

Figure 6.5—Symbols

(+) means exceeds minimum requirements
(0) means meets minimum requirements
(–) means fails to meet minimum requirements

Generally speaking, this system adds little to the evaluation process. If used in a pass/fail environment, it provides too much information, since quality above "meets the minimum requirement" is not germane.

If used for a comparative assessment, it does not provide enough information because it does not permit the evaluators to indicate the relative value of proposals that exceed the minimum requirements.

In a comparative assessment, the result of this system would be that all acceptable proposals are found technically equal, and award would then be made on the basis of low cost or price. This will create problems if you have indicated that the technical factors are more important than the cost/price factors. In such instances, you must justify your decision to award to other than the high technical proposal, and this scoring system will not produce sufficient supporting information to make such a decision.

Computer-Based Evaluations

Computer-based evaluation or decision-modeling systems are also available. Evaluation software is a just another tool in proposal evaluation. If you remember that a computer is nothing more than a bigger and better pencil, and objectively examine the logic behind the system used, you may find computer support useful. You should make use of any tool that will help you do a better job. You must, however, treat computer software as a support tool, not a decision maker. Evaluation software cannot substitute for your own judgment. In the event of a protest, the Comptroller General will not be amused if your excuse is "The computer made me do it." Example 6.8 further illustrates this point.

Example 6.8—Objectively assess the applicability of evaluation software before using it[18]

An award based on low evaluated cost was protested on several grounds, one of which was that the evaluation and adjustment of the protester's proposed labor hours and material costs was improperly based on a rigid, computer-generated, mathematical comparison of the proposed hours and costs to the government's estimate without taking into account the offeror's particular approach to performing the contract.

The computer was programmed to compare each offeror's proposed labor hours and material costs with the government estimate. The program accepted proposed costs within a predetermined percentage of the government estimate. For those costs outside the range, it used a formula that split the difference between the offeror's estimate and the government estimate. This program was automatically applied to all proposals.

Note: The decision contained proprietary information and was subject to a General Accounting Office protective order. Deletions in the quoted text are indicated by "[deleted]."

While a reasonably derived estimate of labor hours and material costs based on historical experience can provide an objective standard against which the realism of proposed costs can be measured, an agency may not mechanically apply that estimate to determine evaluated costs.[19] *In some instances, an estimate has limited applicability to a particular company because of the skill of its labor force, or its innovative work methods, or simply because of the way the offeror prepares its proposal.*[20] *In these cases, any absolute reliance upon the government estimate could have the effect of arbitrarily and unfairly penalizing or rewarding one firm and depriving the government of the benefit available from the different approaches of different firms. Accordingly, in order to undertake a proper cost realism evaluation, the agency must independently analyze the realism of offeror's proposed costs based upon its particular approach, personnel, and other circumstances.*[21]

... Nonetheless, the record shows that every contractor labor hour and material cost estimate within [deleted] percent of the government estimate was accepted, while every contractor estimate outside the [deleted] percent range was automatically adjusted using the "split the difference" formula. Thus, in every instance where an offeror's estimate was [deleted] percent above or below the government estimate, the computer automatically applied the formula and did so no matter how large the disparity between the government's estimate and the offeror's estimate. In our view, there is a high probability that this mechanical analysis skewed the offerors' projected costs which formed the basis for the award decision.

In addition, we think there was an even more fundamental flaw in the Navy's method here. The Navy reports that the cost analyst applied the "split the difference" formula on all contractor estimates outside of the [deleted] percent range on which she determined, consistent with the source selection plan, that the "offeror's estimate is well supported with an equal probability of government or offeror being correct. The Navy's approach did not provide a justification for the adjusted labor hour or material cost estimate that was actually used to calculate an offeror's evaluated cost. Put another way, if an offeror proposed no material cost for a work item and the government estimate included $20,000 in material costs for that work item, we see no rational basis for substituting an estimate of $[deleted]—the adjusted material cost estimate that would be used in the calculation of the contractor's overall projected cost in this example.

The Comptroller General found that, because of the automatic application of the formula, the agency's evaluation did not satisfy the requirement for an independent analysis of each offeror's cost proposal based on its particular approach, personnel, and other circumstances. The Comptroller General sustained the protest and recommended that the agency reevaluate the cost proposals using a method of cost realism analysis that reasonably determines the extent to which each offeror's proposed costs represent what the contract should cost for that offeror to perform. The Comptroller General also recommended another round of discussions and final proposal revisions.

Example 6.8 illustrates what can go wrong if you do not objectively assess the applicability of the evaluation software. Before buying any evaluation software, run a "real world" test on the software using an actual set of contractor proposals to see what results and documentation are really provided. Then, before each use, reassess what you want the software to do against what you know it will do. You may find in some instances that because of the peculiarities of the instant procurement, your standard software will not produce the desired results.

Scoring Plans for the Evaluation of Proposal Risk and Performance Risk

In some instances, additional factors are evaluated separately after the technical evaluation. Two of the more common instances are the evaluation of proposal risk and performance risk. Because these factors represent broader issues than those addressed by the technical evaluation, they may be evaluated by a separate evaluation team, or are evaluated separately by the basic evaluation team.

Proposal Risk

As noted in Chapter 4, proposal risk is the extent of the risk of failure or disruptive problems during contract performance based on the overall proposed technical approach. Proposal risk is evaluated based on the results of the technical evaluation, usually in terms of potential schedule disruption, cost increases, or the degradation of the quality of performance. The following is an example of a scoring plan to assess proposal risk when proposal risk is a separate evaluation factor:

Figure 6.6—Scoring Proposal Risk

High	Likely to cause significant disruption of schedule, increase in cost, or degradation of performance even with special contractor emphasis and close government monitoring.
Moderate	Can potentially cause some disruption of schedule, increase in cost, or degradation of performance. However, special contractor emphasis and close government monitoring will probably be able to overcome difficulties.
Low	Has little potential to cause disruption of schedule, increase in cost, or degradation of performance. Normal contractor effort and normal government monitoring will probably be able to overcome difficulties.

Generally, it is a good idea to indicate your intention to evaluate proposal risk in the RFP—this helps ensure that the offeror will address risk in its proposal. However, the consideration of risk is inherent in the evaluation of technical proposals, and risk may be considered in the evaluation even if it was not specifically cited in the RFP as noted in Examples 6.9 and 6.10.

Example 6.9—Proposal risk is an inherent evaluation factor #1[22]

Furthermore, while the solicitation included as part of the evaluation the consideration of risk based on the offeror's past and present performance, and did not otherwise enumerate risk as an evaluation factor, the agency was not thereby precluded from also considering any risk arising from the offeror's approach or demonstrating lack of understanding. As we have previously recognized, consideration of the risk involved with respect to an offeror's proposal and approach is inherent in the evaluation of technical proposals.[23]

In Example 6.7 performance risk (risk based on past performance) was identified as an evaluation factor, but proposal risk (risk based on proposed technical approach) was not so identified, but the Comptroller General said proposal risk could be evaluated anyway. In Example 6.10 proposal risk was not identified at all, and the Comptroller General explains why proposal risk is an inherent evaluation factor.

Example 6.10—Proposal risk is an inherent evaluation factor #2[24]

In a procurement for telemetry sets, the award decision was based primarily on the risk factor represented by each proposal. Risk was not one of the stated evaluation factors, but everything else was roughly equal and the agency felt that the only significant difference between the proposals was the risk factor represented by each offeror's proposed approach. One proposal (the lowest priced) was rated as a medium risk, and the other proposal, at a slightly higher price, was rated as a low risk. The agency determined that the small savings (2.56 percent) that would result from award to the lowest priced proposal did not justify assuming the risk that the proposal represented. Accordingly, award was made to the higher priced proposal offering the least risk.

The lowest-priced offeror protested on the grounds that the RFP did not provide for consideration of risk factors. The Comptroller General denied the protest.

Agencies have broad discretion in determining the manner and extent to which they will make use of technical and price evaluation results. In reaching an award decision, the agency may make price/technical tradeoffs, subject only to the test of rationality and consistency with established evaluation factors.[25] *In this connection, it is well established that consideration of the risk involved in an offeror's approach is inherent in the evaluation of technical proposals.*[26] *This is because the degree of risk present is clearly related to the technical approach proposed and the ability of the firm to perform the contract.*[27] *Thus an agency properly may find one technical proposal superior to another based on their relative levels of risk, and make a price/technical tradeoff decision in favor of that technically superior proposal. That is what the Navy did here. Given that technical factors were considered as important as cost in the evaluation scheme, moreover, we think the agency reasonably concluded that the relative strength of Symetric's proposal—based on its low risk—under the most important evaluation factor and the two other factors warranted paying Symetric's 2.56 percent higher price.*

Performance Risk

Performance risk is related to the evaluation of past performance. It is an assessment of how an offeror's past performance might affect the proposed contract effort. Performance risk is evaluated based on reports of how well the offeror performed on other similar contracts. Past performance may be evaluated as one of the regular evaluation factors or separately as performance risk. When evaluated separately, the scoring plan is usually the same as was used for the evaluation of proposal risk.

Because the basis for the evaluation of proposal and performance risk is broad, the scoring plan should also be broad; high risk, moderate risk, and low risk is probably all you need to indicate the level of risk. Trying to define risk as "high-high," "high," and "low-high" would not add to the effectiveness of your evaluation.

There is a difference between the evaluation of an offeror's past performance (see Chapters 3 and 12) and the evaluation of performance risk. Past performance evaluates an offeror's actions under previous contracts, including such factors as the offeror's conformance to specifications and standards of good workmanship, its adherence to contract and administrative delivery schedules, and its record for reasonable and cooperative behavior. These factors are not directly related to performance of the proposed contract.

The assessment of performance risk is tied directly to performance of the proposed contract as it relates the contractor's past performance to how it is likely to perform the proposed effort. To avoid confusion, it might be best to clearly indicate in the RFP that the past performance factors will be evaluated as performance risk. This is, after all, what the evaluation of past performance is all about.

EVALUATION FORMULAS

When numeric scoring plans are used, evaluation formulas are often used to develop a final score for each proposal. This facilitates the establishment of the relative ranking of all of the proposals. There are two common types of evaluation formulas: one is used in *technical competitions* in which cost is an unweighted evaluation factor and the other is used in *technical/cost competitions* in which cost is a weighted evaluation factor. It should be noted that the formulas discussed below are not the only evaluation formulas. There is no standard, or best, formula to use. You may use anything you desire, as long as it does not conflict with the stated evaluation criteria and it produces reasonable, supportable results.

Technical Competition

Figure 6.7 demonstrates the application of an evaluation formula in a technical competition in which cost is an *unweighted* evaluation factor.

The points, or scores, assigned to each subfactor have been added to get a total score for each primary evaluation factor. The total score for each factor is then multiplied by the assigned weight for that factor to obtain a weighted factor score. The sum of the weighted scores is the technical score for that particular offeror.

Once the weighted scores are developed for all offerors, they are displayed in an array and serve as a visual tool in the contracting officer's competitive range and source selection decisions.

Figure 6.7—Evaluation Formula—Technical Competition

EVALUATION FACTOR	EVALUATION SCORE	×	ASSIGNED WEIGHT (1)	=	WEIGHTED SCORE
Factor I	92 (Excellent)	×	.67		61.6
Factor II	85 (Very Good)	×	.22	=	18.7
Factor III	78 (Good)	×	.11	=	8.6
					88.9
TECHNICAL SCORE - COMPANY A					89 (2)

(1) Multiply the assigned weight as a percentage in order to get a whole number for the weighted score.

(2) Use whole numbers rather than decimals. Round the weighted score to the nearest whole number. The use of decimals is discouraged because decimals give the appearance of a precision that is not appropriate considering the subjective nature of the evaluation process.

Technical/Cost Competition

Figure 6.8 uses the same formula as used in Chapter 5 to explain the use of cost/price as a weighted evaluation factor. This formula uses the results of the formula in Figure 6.7 and factors in the cost/price score to get a total score.

The formula first establishes the ratio between the estimated cost of the lowest acceptable offer and the offer being evaluated (the cost figures used should be the "evaluated" costs, not the proposed costs). This number is then multiplied by the total number of cost points (the assigned weight) to obtain the cost score.

The weighted technical score is added to the cost score to obtain a total score. The total scores are displayed in an array to be used by the contracting officer in making the competitive range determination and later the source selection decision (based on the evaluation of the final proposal revisions). The formula results can be expected to change as a result of discussions and resulting revisions by the offerors.

Figure 6.8—Evaluation Formula—Technical/Cost Competition

Cost – lowest acceptable offer (1) / Cost – acceptable offer being evaluated (2)	×	Maximum number of cost points [30]	+	Weighted technical score for acceptable offer being evaluated [89 × 70%] (3)	=	Total score for acceptable offeror (4)
$225,000 / $387,000	×	30	+	62	=	79.44
COMPANY A - COMPOSITE SCORE						79

(1) The evaluated cost of the lowest acceptable offer still in contention for award.

(2) The evaluated cost of Company A, the offeror being evaluated.

(3) The weighted technical score multiplied by the technical percentage.

(4) The total scores rounded to the nearest whole number in order to avoid a false impression of precision.

Publishing Evaluation Formulas in the RFP

Some agencies publish evaluation formulas, but not the scoring plans, in the RFP. Although publishing the evaluation formula is not a prohibited practice, do *not* use language that indicates that award will be based on the high score resulting from the application of the evaluation formula. If you do publish the evaluation formula and the source selection official agrees with the scoring, the award must be made in accordance with the established formula, as set forth in the RFP.

If the source selection official disagrees with the scores, how they were assigned, or their significance, the formula results are not binding. A protest is likely, however. The high scoring offeror will be expecting you to award in accordance with the stated formula, because that is what you stated in the RFP. For that reason, you should avoid using a specific award formula in the RFP. If you must publish a formula, then indicate that the formula will be used for ranking purposes only.

You would be better off, however, if you did not publish the evaluation formula at all. Publishing the evaluation formula is not required, as noted in Example 6.11, and could help you avoid a protest.

Example 6.11—Agencies need not disclose price scoring formulas[28]

While the Federal Acquisition Regulation (FAR) requires that price and technical evaluation factors, and their relative importance, be set forth in the solicitation . . . it does not require agencies to disclose the price evaluation formula that will be applied. The use of the type of price scoring formula that the agency utilized here, without disclosure in the RFP of the agency's intention to use it, is relatively common and is not objectionable.[29]

Note: The formula used in this case was similar to the one shown in Figure 6.8.

Competitive range and source selection decisions are based primarily on the evaluator's written narrative technical evaluations. Evaluation decisions are subjective decisions that do not lend themselves to the rigid application of a mathematical formula. Evaluation formulas are useful tools in the display of the relative rankings of proposals and in highlighting the general differences or similarities in proposals, but they should not be used as the primary basis for evaluation decisions.

REVIEW THE BASIS FOR AWARD

Once you have developed your scoring plan, carefully review the SOW, your selection of evaluation factors, their relative weight, the proposal preparation instructions, how you intend to evaluate the proposals, and your scoring plan. This review is necessary to prevent mistakes and to ensure that everything will work together toward an effective evaluation.

References

1. Ralph G. Moore & Assocs., B-270686; B-270686.2, 2/28/96, GCR 109,398.
2. National Steel & Shipbuilding Co., B-250305.2, Mar 23, 1993, 93-1 CPD ¶260; Robert E. Derecktor of Rhode Island, Inc.; Boston Shipyard Corp., B-211922; B-211922.2, Feb 2, 1984, 84-1 CPD ¶140.
3. RCA Service Co., B-208871, 8/22/83, 83-2 CPD 221.
4. Wheeler Industries Inc., B-193883, 7/20/79, 79-2 CPD ¶41.
5. Bell Aerospace Co., 55 Comp. Gen. 244 (1975), 75-2 CPD ¶168.
6. RCA Service Co., B-208871, 8/22/83, 83-2 CPD ¶221.
7. Engineering and Computation Inc., B-261658, 10/16/95, 95-2 CPD ¶176 at 3.
8. Peterson Builders, Inc., B-244614, 11/1/91, 91-2 CPD ¶419, GCR 106,022.
9. Bunker Ramo Corp., 56 Comp. Gen. 712 (1977), 77-1 CPD 427; Ferguson-Williams, Inc., B-231827, 10/12/88, 88-2 CPD ¶344, GCR 102,425.
10. Dynamics Research Corp., B-240809, 12/10/90, 90-2 CPD 471, GCR 104,970; MAXIMUS, B-195806, 4/15/81, 81-1 CPD ¶285.
11. Cardinal Scientific Inc., B-270309, 2/12/96, GCR 109,388.
12. Ferguson-Williams, Inc., 68 CG 25 (1988), 88-2 CPD ¶344.
13. Tennier Indus., Inc., B-252338, 6/18/93, 93-1 CPD ¶471.

14. Moxon, Inc./SRC Division, B-179160, 3/13/74, 74-1 CPD ¶134.
15. 52 Comp. Gen. 59 (1970).
16. 52 Comp. Gen. 382, 387 (1972).
17. B-176761(2), 1/24/73.
18. The Jonathan Corp.; Metro Machine Corp., B-251698.3; B-251698.4, 5/17/93, GCR 107,849.
19. Kinton, Inc., 67 Comp. Gen. 226 (1988), 88-1 CPD ¶112, GCR 101,577.
20. Allied Cleaning Servs., Inc., B-237295, 2/14/90, 90-1 CPD ¶275, GCR 104,103; Kintron, Inc., supra.
21. United Int'l Eng'g Inc.; Morrison Knudsen-Dynamics Research; PRC Inc.; and Science Applications Int'l Corp., 71 Comp. Gen. 177 (1992), 92-1 CPD ¶122, GCR 106,310.
22. Communications International, Inc., B-246076, 2/18/92, 92-1 CPD ¶194, GCR 106,383.
23. Advanced Sys. Technology Inc., Eng'g and Professional Servs., Inc., B-241530; B-241530.2, 2/12/91, 91-1 CPD ¶153; Honeywell, Inc., B-238184, 4/30/90, 90-1 CPD ¶435.
24. Herley Industries, Inc., B-251792.2, 4/16/93, GCR 107,508.
25. Shirley Constr. Corp., 70 Comp. Gen. 62 (1990), 90-2 CPD ¶380.
26. S-TRON, B-244767.2, 5/1/92, 92-1 CPD ¶409.
27. Consolidated Group, B-220050, 1/9/86, 86-1 CPD ¶21.
28. Heimann Systems Inc., B-272182, 9/9/96, GCR 109,652
29. Contex Constr. Co. Inc., B-238777, 6/14/90, 90-1 CPD ¶566; Didactic Sys., Inc., B-190507, 6/7/78, 78-1 CPD ¶418.

CHAPTER 7

Proposal Preparation Instructions[1]

The primary purpose of proposal preparation instructions is to obtain information needed from offerors to effectively evaluate their proposals, such as graphs, charts, and discussion of particular points of interest. Proposal preparation instructions are also used to standardize the format and organization of offeror's proposals to make proposal evaluation more efficient, and to elicit specific information from the offerors when you intend to incorporate all or part of the successful offeror's proposal in your SOW.

Evaluation of proposals that contain voluminous data is difficult and time-consuming. Unnecessarily elaborate proposals also make evaluation difficult, and flashy presentations do not necessarily reflect quality preparation. It is difficult to assess the relative worth of proposals that fail to address the evaluation factors. Competing proposals submitted in differing formats tend to create confusion in evaluation, result in pertinent material being overlooked or not fully evaluated, and make it difficult to fully appreciate the relative worth of the proposals. Proposal preparation instructions help to minimize these problems by providing a standard for the content, organization, and format of the proposals.

The final part of the evaluation plan should include the proposal preparation instructions. They are published in Section L of the RFP. Consolidate all information related to proposal preparation in the proposal preparation instructions, except for the standard solicitation provisions (which go in another part of Section L) and the evaluation criteria (which go in Section M). This makes it easier for the offerors to find the information, helps avoid confusion, and ensures effective communication of your instructions.

OBTAINING EVALUATION INFORMATION

Proposal preparation instructions are used primarily to obtain information needed for evaluation purposes. Your areas of interest, for evaluation purposes, are expressed by the evaluation factors in Section M of the RFP. As noted in Chapter 2, a title and a short narrative describe the evaluation factors and subfactors. The descriptors illustrate the salient characteristics of the factors and explain how they will be evaluated. The proposal preparation instructions expand on these descriptions and explain what general or specific information is needed. This helps offerors understand the kind of information that you expect to see in their proposals, and completes the description of how the proposals will be evaluated. The following paragraphs address how to do this.

Listing the Information Requirements

In the proposal preparation instructions, require each offeror to structure its proposal in the same order as the evaluation factors listed in Section M. This ensures that the offerors will discuss your areas of interest in the same order and with the same level of importance as you will use in evaluation. For example, if you list the technical evaluation factors in Section M in descending order of importance (as shown in Figure 7.1), you should require the offeror to address its proposal to the same factors, in the same order.

Figure 7.1—Section M Listing Of Evaluation Factors

Technical
- A. Technical Approach
- B. Understanding the Requirement

Management
- A. Management Approach
- B. Staffing Plan
- C. Key Personnel

Corporate Experience

Past Performance

Presenting Primary Evaluation Factors

Section M presents each primary evaluation factor with a title and a short narrative illustrating the salient characteristics of the factor. Your proposal preparation instructions should present each primary factor in the same manner. This is redundant, but repeating the narrative description reinforces the connection between Section M and the proposal preparation instructions. You may choose to simply paraphrase the narrative description in Section M. If you do this, exercise care in choosing your wording. A paraphrased description can confuse the offeror, particularly if, in paraphrasing, a requirement appears different from that in Section M.

Presenting Significant Subfactors

The significant subfactors should be presented somewhat differently. Include a general statement (the same as used in Section M) followed by a statement of the specific information requirements. The specific information requirements will vary depending on the circumstances, but they should amplify the general statement, explaining what information you expect to see in the proposals.

Information requirements should specify both form and content. These requirements may address the submission of charts or graphs, a discussion of methods and methodology or specific technical considerations, technical or management plans and schedules, staffing plans, manning levels and labor mix, and any other information you consider necessary to evaluate an offeror's response to a particular evaluation factor. If certain tasks in the SOW require specific supporting information, you must reference that task. For example, in a requirement for a study, the technical factors and significant subfactors could be presented as follows:

- Technical (Primary Factor)
  Proposals will be evaluated on the basis of the soundness and workability of the proposed technical approach, the demonstrated understanding of the require-

ment, and the validity of the technical plan and proposed methodology. [From Section M]

- Technical Approach/Understanding the Requirement (Subfactor)
  The offeror shall demonstrate a sound and workable technical approach that ensures a high probability of successful performance. The offeror shall demonstrate its understanding of the requirement through the degree of thoroughness, soundness, and comprehension expressed by the proposed technical approach. [General statement from Section M]

  The offeror shall describe its technical approach in sufficient detail to demonstrate its soundness and workability. Identify the scope of the study and how its purpose will be accomplished. Provide an analysis of the complexity of the requirement and indicate how any anticipated problems will be resolved. [Specific information requirement]
- Technical Plan/Methodology (Subfactor)
  The offeror's technical plan, schedule, and the methodology to be employed to identify, obtain, research and analyze articles, reports, and other information sources will be evaluated for its appropriateness for this study and the extent of the effort proposed. [General statement from Section M]

  The offeror shall fully describe its plan for the technical approach to comply with the tasks set forth in the statement of work, including the phasing of tasks, scheduling of work effort, staffing, and the methodology to be employed. The discussion of the methodology shall include the methodology to be used for data collection and the methodology to be used to analyze the data and draw conclusions. Identify other methodologies that might have been applicable and indicate why they were not selected. Identify the proposed sources of information to be used and discuss the methods to be used to identify and obtain the information required. Indicate the volume of the anticipated research materials and the research techniques to be used. [Specific information requirement]

Providing a general statement and specifying the specific information requirements for subfactors ensures that the offeror understands how each factor will be evaluated and that you get the information needed for evaluation. You must be as explicit as possible. Instructions that help offerors write good proposals are a plus, not a minus. You want offerors to write proposals that are responsive to your concerns. This makes the evaluation easier. At the same time, you should keep in mind that your job is to evaluate the offeror's technical expertise and ability to perform the contract, not its proposal writing ability.

The following are examples of how you could present other evaluation subfactors in the proposal preparation instructions and indicate some of the types of information that might be needed for evaluation. Tailor the specific requirements for the instant procurement. Do not list something as a requirement unless you are sure that you know how you would evaluate the information submitted.

- Management Approach
  The general statement should require offerors to provide a detailed discussion of their approach to the overall management and integration of all activities required by the SOW. It should include a discussion of management objectives and techniques that demonstrate how the work requirements will be met.

  Specific information requirements might include submission of organization charts, discussion of the lines of authority and responsibility, and a demonstration of how the proposed organization will be prepared to respond promptly to problems or program changes. Other useful information might be how the proposed project manager will obtain support from other corporate elements and subcontractors, and his or her ability to access the higher levels of corporate management.

- Staffing Plan
  The general statement should require offerors to describe the proposed staffing plan, including how long it will take to fully staff the contract, and how peak workloads, overlapping or simultaneous task assignments, and sick leave and vacations will be covered.
  The specific information requirements might include a discussion of how the offeror's resources are allocated, how the offeror plans to retain the proposed staffing levels, information on the turnover rates and related recruiting efforts, and, when appropriate, how the offeror plans to maintain the required level of personnel with security clearances.
- Key Personnel
  The general statement should require the offeror to describe the educational background, directly related work experience, professional development, and demonstrated performance record of the proposed key personnel.
  Specific information requirements usually include a description of what is required in the resumes of key personnel, such as information demonstrating that the individual meets the minimum qualification criteria described in the SOW. You should also obtain information on the current employment status of the proposed key personnel. If an individual is not currently employed full-time by the offeror, require a letter of commitment or some other indication of the individual's commitment to work under the contract and an authorization to use the individual's resume in the proposal. You may also want the offeror to indicate the amount of time (usually as a percentage) that each key individual will devote exclusively to work under the contract. It is important to identify any other contracts to which the individual is committed because you could have a problem if the individual is already fully or substantially committed to other work.

If past performance is also an evaluation factor, require the offeror to indicate any involvement of proposed key personnel with any of the contracts referenced for past performance. You may want to question an offeror about the involvement of proposed key personnel in a contract that receives an adverse past performance report. Such questions, however, should be reserved for discussions (after establishment of the competitive range) because the offeror's response might require a proposal revision, and generally would not, in and of itself, require a proposal rejection.

- Corporate Experience
  The general statement should require the offeror to describe the corporate experience that demonstrates the offeror's ability to efficiently perform the tasks required under the contract.

  The specific information requirements usually include a requirement for the offeror to demonstrate previous experience similar to the current requirement. Require the offeror to identify the contract number, type of work done, contract type and dollar value, and the name and telephone number of the COTR for each referenced contract. Require the offeror to demonstrate how each previous contract relates to the proposed effort. To ensure that the corporate experience is relevant, place a limit on the applicable time period. Typical time periods used are three to five years, depending on how technological changes or other events have affected the relevance of past contracts.
- Past Performance
  The general statement should require the offeror to identify current and past contracts that demonstrate the offeror's ability to successfully perform the required effort. Specific information requirements usually include a requirement for the offeror to demonstrate previous experience similar to the current requirement. Require the offeror to identify current and past contracts for the same or similar work, including the contract number, dollar value, dates, name of the contracting agency, a contact telephone number and a brief description of the

work effort that demonstrates how the referenced contract relates to the proposed effort.

Require offerors to identify any performance problems with the referenced contracts and the corrective action taken. Indicate that the offeror must provide evidence of the cause of the problem and demonstrate that the problem has been resolved. Inform offerors that if past problems are not fully addressed, the government will assume that they still exist.

To ensure that the past performance information is relevant, limit the references to current contracts and contracts that have been completed within the past three to five years, depending on how technological changes or other events have affected the relevance of past contracts.

USING A STANDARDIZED PROPOSAL FORMAT

While the primary purpose of the proposal preparation instructions is to obtain information for evaluation, a secondary purpose is to make the evaluation process easier by standardizing the proposal format. Requiring adherence to the outline of the evaluation factors in section M helps ensure this. Standardization makes the evaluation process easier because the evaluators will not need to search through differing proposal formats to find the necessary information. Standardization also assists offerors in their proposal preparation by eliminating the need for them to guess the proposal format that would be most acceptable to the government. This leads to better proposals.

Separating Technical and Pricing Information

Proposal preparation instructions usually indicate that proposals are to be submitted in at least two volumes. The first volume contains the technical proposal and other related material. The second volume contains the pricing proposal. This format facilitates the initial evaluation in which the technical proposal is evaluated by a technical evaluation team and the cost or pricing proposal is evaluated by the contracting officer or a cost evaluation team. Figure 7.2 indicates one way to present a standardized proposal format.

Figure 7.2—Standardized Proposal Format

*Format For The Technical Proposal Volume**

Part 1—Technical
- A. Technical Approach
- B. Understanding the Requirement

Part 2—Management
- A. Management Approach
- B. Staffing Plan
- C. Key Personnel

Part 3—Corporate Experience

Part 4—Past Performance

Format for the Cost Volume

Part 1—Cost or Price Proposal

Part 2—Support Documentation

*The format for the Technical Proposal Volume is always the same as the listing of the evaluation factors in Section M.

The instructions should include a statement that pricing information is to be provided *only* in the pricing volume. This protects the objectivity of the technical evaluation. Knowledge of the pricing can bias the technical evaluators. In most instances, the technical evaluators know how much funding is available. When the evaluators know that the proposal price varies significantly from the funds available, it is difficult for them to evaluate a proposal objectively.

Additional Proposal Volumes

With more complex proposals, the need for additional proposal volumes increases. Often, a management volume is required in addition to the technical and pricing volumes. Large, complex requirements may require additional volumes dealing with specific areas, such as specific tasks in a large multitasked requirement. An examination of the evaluation plan can help determine how many volumes are required. If the plan indicates that the use of a number of different evaluation teams is planned, each team should have its own volume, if feasible.

In some instances you may wish to have an executive summary as a separate volume. Be careful with executive summaries, they are usually of little actual value. If you do require the submission of an executive summary, you must define this requirement carefully—make sure that the offerors understand that the purpose of this document is simply to provide an overview of what is in the proposal itself. Instruct offerors not to include pricing information in the executive summary. It would also be a good idea to place a stringent page limitation on this document.

Other Considerations

Standardizing proposal format involves more than just providing an outline to follow and establishing the number of required proposal volumes. Standardization also includes indicating the number of copies to be provided, setting page and type size preferences, and, when appropriate, limiting the number of proposal pages.

Number of Copies

The number of copies to be provided is a function of the number of evaluation teams and how you will conduct the evaluation. Generally you should require enough copies so that each evaluator has a copy; however, if you do not plan to have each evaluator evaluate each proposal, you will not need that many. Do not require more copies than will actually be used in evaluation. Proposals must be safeguarded in a manner similar to classified material, and you do not want extra copies lying around.

Paper Size, Type Size, and Font Styles

Indicate the paper size, type size, and font style or styles to be used in the proposal. This helps avoid unnecessarily elaborate or hard to read proposals. Such standardization is also needed when page limitations are used.

Paper size is usually established as the standard 8 1/2 x 11 inches to discourage the use of legal-sized paper. You may also want to limit the size of fold-out pages. Fold-out pages are usually limited to nontext information such as charts, tables, or diagrams and the size is commonly 11 x 17 inches. Margins are often set at 1 inch. Some agencies require that proposal printing be double spaced rather than single spaced. Other agencies have dictated the maximum number of lines that may be printed on a page.

Type size is usually set at no smaller than 10-point character height (vertical size) and no more than an average of 12-characters per inch to avoid the use of small print that is difficult to read.

Font styles are usually established only where provisions are made for proposals to be submitted in both hard copy and on diskette or where page limitations are set. If offerors will submit proposals on diskettes, the fonts (and the word processing program used) must be compatible with your machines.

Page Limitations

Page limitations are used to preclude the submission of unnecessarily elaborate or lengthy proposals. A necessary prerequisite to the use of page limitations is, of course, that you know how many pages constitute a reasonable proposal for your particular requirement. If you set the page limitation too low, you may not get all of the information you need. If you set the page limitation too high, you are encouraging elaborate proposals. The best guideline to use is the complexity of your requirement. If you have a complex requirement (this will be reflected in the size of your SOW) you should probably establish a page limitation. Examine previously submitted proposals for similar efforts to see if an average can be established, or simply use your best judgment. If the requirement is not complex, page limitations are not necessary.

Evaluating Page and Format Limitations

When using page limitations, specify exactly what counts as a page. Generally, page limitations are applied only against the basic text of the technical and management proposals. Attachments may or may not be included in the page limitation. You may want to include page limitations for attachments that amplify information in the technical and management proposals, otherwise you may end up with slim proposals and fat attachments. You may also want to limit the types of information included in attachments to technical supporting information that would not influence the evaluation of the technical and management proposals. Pricing proposals are usually not included in page limitations.

In addition, you must state how you will determine which pages are excess and what will happen to excess pages. Typically, excess pages are determined by counting from the first page of the proposal. When the count reaches the page limitation, the counting stops. Pages in excess of the page limitation are physically removed from the proposal (before the evaluation starts) and returned to the offeror.

Where you find formatting problems, such as the wrong type size, too many lines per page, and wrong page size, you should either recalculate the page count based on what it would be if done as directed, or simply remove the offending pages.

The use of page and format limitations depends on local circumstances. You should, however, have a valid reason for the limitations you do use. Keep in mind that while you are doing this to make the evaluation easier, you should not be overly restrictive. It would also be a good idea to point out to offerors that when excess pages are removed and not evaluated, this usually results in substantial proposal deficiencies.

If you decide to use page and format limitations, they must be appropriate to the requirements because such limitations must be followed in the evaluation and they cannot be waived, unless the RFP is amended to revise the limitations for all offerors. If your limitations are too restrictive or confusing, you may end up rejecting what was otherwise a winning proposal. The Comptroller General insists that page and format limitations be scrupulously followed, as shown in Example 7.1.

Example 7.1—Offerors must adhere to page and format limitations[2]

Infotec accepted the page and line limits of the RFP without protesting. By choosing to format its proposal as it did, Infotec assumed the risk that its pages would be rejected for noncompliance with the limits. See Kinton Inc., et al.[3] In Kinton, the protester's sample videotape was rejected in part because it was not submitted on 1-inch format tape as required by the RFP. The protester contended that it had a 1-inch tape available but did not submit it. We concluded that the burden rested on the protester, as it did on the other offerors, to submit a sample which met all specifications. Here, Infotec notes that it used a larger type size than the specified minimum, and that it could "easily" reformat the rejected pages. However, Infotec assumed the responsibility to establish, within the RFP format limitations, the suitability and desirability of its proposal and it was by its own choice and business judgment that it used the format that it did. We believe that only by demonstrating the merit of its proposal within the established format would Infotec have been entitled to a further opportunity to expand or correct its proposal through discussions.[4]

Under these circumstances, waiving the deviations or allowing their correction as clarifications would have prejudiced other offerors whose proposals had to meet the same requirements and which had pages removed for violating the limits.

As the Comptroller General points out, offerors must adhere to page and format limitations set forth in the proposal preparation instructions. If offerors choose not to comply, they take the responsibility that their proposals may be rejected.

You should note, however, that a proposal is not rejected simply because it exceeds page or format limitations. A proposal is only rejected when, after removing the excess pages, evaluation of the remaining proposal pages results in a determination that the deficiencies are so great that the proposal does not have a reasonable chance for award. *The deficiencies that result when only part of a proposal is evaluated cause the rejection, not the failure to adhere to the page limitations.*

Offerors are required to comply with page and formatting limitations when the proposal is submitted, not at some later point. A failure to adhere to proposal preparation instructions is not a minor informality—to waive such failures would give an offeror a potential competitive advantage because it would be allowed to have its noncompliant proposal evaluated as is, while other offerors were constrained to follow the instructions. If the evaluation finds the proposal substantially deficient, because of the application of the page and formatting limitations, the proposal must be rejected. Rejection of the proposal is required because a technically unacceptable proposal is not subject to correction; to do so would prejudice other offerors.

PROVIDING SPECIFIC INFORMATION

The proposal preparation instructions may also be used to elicit specific information that can then be used to amplify your initial SOW. This is usually done where you intend to incorporate all or part of the successful offeror's proposal in your SOW.

Some requirements are difficult to describe. You may not know how to go about meeting the requirement because of its technical complexity (as in software development). You may not be sure that the requirement can be met and part of the purpose of your requirement is to find out (as in R&D). There may be a number of different ways to meet the requirement and you do not want to predetermine the way by specifying it in the SOW. You must, therefore, get the offerors to provide the necessary details in their technical proposals.

In such instances, you must provide a broad functional description of your requirement in your initial SOW and use the proposal preparation instructions to require offerors to explain the details of how the work will be done. The successful offeror's proposal would then be incorporated by reference (in whole or in part) into the final SOW.

To successfully follow this approach, you must tell the offerors the level of detail to be provided, such as the technical approach, work plans, methodology, analytic techniques, management reporting formats, or other details as to how the requirement will be met. Then, as appropriate, you may incorporate the information by reference in your final SOW. This converts the offeror's proposal promises into enforceable contract requirements.

FORMATTING INSTRUCTIONS

The purpose of proposal preparation instructions is to provide guidance to the offerors as to the format and content of their proposals. How you provide this guidance is a matter of choice. The important thing to remember is that the instructions should be grouped together in a logical manner, be clearly marked as proposal preparation instructions, and contain only information related to the development of the offeror's proposal. Do not include any information that applies to activities taking place after contract award. Information of this nature belongs in either the SOW or a contract clause, as appropriate. There are a number of ways to express the proposal preparation instructions. Figure 7.3 provides one example of how it can be done:

Figure 7.3—Sample Format for Proposal Preparation Instructions

Introduction

- Make a statement to the effect that unnecessarily elaborate or lengthy proposals are not desired and will reflect adversely on the evaluation of the offeror's understanding of the requirement.

- Require the offeror to provide the technical and management information in a separate volume from the pricing information. Additional volumes may be required as necessary.
- Indicate the number of proposal copies required.
- If you intend to limit the number of proposal pages, indicate the page limitation, how it will be applied, and how you will handle excess pages.

Note: The information above is often presented in a table, such as:

Volume	*Title*	*No. Copies*	*Page Limitations*
I	Technical Proposal	10	100
II	Management Proposal	10	15
II	Corporate Experience	10	2
IV	Past Performance	10	2
III	Cost Proposal	4	None

Instructions

- Require the offerors to present the proposal in the same format as the evaluation factors listed in Section M. For example, if the following evaluation factors were listed in Section M, the instructions should require that the proposal format follow the same order and address the same factors:

Technical Factors
- Technical Approach
- Understanding the Requirement

Management Factors
- Management Approach

Corporate Experience
Past performance
Cost

- For each evaluation factor and subfactor, identify the data or other information required. This includes such information as staffing plans, organization plans, graphs, charts, and other technical information that you need for evaluation purposes. It also includes information needed to complete the description of your requirement, such as work plans and schedules, proposed methodologies, proposed test plans, and other necessary information.

CHECKING YOUR WORK CAREFULLY

The proposal preparation instructions are an important part of the solicitation process. The contractor relies on this information in the preparation of its proposal. The efficiency of the evaluation process depends on how well the proposal preparation instructions direct the contractor to provide relevant information and a proposal format that facilitates the evaluation. Check your proposal preparation instructions carefully before the RFP is issued to ensure that the instructions are properly presented. Ambiguities, inconsistencies, or outright errors in the proposal preparation instructions can cause considerable confusion among the competing offerors and can result in the disqualification of an otherwise qualified offeror. Check the proposal preparation instructions against the RFP as a whole, but particular attention should be paid to the SOW requirements and the evaluation criteria and procedures listed in Section M to ensure that they are compatible.

The following is a list of some of the information that you might want to require offerors to provide in their proposals:

- Discuss specific work elements of particular interest (indicate if this information will be incorporated in the final SOW).
- Provide specific technical information such as graphs, drawings, charts, and other technical information needed for evaluation.
- Discuss technical performance problems that the government has identified in the SOW or are otherwise known to the offeror and how they might be resolved.
- Provide details of the proposed effort to demonstrate how the offeror will meet your functional description of the requirement.
- Discuss the proposed methodology or technical approach to be used, including an explanation of why the particular methodology or technical approach was selected, where more than one is available.

- Provide a risk assessment that identifies risk areas, and recommends approaches to minimize the impact of the risks on the overall success of the contract.
- Provide a performance assessment, as appropriate, on past or current contracts which identifies contract performance problems and indicates how they were, or will be, corrected.
- Discuss how the offeror proposes to manage the contract effort and propose the format and content of the management reports it will submit during contract performance, including a discussion of how the offeror prepares its reports and how long it takes.
- Provide specific management data such as organization charts and staffing plans, as well as a discussion of the corporate lines of authority and communication, and how these will help the offeror respond quickly to performance problems and changes.
- Define milestones or specific work schedules, including a work plan and performance schedule.
- Provide information on its corporate experience, including a requirement to specifically identify past contracts and demonstrate how they are applicable to the projected effort.
- Provide information on its past performance, including references to current and past contracts that demonstrate how the offeror performed on work of the same or similar nature.
- Address its proposed staffing plan, including information on the allocation of resources, turnover rates, and recruiting procedures.
- Propose questions or areas of interest for a study when these are not provided in the SOW.
- Provide details of the data collection effort, methodology, and analytic techniques to be employed when acquiring a study effort.
- Propose details of scheduled technical meetings (purpose, when, where, who attends, etc.), when this is not dictated by the government in the SOW.

- Propose the technical data to be provided, and its format.
- Propose a quality assurance program.
- Propose a test plan, including information on how the test will be conducted and the test results analyzed.
- Identify key personnel, demonstrate how they meet the requisite qualifications and indicate the percentage of time key personnel will devote to the contract.

An offeror's proposal cannot be rejected solely for failing to follow the proposal preparation instructions, but it can be rejected if the failure results in a substantially deficient proposal, as often happens when an offeror fails to heed page limitations. Most offerors will follow the suggested format and content because they realize that proposals tend to get lower scores in evaluation if the evaluators have difficulty in locating pertinent information due to a differing format, or if required information is not provided.

An offeror appreciates and benefits from clear, thorough proposal preparation instructions because the more the offeror knows about what the government wants to see in the proposal, the better it can respond to the government's concerns. Both the government and the offeror benefit from a responsive proposal.

The proposal preparation instructions are the final part of the evaluation plan. Keep in mind that the evaluation factors, their relative importance, and the proposal preparation instructions are published in the solicitation. This enables you to influence the structure and content of the proposals and to expedite the evaluation process by reducing the possibility of confusing and conflicting proposal structures.

References

1. Much of the material in this chapter is taken from Chapter 1 of *How to Write a Statement of Work Fourth Edition,* by Peter S. Cole, published by Management Concepts, Inc. (1999).

2. Infotec Development, Inc., B-238980, 7/20/90, 90-2 CPD ¶58, GCR 104,561.
3. Kinton Inc., B-228233, et al., 1/28/88, 88-1 CPD ¶86, GCR 101,551.
4. Todd Pacific Shipyards Corp., B-214160, 11/13/84, 84-2 CPD ¶519.

CHAPTER 8

Reviewing What Has Been Done

Before finalizing the evaluation plan, review the entire RFP to ensure that the evaluation criteria and the evaluation process have been clearly described and are compatible with the rest of the RFP. The contracting personnel involved with the procurement and the technical personnel who developed the requirement and the SOW (at this point in time the technical evaluation team may not have been identified) should perform this review.

REVIEW THE EVALUATION FACTORS

Review your evaluation factors to ensure that there are no conflicts or duplications in the evaluation process and that the method of evaluation is consistent. Conflicts and duplication can occur where evaluation factors are not clearly defined and it appears that two factors are evaluating the same thing. For example, the evaluation of corporate experience and past performance can appear duplicative or in conflict. You must check your evaluation factors to ensure that they have been clearly described and that you have explained how each will be evaluated.

Make sure that the technical evaluation factors will enable evaluators to identify and document the relative strengths, deficiencies, significant weaknesses, and risks in each proposal. This information provides the basis for the establishment of the competitive range, the negotiations, and the final source selection decision. A failure to document this information properly is a fatal weakness. The Comptroller General has consistently ruled that evaluation results must be fully documented in the contract file and support the source selection decision as shown in Example 8.1.

Example 8.1—Evaluation results must be fully documented[1]

While adjectival ratings and point scores are useful as guides to decision-making, they generally are not controlling, but rather, must be supported by documentation of the relative differences between proposals, their weaknesses, and risks, and the basis and reasons for the selection decision.[2]

The need to fully document the evaluation and to retain this documentation in the contract file cannot be stressed enough. A failure here may result in a failed procurement.

If technical excellence is your primary concern, make sure the evaluation factors will highlight proposal differences and assist you in identifying the proposal with the greatest technical value. The evaluation factors, their relative importance, and the manner of scoring must be consistent with this goal. In addition, ensure that the evaluation is done by a comparative assessment rather than using pass/fail criteria.

If price is your primary concern and technical quality above a specified minimum is not a concern, make sure that your evaluation factors permit you to distinguish the acceptable technical proposals from those that are not acceptable. When awarding on the basis of the lowest priced technically acceptable proposal, your evaluation is not concerned with the quality of the proposals other than distinguishing acceptable proposals from unacceptable proposals. Your evaluation criteria should establish the minimum acceptable levels but need not go beyond that. In such instances, the use of pass/fail criteria is appropriate.

If using both a comparative assessment and pass/fail factors, make sure that these are separately explained and listed in the RFP. These factors must not be combined unless you plan to first apply the pass/fail criteria and then do a comparative assessment of the acceptable proposals. You must explain the process clearly.

REVIEW THE DESCRIPTION OF THE EVALUATION FACTORS

The evaluation factors must effectively communicate your intentions to the offerors. The description of the evaluation factors must tell the offerors what you want them to address in their proposals in as much detail as possible. This is done through a narrative description of each factor and significant subfactor and by using the proposal preparation instructions to require the submission of pertinent information. Make sure that the evaluation criteria in Section M are compatible with the proposal preparation instructions in Section L.

Do not, however, overlook the basic purpose of the evaluation factors, which is to facilitate the discrimination between proposals by establishing criteria for judging the relative worth or value of the competing proposals. The evaluation factors must be viewed as a whole and must interact properly to ensure reasonable and rational results. They provide the basis for the overall evaluation process, the purpose of which is to select the offeror who best meets your requirements (i.e., offers the best value).

REVIEW HOW THE EVALUATION SCHEME IS DESCRIBED

In addition to the description of the individual evaluation factors and subfactors, Section M should include a statement describing the overall evaluation scheme. This should be done in a narrative separate from the listing of evaluation factors and subfactors and should indicate the basis for award and generally, how the evaluation will be conducted.

Ensuring that offerors understand how their proposals will be evaluated is to your advantage as well as the offerors. Knowing how the evaluation will be conducted helps the offerors provide proposals that fit within the evaluation scheme. This not only helps expedite the evaluation process but also helps ensure that you get the information you want.

Review How the Evaluation Will Be Conducted

If the evaluation is conducted on the basis of a comparative assessment, you must indicate that all proposals will be evaluated, ranked, and rated on the basis of their comparative value. If the evaluation is on a pass/fail basis, you must indicate that proposals will be evaluated only to determine their acceptability, and that technical quality in excess of the minimum requirements will not be evaluated. As noted earlier, if the evaluation is on the basis of a combination of pass/fail and comparative assessment, the evaluation factors must be identified and grouped by how they will be evaluated. If a specific evaluation factor will be evaluated both ways, indicate that it will be first evaluated to the pass/fail criteria. If it passes, it will then be evaluated by comparative assessment.

Review the Relationship of the Technical Factors and the Cost or Price Factor

The solicitation must state the relationship between cost or price and the noncost (technical) evaluation factors, indicating whether the noncost factors are significantly more important than cost or price; approximately equal to cost or price; or significantly less important than cost or price. A failure to meet this requirement could result in a protest. Generally, if the relationship is not stated, the Comptroller General will consider technical and cost to be of equal value.

Review How Cost Will Be Evaluated

If cost is a weighted factor, you must indicate its relative importance, such as Technical 70 percent - Cost 30 percent. If cost is an unweighted factor, you must indicate this and state that its importance will increase if the technical factors are evaluated as being roughly equal and that cost could become the determining factor.

Review the Basis for Award

You must ensure that the basis for award is explicitly stated.

Award to the Lowest Priced, Technically Acceptable Proposal

Ensure the factors that establish the technical requirements for acceptability are set forth and state that award will be made to the technically acceptable proposal offering the lowest evaluated price.

Award Based on Best Value

You must indicate that award will be based on best value and state that award may be made to other than the lowest price or to other than the highest technical rating depending on the government's determination as to the proposal offering the best value to the government. If you intend to make a cost/technical tradeoff (and this is usually done in a best value procurement), specifically state that this will be done—particularly if you intend to adjust the offeror's cost or price figures in developing your evaluated cost or price. A simple mention of "best value" in the RFP is not sufficient to put offerors on notice that you will be making adjustments because there are differing methods of doing this. For example, some agencies have discounted costs by the amount that they exceed the minimum requirements; other agencies have increased costs to account for what they consider to be understated costs. You should indicate, preferably without the use of mathematical formulas, how you intend to do this (see Chapter 13).

Ensure a Common Basis for Proposal Submission and Evaluation Is Provided

Offerors must be provided with a common basis for the submission and evaluation of proposals. Once established, award must be based on these requirements. Any changes to the evaluation scheme must be formalized by an amendment to the RFP that provides an opportunity for all offerors to make revisions appropriate to the change. The government cannot make selective, unwritten changes, or accept deviations from the evaluation criteria for individual offerors. Just as an offeror is required to respond to the published requirements of the RFP, the government must evaluate strictly in accordance with the published evaluation procedures, as shown in Example 8.2.

Example 8.2—Offerors must be provided with a common basis for the submission and evaluation of proposals[3]

It is a fundamental principle of competitive procurement that offerors be provided with a common basis for the submission and evaluation of proposals.[4] Award therefore must be based on the requirements contained in the solicitation, and where the solicitation requires prospective contractors to furnish specific information bearing on their ability to perform the work as a prerequisite to an award, an agency does not have discretion to disregard an offeror's failure to satisfy such a requirement.[5] Where the agency determines, however, that the ground rules of a solicitation no longer reflect its needs and can be relaxed, it should amend the RFP and afford all eligible offerors the opportunity to revise their proposals accordingly, particularly where the failure to adhere to those ground rules would prejudice one or more offerors.[6]

SAY WHAT YOU MEAN AND MEAN WHAT YOU SAY

You should exercise care in how you word and structure the evaluation criteria in Section M of the RFP. You must set forth all evaluation factors and significant subfactors, and their relative importance. If you fail to do this, you may find yourself in a bind when offerors are technically equal. If offers are technically equal, cost/price becomes the decision maker. You cannot then bring up other factors to avoid awarding to the lowest price, as shown in Example 8.3.

Example 8.3—Select and word evaluation factors carefully[7]

It is fundamental that offerors must be advised of the bases upon which their proposals will be evaluated.[8] *In particular, contracting agencies are required by statute to set forth at a minimum, all significant evaluation factors (and significant subfactors). . . including cost or price, cost-or price-related factors, and noncost- or nonprice-related factors, and their relative importance.*[9] *An agency may not give importance to specific criteria beyond that which would reasonably be expected by offerors.*

Here, although the agency's selection of Beneco was based on Beneco's lower assessed performance risk, the RFP provided only that performance risk would be a "general consideration" in the integrated assessment of proposals. The RFP did not provide the relative importance of the performance risk assessment (or other general considerations) vis-à-vis the evaluation factors specifically identified and listed in descending order of importance, in the RFP. Thus under the RFP this "general consideration" could not be given significant weight in the award selection.[10] *Consequently, the agency could not properly make award to Beneco merely because of its lower performance risk, where Beneco's offer, under the solicitation's stated and weighted evaluation criteria, was technically equal to, but higher in price than HJ's offer. Indeed, given HJ's technically equal "blue" rated proposal, low proposal risk rating, and low price, the record fairly shows that HJ would have been selected for award under the RFP.*

If the Air Force believes that past performance as it relates to the probability of successfully performing the contract should be separately evaluated, we recommend that it list and define this element as an evaluation factor for technical proposals, and state the relative weight that the factor will be accorded in the technical evaluation (and in a footnote - "This determination should include an assessment of the extent to which that factor is already included within the assessment of the company experience technical evaluation factor."). The agency should then reopen discussions and solicit revised proposals from the competitive range offerors. If, upon review, the agency concludes that past performance was adequately addressed under the company experience technical evaluation factor, so that the RFP reflects the government's actual requirements, it should terminate Beneco's contract and make award to HJ.

In this case the contracting agency acted improperly in awarding a contract to an offeror under an evaluation factor which was said to be a "general consideration," whose relative importance was not disclosed vis-à-vis the evaluation factors specifically identified and listed in the RFP in descending order of importance. The fact that the awardee's proposal was technically equal to but higher in price than the protester's proposal compounded this problem.

It should also be noted that the Comptroller General indicated a possible relationship between performance risk and the company experience evaluation factor. Do not be misled by the Comptroller General's wording in this example. The problem was that none of the evaluation factors were well defined. In fact, there should be no relationship between past performance (expressed as performance risk) and corporate experience (see Chapter 4, Proposal Risk, where performance risk is defined in relation to proposal risk, and Chapter 3, Past Performance Versus Corporate Experience, where the differences between past performance and corporate experience are discussed). The key point here is that the evaluation factors must be defined to show what will be evaluated and the relative importance of each factor must also be set forth.

Once you have established how you are going to evaluate proposals, you should carefully assess what you have done to see if you have created a problem, as in Example 8.3. Do not throw in some factor as a "general consideration." If some factor will be evaluated, it must be specifically identified as described above. Do not generalize to give yourself "flexibility." This will only cause problems. In short, *say what you mean, and mean what you say, because you must evaluate the proposals exactly as set forth in the RFP.*

REVIEW THE OVERALL EVALUATION PLAN

The overall evaluation plan must be reviewed objectively. Try to keep the evaluation plan as simple as possible. Generally, complex evaluation plans are undesirable. The more complex the plan, the harder it will be for the evaluators to make valid judgments. Complex plans tend to generate a need for mathematical formulas. The evaluators then often place more reliance on numbers than on an actual assessment of the problems and strengths of competing proposals. The evaluation results must be supported by a written rationale that is reasonable and supported by the numbers rather than the other way around.

Complex plans, with multiple evaluation factors and subfactors, also tend to level out the evaluation results. Scoring often becomes diluted if a large number of factors are used, as the highs and lows tend to make the bottom lines roughly equal. The leveling effect makes it difficult to distinguish between the proposals and to identify the proposal offering the best value. This is often a problem in procurements stating that technical considerations are paramount and cost, while considered, is less important or is not a weighted and scored evaluation factor. In such instances, if the technical evaluations level out, *cost becomes the discriminating factor.* Offerors who have concentrated on technical excellence and find themselves losing a contract because of pricing factors may protest. Keeping the evaluation plan as simple as possible minimizes this kind of problem.

REVIEW THE ENTIRE RFP

In addition to checking the consistency of the evaluation factors, one to another, you must check the evaluation factors and your overall evaluation scheme against the SOW and the RFP's clauses and provisions. No conflicts should exist between them. This is important because generally, technical personnel develop the SOW and the evaluation criteria and contracting personnel develop the clauses and provisions in the RFP. Conflicts may develop if nobody checks the overall picture, as illustrated by Example 8.4.

Example 8.4—Conflicts between the SOW, evaluation criteria, and RFP provisions may lead to protests[11]

Clause 1.2 of an SOW stated that "for pricing purposes the offeror may choose to recoup equipment costs under line item 0001 or amortize the costs over the options."

The RFP also contained FAR provision 52.215-16, Contract Award, which stated that the government could reject an offer as unacceptable if the prices proposed were materially unbalanced between line items.

The low offeror was rejected for submitting materially unbalanced pricing (the price for line item 0001 included the offeror's up-front costs incurred for equipment, freight, engineering and installation, warranties, required spare parts, and combined overhead and profit). The contracting officer felt that the pricing was unbalanced because if the agency did not exercise all of the options, the offer would not result in the lowest overall cost to the government. The rejected offeror protested this decision and the Comptroller General sustained the protest.

An offer is materially unbalanced where it is mathematically unbalanced (each item does not carry its share of the cost of the work specified for that item as well as overhead and profit, and the offer is based on nominal prices for some of the work and enhanced prices for other work) and will not result in the lowest cost to the government. A grossly front-loaded offer, that is, one that includes a significantly disproportionate share of total evaluated contract costs in a line item for which payment will be made prior to performance of work required by other line items, typically is regarded as mathematically unbalanced on its face. Although the front-loaded pricing may reflect start-up and equipment costs, the government expects such costs to be apportioned over the entire evaluated contract period; offerors who front-load costs are in effect shifting the risk from themselves to the government that the contract will not extend through the entire evaluation period. As we stated in Westbrook,[12] *the government generally is under no obligation to accept that risk.*

In this case, the solicitation expressly invited frontloading. Clause 1.2 of the SOW permitted offerors to recoup their equipment costs under line item 0001 instead of amortizing them over the base and option periods of the contract, and there is no suggestion in the record that Westbrook's item 0001 costs exceed the costs of the equipment it would furnish plus other costs associated with the installation. We do not think an agency can invite offers on a particular basis and then reject an offer precisely because it is submitted on that basis. . . accordingly we sustain the protest...

The problem in Example 8.4 is a common one. The RFP was not carefully reviewed to detect conflicts between the SOW, the evaluation criteria, and the RFP clauses and provisions. There should be two such reviews. The contracting officer and the author of the SOW should conduct the first review before the RFP is issued. The evaluation team conducts the second review before the evaluation is started (this will be discussed in more detail in Chapter 10). Had either one of these reviews been done properly, the matter could have been resolved before the evaluation process started.

You can resolve a problem found before the evaluation process starts by issuing an amendment to the RFP that makes the correction and permits offerors to revise their proposals accordingly. This will cost you the time it takes to find and fix the problem plus a week or so for the offerors to revise their proposals.

A protest is more costly. Preparing a response to a protest costs significant time and effort. If the protest is sustained, there is the additional cost of the time and effort to fix the problem, to reevaluate the proposals, to make another award decision, and possibly even pay the offeror's filing costs and attorney's fees.

It is worth the time and effort to "do it right" in the first place. Reviewing what has been done, including the evaluation plan, the SOW, the evaluation criteria, the proposal preparation instructions and the RFP provisions, to ensure that they are consistent will help minimize problems later in the procurement process.

References

1. Biospheres Inc., B-278508.4; B-278508.5; B-278508.6, 10/6/98, GCR 110,428.
2. Century Envtl. Hygiene, Inc., B-279378, 6/5/98, 98-1 CPD ¶164 at 4; Engineering and Computation Inc., B-261658, 10/16/95, 95-2 CPD ¶176 at 3.
3. Pasco Realty, B-245705, 1/8/92, 92-1 CPD ¶39, GCR 106,229.
4. E.C. Campbell, Inc., B-222197, 6/19/86, 86-1 CPD ¶565.
5. United Materials, Inc., B-243669, 8/16/91, 91-2 CPD ¶161, GCR 105,773.

6. DynaLantic Corp, 68 Comp. Gen. 413 (1989), 89-1 CPD ¶421, GCR 103,141.
7. H.J. Group Ventures, Inc., B-246139, 2/19/92, 92-1 CPD ¶203, GCR 106,410.
8. Republic Realty Servs., Inc., B-242629, 5/7/91, 91-1 CPD ¶446, GCR 105,466.
9. 10 USCA 2305(a)(2)(A) (West Supp. 1991).
10. Laser Power Techs., Inc., B-233369 and B-233369.2, 3/13/89, 89-1 CPD ¶267, GCR 102,987; see also Devres, Inc., 66 Comp. Gen. 121 (1986), 86-2 CPD ¶652, GCR 100,119.
11. Glen Industrial Communications, Inc., B-248223, 5/19/92, 92-1 CPD ¶453, GCR 106,641.
12. Westbrook Indus., B-245019.2, 1/7/92, 92-1 CPD ¶30, GCR 106,215.

CHAPTER 9

Oral Presentations[1]

An oral presentation is a verbal presentation, or briefing, by an offeror designed to present specific proposal information as directed by the government. This information is presented orally in lieu of presenting the same information in the written proposal, but may also be used to supplement written proposal material under certain circumstances, such as where past performance references are required in writing, and oral presentations are used to expand on past performance. Oral presentations can be made at any time during the acquisition process but are most often used during the initial evaluation prior to the determination of the competitive range or prior to making an award without discussions. Oral presentations may also be used during discussions after establishment of the competitive range.

The purpose of oral presentations is to eliminate, or reduce, the need for written information where the information can be conveyed in a more meaningful and efficient way through verbal means. The concept presumes that certain evaluation information can be presented more efficiently and at less cost to the offeror by verbal means than through the written proposal. It also presumes that the information in oral presentations can be evaluated easier and faster than if the same information was included in the written proposal.

WHAT IS THE RELATIONSHIP BETWEEN ORAL PRESENTATIONS AND THE WRITTEN PROPOSALS?

Oral presentations are used to evaluate how the *offeror plans to perform the work*, such as the technical approach, the offeror's understanding of the requirement, the management approach, staffing plans, resource use and allocation, and any other areas that demonstrate how the offeror will meet its commitment to perform, but are not part of the offeror's contractual commitment to perform. For example, staffing and resource allocation relates to how the offeror plans to perform and as such can be addressed orally.

However, if the oral presentation includes information that the parties intend to include in the contract as material terms or conditions, this information must be put in writing and should not be a topic of an oral presentation. Oral statements may not be incorporated by reference. If, during an oral presentation, the dialogue between the government and the offeror constitutes discussions, whether intended or not, the government must comply with the rules for negotiation.

Oral presentations are a part of the overall evaluation process, as are the written proposals, but are evaluated separately from the written proposals. Specific evaluation criteria and scoring procedures are used to evaluate oral presentations. The information to be evaluated is information that would otherwise be included in the written proposals.

Written proposals are used to evaluate those things related to an *offeror's contractual commitment* such as cost or pricing information, representations and certifications, past performance or corporate experience references, facility availability, resumes of key personnel, commitments to specific SOW requirements, and any other areas that demonstrate the offeror's contractual commitment to perform in accordance with the statement of work. If the SOW calls for the use of specific techniques, processes, equipment, staffing levels or qualifications, the offeror's response must be included in the written portion of the proposal because the offeror must specifically commit itself to perform in this manner. If it is intended to incorporate parts of the offeror's proposal into the SOW, this information must also be contained in the written proposal.

Generally, the same information is not evaluated in both the written and the oral format. However, while the references and explanations with respect to past performance and corporate experience should be in writing, an oral explanation of the relevance of such information and how it demonstrates the offeror's competence to perform the contract work may supplement this information.

DECIDING WHETHER TO USE ORAL PRESENTATIONS

Oral presentations should be used only where it can be determined that their use will enhance the efficiency and effectiveness of the procurement. The following factors should be considered.

Facilities

Determine if the agency has adequate presentation facilities. Normally, oral presentations are made at the agency's facilities (this helps avoid problems with superior versus inferior facilities). The agency must have, or be able to obtain, presentation space that will be large enough to accommodate all participants and have the resources (video/audio equipment, black/whiteboards, other audio-visual aides, and adequate supplies and furniture) for the presentations. This space must be readily available for the time necessary to make all of the presentations, including specified time periods prior to the presentations for offerors to familiarize themselves with the facilities.

Oral presentations may also be conducted at an offeror's facility. This might be appropriate where the presentation can be combined with a planned site visit or other demonstration that must be performed at the offeror's facility. Consideration might also be given to teleconferencing or video teleconferencing if both the government and the offerors have the appropriate equipment.

Time Considerations

Determine if there is enough time to conduct oral presentations. Do not assume that oral presentations will shorten the procurement process without first addressing the time factors. The time factors encompass two main areas, the time to conduct the presentations and the time to evaluate the presentations.

Time to Conduct the Presentations

This time consideration involves both the time for the individual presentations and the number of presentations that will be required. For example, offerors should be afforded at least one hour to make their presentations, and one-half hour for a question and answer (Q&A) period. This may not be a problem if only a few proposals are expected, but if 20 proposals are expected, or 200 (see Example 9.1), this time factor could be important.

Time to Evaluate the Presentations

This time consideration involves both the time necessary to evaluate the oral presentations and the availability of the evaluators during this period. Generally, a minimum of at least one-half hour of evaluation time should be allotted for each hour of presentation time. This should give the evaluators time to fill out their evaluation forms and to caucus with the other evaluators to ensure consistency in the evaluation.

Evaluators have full-time jobs; generally, they are assigned to evaluations on a part-time basis. While some agencies assign evaluators full-time for major acquisitions, this is not usually done for less-than-major acquisitions. So, in addition to considering the time necessary to conduct the evaluations, there must be some assurance that all of the evaluators will be available when needed or that an accommodation will be made for those who are absent—such as viewing a video/tape recording of the presentation and doing their evaluation at a later time. It should be noted, however, that later viewing by some of the evaluators may adversely affect the effectiveness of the Q&A period. Later viewing may also extend the evaluation time while waiting for the absent evaluators to conduct their evaluation.

Even assuming a best case scenario—one hour for the presentation, one-half hour for a Q&A period, and one-half hour to evaluate the presentation—two hours per presentation times the number of offerors, can amount to a significant amount of time, particularly considering that these same evaluators must also evaluate the written proposals as well. These time factors must be considered when planning to use oral presentations as part of the evaluation scheme. If time is of the essence and the procurement is highly competitive, time factors may preclude the use of oral presentations.

Types of Effort Most Appropriate for Oral Presentations

Oral presentations are most effective when used in conjunction with a functional statement of work where an offeror's qualifications to perform the work and its understanding of the requirement are the primary evaluation criteria.

Task Type Contracts

Oral presentations are most effectively used with task type contracts, in which a significant part of the evaluation centers on the offeror's response to how it would perform one or more sample tasks. A description of how an offeror would plan, staff, and perform a sample task lends itself to an oral presentation, particularly if the presenter is the project manager who will be responsible for the performance. While a sample task is fictional, it must be realistic (based on a likely future task or previous effort that will likely recur), fully described (i.e., a complete task order SOW), and the government should have a reasonably firm idea about how the effort should be conducted. In addition to describing the task, the RFP should specify the kinds of information to be presented. The description of the information required should include everything that will be evaluated, such as the following, when applicable:

- Any technical considerations (technical approach/technical understanding)
- Management considerations (organization, authority, oversight)

- Staffing considerations (who, how many, specific qualifications, staffing allocation and reallocation, reaction time, etc.)
- Facilities and resources (availability of facilities/resources other than personnel, how the facilities/resources will be used, allocation and use of equipment and supplies, availability of backup facilities/resources, etc.).

Performance-Based Service Contracts

Oral presentations can be effectively used in conjunction with performance-based service contracts where (1) a functional statement of work is used in which the kinds of services required and the expected results are described, but the details of how to do the work are left to the offeror to describe in its written proposal or oral presentation, (2) performance standards are established in the statement of work to measure how well the contractor performs, such as quality of work, timeliness, quantity, and other performance attributes deemed significant to successful contract performance, and (3) the performance standards are tied to quality-related evaluation factors such as technical and management capabilities.

Research and Development Contracts

Oral presentations may be used for research and development contracts, but care must be taken to ensure that the oral presentations address only issues related to how the offeror plans to meet the requirement. The greatest problem will be ensuring that the Q&A session after the presentation does not go beyond clarification of the presentation and turn into discussions. It is difficult to limit questions about technical issues to only clarification matters and still get meaningful results.

Supply Contracts

Oral presentations are less effective for supply contracts, particularly fixed-price contracts, because technical and management issues are often not major discriminators or are so closely tied to contract compliance issues that it is difficult to effectively separate them. However, oral presentations to supplement past performance and corporate experience matters might be considered.

PLANNING FOR ORAL PRESENTATIONS

A number of decisions must be made in planning for oral presentations.

Decide When the Oral Presentations Will Be Made

Oral presentations may be made before an award without discussions, before the determination of the competitive range, or as a part of the discussions after the determination of the competitive range. Where oral presentations are made prior to an award without discussions or prior to the determination of the competitive range, the presentations should be scheduled as soon as possible after completion of the initial evaluation of the written proposals. Evaluators should be familiar with an offeror's written proposal before they hear the oral presentation. This familiarity will help them understand what is being presented and to ask pertinent questions.

When oral presentations are used after establishment of the competitive range, they should be conducted as a part of the initial discussions so that any proposal problems that surfaced during the oral presentations may be addressed in any further discussions or in the offeror's final proposal revision.

Decide What Material Is to Be Covered in the Oral Presentations

Certain information must be in writing, such as cost or pricing information, representations and certifications, past performance and corporate experience references, personnel resumes, and information demonstrating compliance with the statement of work and other terms and conditions set forth in the RFP. Other information may be provided orally or in writing, such as the relevance of the past performance and corporate experience references, information demonstrating the offeror's understanding of the requirement (business and management approach, staffing, scheduling, etc.) and how the offeror would perform sample tasks.

After considering the nature of the requirement and when the oral presentations will be made, select that information that could be best presented within the time to be allotted for the oral presentations.

Decide Who Will Make the Presentations

Presenters should be the key personnel who will be assigned to manage and direct contract performance (project manager, task leader, etc.). If such personnel are not available, the presenter should be from the offeror's in-house staff and not hired outside specialists. If subcontractors will be performing significant portions of the work to be addressed by an oral presentation, the presenter should be the subcontractor project manager, task leader, etc. While there may be more than one presenter, contractor attendance at oral presentations should be limited to only those contractor or subcontractor personnel actually making presentations. Require offerors to identify the presenters in their written proposals. Substitutions after submission of the written proposal must be justified prior to the presentation and the substitutes must fit the profile indicated above.

Decide Which Government Personnel Will Attend the Presentations

Generally, all evaluators, the contracting officer, and the source selection official (if other than the contracting officer) should attend each presentation. However, if the presentations are to be taped for later evaluation at a minimum, the head of the evaluation team, the contracting officer, and any available evaluators should attend. You must ensure that enough evaluators attend each presentation to make the Q&A session worthwhile.

Establish Specific Evaluation Criteria for Use With the Oral Presentations

The evaluation criteria should consist of factors that help determine the offeror's qualifications to perform all aspects of the work, how well the offeror understands the requirement, and how the offeror will approach accomplishment of the required tasks.

Section M of the solicitation should clearly indicate which evaluation factors will be used in the evaluation of the written proposals and which will be used in the evaluation of the oral presentations. In both cases, the evaluation factors and their relative importance must be identified, defined, and an explanation provided as to how the evaluation will be conducted. Generally, the same evaluation factors that would be used to evaluate the information if it were in a written format would be used to evaluate the information in an oral format.

Decide the Ground Rules Governing the Presentations

The ground rules governing the oral presentations must be decided upon before issuance of the solicitation and should be published as a part of the proposal preparation instructions.

Order of Presentation

The government determines the order of presentations, usually by a lottery. After receipt of the proposals, the contracting officer will notify each offeror of the time and place for its presentation. Presentations must be made in the order designated and at the time specified. Generally, changes will not be allowed. Offerors are informed only of the time of their presentation. Information regarding the identity or number of other offerors must not be released.

Presentation Time

The government specifies the amount of time allotted to each presentation. This time period shall be the same for each offeror. Offerors must complete their presentations within the time specified. Additional time will not be permitted.

As noted earlier, presentation time should be commensurate with the complexity of the procurement and must be published in the RFP. Time can be controlled in terms of hours allotted, amount of presentation material that may be used, or both. Be careful with limitations on the amount of presentation material that may be used. Such limitations presume that the government knows the appropriate amount. Give the offeror as much leeway as possible in how the material will be presented. The quality of the presentation will influence the evaluation, so let the offeror be responsible for the quality. When time limits are used, they should apply to the overall presentation. Do not attempt to dictate time limits on individual components of the overall presentation.

Communications

Generally, after receipt of the proposals and prior to the presentation itself, no communications regarding the oral presentations are allowed. However, written questions that are directed at clarification of the presentation process should be accepted and the answers to such questions provided to all offerors.

Presentation Content

Restrict all oral presentations to verbal presentations. The use of offeror-prepared video tapes or other media forms in addition to the verbal presentation should not be permitted, although such material may be submitted with the written proposal. Offerors should be put on notice of the following:

- The oral presentations are restricted to the topics identified in Sections L and M of the RFP. No additional topics or information may be provided.
- The oral presentation may not address information provided in the written proposal, particularly cost or pricing information.
- The offeror may not reference the written proposal as support for information furnished. If the offeror finds it

necessary to address information that is also in the written proposal, the written information must be fully presented. The evaluation of an oral presentation is restricted to only the information presented verbally.

Presentation Materials

You may place restrictions on the type of presentation material and the manner of presentation (usually these are related to the facilities and equipment that will be available for use). You may also place limits on the amount of presentation material (i.e., only 20 slides per task), but this should be the exception rather than the rule. It is up to the offeror to develop a successful presentation within the time allotted, and the offeror should be permitted to use its own judgment in this area.

Require the offeror to deliver copies of all presentation materials (i.e., hard copies of slides and other briefing material) as part of the initial proposal submission. This material should include identification of the presenter(s). If more than one presenter will be used, each presenter and the material that presenter will cover must be identified. Tell the offeror that additional material or changes to material submitted shall not be permitted after the date set for receipt of proposals and that the presentation itself may not address matters not covered by the material submitted. This is necessary to permit the evaluators to become familiar with the material before the presentation is made and to comply with the FAR requirement that once proposals are submitted they may not be changed until after discussions commence.

Develop Specific Proposal Preparation Instructions

The proposal preparation instructions in Section L of the solicitation should state that oral presentations will be required and provide instructions and guidance regarding the nature and extent of the process involved, such as the following:

- Describe the ground rules for the oral presentations.

- Describe the applicable evaluation factors and the specific topics to be discussed in the oral presentation. Be as specific as possible about the topics to be addressed. For example, if staffing levels and allocation of resources is to be addressed, you should indicate any particular concerns you have, such as how peak workloads would be met without jeopardizing other ongoing work and how personnel and other resources would be shifted to meet workload peaks.
- Identify place of the oral presentations, how the presentations will be scheduled (usually by a lottery), and the total amount of time allocated for each presentation. Warn offerors that the presentations must be made as scheduled and be completed within the time allotted. No changes or extensions will be permitted.
- Describe the rules governing the use of presentation media, particularly if there are any restrictions involved, such as prohibitions on unnecessarily elaborate presentations or presentation materials, restrictions due to a lack of specific equipment, etc., and requirements for and any limitations on the use of written material or other media to supplement the presentation.
- Describe the format and content of presentation documentation and when it shall be delivered to the government (usually as part of the written proposal submission).
- Describe the rules governing who shall make the presentations and identify the numbers and types of government personnel who will attend.
- Describe the location and physical characteristics of the presentation facility and the resources (types of equipment, etc.) to be made available. Indicate when the facility will be available for inspection and how to obtain permission to inspect it.
- Specifically state whether the presentation will encompass price or cost and fee. Generally, cost or pricing issues should not be part of the oral presentations and offerors should specifically be informed of this.

- Describe whether the presentation will constitute discussions. If presentations are made before the establishment of the competitive range, indicate that any communications will be for clarification only and will not constitute discussions as defined by FAR 15.306. If presentations are made after establishment of the competitive range, any exchanges will constitute discussions. Identify the limitations on government-offeror interaction before, during, and after the presentation.
- Indicate that written questions about the oral presentation process may be submitted before the presentations, and that the answers will be provided to all offerors.
- Describe the question and answer period that follows the presentation and indicate that it does not count against the overall time limit.
- State that after the oral presentation is completed there will be no further communications about the presentation and no changes in the presentation material will be permitted. However, presentation information may be addressed during the discussions after establishment of the competitive range.
- State how the presentation will be recorded (videotaped, audiotaped, written transcript, etc.). Generally each offeror will be provided a copy of the record of its own presentation.

CONDUCTING ORAL PRESENTATIONS

Several factors must be considered in conducting oral presentations.

Controlling the Presentations

Regardless of where the oral presentations are conducted, they must be closely controlled to ensure that they are made within the established ground rules. This is particularly important with respect to who is permitted to make the presentations, the time allotted for the presentation, and the presentation content. As noted earlier, the government determines the order of the presentations and the presentations must be made at the time specified. The time set for the presentations is similar to the time set for receipt of proposals and generally, the same rules regarding lateness would apply.

Question and Answer Period

Normally, a Q&A period follows each presentation. The Q&A time does not count against the presentation time allotted. All questions must be related to the material presented. The government may point out areas that need improvement, but cannot discuss how to make such improvements. The offeror may provide verbal answers to the questions asked, but may not provide any additional written material. The government will evaluate only the material presented and the results of the Q&A. While an offeror may be permitted to revise its written proposal as a result of discussions, the submission of additional or supplemental information related to the oral presentation is not permitted.

Clarifications Versus Discussions

When oral presentations are conducted before the establishment of the competitive range, a potential problem arises with respect to what can be discussed during the Q&A. The problem is this—while one of the purposes of oral presentations is to create a dialogue between the evaluators and the offeror, the dialogue may not reach the level of discussions as defined in FAR Part 15.306(d).

Making the distinction between clarifications, which are allowed, and discussions, which are not allowed, is not easy. Clarifications [FAR 15.306(a)] and communications [FAR 15.306(b)] are exchanges between the government and offerors for the purpose of enhancing the government's understanding and interpretation of proposals and do not involve information that might lead an offeror to revise its proposal. Discussions [FAR 15.306(d)] are exchanges between the government and an offeror that involve information essential for determining the acceptability of a proposal and/or provide the offeror an opportunity to revise or modify its proposal.

So, how do you do one, but not the other? The OFPP publication *Guidelines for the Use of Oral Presentations* recommends that the RFP contain disclaimer language indicating that any communications during the Q&A period are clarifications and not discussions. It should be noted, however, that this disclaimer is meaningless if discussions actually occur. The most effective way to avoid the clarifications versus discussions problem is to ensure that the questions asked do not suggest ways to resolve proposal problems. For example, an offeror could be asked to explain how the proposed staffing will handle certain situations (i.e., workload peaks or emergencies), but the evaluators may not comment on or further discuss the offeror's response or otherwise indicate whether the response was adequate or inadequate. It is also improper for evaluators to continue to ask the same questions until the presenter "gets it right." The contracting officer must control the Q&A dialogue carefully to avoid entering into discussions. This could be a fatal error in the event of a protest.

It should be noted that the problem with discussions is minimized where the oral presentation centers on how an offeror would perform a sample task. A sample task is fictional and does not represent a firm contractual requirement. Since the evaluation will be aimed at the offeror's demonstrated capability to perform a task of the nature described, the normal rules governing discussions do not apply. Offerors can be questioned more closely and in more detail, as long as the questions are restricted to what the offeror would do and do not result in a dialog about how it should be done. There is more leeway to ask "what if" questions when addressing sample tasks, but these questions must be restricted to how the offeror would perform.

It should be noted, however, that discussion problems apply only when the oral presentations are given before the establishment of the competitive range. If the oral presentations are made after the establishment of the competitive range and before submission of the final proposal revisions, any communications are automatically discussions. The only problems then are to avoid technical leveling by giving the offeror an indication of how to fix perceived problems or technical transfusion by telling an offeror about how a competitor proposed to resolve the problem.

Evaluating Oral Presentations

The evaluation of oral presentations must be done strictly in accordance with the stated evaluation factors. Generally, evaluation scoring should use the same scoring method as used for the evaluation of the written proposals. To facilitate the evaluation, evaluators should be provided with an evaluation form that outlines the RFP's evaluation factors and identifies the key points that should be made during the oral presentation. This will not only assist in the evaluation itself, but will also help evaluators to formulate questions for the Q&A period to follow the presentation.

The evaluators should meet to evaluate each oral presentation immediately after the presentation. If this is not possible, at a minimum, the evaluators should caucus following each presentation to exchange reactions, summarize potential strengths and weaknesses, and verify perceptions and understandings. The individual evaluations and team meeting for consensus may occur at a later date. It should be noted, however, that one of the reasons for the use of oral presentations is to expedite the procurement process. This is not likely to happen if the evaluations are put off to a later date.

Where oral presentations are made before the establishment of the competitive range, the evaluation must be done as soon as each presentation is completed. Any delay at this point will reduce the effectiveness of the use of oral presentations.

Where oral presentations are made after the establishment of the competitive range, any deficiencies and weaknesses found as a result of the oral presentations should be recorded and provided to the offerors during discussions.

Oral presentations can be an effective evaluation technique if carried out properly. Sometimes, however, you can lose control of the process as shown in Example 9.1.

Example 9.1—Do not get carried away with the use of oral presentations[2]

In a solicitation for the award of multiple indefinite-delivery, indefinite-quantity, government-wide acquisition contracts for information technology services and products, the RFP provided for award without discussions, on a cost/technical tradeoff basis. The RFP contemplated awards in three functional areas: information systems engineering (ISE); information systems security (ISS); and systems operations and management (SOM), and stated the following evaluation criteria for award:

Non-Price Factors

1. Past Performance
   a. Quality Recognition/Certifications (QRC)
   b. Past Performance Management (PPM)
2. Team Composition

Price Factors

1. Realism
2. Reasonableness

The RFP stated that it was the agency's intention to provide each offeror with an opportunity to make a one-hour oral presentation and indicated the topics to be covered.

The Commerce Department had anticipated receiving 40 to 60 proposals in response to the RFP. It actually received over 200. Because the agency believed it would be impossible to invite all offerors to make oral presentations, it decided to limit oral presentations to only the "most competitive offerors." Acting alone, the co-chairs of the source selection evaluation board (SSEB) then "screened" all proposals against the evaluation criteria to determine the greatest number of proposals that would permit an efficient competition among the most highly rated proposals.

In performing this review, the SSEB chairs assigned letter ratings (from A+ to C–) under the two past performance subfactors (QRC and PPM) and either a "+" or "–" under the team composition factor. No narrative explanations for these ratings were prepared. An initial screening matrix prepared for each functional area ranked offerors according to their relative ratings under the QRC subfactor; this document also noted each offeror's rating under the PPM subfactor and team composition factor and each offeror's average loaded hourly labor rate. The contracting officer reviewed the offeror's average loaded labor rates for realism and reasonableness and determined that all of the average rates were reasonable.

For each functional area, and based only on the offerors' QRC subfactor ratings, the SSEB chairs recommended a cutoff that would provide for a "sufficient, high-quality competition." They recommended to the two SSAs (who were acting jointly) that only those offerors that received a B+ or higher under the QRC subfactor be permitted to make an oral presentation. The SSAs agreed. Price was not considered in determining which offeror would be invited to make an oral presentation.

The complete SSEB then evaluated the proposals of those offerors that were selected to provide an oral presentation. It should be noted that the SSEB did not have access to the earlier screening evaluation. Upon completion of each oral presentation, the SSEB contacted the offeror's past performance references to confirm proposal claims concerning past performance management. The SSEB prepared evaluation worksheets that summarized the significant aspects of the proposals and identified any notable strengths or weaknesses. The group then prepared an evaluation report that was presented to the SSAs for their consideration.

In reviewing the evaluations of the respective proposals, the SSAs considered for award only those offerors whose proposals were considered highly competitive, that is, those offerors selected by the SSEB co-chairs to make oral presentations. Price was not a discriminator in this source selection process, because, according to the SSAs, the prices had been evaluated for price reasonableness and realism when the technical proposals were evaluated.

When the award selections were announced, Kathpal Technologies and Computer & Hi-Tech Management protested. They argued that Commerce had failed to consider the protesters' entire proposals in determining that they should be removed from the competition without making oral presentations (each had received only a B under the QRC factor), that is, Commerce did not consider the offerors' proposed pricing and complete technical proposals.

Commerce responded that it had evaluated the offerors' complete proposals in determining which offerors were "highly competitive" and would be allowed to make oral presentations. Commerce acknowledged that only the offerors' ratings under the QRC subfactor were considered in determining which offerors were "highly competitive" but that they were not required to consider price in the initial screening because at this stage the agency was only establishing which offerors would make oral presentations.

The Comptroller General did not agree with the agency and sustained the protest.

First, we disagree with the agency that it could ignore price in its initial screening evaluation. Cost or price to the government must be included in every RFP as an evaluation factor, and agencies must consider cost or price to the government in evaluating competitive proposals.[3]

This requirement means that an agency cannot eliminate a technically acceptable proposal from consideration for award without taking into account the relative cost of that proposal to the government.[4]

Here, despite the agency's attempts to portray the initial screening evaluation as only establishing which offerors would make oral presentations, the record shows that the initial screening resulted in technically acceptable offers, including those of Kathpal and CHM, being eliminated from any consideration for award. That is, the SSAs considered for award only those offerors that were deemed "highly competitive" as a result of the initial screening, which included only those offerors that were allowed to make oral presentations. Indeed, the agency acknowledges in its report on Kathpal's protest that "it was reasonable for the agency to eliminate protester from the competition" on the basis of its B rating under the QRC subfactor. Accordingly, it is clear that the agency's determination in the initial screening evaluation that an offeror was not highly competitive and would not be invited to make an oral presentation actually meant that those proposals were eliminated from consideration for award.

It is also unrebutted, as described above, that, apart from assessing the realism and reasonableness of the offerors' loaded labor rates, the agency did not meaningfully consider price in its decision to eliminate the protesters and others from the competition. Rather, the only consideration in determining which offers were highly competitive was the rating that offers received under the QRC subfactor. Although agencies have considerable discretion in determining the appropriate method for evaluation of cost or price, they do not have the discretion to eliminate technically acceptable offers from competition without meaningful consideration of price.[5] In this regard, we have found that merely assessing the reasonableness of proposal pricing does not satisfy this obligation to consider price in evaluating proposals.

Next, we find, consistent with the protesters' arguments, that Commerce failed to evaluate the protesters' technical proposals in accordance with all of the stated evaluation criteria. As described above, the RFP provided that technical proposals would be evaluated under two evaluation factors—past performance and team composition—and that the past performance factor consisted of two subfactors—QRC and PPM. Here, however, Commerce considered only the proposals' ratings under the QRC subfactor in determining which offers would be further considered for award. The failure to consider offerors' proposal ratings under all the stated evaluation criteria in eliminating technically acceptable proposals from the competition is not reasonable and violates the statutory requirement that proposals be evaluated under the factors stated in the solicitation.[6]

We recognize that Commerce believed that limiting competition to only those offerors that were considered "highly competitive" was justified because "of the number of highly qualified proposals received" and because it "had sufficient competition in each of the functional areas." Given the large number of proposals received, limiting the burden of proposal evaluation was a sensible approach. Once it realized how many firms were interested in competing, the agency could have elected to amend the solicitation to eliminate the oral presentation (and perhaps even one of the evaluation factors or subfactors) from the initial evaluation. If Commerce had decided to conduct discussions, it could have (after evaluation of the proposals under all factors, including price) limited the competitive range for purposes of those discussions more strictly than in the past. Specifically, pursuant to 41 U.S.C 253b(d)(2), as implemented in FAR 15.306(c), the agency could have limited the competitive range (otherwise comprised of all the most highly rated proposals) for purposes of efficiency, which could have been a sensible way to handle the large number of proposals received here.

Commerce could not, however, properly limit the competition as it did here. It could not eliminate proposals from consideration without evaluating them under all of the solicitation's evaluation criteria, including price. Moreover, since the agency did not establish a competitive range, it never had occasion to take advantage of the possibility of limiting the competitive range for the sake of efficiency.

It is likely that the agency's desire to use oral presentations and the unanticipated number of proposals caused it to overlook sound procurement processes. First, its original estimate of 40 to 60 proposals should have been an early indication that the use of oral presentations might not be an effective approach. Then, when over 200 proposals were received, its attempt to save the oral presentation approach led it to make a series of bad decisions that only compounded the problem, as outlined by the Comptroller General. Oral presentations can be an effective evaluation technique, but only when used appropriately.

DOCUMENTING ORAL PRESENTATIONS

The government must maintain a record of each oral presentation. The method and level of detail of the record is at the discretion of the SSA but it must be sufficient to document what the government relied upon in making its decisions. A copy of the record placed in the file should be provided to the offeror.

A video or audio tape recording is the most effective documentation method. If the oral presentation will be videotaped or audiotaped, an audio-visual specialist should perform the work and be consulted about the selection of the place of presentation to ensure that it will accommodate effective audio-visual requirements. Each offeror should be provided with a copy of the video/audio tape for its own records. The master tape should be sealed and securely stored once any necessary copies are made. Copies may be made for evaluators, but these copies should be numbered, accounted for by signature, and all such copies should be destroyed after award. After award, only the master copy is retained in the official contract file.

References

1. Much of the material in this chapter is based on the publication, *Guidelines for the Use of Oral Presentations*, developed by the Procurement Executives Association in partnership with the Office of Federal Procurement Policy (March 1996).
2. Kathpal Technologies, Inc.; Computer & Hi-Tech Management, Inc., B-283137.3; B-283137.4; B-283137.5; B-283137.6, 12/30/99.
3. 41 U.S.C. 253a(c)(1)(B) (1994); FAR 15.304(c)(1); S.J. Thomas, Inc., B-283192, 10/20/99.
4. SCIENTECH, Inc., B-277805.2, 1/20/98, 98-1 CPD ¶33 at 7.
5. SCIENTECH, Inc., supra at 7.
6. 41 U.S.C. 253b(a); Foundation Health Fed. Servs., Inc.; QualMed, Inc., B-254397.4 et al., 12/20/93, 94-1 CPD ¶3 at 37, 41.

CHAPTER 10

Preparing for the Evaluation

Before starting the actual evaluation, the contracting officer should convene the entire evaluation team for a preparation briefing and orientation. This should take place as soon as possible after the receipt of proposals. Each evaluation should be treated as a unique event. It should not be assumed that the evaluators will understand how the evaluation process works, even if some of them have participated in other evaluations. The briefing and orientation should be designed to help ensure that all evaluators understand how to conduct the particular evaluation at hand. Once the briefing and orientation are completed, the proposals should be distributed to the evaluators.

PREPARATION BRIEFING

The first step in the preparation briefing should provide an overview on how the evaluation process works.

Provide an Overview of the Evaluation Process

An overview of the evaluation process will help explain how the process works and how the evaluation results are used. This is particularly important since the FAR 15 rewrite has made some significant changes in the evaluation process.

Initial Technical Evaluation

The evaluation process begins with the initial technical evaluation. The purpose of the initial evaluation is to evaluate all proposals in detail to determine which proposals should be in the competitive range. The evaluators first conduct individual evaluations and then meet as a team to develop a consensus on the ratings and ranking of the proposals. The initial evaluation report provides the basis for the determination of the competitive range (see Chapter 11).

Determination of the Competitive Range

Based on the results of the initial technical evaluation and the recommendations of the evaluators, the contracting officer makes a determination of the competitive range. The competitive range consists of only the most highly rated proposals. Proposals not in the competitive range are rejected and the offerors are not permitted to participate further. Competitive range decisions, both positive and negative, must be fully documented. See Chapter 15.

Discussions and Final Proposal Revisions

Discussions are conducted with all offerors in the competitive range. A letter from the contracting officer usually initiates the discussions, citing the discussion questions developed during the initial evaluation that the offeror must address. Individual offerors may be permitted to make proposal revisions during discussions, but all offerors still in the competitive range must be afforded an opportunity to make a final proposal revision upon completion of the discussions. Offerors may be rejected during discussions if, as a result of the discussions, it is determined that they no longer have a reasonable chance for award. Discussions are closed by a written request for final proposal revisions that establishes a common date for the receipt of the final proposal revisions. This is the last chance offerors have to revise their proposals. No further discussions are conducted or revisions accepted after the final proposal revisions are received (see Chapter 16).

Final Technical Evaluation

The final evaluation is conducted as soon as possible after the discussions are concluded and the final proposal revisions are received. The purpose of the final evaluation is to evaluate the proposal changes resulting from discussions, to adjust the scoring and ranking accordingly, and to make a recommendation as to which proposal, or proposals, should be selected for award. In addition to providing the basis for the source selection decision, the results of both the initial and final evaluations serve as the basis for the debriefing of unsuccessful offerors (see Chapter 17).

Source Selection Decision

The source selection official makes a source selection decision based on the results of the final technical evaluation, the pricing evaluation and, often, a cost/technical tradeoff (see Chapter 18). The cost/technical tradeoff, which is in addition to the evaluation results, assesses the significance of the pricing and technical differences between the offerors to determine which offer represents the best value to the government. While the source selection official is not bound by the recommendations of the evaluators, the source selection decision must be reasonable, in accordance with the stated evaluation criteria, and must be fully documented (see Chapter 19).

Debriefing

The evaluation process is not complete until the unsuccessful offerors have been debriefed. Debriefings of those offerors eliminated from the competitive range may be conducted before the award decision is made. Debriefings of the offerors in the competitive range must be conducted as soon as possible after award. Debriefings are designed to tell the offeror about those areas of its proposal that were deficient or otherwise caused the offeror to be unsuccessful. They are also used to assure the offeror that the evaluation was conducted fairly and to provide the offeror information useful in improving the quality of its future proposals (see Chapter 20).

Once the evaluators have been given an overview of the evaluation process, they should be briefed on other evaluation considerations such as the constraints on evaluator presumptions, the offeror's responsibilities, documentation requirements, and, as applicable, the forms to be used in the evaluation process.

Discuss the Constraints on Evaluator Presumptions

Evaluators are constrained to evaluate only what is found within the four corners of the proposal. They cannot presume things not actually stated in the proposal on the basis of their knowledge of what the offeror has done in the past or other personal experience with the offeror. The Comptroller General has ruled the following:[1]

An agency must base its technical evaluation solely upon the information furnished in the proposal rather than on presumptions favoring an offeror on the basis of past performance.

Past performance, in this instance, refers to an evaluator's past experience with work the offeror has performed. The ruling above does not mean that evaluators cannot go outside of the proposal for information on such things as past performance or corporate experience. The Comptroller General's ruling has to do with inferring something not substantiated by what was in the proposal, based on the evaluator's personal knowledge or past experience with the offeror. In other words, if the RFP requires an offeror to demonstrate certain capabilities in the proposal, and the offeror fails to do this, an evaluator cannot presume the capability exists, as shown in Examples 10.1 through 10.4.

Example 10.1—Presumptions-past experience[2]

An RFP required substantiation of the experience of the offeror's material supplier. The offeror cited a particular project to establish its own experience, but failed to specifically identify the material supplier that would be used on the proposed contract. The contracting agency accepted this, presuming that the supplier was the same supplier that had been used on the project cited by the offeror. The Comptroller General did not agree.

GSA could not reasonably assume EPS/VSL was using the same material supplier that EPS had previously used on the water tower project. Therefore, we find that GSA, in effect, waived for EPS/VSL the mandatory requirement that the material supplier have produced material incorporated into seismic isolation bearings that have been in use for not less than 3 years. Further, since the record of the evaluation indicates that the TEB attributed 4 points to this subfactor and that EPS/VSL's technical proposal received a perfect score, this aspect of the evaluation was unreasonable.

The RFP specifically required substantiation of the material supplier's experience. Presuming an offeror will meet a material requirement that is not substantiated in the proposal is, in effect, a waiver of the substantiation requirement for that offeror but not for any other offeror. This is not proper.

Example 10.2—Presumptions-incumbency #1[3]

Presumptions are often encountered in the evaluation of an incumbent's proposal where the incumbent has been performing well. In this respect, the Comptroller General has ruled the following:

We note that All Star, the incumbent contractor, appears to argue that its offer should have been included in the competitive range regardless of any deficiencies in its proposal because of the agency's familiarity with its past and current performance, which All Star characterizes as "superior." All Star's apparent reliance on its status as the incumbent is misplaced. An agency's technical evaluation is dependent upon the information furnished in the proposal.[4] There is no legal basis for favoring a firm with presumptions on the basis of the offeror' prior performance; rather, all offerors must demonstrate their capabilities in their proposals.

As in Example 10.1, the Comptroller General's reference to past performance referred to experience with the offeror's performance—not a past performance evaluation as is done now. Because an incumbent has done well in the past does not mean that it can submit a less than adequate proposal and expect its reputation to "fill in the gaps." If a proposal fails to address a material requirement, you cannot presume the offeror can meet that requirement because of its reputation.

Example 10.3—Presumptions-incumbency #2[5]

Periodically, problems arise concerning whether the incumbent contractor has an unfair competitive advantage based on its incumbency and what should be done to resolve the issue. The answer is to *treat the incumbent like any other offeror and evaluate only what is provided in the proposal.* Any competitive advantage that might accrue to an incumbent is part of the normal competitive process and does not require "corrective" action, as long as the advantage has not resulted from an unfair action on the part of the government. In this regard, the Comptroller General has ruled the following:

We also conclude that Coopers & Lybrand did not have an unfair competitive advantage based on its performance of the earlier contract. There is no requirement that an agency equalize competition with respect to the advantages that an incumbent contractor may have, as long as those advantages do not result from unfair action by the government.[6] Although Coopers & Lybrand may have had a better understanding of NCUA's requirements due to the earlier contract, we have no basis to conclude that those advantages were the result of any improper action on the part of NUCA.

Example 10.4—Presumptions-lack of detail[7]

A contractor with a long history of experience relevant to the task area protested about being rejected from the competitive range because its proposal lacked sufficient detail (the evaluators found that the proposal merely parroted the RFP requirements identifying the problem areas but did not propose any solutions). The Comptroller General denied the protest.

IRA responds that it should have been afforded discussions in order to address any instances where its proposal may have lacked adequate detail. IRA, which for over 12 years has provided HHS with many of the services listed under the Migrant Programs Branch requirements, seems to believe that its proposed methodology should have been evident from this prior experience. However, responses that are essentially blanket offers of compliance are not adequate substitutes for the detailed and complete technical information necessary to establish that what the offeror proposes will meet the agency's needs.[8] An offeror must demonstrate affirmatively the merits of its proposal, and it runs the risk of rejection if it fails to do so.[9] Here, the agency properly evaluated IRA's methodology on the basis of the material contained in IRA's proposal, rather than on the basis of assumptions arising from IRA's past performance. Our review of the record confirms that the agency reasonably concluded that IRA failed to demonstrate how it would perform the required tasks.

As you would with incumbents, you must exercise care when evaluating the proposals of firms that have done business with your agency for a length of time. Constraining an evaluator's presumptions about an offeror's capabilities is an important factor in a successful evaluation. This should be a key point in the preparation briefing.

Discuss the Offeror's Responsibilities

Ensure that the evaluators understand the offeror's responsibilities with respect to the proposal submitted. The offeror is responsible for submitting an adequately written and fully documented proposal or proposal revision. The offeror that fails to do so runs the risk of rejection. Contracting agencies may evaluate only what is found in the proposal and are not obligated to search out information or qualifications that offerors may have omitted from their proposals, as shown in Example 10.5.

Example 10.5—Offerors are responsible for submitting adequate proposals[10]

Offerors are responsible for preparing their proposals in a manner which establishes that what is offered will best meet the government's needs and that the offeror is the most qualified to do so. Agencies are not obligated to search out information or qualifications that an offeror may have omitted from its proposal. When an offeror fails to furnish sufficient information in its proposal to establish its technical acceptability, the agency can reasonably conclude that the offeror is technically unacceptable and exclude it from the competitive range.[11]

The point here is that to be included in the competitive range the offeror must submit an acceptable initial proposal. When evaluating the proposal, the government is *not required* to infer, deduce, or otherwise look beyond the information provided.

Discuss the Basis for Proposal Rejection

The evaluators need to be briefed on what will be done with the results of their evaluation (i.e., how the competitive range is determined). The briefing should instruct them of the following points:

- A proposal must be rejected if it is so technically inferior that meaningful discussions could not be conducted unless the offeror first submitted a substantially revised proposal, tantamount to a new proposal.
- A proposal must be rejected if it is so out of line in price that it could be brought in line only by making technical changes that would substantially revise the proposal, making the revisions tantamount to the submission of a new proposal.
- A proposal should be rejected, even if it is otherwise acceptable, if the offeror's low score, in comparison to the array of scores of other offerors, demonstrates that the proposal does not have a reasonable chance for award. These are what would otherwise be called marginal proposals. The FAR 15 rewrite eliminated the concept that proposals susceptible to being made acceptable should be included in the competitive range.
- Since the competitive range will consist of only the most highly rated proposals, a final cut should be made among the remaining proposals to eliminate those proposals that are acceptable, but not the most highly rated.

Evaluators should be cautioned that when scoring proposals, the scores must be compatible with the language of the technical narratives. This will make it easier for the contracting officer to follow their advice when establishing the competitive range.

Discuss the Documentation Requirements

You must brief the evaluators on the documentation requirements because the results of the initial evaluation must be fully documented. This is very important. If the evaluators understand the documentation requirements before the evaluation begins, they will be better prepared to provide the necessary information in the proper format.

The FAR 15 rewrite spread the documentation requirements over a number of paragraphs. The following are the documentation requirements as related to contract negotiation.

- **FAR 15.305 (a)**—The relative strengths, deficiencies, significant weaknesses, and risks supporting proposal evaluation shall be documented in the contract file.
- **FAR 15.305(a)(1)**—The contracting officer shall document the cost or price evaluation.
- **FAR 15.305(a)(3)**—When tradeoffs are performed, the source selection records shall indicate (i) an assessment of each offeror's ability to accomplish the technical requirements, and (ii) a summary, matrix, or quantitative ranking along with appropriate supporting narrative, of each technical proposal using the evaluation factors.
- **FAR 15.306(a)(3)**—If the solicitation contains such a notice [to award without discussions] and the government determines it necessary to conduct discussions, the rationale for doing so shall be documented in the contract file.
- **FAR 15.308**—The source selection decision shall be documented, and the documentation shall include the rationale for any business judgments and tradeoffs made or relied on by the SSA including benefits associated with additional costs.

It should be noted that all of the information required to be documented has its basis in the initial evaluation.

In the initial evaluation of individual proposals, evaluators must develop a written technical narrative that identifies the proposal problems (categorized as deficiencies, weaknesses, errors, omissions, and misunderstandings) as well as the proposal strong points for each proposal evaluated. The narrative must document the reasons the problems were so categorized and assess the impact on the acceptability of the proposal (risk assessment) if the problems are not corrected. In addition, the technical narrative must indicate the scores and ratings assigned to each proposal and include a set of discussion questions for each offeror, based on the problems found (see Chapter 11).

Upon completion of the individual evaluations, the evaluators must meet to develop the initial evaluation report. The initial evaluation report reflects the consensus opinion of the team members on the evaluation of each proposal, indicating which proposals should be rejected, and why, and which should be included in the competitive range. The report also contains the team consensus on the discussion questions to be provided to each offeror, and copies of the individual technical narratives and related scoring.

In general, the contracting agency is responsible for deciding how the evaluation is to be conducted. The agency, however, is also charged with fully documenting the evaluation results to substantiate its decisions and to show that the evaluation results were reasonable, were conducted in accordance with the stated evaluation criteria, and were not in violation of procurement laws and regulations. Example 10.6 illustrates the Comptroller General's view.

Example 10.6—Comptroller General bases decisions on the evaluation documentation[12]

The evaluation of technical proposals is primarily within the discretion of the contracting agency, which is responsible for defining its needs and the best method of accommodating them, and must bear the consequences of a defective evaluation.[13] Consequently we will not engage in an independent evaluation of technical proposals, but will examine the agency's evaluation only to ensure that it had a reasonable basis and was consistent with the stated evaluation criteria. The fact that a protester disagrees with the agency's conclusion does not establish that the evaluation was unreasonable.

Thus, in the event of a protest, the Comptroller General will not second-guess the evaluation factors or how they were used, as long as what was done was within law and regulation. The evaluation record will be examined, however, to determine if the decisions made were reasonable and in accordance with the RFP's stated evaluation scheme. The key, therefore, is to carefully document all evaluation actions.

If you fail to fully document the evaluation process, the Comptroller General will generally sustain a protest concerning how the evaluation was conducted, as shown in Example 10.7.

Example 10.7—Evaluation documentation must be complete #1[14]

In sum, the agency substantially reduced Son's score under the most important evaluation factors based on improper considerations. We emphasize that our findings regarding the evaluation are based on the evaluation record supplied by the Air Force, which consisted only of the individual evaluator's worksheets and a brief decision document. FAR 15.612(d)(2) requires agencies to document the reasons for their selection decisions. Here, however, the record did not include any type of comparison of the relative differences between proposals or otherwise articulate the basis of the Air Force's decision. The selection document noted only that "the proposal submitted by Good Food Service was superior to all the others," and that Good Food Service received a higher combined score than Son's. Similarly, the narrative comments on the evaluation worksheets contain very few comments in support of the ultimate decision; in fact the worksheets do not even indicate the basis for large reductions in Son's score under certain evaluation factors. The Air Force's position is based in part on its finding that Son's proposal contained inadequate detail. As with the rest of the record, however, there is no indication of where detail is lacking or the impact of the absence of any particular detail. Further, our own review of the two proposals reveals no obvious material differences in the amount of detail provided. We are obligated to object to a decision that one offeror is technically superior to another when a reasonable basis is not evident from the record.[15]

Note: The FAR reference noted above is now 15.308.

The basis for the Comptroller General's decision in Example 10.7 was the agency's failure to adequately document the evaluation and the source selection decision. Since the evaluation results and the source selection decision were not substantiated in the record, the Comptroller General had no choice but to rule for the protester. It is the contracting agency's responsibility to adequately document its decisions.

Example 10.8 provides an example of how *not* to document an evaluation. Needless to say, the agency was required to conduct this evaluation over again.

Example 10.8—Evaluation documentation must be complete #2[16]

The only documents supporting the technical evaluations are what appear to be consensus reports stating only the evaluation board's overall adjectival rating and a total point score for each proposal for each of the technical evaluation factors. In rare instances, there are very brief notations on the original evaluation documents showing that a particular proposal's initial score was adjusted upon evaluation of BAFOs. However, there are no scoresheets, narratives, notes or any other documents showing what the individual evaluators thought of each proposal. Furthermore, there are no descriptions stating why any proposal received a particular rating for a particular evaluation factor, no statements detailing the various strengths and weaknesses of any proposal, and no assessments of risk inherent in any proposal.

The typewritten evaluation documents purport to contain narratives describing the strengths and weaknesses of proposals and rating the proposals on technical merit (i.e., poor, good, or excellent). However, examination of all of the technical evaluation documentation reveals that: (1) the purported narratives are generic in nature and were prepared prior to evaluating the proposals; (2) the evaluation document for every proposal contains the exact same, preprinted, generic narratives; (3) each generic narrative represented a range of point scores (for example, the narrative labeled "excellent" might represent a range of 11 to 15 technical evaluation points) and that the source evaluation board merely wrote in a consensus point total above the preprinted narrative that matched the consensus point total; and (4) there are no descriptions or narrative discussions prepared after evaluation of any of the proposals.

Example 10.8 illustrates the problems that can result when an agency does not pay attention to business. What is even more disturbing is that the same agency had the same problem, with the same results, involving some of the same contractors a year previous to the decision above. From the description in the Comptroller General's statement, it appears that the agency used a scoring table, similar to that in Chapter 6, Figure 6.1, as the primary evaluation document. Figure 6.1 is only a guide and cannot substitute for a written narrative outlining the specific proposal problems and strong points. A scoring table, like Figure 6.1, is only used to assign scores and ratings.

Caution evaluators that they must fully document the evaluation record at the time of the evaluation. In the event of a protest, contemporaneous documentation is the best way to substantiate decisions made during the evaluation process, as shown in Example 10.9.

Example 10.9—Evaluation results cannot be supported without contemporaneous documentation or other explanation[17]

In reviewing protests against allegedly improper evaluations, our Office will examine the record to determine whether the agency's determination was reasonable and consistent with the evaluation criteria listed in the solicitation.[18] Implicit in the foregoing is that the agency must document these judgments in sufficient detail to show that they were not arbitrary.[19]

... Numerical point scores, while useful as guides to decision-making, do not of themselves supply the basis and reason for the award decision.[20] Where there is inadequate supporting documentation for an award decision, we cannot conclude that the agency had a reasonable basis for the decision.[21]

Here, the Department of State has provided only the final technical scores received by USDS and Group 4, unaccompanied by any contemporaneous evaluation documentation or narratives that would support these scores. The agency, in response to inquiries from our Office, has confirmed that no other documentation exists. Thus, the record does not indicate that the agency did anything other than arbitrarily award the scores without regard to the comparative merit of the competing technical proposals. Under the circumstances, the agency has not satisfied its obligation to document the evaluation and award selection decision adequately.[22]

While we have at times accepted explanations in agency reports justifying a source selection in the absence of adequate contemporaneous evaluation documentation, these later explanations must provide sufficient detail by which the rationality of the agency's evaluation decision can be judged.[23] (And in a footnote—However, we accord greater weight to contemporaneous source selection materials rather than documents prepared in response to protest contentions.[24]) In this case, the agency report fails to address with any specificity the reasons underlying its evaluation of Group 4's or USDS' proposals. Instead, the agency has defended its position in generalities and conclusory statements, which provide no basis to determine the reasonableness of the evaluation.

... Because the record contains no adequate support for the agency's source selection decision, either in contemporaneous evaluation documentation or later report explanations, we cannot determine that the evaluation and award selection were reasonable and consistent with the stated criteria. Neither does our review of the proposals themselves disclose the basis for the source selection decision. Consequently, we sustain the protest on this basis.

Note that while the Comptroller General prefers contemporaneous documentation to support evaluation results, later reports and arguments may be acceptable if they support the decisions made and they would have been valid at the time the decisions were made, as shown in Example 10.10.

Example 10.10—Agency explanations can overcome a lack of contemporaneous evaluation documentation[25]

While there is no contemporaneous documentation regarding BOP's evaluation of its proposals, our review must consider the entire record, including statements and arguments made in response to the protest.[26] *The fact that the agency's explanation was not contained in the contemporaneous record does not provide a basis to disregard it in our review.*[27] *Furthermore, even if the reasons initially advanced by BOP to reject Bannum's proposals were improper, an agency may justify its actions on new grounds so long as those grounds would have provided proper support at the time the action was taken.*[28] *Because the record reasonably supports that Bannum's proposals were seriously deficient in addressing the SOW requirements, we would not sustain its protest, even accepting Bannum's assertion that the initial reason for rejecting its proposals was insufficient or otherwise improper.*

Discuss the Safeguarding of Proposals and Proposal Information

The need to properly safeguard the proposals and the information they contain must be discussed. The safeguarding procedures are designed to ensure that no unauthorized government or nongovernment personnel have access to the proposals' contents. Even a hint of an information leak can seriously jeopardize the evaluation process and possibly lead to a cancellation of the procurement.

The contracting officer and members of the evaluation team are the only personnel with authorized access to the proposals. When not in use, proposals should be kept under lock and key, even in secure areas. Proposals must be kept at the contracting agency's facility and cannot be taken home at night.

If the evaluation is conducted at a facility other than the contracting agency's facility, you must make arrangements for safeguarding the proposals at that facility or appoint someone to return the proposals to the contracting agency's facility at the end of each working day.

The evaluators should also be instructed that they may not reveal who has submitted proposals, how many proposals have been submitted, or anything about the contents of the proposals to anyone not actually participating in the evaluation, including the evaluator's supervisors and other agency management personnel not assigned specific evaluation duties. The contracting officer is the only person authorized to discuss any aspect of the competition.

Brief Evaluators on the Forms Used in the Evaluation

When applicable, the preparation briefing should describe the forms to be used during the evaluation. Some agencies provide standardized forms for the individual evaluation reports as well as the initial and final evaluation reports. These forms help ensure that all of the evaluators are conducting their evaluations in the same manner.

It should be noted that standardized forms can create problems. Some agencies use preprinted "fill in the blanks" forms that contain both format and standardized content. These tend to inhibit creativity and objective analysis as evaluators try to fit their evaluation comments and results to the words in the form. This is not always possible and can lead to inadequate documentation.

The most effective forms are those that standardize the evaluation format, but not the content. These forms simply identify the subjects to be addressed and the broad format to be used. Such forms ensure that the evaluators provide all of the necessary information, but permit them to use their own words. A similar format could be used for the initial evaluation report that represents the consensus findings of the evaluation team. If you do not have prepared forms or formats to use, you should ensure that the evaluators understand their responsibilities, particularly with respect to what must be documented for the record.

ORIENTATION

Orientation begins once the preparation briefing is completed. The preparation briefing concerns evaluation issues; the orientation involves familiarization with the instant procurement and how it is to be evaluated. Orientation involves the entire evaluation team in reading and discussing the RFP and related documentation with an emphasis on the SOW, the evaluation factors and their relative importance, proposal preparation instructions, the scoring plan and standards, and any special conditions or restrictions required by the RFP's solicitation provisions or contract clauses.

The orientation process helps ensure complete and mutual familiarity with the requirement, the evaluation factors to be applied, and the terms and conditions each offeror's proposal must meet. Discussion among team members also helps ensure a common understanding of what the evaluators are to look for, how they are to interpret what they find, and the procedures they are to follow.

Do not assume that the evaluators will intuitively understand how to conduct the evaluation. Generally, technical personnel do not conduct evaluations frequently enough to remember all the details required. The initial preparation briefing and orientation is designed to provide a common script for each evaluator to follow, both in terms of what to look for and how to document the findings. If you do not take the time to ensure that the evaluators have a common understanding of what is to be done, you may be unpleasantly surprised at the results.

DISTRIBUTING PROPOSALS

Upon completion of the orientation, distribute the proposals among the evaluators. This may be done in any number of ways, depending on the complexity of the evaluation.

Techniques range from the simpler evaluation in which each evaluator reads and evaluates each technical proposal to a more complex evaluation in which each proposal is broken down into technical subparts for evaluation by individuals with expertise in a particular area.

There is no standard technique for the distribution of proposals, but whatever technique is used, you must ensure that at least two different individuals evaluate each proposal. This helps to minimize bias or misunderstandings. Later in the evaluation process, the evaluators conduct team discussions to attempt to identify significant scoring differences and to obtain a scoring and ranking consensus. This would be difficult to do if only one individual evaluates the proposals.

References

1. Robert Slye Elecs., Inc., B-243272, 7/5/91, 91-2 CPD ¶28, GCR 105,635.
2. Dynamic Isolation Systems, Inc., B-247047, 4/28/92, 92-1 CPD ¶399, GCR 106,587.
3. All Star Maintenance, Inc., B-244143, 9/26/91, 91-2 CPD ¶294, GCR 105,882, f 5.
4. Inter-Con Sec., Sys. Inc., B-235248; B-235248.2, 8/17/89, 89-2 CPD ¶148, GCR103,458.
5. National Credit Union Admin.; Schreiner, Legge & Co.— Recon., B-244680.2; B-244680.3, 4/1/92, 92-1 CPD ¶329, GCR 106,517.
6. ADT Facilities Mgmt. Inc., B-236122.2, 12/12/89, 89-2 CPD ¶541.
7. InterAmerican Research Associates, Inc., B-253698.2, 11/19/93, GCR 107,943.
8. M.C. Dean Elec. Contracting, Inc., B-246193, 2/24/92, 92-1 CPD ¶219, GCR 106,404.
9. Vista Videocassette Servs., Inc., B-230699, 7/15/88, 88-2 CPD ¶55, GCR 102,132.
10. Sunbelt Properties, Inc., B-245729.3, 3/12/92, 92-1 CPD ¶278, GCR 106,466.

11. Inter-Con. Sec. Sys., B-235248; B-235248.2, 8/17/89, 89-2 CPD ¶148, GCR 103,458.
12. Dynamic Isolation Systems, Inc., B-247047, 4/28/92, 92-1 CPD ¶399, GCR 106,587.
13. Mar Inc., B-242465, 5/6/91, 91-1 CPD ¶437.
14. Son's Quality Food Co., B-244528.2, 11/4/91, 91-2 CPD ¶424, GCR 106,028.
15. Pharm Chem Laboratories, Inc., B-244385, 10/8/91, GCR 105,922; Avanco Int'l, Inc., B-241007.2, 3/13/91, 91-1 CPD ¶276, GCR 105,284.
16. DNL Properties, Inc.; Crawford/Edgewood Managers, Inc.; Pearl Properties, B-253614.2; B-253614.3; B-253614.5; B-253734, 10/12/93, GCR 107,953.
17. U.S. Defense Systems Inc., B-245563, 1/17/92, GCR 110,280.
18. Hattal & Assocs., 70 Comp. Gen. 632 (1991), 91-2 CPD ¶90; American President Lines, Ltd., B-236834.3, 7/20/90, 90-2 CPD ¶53.
19. American President Lines, Ltd., supra.
20. S&M Prop. Mgmt., B-243051, 6/28/91, 91-1 CPD ¶615.
21. Hattal & Assocs., supra.
22. S&M Prop. Mgmt., supra; Universal Shipping Co., B-223905.2, 4/20/87, 87-1 CPD ¶424.
23. Hydraudyne Sys. and Eng'g. B.V., B-241236; B-241236.2, 1/30/91, 91-1 CPD ¶88.
24. Dyncorp, B-245289; B-245289.2, 12/23/91, 91 -2 CPD ¶575.
25. Bannum, Inc., B-271075; B-271076; B-271117, 5/22/96, GCR 109,497.
26. ROH, Inc., B-261132, 8/8/95, 95-2 CPD ¶169.
27. Sociometrics, Inc., B-261367.2; B-261367.3, 11/1/95, 95-2 CPD ¶201.
28. 71-72 Corp., B-213424, 4/10/84, 84-1 CPD ¶407; NonPublic Educ. Serv., Inc., B-207751, 3/8/83, 83-1 CPD ¶232.

CHAPTER 11

Conducting the Initial Evaluation

The initial evaluation provides a basis for the contracting officer's determination of the competitive range and the discussions to follow. The results of the initial evaluation are used to rank and rate each proposal and to identify the most highly rated proposals for inclusion in the competitive range. The discussions that follow the establishment of the competitive range are based on discussion questions developed during the initial evaluation. The discussion questions articulate the deficiencies, weaknesses, and other proposal problems that must be revealed to each offeror in the competitive range as well as the errors, omissions, and misunderstandings that must be clarified during the discussions. The documentation of the initial evaluation results is used throughout the remainder of the procurement process, including the source selection and debriefings.

GENERAL REQUIREMENTS

Evaluators should be aware of certain general requirements before beginning the evaluation.

Page Limitations

If the RFP imposes page limitations, the contracting officer must examine each proposal for compliance before distributing the proposals for evaluation. Evaluators are not permitted to evaluate any pages in excess of the page limitation. It is necessary, therefore, that you remove the excess pages and return them to the offeror, before the initial evaluation begins.

First Reading

The evaluation of a proposal begins with a light reading or scanning from front to back. Do not take notes at this point. This first reading is not for evaluation; it is a reading for content only—to gain an overall familiarity with the proposal. To attempt an evaluation on the first reading would not be fair to the offeror. It is difficult to erase a negative first impression if you score a proposal down early in the reading for "missing" information that is later found in the back of the proposal. Therefore the first reading is for content only. Once you are familiar with the contents of the proposal, you are ready to begin the proposal evaluation.

Second Reading

The second reading is for evaluation purposes. Unlike in the first reading, you should take notes during this reading, commenting on each problem or strong point as you read. Each comment should make note of the proposal page/paragraph number for later reference. Write your notes on a separate piece of paper, not on the proposal itself. Notes recorded on the proposal itself could affect the objectivity of the next evaluator to read the proposal.

Do Not Make Comparisons

When evaluating multiple proposals, do not evaluate on the basis of comparisons between proposals. Evaluate each proposal on its own merits, as though it was the only proposal received. Comparisons and the relative rankings of proposals come later, after all of the proposals have been evaluated. Comparisons between proposals are based on the results of your completed evaluations. This helps ensure objectivity in the initial evaluation.

Stick to the Proposal Contents

Evaluate only what is actually written in the proposal. Do not assume that the offeror will do, or not do, something unless it is specifically stated so in the proposal. You may not substitute your personal knowledge or judgment for what is written in the proposal.

Follow the Evaluation Criteria Published in the RFP

The initial evaluation must be conducted strictly in accordance with the established evaluation factors and procedures published in the RFP. Do not add, subtract, or change any of the published evaluation factors. If you find what you consider to be a deficiency or weakness in a proposal, but it is not explicitly covered by a published evaluation factor, make a note of it for a later determination as to its status. You may determine that such deficiencies or weaknesses are inherently related to one of the published evaluation factors (see the discussion of unstated subfactors in Chapter 2). If so, they may be considered in the evaluation. If not, you should note it as something to be addressed during discussions, but do not use the perceived problem for scoring or ranking purposes.

Read each proposal carefully to gain an understanding of how the offeror proposes to meet the RFP requirements. Match this against the published evaluation factors, the SOW requirements, and the proposal preparation instructions. Note the proposal problems and strong points and then score the proposal in accordance with the scoring plan. Do not attempt to score the proposal as you evaluate. First complete the evaluation and then apply the scoring based on your written notes.

EVALUATE THOSE AREAS ADDRESSED BY SPECIFIC EVALUATION FACTORS

If you have prepared the proposal preparation instructions properly and the offeror has responded accordingly, the technical proposal will be organized in the same order as you described the evaluation factors in Section M of the RFP. This will facilitate your evaluation. During the evaluation, determine if the offeror has provided the information required and note information that has not been provided or is inadequate.

You must evaluate strictly in accordance with the published evaluation factors and subfactors. The following paragraphs address what to look for with respect to some of the more common evaluation factors.

Technical Approach

The proposed technical approach must be carefully examined. The SOW indicates *what* is to be done; the offeror's technical proposal is supposed to explain *how* it will be done. You must ensure that all aspects of the requirements set forth in the SOW, including equipment and material, are addressed. Make an assessment of how well the proposal meets the SOW requirements. This assessment should include such things as the soundness and workability of the technical approach, the validity of the proposed methodology or techniques, the likelihood of success, and the risk of failure or disruptive problems during contract performance associated with the proposed approach.

Technical Plan

Examine the offeror's plans for meeting the requirement. You must examine the scheduling, sequencing, and timing of proposed contract activities with respect to the proposed methodology or techniques, and the planned use of equipment, material, and personnel, particularly if the offeror proposes an innovative approach to accomplishing the work. Examine such things as the proposed use of contingency planning and the extent of proposed subcontracting to assess their impact on contract performance. You should also assess whether the offeror can perform as promised, including in your assessment both the probability of technical success and of completing the work within the required contractual time frames.

A poorly written SOW can lead to problems in this area. If you find a proposal problem, you must check your SOW before assuming that it is the offeror's problem. It is possible that an offeror's response will reveal problems in the wording of your SOW that were not obvious when the SOW was written. This is particularly important if a number of offerors are misleading the requirements of the SOW. If the SOW is part of the problem, fix it by amending the RFP and permitting revised proposals before establishing the competitive range.

A warning: Do not assume that an offeror will do something that is not specifically addressed in the proposal. You must watch for technical promises that lack substantiating details, technical data, or discussion. Promising something without explaining exactly how it will be accomplished is not acceptable.

Technical Understanding

An offeror demonstrates technical understanding by the thoroughness, soundness, and comprehension of the technical proposal and, when appropriate, the proposal's cost realism. You can assess how well the offeror has demonstrated its understanding of the requirement through its analysis of the requirement, its identification of potential problems and suggested solutions, the applicability of the proposed technical approach, and the proposed use of innovative approaches and state-of-the-art advances.

Technical understanding often serves as the "catch-all" technical evaluation factor. If a perceived problem cannot be categorized as a problem under one of the other technical evaluation factors, it often can be accounted for under technical understanding, or lack thereof.

Management Plans

Review the proposed management plan to determine if the proposed organization, lines of authority, lines of responsibility and communications, and management approach are workable for the proposed effort and if they will facilitate the early identification and resolution of problems and allow the offeror to promptly respond to contract changes. You can assess the offeror's commitment to program success as demonstrated by the corporate level of the proposed project manager, that individual's access to upper management, and the degree to which upper management is committed to providing assistance in the event of problems.

Staffing Plans

Assess the proposed staffing and labor mix to determine if the offeror has proposed the appropriate kinds and numbers of personnel. You must also determine if the staffing plan reflects the technical input and ability to react to workload fluctuations in a timely manner.

Do not assume that perceived staffing deficiencies are a problem until you have examined how the proposed staffing will be used. Innovative staffing techniques, methodology, or equipment use may result in lower, but acceptable, staffing levels.

As appropriate, examine the offeror's proposed recruitment, compensation, and training plans to assess the impact of these factors on the offeror's ability to recruit and maintain an adequate staffing level. If your requirement involves work effort that typically experiences high turnover rates (such as janitorial and guard services) or if personnel fluctuations may jeopardize effective contract performance (as with technical support services or R&D), these factors can be critical.

Assess the proposed organization and method of performance and its impact on the staffing requirements. Contractors often operate with lower staffing levels than the government, using cross-utilization (workers trained for more than one task and moved around depending on the workload) to handle peak workload conditions. If an offeror's proposed staffing does not match the government estimate, do not automatically assume the offeror is wrong—the offeror may simply have a better way of getting the job done.

Key Personnel

Review the qualifications of proposed key personnel and match them to the qualifications listed in the RFP. Determine if they have the requisite education, experience, and expertise and are actually committed to contract performance. Ensure that proposed key personnel who are not employed full-time by the offeror have committed themselves, in writing, to work on the contract if awarded. As appropriate, you should examine the extent of time the key personnel will devote to the proposed effort and assess the impact (positive or negative) that this might have on contract performance.

The proposal preparation instructions should have required the offeror to indicate if any of the proposed key personnel were involved in contracts referenced for past performance purposes. If there is adverse past performance information about a contract involving proposed key personnel, you should note this and make the level of involvement a discussion question. Generally, you should not use such involvement to downgrade a proposal in the initial evaluation. This can be a complex issue and is better left for discussions. It cannot be assumed that the named individual was responsible for the adverse past performance without more information. The offeror's response to the discussion question will permit an assessment of such involvement in the final evaluation.

Corporate Experience

You should check the contracts the offeror listed to determine its corporate experience by contacting the contracting agencies involved. Verify that the referenced effort is pertinent to the current requirement. A proposal can be downgraded under the corporate experience factor if the offeror fails to demonstrate that its past experience is pertinent to the current requirement.

You are not limited to checking only the referenced contracts. You may check on contracts the offeror performed for your agency or other agencies, but did not reference. Keep in mind, however, that corporate experience has nothing to do with how well the offeror performed, only with whether the offeror has performed work of the same or similar nature as the current requirement. Corporate experience may also be evaluated through the experience of key management and technical personnel where specific corporate experience is lacking. This is particularly important when evaluating the corporate experience of a newly formed business.

Past Performance

When you use past performance as an evaluation factor or subfactor, you must assess the relationship of the offeror's past performance to the current requirement and its likely impact on how the offeror will perform.

Check the contracts the offeror has referenced as being indicative of its past performance by contacting the contracting agencies involved. Generally, you obtain past performance information through questionnaires sent to the pertinent contracting agencies. It would be beneficial, however, to contact the agencies first by telephone and talk to the technical and contracting personnel who were actually involved in the performance of the referenced contracts. You are more likely to get a response to your questionnaire if the respondent knows it is coming.

The assessment of past performance is not limited to only those contracts referenced by the offeror. You may use other sources of information such as the procurement data systems at the Federal and agency level. You may also query private sources such as subcontractors, suppliers, financial institutions, and the offeror's commercial customers. When using private sources, ensure that any comments made are supported by a written document.

It should be noted that you are obligated to use past performance information that is "close at hand," such as an evaluator's personal and direct knowledge about a contract the offeror performed, and information about the offeror's contracts with your own agency that were not referenced in the offeror's proposal (see Examples 12.8 through 12.11 in Chapter 12).

Negative responses about past performance must be in writing if they are to be used in the evaluation. When negative responses are received, try to find out what went wrong and why. Keep in mind that an offeror must be advised of adverse past performance information to which it has not had a prior opportunity to respond and be given a chance to comment—before establishment of the competitive range. The more you know about the background of the negative responses, the better you will be able to evaluate the offeror's comments when informed of the negative information. Chapter 12, Evaluating Past Performance, has more information on this subject.

Pricing

Price or cost to the government shall be evaluated in every source selection [15.304(c)(1)].

Regardless of how the evaluation is to be conducted, cost or price must be an evaluation factor to be considered before the establishment of the competitive range, as shown in Example 11.1.

Example 11.1—Cost or price must be evaluated[1]

In a solicitation for advisory and assistance services, the RFP stated that the cost/rate criterion would not be point scored or adjectivally rated; instead cost/rate proposals were to be evaluated for reasonableness and appropriateness of proposed rates. A financial advisor who evaluated the cost/rate proposals for reasonableness but did not compare or rank the offeror's proposed prices or labor rates briefed the Score Evaluation Panel (SEP). The SEP then examined the technical rankings and decided that there was a breakpoint between the seventh and eighth ranked proposals and determined that only the top seven proposals would be included in the competitive range.

An unsuccessful offeror, whose proposal was considered technically acceptable but not within the top seven proposals, protested. The protester argued that, among other things, the agency failed to consider relative proposed prices of the offers in making its competitive range determination. Since its labor rates were substantially lower than some of the offerors included in the competitive range, the protester contended that if pricing had been considered it would have been included in the competition. The Comptroller General agreed.

Cost or price must be considered as a factor; it is improper to exclude an offeror from the competitive range solely on the basis of technical considerations, unless the proposal is technically unacceptable.[2]

The failure to consider cost in competitive range and award decisions is improper. Agencies must consider cost to the government in evaluating competing proposals.[3] *Agencies have considerable discretion in determining the appropriate method for taking cost into account; they do not have discretion, however, not to consider cost at all, as happened here.*[4]

In this case, the cost/rate proposals were evaluated for reasonableness, but no comparison of the offeror's costs was made as part of the competitive range determination (which was based solely on the technical rankings). Had the agency compared rates, done a cost realism analysis, or taken some other action that would have factored in the pricing along with the technical considerations, this problem would not have come up. When establishing the competitive range the comparative pricing must be considered before a proposal is rejected—unless it is rejected as technically unacceptable.

IDENTIFY AND CATEGORIZE PROPOSAL PROBLEMS

As you read the proposal for evaluation purposes, you must make a written note of anything you regard as a problem. Proposal problems are categorized as deficiencies that must be corrected, weaknesses that should be corrected, and errors, omissions, or misunderstandings that should be fixed or otherwise clarified. Your notes should reference the proposal page and paragraph number of the problem and, if the problem is related to a specific RFP requirement, the RFP page and paragraph number, too. These notes will make it easier to review your evaluation when scoring the proposal, to address the problems when reaching an evaluation consensus and citing the problems during discussions.

Deficiencies

Proposal deficiencies must be identified. The FAR defines a deficiency as "a material failure of a proposal to meet a government requirement or a combination of significant weaknesses that increases the risk of unsuccessful contract performance to an unacceptable level." A deficiency is a problem or a combination of problems that must be corrected prior to contract award.

A deficiency relates to substantive issues, such as where an offeror proposes staffing, equipment, or material that does not meet the capability requirements of the SOW, or where the methodology or techniques proposed for use are not considered to be adequate. A deficiency can also be an informational inadequacy such as the offeror's failure to address an issue sufficiently for the evaluator to determine the acceptability of the offeror's approach. Basically, a deficiency exists wherever the offeror fails to demonstrate that it will meet the contractual requirements or fails to provide sufficient information to permit evaluators to ascertain exactly what the offeror is proposing to do and whether it will meet the contractual requirements.

Identify each deficiency and note its relative importance and impact on the acceptability of the proposal if the deficiency is not corrected. Further, you should categorize the deficiency as either susceptible to correction or as one requiring a significant revision to the proposal, tantamount to a new or almost entirely different proposal. This categorization is important because, as noted in Chapter 10, an initial proposal must be rejected if the deficiencies are such that meaningful discussions cannot be conducted unless the offeror first submits a substantially revised proposal, tantamount to a new proposal.

The identification of deficiencies is also important because the contracting officer is required to reveal proposal deficiencies to each offeror during discussions. Specifically noting the deficiencies helps ensure that offerors will be properly notified of the proposal problems.

Weaknesses

Proposal weaknesses must also be identified. The FAR defines a "weakness" as a flaw in the proposal that increases the risk of unsuccessful contract performance and a "significant weakness" as a flaw that appreciably increases the risk of unsuccessful contract performance.

The FAR definition can be misunderstood because it creates two levels of weaknesses with little to distinguish one from the other. The following is suggested. Categorize weaknesses as "significant" or "minor." A significant weakness is one that has a significant adverse impact on the proposal's score, the correction of which (or failure to correct) might affect the offeror's ability to win the contract. A minor weakness is one that would result in a relatively small reduction in the proposal's score, the correction of which would not significantly affect the offeror's competitive position or adversely affect contract performance. Do not categorize weaknesses until after your evaluation is completed. Then, go back over your notes to determine whether the noted weaknesses are significant or minor. This is necessary because a combination of weaknesses could be categorized as a deficiency if the net effect of the combined weaknesses increases the risk of unsuccessful contract performance to an unacceptable level.

Offerors must be notified of significant weaknesses during discussions, so the contracting officer needs this information to properly prepare for the discussions. The contracting officer is not required to discuss minor weaknesses.

Significant weaknesses are areas of a proposal that are not so bad as to be categorized as deficiencies, but do result in the lowering of the proposal's score. While a deficiency must be corrected for the proposal to be acceptable, a weakness, in and of itself, does not make the proposal unacceptable—but is an area that should be corrected or clarified.

For example, a weakness exists (rather than a deficiency) where the offeror makes only a minimal response to an RFP requirement, such as the following:

- Offering staffing levels below the level expected, but still at a minimally acceptable level
- Offering a standard rather than an innovative approach where the SOW indicates a preference for an innovative approach
- Offering a methodology or technique that will "do the job," but only with difficulty or with less than optimal results.

When noting a weakness, you should explain how the weakness will, if uncorrected, affect the acceptability of the proposal and what kind of weakness it is; for example, an informational weakness (a failure to provide required information or adequately explain something); an historical weakness (one that relates to past history, such as inadequate corporate experience or poor past performance); or an inherent weakness in the proposal's approach due to the offeror's lack of diligence, competence, or inventiveness in preparing the proposal.

Offerors can usually correct informational weaknesses by submitting the required information. Historical weaknesses cannot be corrected, but sometimes they can be satisfactorily explained. Inherent weaknesses may be correctable, but they often indicate potential problem areas that should be examined closely.

Errors, Omissions, or Misunderstandings

Identify errors, omissions, or misunderstandings that should be corrected or clarified during discussions. *Errors* are such things as mathematical or typographical mistakes.

Omissions are the failure to provide necessary data, such as charts or graphs, or other supporting information, which appear to be the result of an oversight rather than a lack of understanding of the requirement for such information. *Misunderstandings* occur where the offeror has obviously misinterpreted an RFP requirement and the misinterpretation does not reflect a lack of the offeror's experience, expertise, or overall understanding of the requirement.

To qualify as an error, omission, or misunderstanding, the problem must be correctable without a basic change to the substance of the offeror's proposal. These problems can be treated as minor irregularities, informalities, or apparent clerical errors, and clarified prior to the establishment of the competitive range or during discussions.

Communications Prior to the Establishment of the Competitive Range

The FAR 15 rewrite (see FAR 15.306(b)(3)(i)) permits deficiencies, weaknesses, errors, omissions, and misunderstandings to be addressed before the establishment of the competitive range. This action is not recommended, however, unless you are sure that the problem area can be explained and would not result in the need for a proposal revision. Proposal revisions are not permitted at this stage of the procurement process. If the corrective action might require a proposal revision, the premature revelation of such problems could be viewed as giving an offeror an unfair competitive advantage through advance knowledge of a deficiency or significant weakness. This action could generate protests.

Communications with offerors prior to the establishment of the competitive range should be kept to a minimum, except communications related to past performance—which are required. Such communications are inefficient for the following reasons:

(1) They add time to the procurement process.

(2) If the problems were such that they could be corrected by an explanation only, it is not likely that they would materially affect an offeror's inclusion in the competitive range.
(3) At this point you do not know which offerors will be included in the competitive range. Why take the time to have communications with offerors who might not be included in the competitive range?

Such exchanges are better handled during discussions, with only those most highly rated offerors included in the competitive range. You should note, however, that communications prior to the establishment of the competitive range are appropriate if they are necessary to determine whether an offeror should be included in the competitive range.

Other Problem Areas

There are other problem areas, not related to specific evaluation factors that bear attention. These apply primarily to how the offeror wrote its proposal and are usually assessed as an indicator of an offeror's technical understanding, but may be applied to other evaluation factors as appropriate.

- *Watch for the use of words and phrases that sound good but do not say anything,* such as flowery words or flattery or the latest catch phrases or buzz words. This is often a reflection of how much the offeror actually knows and can be accounted for under technical understanding, or lack thereof.
- *Watch for the offeror who simply quotes back the wording of the SOW.* This usually indicates a lack of technical understanding if the offeror does not offer anything else of substance. Generally, an offeror who responds in this manner and fails to address the RFP requirements should be rejected.

- *Watch for ambiguities and inconsistencies.* This can indicate a lack of technical expertise, a misunderstanding, or both. However, before you assume that this is strictly the offeror's problem, check the wording of the SOW to see if it has contributed to the problem. As noted earlier, if the SOW is part of the problem, you can fix it by amending the RFP and permitting the submission of revised proposals before the establishment of the competitive range. Check the resulting proposal revisions carefully to ensure that the ambiguity or inconsistency has been resolved.

Generally, ambiguities and inconsistencies should be regarded as deficiencies, but may be considered as weaknesses if their net effect does not increase the risk of unsuccessful performance to an unacceptable level. You should look at such problems closely because they may mask even greater problems.

Be particularly careful to resolve all proposal ambiguities or inconsistencies especially if you intend to incorporate all or part of the successful offeror's proposal into the SOW. You do not want to incorporate additional problems into the SOW.

IDENTIFY PROPOSAL STRONG POINTS

Do not forget to look for strong points in the offeror's proposal—areas of the proposal that significantly exceed the minimum requirements or demonstrate particular capabilities that offer advantages to the government. Identify each proposal strong point and explain why it is important to the success of the contract. In the initial evaluation, the identification of proposal strong points is important in ranking proposals and preparing for discussions. In the final evaluation, it is important in the best value determination and source selection. Example 11.2 demonstrates the usefulness of identifying proposal strong points.

Example 11.2—Proposal strong points can be used to determine the competitive range[5]

An offeror was informed that its proposal was not included in the competitive range because the proposal weaknesses, combined with a lack of significant major strengths, indicated that the proposal did not have a reasonable chance of being selected for award. The offeror protested that its weaknesses were minor and did not concern its capability to perform the contract.

The agency reported that the protester's relatively low score was based not only on the proposal's weaknesses, which the agency admitted were relatively minor, but also on the absence of any significant major strengths in the proposal. Basing its decision on the relatively low scores received by the lowest scored proposals and the strengths found in the highest five proposals, the evaluation panel determined that it would not be fair or reasonable to subject the lower ranked proposals to the added expense of going through the final competition. The Comptroller General agreed with the agency and denied the protest.

We think the agency's determination was reasonable. Even without the admittedly minor deficiencies in Curry's proposal, in the evaluators' view the proposal was technically inferior to several others because it offered no particular strengths while other proposals did. In this regard, the SEP found that five other offerors demonstrated a more complete understanding of the RFP's requirements and offered certain advantages in their approaches to the work, such as an automated work control system that could be adapted to this contract, an automated reporting system, and innovative management techniques. The protester has not challenged the evaluation of these other offerors and we find nothing in the record which would support a conclusion that these evaluation results were unreasonable. Therefore, given the technical superiority of several other firms and the fact that there is no advantage to Curry's price, the agency could properly conclude that Curry's proposal had no reasonable chance for award.

In Example 11.2, the competitive range determination turned on the strengths, not the weaknesses, found in the competing proposals. This is somewhat unusual; proposal strengths are not usually the determining factor in a competitive range determination. It does point out, however, the need to identify and document proposal strengths in the initial evaluation.

This case predated the FAR 15 rewrite, but it demonstrates one of the key points in the rewrite—that the competitive range should include only the most highly rated proposals, even if this means that otherwise acceptable, but lower rated, proposals would be excluded.

ASSESS COST REALISM

As noted in Chapter 4, you must assess the realism of proposed costs when evaluating cost-reimbursement proposals. You should also consider assessing cost or price realism in other contract types where the requirement is complex, or labor intensive, or where doing so will otherwise help you evaluate the offeror's understanding of the requirement.

Generally, cost or price is evaluated by a separate evaluation team consisting of personnel whose expertise is cost or price analysis. These teams often have technical personnel assigned to help relate the technical aspects of the proposal to the cost/price analysis.

The assessment of cost realism, however, is different. Here, the emphasis is more technically oriented than cost oriented. Cost realism analysis involves examining the relationship between the proposed costs and the proposed technical approach to see how well they match. The technical evaluation team, supported by members of the cost evaluation team, should conduct the cost realism analysis. Keep in mind that the proposed costs, not the evaluated costs, are being matched with the proposed technical effort. If there are differences, or disconnects, between the proposed costs and the technical approach, the proposed costs should be considered as unrealistic. This should be reflected in the technical evaluation and the discussion questions to be addressed during discussions, after the establishment of the competitive range.

It should be noted that it is not improper double-counting to downgrade a proposal for a lack of technical understanding and for having unrealistic costs, where both are stated evaluation factors. Problems with cost realism must be noted, not only with respect to rating and ranking the proposal, but also for discussion questions in the event the offeror is included in the competitive range.

The following paragraphs address some of the areas considered in assessing cost realism. A lack of cost realism may be regarded as a significant weakness or a deficiency depending on your assessment of how it affects the offeror's ability to perform the contract. At a minimum problems with cost realism should be addressed during discussions.

Direct Labor/Engineering Costs

Assess the proposed direct labor/engineering costs to determine if these costs represent the application of sufficient labor hours and an appropriate labor mix for the proposed technical approach. The number of labor hours by labor category can be determined from the cost proposal. The proposed hours and labor mix should agree with what the offeror has proposed in its technical approach. If not, this inconsistency must be questioned. An inconsistency here usually indicates that the offeror does not fully understand the requirement and that the offeror will have difficulty providing what it promised to provide in its technical proposal.

For example, the proposed technical approach indicates a high level approach, using senior personnel and advanced techniques and facilities. The cost proposal, however, indicates a low level approach using minimal facilities and junior personnel incapable of applying the advanced techniques. The inconsistency between the proposed costs and the proposed technical approach indicates a lack of cost realism and should be questioned to determine how well the offeror understands the requirements.

You should also match the labor hours and mix to the government estimate to see how well they agree. If there is an inconsistency here, first verify the correctness of the government estimate. Then examine the proposal to see if the inconsistency can be explained by differences in the technical approach, the use or application of advanced technology, or innovations in the amounts and types of resources applied. If the differences cannot be accounted for, the proposed costs may be considered to be unrealistic.

Material and Equipment Costs

Assess the proposed material and equipment costs to determine if these costs indicate that the quantity, quality, and type of material and equipment proposed for use are consistent with the offeror's proposed technical approach and sufficient to meet the government requirement.

If the technical proposal promises high quality material and sophisticated equipment, but the proposed costs indicate that lower quality material and equipment will be acquired, this is an inconsistency that demonstrates a lack of cost realism. Such inconsistencies indicate either a lack of technical understanding or a potential problem in the proposed technical approach and should be questioned during discussions to determine how well the offeror understands the requirements.

Other Direct Costs

The other proposed direct costs such as travel, per diem, and rentals should be assessed to determine if they are realistic with respect to the proposed technical approach and the government requirement. As noted earlier, inconsistencies here indicate either a lack of technical understanding or a problem in the technical approach and such inconsistencies should be questioned during discussions.

MAKE COST REALISM ADJUSTMENTS

In addition to determining how well proposed costs match the proposed technical approach, the cost realism assessment can help determine the probable cost consequences of an award decision. You can arrive at the probable cost consequences by adjusting the proposed costs to reflect the results of the cost realism analysis. These adjustments are designed to provide an evaluated cost that more closely represents the performance costs of the proposed technical approach. The results of the cost realism analysis must be coordinated with the cost analysis performed by the cost evaluation team to ensure that the adjustments also reflect the results of the cost analysis and that all pricing inconsistencies are accounted for.

Cost realism adjustments may be done twice in the evaluation process: first in the initial evaluation and again in the final evaluation. It is not unusual for both technical and cost changes to be made as a result of discussions, and the final evaluation must account for these changes.

It should be noted that these adjustments are for evaluation purposes only—to determine the relative worth of a proposal in comparison with other proposals. The contract itself will be awarded at the proposed price.

The following paragraphs discuss some examples of cost realism adjustments and their associated problems.

Independent Analysis

An independent analysis of each offeror's cost proposal is necessary to determine the likely realism of proposed costs. You must ensure that cost realism adjustments are reasonable and that the rationale for the adjustment is fully documented in the record. Examine the proposed technical approach carefully, particularly where there are significant pricing differences between the proposals. The technical approach can have a substantial effect on the pricing, as shown in Example 11.3.

Example 11.3—You must document your cost realism analysis[6]

Two proposals were received and evaluated. Award was made to the high technical, lowest priced offer under an RFP that stated that price and technical merit were approximately equal in importance. The unsuccessful offeror protested the award on the grounds that the awardee's price was unrealistically low (by almost $40 million) and therefore not acceptable. The Comptroller General Denied the protest.

Price realism determinations are necessarily judgmental and unless shown to be clearly unreasonable, will not be subject to objection by our Office.[7] Having examined the record here, we have no basis to find the agency's price realism analysis of UXB's proposal unreasonable. The agency reports that following receipt of initial proposals, it was concerned over the relatively large disparity between the offerors' proposed prices and the government estimate. As a result, an analysis was undertaken in which the RFP and the proposals were reexamined in an effort to determine an explanation for these disparities. Based on this analysis, the agency concluded that the difference in prices was attributed to the widely differing technical approaches taken by the two offerors. In particular, the agency found that UXB's proposed approach to satisfying the range clean-up requirements under Annex 4 of the RFP was premised upon a unique and innovative use of specialized equipment, whereas Spectrum chose to rely much more heavily on manual labor. Thus the agency concluded that UXB's lower pricing, especially for Annex 4, reflected much lower labor costs than were included in either Spectrum's proposal or in the government estimate. Additionally, the TEB determined that both offeror's technical proposals demonstrated a consistent understanding of the RFP requirements, but that UXB's proposal simply reflected an innovative technical approach to meeting these requirements.

The record demonstrated that the offerors did in fact base their proposals on differing technical approaches. We find it reasonable to attribute UXB's lower costs to the particular technical approach reflected in its proposal. We accordingly have no basis to question the price realism analysis conducted in this case.

In this case the agency did the right thing by noting the large pricing difference, reviewing the pricing, and accounting for the differences before making the award. You should evaluate proposals offering different technical approaches on the basis of the approach proposed to determine the cost realism of each approach and ensure that any pricing adjustments reflect the differing technical approaches.

Agencies often opt for a standard, across-the-board adjustment (normalization) rather than making an independent analysis. Standard adjustments, however, may not be applicable in all instances, as shown in Example 11.4.

Example 11.4—Do not substitute a mechanical formula or standard adjustment for an independent analysis[8]

An agency analyzed management salaries by comparing the proposed pay rates for management positions to a government estimate of pay rates for those positions. In instances where the offeror's rate was lower than the government estimate, the agency adjusted the rate upward. Where the offeror's proposed rate was higher than the government estimate, the agency used the proposed rate. The Comptroller General found this to be improper.

In our view, the Marine Corps's mechanical application of estimates to every management category in the solicitation is not a reasonable normalization of costs because it does not meet the standard required when reviewing competing cost proposals—i.e., an agency must make an independent analysis of each offeror's cost proposal to determine the likely realism of proposed costs, particularly when the agency makes award on the basis of initial proposals without discussions.[9] An offeror's proposed management employees and issues such as how senior they must be, and how they are to be compensated, will clearly differ from one company to the next. In a blanket adjustment of all offerors, the Marine Corps makes no allowance for different management approaches and the possible use of different skill levels to serve in management positions. In Kinton, we sustained a protest against just such an upward adjustment to a government estimate of proposed staff hours without considering the special skills of proposed individuals reflected in the offeror's higher per hour rate. Therefore, we find that the Marine Corps' adjustment of all offeror's management employees—including Bendix's—to a preestablished, but unpublished estimate, is unreasonable without further analysis of the reasons for the variations among proposals.[10]

The agency's desire to simplify the evaluation by substituting a normalization formula for independent analysis led it to use an improper evaluation scheme. This problem could have been avoided had the agency conducted an objective review of how the evaluation scheme would be applied, and its possible effect on differing proposals, before the RFP was issued.

Normalization

Normalization is a technique that involves the establishment of a cost standard, or baseline, against which all proposed costs are measured (see Chapter 5, Using Normalization). Normalization is used to develop a "should cost" estimate for each proposal from a base common to all proposals, thereby permitting the agency to use the same formula, or approach, in making adjustments to each proposal. Normalization techniques can also be applied to other evaluation areas, such as labor hours, when evaluating time-and-materials or labor hour proposals. Normalization is popular because making standard across-the-board adjustments appears to be equitable and simple to use, and it requires a minimum of analytical effort on the part of the evaluators.

Normalization can be effective, but only if all the proposed technical approaches have enough similarities that the adjustment technique used applies uniformly to all offerors.

Do not use normalization in an attempt to equate the costs of dissimilar proposals. Differing technical approaches, differing levels of personnel experience, and differing staffing approaches are just some of the things that preclude the effective use of normalization.

The following examples show what can go wrong in making cost realism adjustments using normalization.

Adjustments to Account for the Use of Uncompensated Overtime

Uncompensated overtime refers to the overtime hours (hours in excess of 40 hours per week) incurred by salaried employees who are exempt from the coverage of the Fair Labor Standards Act, 29 U.S.C. 202 (1988). No law or regulation prohibits the use of uncompensated overtime, but the offeror must use an accounting system that properly accounts for uncompensated overtime by exempt employees. Therefore, unless the RFP expressly prohibits its use, an offeror may propose on the basis of uncompensated overtime

When an offeror uses uncompensated overtime, where other offerors do not, the dissimilar approaches make the evaluation more complicated. Do not, however, attempt to normalize such costs in the manner shown in Example 11.5.

Example 11.5—Normalization pitfalls—Adjustments to account for the use of uncompensated overtime[11]

In response to a solicitation that did not prohibit the use of uncompensated overtime, an offeror proposed using uncompensated overtime on the basis of a 45-hour workweek. The offeror's proposal demonstrated that it accounted for the uncompensated overtime using a method of accounting that was deemed acceptable by the Defense Contract Audit Agency (DCAA).

The other offeror proposed on the basis of a 40-hour workweek. The contracting agency normalized the first offeror's 45-hour workweek to a 40-hour workweek, so both proposals could be evaluated on the same basis. The resulting cost adjustment changed the first offeror's evaluated costs to the extent that it was no longer low and award was made to the other firm. The first offeror protested and the Comptroller General not only sustained the protest, but recommended that the awarded contract be terminated and award made to the protester.

The agency also argues that it was necessary to "normalize" GRC's proposed labor rates to a 40-hour workweek so that, to be fair, all offerors would be evaluated on the basis of a 40-hour workweek. We do not agree. Normalization is a technique sometimes used within the cost adjustment process in an attempt to arrive at a greater degree of cost realism. It involves measuring offerors against the same cost standard or baseline in circumstances where there are no logical differences in approach or in situations where insufficient information is provided in the proposals, leading to the establishment of a common "should have bid" estimate by the agency.[12]

There is no basis on this record for the agency to "normalize" the two offeror's proposed labor costs to a 40-hour workweek, since the offerors proposed differing approaches to accomplishing the contract work. AMS proposed a 40-hour workweek, while GRC offered to satisfy the RFP requirements with uncompensated overtime. Since there is no prohibition in the RFP to the use of uncompensated overtime, and its use is consistent with GRC's standard accounting practices, we see no basis for the agency to "normalize" labor rates that actually reflect the firm's bidding strategies. Furthermore, such an adjustment serves to artificially inflate GRC's labor rates beyond those that would have been billed under GRC's full time accounting system and appears to violate Cost Accounting Standard 401, which requires offerors' estimates of proposal costs to be consistent with their standard accounting practices.[13]

As noted earlier, normalization should not be used as an attempt to equate the evaluated costs of dissimilar proposals. Normalization appears to be easier, but the agency's warning bells should have gone off once the low offeror was displaced because of the evaluation technique used.

Adjustments to Labor Rates

Labor rates are subject to a number of adjustments. They may be adjusted during cost analysis to make them conform to the offeror's accounting system. They may be adjusted again if the cost realism analysis indicates that the costs are not realistic with respect to the types or numbers of personnel proposed. Finally they may be adjusted by a normalization technique to establish an evaluation standard. This leaves plenty of room for error, as shown in Example 11.6.

Example 11.6—Normalization pitfalls—Adjustments to labor rates[14]

An RFP required offerors to provide loaded hourly rates for each of six categories of labor for a contract under which the work would be ordered, when required, through the issuance of delivery orders. The agency evaluated the labor rates based on an "average hourly rate" calculated by adding the labor costs submitted in each of the six categories and dividing by six. This technique was protested and the Comptroller General agreed that it was improper.

In this regard, the price of each delivery order under the contract will not be based on the contractor's average rate. According to the solicitation, delivery orders are to be based on the loaded rates for the mix of labor categories which is determined by the agency's needs for the particular tasks to be ordered. This means that over the period covered by the contract the agency will require different amounts of each of the various labor categories. For example, the record indicates that on the predecessor contract, the contractor used approximately 1,300 hours of Senior level staff, 500 hours of Junior level staff and approximately 300 hours of Support staff in performing the delivery orders. Using this and other information available from the predecessor contract, the agency should have created and applied in the price evaluation realistic estimates of the number of labor hours expected to be used in each category. Without using such estimates, there is nothing to assure that the evaluation would account for the possible wide disparity in labor hour usage between the various labor categories and, as a result, there is no direct relationship between the evaluated price of a particular offeror and the actual price of performance by that offeror.[15]

The contracting agency must decide on some appropriate, reasonable method for proposal evaluation; however, an evaluation method that produces a misleading result cannot be used. In this instance, the use of an average hourly rate produced a misleading result because the contract tasks would use the actual rates and call for varying labor mixes. Thus there is no direct relationship between the "average hourly rate" and the likely actual costs.

Example 11.6 illustrates what happens when there is no objective management review of an RFP before it is issued. When briefing the evaluators before beginning the evaluation, you should go over the evaluation scheme to ensure that its application will yield supportable results and that the evaluators understand the calculations to be used. It is much easier to avoid a problem than to fix it later.

The case noted in Example 11.6 contained another common evaluation error, as shown in Example 11.7.

Example 11.7—Normalization pitfalls—Faulty calculations

In the case cited in Example 11.6, an offeror proposed one of the labor categories, Support staff, at no charge. The agency divided the total of the offeror's six proposed hourly rates ($234)—which included $00 for Support staff—by five instead of six as set forth in the solicitation and applied to the other offerors. This resulted in an average hourly rate of $46.80. The offeror protested and the Comptroller General agreed that the calculations were improper.

This simply makes no sense. As the agency notes, the solicitation states that to determine average hourly rates each offeror's "rates will be added together and divided by all categories of labor." Apex's proposal did not take exception to the requirement of proposing support services personnel and the agency does not suggest that Apex did so; rather Apex simply proposed to provide Support staff at no charge to the government. Under the circumstances, since Apex proposed staff in all six required categories, in evaluating Apex's proposal, the agency should have divided the total of Apex's hourly rates ($234) by six (the number of labor categories which the firm proposed). Under a correct calculation, Apex's average hourly rate should have been $39 and under the scoring system used by the agency, its overall score should have been higher.

Typically, once you have a problem it keeps getting worse, rather than better. All calculations should be checked before any evaluation decisions are made. This includes the supporting concept for the calculations as well as the mathematics. Such errors are not uncommon, usually because of time pressures. It is very difficult to defend mathematical errors, particularly if they affect award decisions.

Adjustments to Labor Escalation Costs

The labor costs of contracts that extend to more than one year are usually subject to adjustments to account for escalation. Normally offerors will propose escalation rates, and these may be adjusted by evaluators if deemed necessary. Give some thought to how escalation will be handled in the evaluation. Example 11.8 shows what can go wrong if you don't.

Example 11.8—Normalization pitfalls—Adjustments to labor escalation costs[16]

An unsuccessful offeror had failed to include labor escalation in its proposal. The agency adjusted for this by removing the proposed labor escalation costs from the awardee's proposal. The unsuccessful offeror protested this method of adjustment and the Comptroller General sustained the protest.

We also question the method by which DSS-W's "normalized" labor escalation in the firms' offers. It is true that GRC failed to bid labor escalation while AMS did, and it was therefore appropriate for DSS-W to seek to normalize the two offers based on the agency's reasonable determination that labor rates would escalate over the option periods of the contract.[17] However, simply removing the costs of labor escalation from AMS's proposed costs was not a reasonable method of normalizing these costs.

Labor escalation, which provides for the increase in labor costs due to inflation or other salary increases over the life of the contract, is accomplished by the use of a percentage multiplier that is applied to an offeror's proposed direct labor costs. The two offerors did not bid the same direct labor costs, and GRC's labor costs are lower than AMS's. Accordingly, assuming the same labor escalator is applied to both offerors, GRC's labor escalation would be lower than AMS's.

Thus GRC's proposed labor costs should be multiplied by the same labor escalator as proposed by AMS, as recommended and calculated by DCAA.

Here, the agency correctly assumed that the labor rates would escalate over time, but then proceeded to calculate the escalation backwards. Generally, labor escalation is an additive, used to increase labor costs. By removing the labor escalation costs from the awardee's proposal, the agency, in effect, said that there would be no escalation, even though the awardee had proposed it. This is clearly unreasonable. As the Comptroller General pointed out, the proper procedure would have been to upwardly adjust the protester's proposed labor rates by the same percentage as proposed by the awardee—keep in mind that these adjustments are made for evaluation purposes only and do not affect the award price.

Adjustments to Labor Union Costs

FAR 22.1002-3 requires consideration of the terms of a collective bargaining agreement (CBA) when evaluating a service contract proposal. This must be considered when making adjustments to labor costs, as shown in Example 11.9.

Example 11.9—Normalization pitfalls—Adjustments to labor union costs[18]

An unsuccessful offeror (the incumbent contractor) protested that its proposal was unfairly evaluated because of improper adjustments to its hourly union labor rates. The agency had upwardly adjusted hourly labor rates covered by a CBA to a higher government estimate, despite the fact that the protester already had employees in place and was subject to a legally binding agreement with the employees for the amount of their wages. The Comptroller General agreed that this was improper.

We consider first Bendix's claim that it was unreasonable to increase its hourly union labor rates above the amounts in the CBA for the period the CBA would be in effect . . . we find that a contracting agency may not impose a government estimate to upwardly adjust labor categories proposed by an incumbent contractor which has a binding negotiated agreement with its employees to perform the services at a lower rate.

When beginning a procurement for a service contract, you should check to see if the incumbent has a CBA that would be in effect after the anticipated date of contract award. This may affect how labor costs are evaluated because the competing contractors must pay wages and fringe benefits at least equal to those contained in the incumbent's current CBA. Knowledge of an existing CBA will also help avoid the problem outlined above.

Adjustments to Travel Costs

Proposed costs should not be adjusted unless you have a valid rationale. This is particularly true of proposed travel costs, which can vary widely depending on the technical approach. If travel requirements are not clear, you should analyze what the offeror proposes, but apply any adjustments individually, based on what each offeror is proposing, rather than a blanket adjustment for all offerors. Example 11.10 shows the effect of not paying attention to the way travel costs are handled.

Example 11.10—Normalization pitfalls—Adjustments to travel costs[19]

In its cost realism analysis of travel costs, an agency accepted the proposed travel costs of the protester and the awardee, despite the fact that the protester's proposed travel costs were nearly $400,000 higher than the awardee. Yet in the evaluation of three other proposals, the agency substituted a government estimate of travel costs for the amounts proposed. The four offerors whose travel costs were accepted proposed costs ranging from approximately $420,000 to $900,000. The three offerors whose travel costs were rejected and replaced with the government estimate proposed travel costs from $0 to approximately $500,000. The government estimate for travel costs was over $1 million. An offeror protested based on the way the travel costs were evaluated. The Comptroller General sustained the protest.

In short, we find that the agency should not have permitted offerors' proposed travel costs to become a factor in determining award, especially when the agency itself admits that it was impossible to predict the amount of travel required by this contract. Therefore, we conclude that the agency's adjustments here are irrational and fail to equally adjust differences between offerors where the solicitation contained insufficient information to permit offerors to submit informed proposed travel costs. See Kirschner Assocs.[20] *(agency unreasonably permitted widely varying proposed travel costs to play a role in its decision to award a cost-plus-fixed-fee contract to the low cost offeror, even though the solicitation failed to provide sufficient and unambiguous information permitting competition on an equal basis) and Moshman Assocs.*[21] *(protest sustained where agency failed to normalize travel costs given uncertainties in solicitation).*

There are two problems here. First, the agency did not treat the offerors equitably—accepting some offerors' proposed travel costs and adjusting the proposed costs of others with no clear rationale for these actions. This is not proper. Second, the solicitation failed to provide a clear and definitive description of the travel requirements so offerors could submit informed proposed travel costs. In such instances, you should either not evaluate travel costs at all, or evaluate them individually, based on each offeror's proposed technical approach and any other information provided by the offeror. Normalization is not appropriate where there is no common basis.

Adjustments to Proposed Fees

Do not adjust proposed fees in cost-reimbursement solicitations as part of a cost realism analysis. The purpose of cost realism is to examine the proposed costs as related to the offeror's proposed technical approach. The fee amounts have nothing to do with analyzing an offeror's probable costs of contract performance, as shown in Example 11.11.

Example 11.11—Normalization pitfalls—Adjustments to proposed fees[22]

An RFP contemplated award of a cost-plus-award fee contract with both a base fee and an award fee. In calculating the evaluated cost, the agency first determined the amount of the upward adjustment to be applied to each offeror's proposed costs, then calculated the amount of additional fee (based on the percentages the offeror used to calculate its award fee), and added that figure to the upward adjustment. An unsuccessful offeror protested that this adjustment technique was improper and the Comptroller General agreed.

Our prior decision in Booz, Allen & Hamilton,[23] *stated that it is irrational for agencies to increase offerors proposed fees as part of a cost realism analysis. When an agency performs a cost realism analysis, it is required by regulation to attempt to ascertain its most probable costs as a result of the offeror's approach.*[24] *As we explained in Booz, Allen, upward adjustments to such proposed fees shed little light on the issue of whether the costs proposed by an offeror are a realistic assessment of the costs the agency will be required to reimburse. In addition, when agencies make award on initial proposals without discussions, the proposed award fee, if otherwise permissible, will not vary from the amount in the proposal.*[25] *Thus we conclude that the Marine Corps improperly adjusted Bendix's proposed award fee as part of its cost realism analysis.*

In short, proposed fees are not part of the proposed costs and should not be adjusted as part of the evaluation of cost.

DEVELOP THE WRITTEN TECHNICAL NARRATIVE

Make notes as you evaluate each proposal and reference the notes to the specific proposal page and paragraph for later review. These notes make up the written technical narrative and are the most important product of the evaluation. It is the technical narratives, not the numerical scores or color codes, that provide the basis for all evaluation decisions and eventually, for the source selection decision.

While reading for evaluation, concentrate on developing the technical narrative. Do not attempt to score the proposal as you evaluate. Scoring would be premature at this point. You may find that something you didn't like early in the proposal is resolved satisfactorily at a later point.

The technical narrative should address both proposal strengths and problems with respect to each evaluation factor and subfactor. Where possible, the technical narrative should use words similar to those set forth in the scoring standards to ensure that each proposal is scored using the same standards (see Chapter 6, Figure 6.1, for example). Do not, however, simply copy the wording of the scoring standard. Technical notes that clearly show how the standards apply must support each comment.

The narrative must be comprehensive enough to support the scoring and rating of the proposal and to serve as the basis for the development of discussion questions. For example, if the scoring scheme provides for a range of numerical scores in relation to a particular adjectival rating, the technical narrative should include comments that will support the scoring, whether at the low end or the high end of the scoring range.

After completing the initial evaluation, it helps to take a break to clear your head and then come back and review your technical narrative to ensure that your comments are consistent, complete, and correct. Do this before you start to score the proposal.

SCORE THE PROPOSAL

After completing your evaluation, go back over the proposal and narrative notes and score the proposal. Ensure that the scoring process adheres to the scoring plan and standards established in the evaluation plan (see Chapter 6), and that it applies consistently to all offerors. After the scoring is completed, check to ensure that each score is clearly supported by the technical narrative. If there is a discrepancy, change the score, not the technical narrative. Adjusting the technical narrative to support the scores gives the impression of favoritism and can lead to a protest.

DEVELOP DISCUSSION QUESTIONS

After evaluating and scoring each proposal, review the technical narrative and develop questions to be used in discussions with each offeror. While this entails what might appear to be unnecessary work (only the most highly rated proposals will be included in the competitive range and discussions), the development of discussion questions enhances the evaluation and helps ensure a complete and comprehensive analysis of all proposals when the evaluation team meets to develop an evaluation consensus.

The term *discussion question* is a general term (some agencies use other terms) referring to the identification of a proposal's problem areas that must be satisfactorily addressed by the offeror during discussions. The contracting officer is required to put the offeror on notice of all proposal deficiencies, significant weaknesses, errors, omissions, and misunderstandings during the discussions. This is done through the discussion questions provided to each offeror before the start of discussions.

Translate the deficiencies, significant weaknesses, errors, omissions, misunderstandings and any other noted risks inherent in each proposal into discussion questions (they do not have to be in the form of a question if another format is more appropriate). Discussion questions must be tailored to each offeror and be pertinent to the perceived proposal deficiencies and weaknesses. This ensures that the discussions to follow are meaningful, that is, to the point. The discussion questions, therefore, should identify a perceived problem as specifically as possible and, at a minimum, must be sufficient to lead the offeror into the areas of its proposal that are of concern. Generally worded discussion questions can lead to unfortunate results, as shown in Example 11.12.

Example 11.12—Word discussion questions to elicit clear, specific answers[26]

Two best and final offers were received for tetrode-type power amplifier tubes (PATS). After award, the unsuccessful offeror protested the agency's conduct of discussions and evaluation with respect to six specific areas of its proposal.

One of these areas was parts cleaning. Offerors were required to demonstrate a thorough understanding of the materials, methods, techniques, equipment, and tools needed to ensure PAT conformance with RFP operating life requirements. The Proposal Evaluation Committee (PEC) faulted the protester's proposal for not addressing the cleaning of parts in sufficient detail under this subfactor and asked the following question: "What is your technical approach to the processing of parts, subassemblies and assemblies that will assure conformance with the operating life requirements and conditions?"

The protester argued that while it recognizes that the cleaning of parts is a routine, albeit important, matter in PAT production, if the agency wanted a detailed discussion of parts cleaning, it should have asked clearly and directly for the information.

The agency maintained that the "processing of parts" as used in the discussion question included parts cleaning and that, therefore, discussions were adequate in that they led the protester into the area of the proposal in need of amplification.

The Comptroller General disagreed with the agency and sustained the protest.

Contracting officers are required to conduct discussions with all offerors in the competitive range,[27] *and although agencies are not required to afford all-encompassing discussions, the discussions must be meaningful and, in general, that means that agencies must lead offerors into areas of their proposals which are of concern to the evaluators and which require amplification or correction.*[28] *In this regard, discussions should be as specific as practical considerations will permit and, where they are unnecessarily general, we will sustain a protest, and in most instances recommend reopening negotiations.*[29] *This is especially true where proposal defects are largely informational in nature, in which case it is incumbent upon the agency to be as clear and precise as possible in informing an offeror of informational gaps in its proposal.*[30] *In addition, an agency may not inadvertently mislead an offeror through the framing of a discussion question into responding in a manner which does not address the agency's concerns.*[31] *In this connection, we find that of the six disputed areas, the agency failed to conduct meaningful discussions in two: parts cleaning and parts traceability.*

In the Navy's report on this matter, the agency recognizes that "parts processing" includes, in addition to cleaning, inspection, deburring, vacuum firing, hydrogen firing, storage and protection, "etc." The RFP nowhere asked for a specific discussion of parts cleaning and the discussion question posed to ITT also did not specifically mention it. Further, the agency does not argue that ITT was downgraded because it thought that the firm did not understand that parts cleaning was a necessary process; it argues only that ITT's discussion of the subject lacked sufficient detail. Thus in the context of this procurement, we fail to see how an offeror such as ITT was reasonably on notice that, of the variety of elements comprising parts processing, the Navy believed its proposal was deficient as a result of a failure to provide information about how it proposed to clean parts unless a specific question mentioning the term "cleaning" was presented. The problem perceived with ITT's proposal was largely informational in nature, and especially since the RFP did not specifically mention parts cleaning, we fail to see why the agency should not have informed ITT about the informational gap in its proposal in a clear and precise manner.[32] Under these circumstances we find that meaningful discussions were not conducted because the question presented to the protester lacked sufficient specificity.[33]

This example points out the need to ensure that discussion questions are straightforward and specifically identify what you perceive to be a problem. If the questions are vague or misleading, the offeror is not being fairly treated.

You must be careful, however, in the wording of discussion questions. Discussion questions should identify the problem, not the solution. For example, if you believe that the proposed staffing is inadequate, the discussion question should only indicate that the staffing level is not adequate in the area in question. Ask the offeror to explain how the proposed staffing will ensure that all requirements are met, but do not indicate what will be considered an adequate response. State the question, not the answer. The offeror's ability to respond to the question is a measure of its understanding of the requirement.

After developing each question, you should separately indicate what is expected as an answer (if this is possible) and the likely impact of an inadequate response on the acceptability of the proposal. The discussion question and the answer/impact statement should not be combined in the same document. The discussion questions are provided to the offerors; the answer/impact statements are retained and used in the evaluation of the offeror's response.

DEVELOP A TEAM CONSENSUS AND THE INITIAL EVALUATION REPORT

Once the individual evaluations are completed, all evaluators must meet to determine a team consensus on the overall evaluation of the proposals and develop the initial evaluation report. If differences among the evaluators cannot be resolved, a minority report should be included in the initial evaluation report. This is needed to ensure that the contracting officer receives a full report on the evaluation, including any differing opinions.

Team Consensus

Reaching a consensus means coming to a general agreement. The evaluation team, as a whole, must come to an agreement on all aspects of the evaluation. For each proposal, consensus must be reached on the following:

- Identification of the deficiencies, significant weaknesses, errors, omissions, misunderstandings, and other risk areas and a rationale to support them. The rationale should show why each problem was categorized as it was, whether it is correctable, and how it should be corrected (if known). It should also provide an assessment of each problem's impact on the acceptability of the proposal if not corrected. This, along with the proposal strong points, is the written technical narrative to support the consensus findings.
- The strong points to be identified along with comments that support the importance of each.

- The scores and ranking to be assigned, given the rationale developed under the first bullet above.
- The wording of the discussion questions to be provided to each offeror and an answer/impact statement to support each.
- The wording of the initial evaluation report and any recommendations to be made.

Note that the team evaluation report addresses the same subjects as the individual evaluation reports, but from a consensus viewpoint. Reaching a consensus can only be achieved by discussing each evaluator's findings and a resolution of a difference of opinion, as shown in Example 11.13.

Example 11.13—Reaching evaluation consensus[34]

In response to a protest arguing that the differences between the individual scoring and the consensus scoring indicated that the evaluation was not properly conducted, the Comptroller General ruled:

It is not unusual for individual evaluators to have disparate, subjective judgments on the relative strengths and weaknesses of a technical proposal.[35] Consequently, disparities in evaluator ratings do not establish that the evaluation process was flawed or otherwise irrational.[36] Moreover, there is nothing improper in technical evaluators discussing the relative strengths and weaknesses of proposals to reach a consensus rating.

Here, we find no basis for objecting to the process the EPA used to arrive at its consensus scores for the proposals. We believe that agency evaluators should discuss their individual evaluations with each other to reach a valid consensus since such discussions generally operate to correct mistakes or misconceptions that may have occurred in the initial evaluation. In short, the overriding concern in the evaluation process should be that the final scores assigned accurately reflect the actual merits of the proposals submitted—not that the scores may be mechanically traced back through some arithmetic calculation to the scores initially given by the individual evaluators. We do not find that the EPA's process for determining consensus scores was flawed in this respect.

Reaching a consensus is more than just agreeing on scores. Its primary purpose is to ensure a balanced evaluation. Problems that might otherwise be overlooked may surface during the discussions that take place among the evaluators while reaching a consensus.

For example, in the evaluation of a proposal, each of three evaluators found one deficiency and each gave the proposal a score of 90. When they met to reach a consensus, however, they found that each of them had found a different deficiency. Was the proposal properly scored at 90? Probably not. The consensus discussion might well find that there were, indeed, three deficiencies rather than one and adjust the proposal evaluation accordingly.

It is not unusual for the consensus evaluation results to differ from the individual evaluation results. Different evaluators can have different viewpoints, no matter how well they are briefed about how to conduct the evaluation. The consensus process permits these different viewpoints to be surfaced, discussed, and eventually a team agreement is reached and documented.

Initial Evaluation Report

The initial evaluation report consolidates the individual evaluation results into a single document, based on the consensus reached by the evaluators. The report normally contains the consensus findings noted above, any dissenting or minority findings, discussion questions for each offeror, an answer/impact statement to support each question, and a copy of each evaluator's individual technical evaluation narrative and scoring for each proposal evaluated.

Usually, the initial evaluation report also contains recommendations as to the offerors to be included in the competitive range or the source selection if award is to be made without discussions. While the contracting officer is not legally bound by such recommendations, it is unusual for the contracting officer to ignore the recommendations if they are fully substantiated by the record.

The contracting officer uses the initial evaluation report as the basis for decisions regarding the determination of the competitive range (or source selection if award is made without discussions). The discussion questions in the initial evaluation report set up the discussions that follow the competition range determination. The answer/impact statements are used both during the discussions and in the final evaluation. In addition, the initial evaluation report is used in the final evaluation to evaluate the extent to which offerors have corrected the problems found by the initial evaluation. Finally the contracting officer uses the initial evaluation report and the final evaluation report when making the source selection decision.

The initial evaluation report is the end product of the initial evaluation process. Evaluators should keep in mind the intended uses of this report while conducting their evaluations.

References

1. SCIENTECH, Inc., B-277805.2, 1/20/98, GCR 110,190.
2. S&M Property Management, B-243051, 6/28/91, 91-1 CPD ¶615 at 4; HCA Gov't Servs., Inc., B-224434, 11/25/86, 86-2 CPD ¶611 at 3-4.
3. 41 U.S.C. 253a(b)(1)(1994).
4. Health Servs. Int'l, Inc.; Apex Envtl., Inc., B-247433; B-247433.2, 6/5/92, 92-1 CPD ¶493 at 4.
5. Curry Construction Co., Inc., B-254355, 12/13/93, GCR 107,991.
6. Spectrum Sciences & Software, Inc., B-243792, 8/14/91, 91-2 CPD ¶147, GCR 105,761
7. Waukesha Alaska Corp., et al, B-229918; B-229918.2, 4/27/88; 88-1 CPD ¶412, GCR 101,873.
8. Bendix Field Engineering Corp., B-246236, 2/25/92, 92-1 CPD ¶227, GCR 106,416.
9. Kinton, Inc., 67 Comp. Gen. 226 (1988), 88-1 CPD ¶112.
10. Optimatrics, Inc.; NU-TEK Precision Optical Corp., 68 Comp. Gen. 714 (1989), 89-2 CPD ¶266.
11. General Research Corp., B-241569, 2/19/91, GCR 105,198.

12. Dynalectron Corp., et al. 54 Comp. Gen. 562 (1975), 75-1 CPD ¶17.
13. FAR 30.410; CACI Federal, Inc., 64 Comp. Gen. 71 (1984), 84-2 CPD ¶542.
14. Health Services Int'l, Inc.; Apex Environmental, Inc., B-247433, 6/5/92, 92-1 CPD ¶493, GCR 106,679.
15. R.P. Densen Contractors, Inc., 66 Comp. Gen. 31 (1986), 86-2 CPD ¶401.
16. General Research Corp., Inc., B-241569, 2/19/91, GCR 105,198.
17. Dynalectron Corp., et al. 54 Comp. Gen. 562 (1975), 75-1 CPD ¶17.
18. Bendix Field Engineering Corp., B-246236, 2/25/92, 92-1 CPD ¶27, GCR 106,416.
19. Bendix Field Engineering Corp., B-246236, 2/25/92, 92-1 CPD ¶27, GCR 106,416.
20. Kirschner Assocs., Inc., B-199547.2, 8/26/81, 81-2 CPD ¶178, aff'd, B-199547.3, 12/1/81, 81-2 CPD ¶435.
21. Moshman Assocs., Inc., B-192008, 1/16/79, 79-1 CPD ¶23.
22. Bendix Field Engineering Corp., B-246236, 2/25/92, 92-1 CPD ¶27, GCR 106,416.
23. Booz Allen & Hamilton, B-213665, 9/24/84, 84-2 CPD ¶329.
24. FAR 15.605(d).
25. CACI, Inc., - Fed., 64 Comp. Gen. 439 (1985), 85-1 CPD ¶363.
26. ITT Electron Technology Division, B-242289, 4/18/91, GCR 105,388.
27. FAR 15.610 [now 15.306(d)(1)].
28. Jaycor, B-240029.2, 10/31/90, 90-2 CPD ¶354, GCR 104,851.
29. Data Preparation, B-233569, 3/24/89, 89-1 CPD ¶300, GCR 103,020.
30. Techniarts Eng'g, B-234434, 6/7/89, 89-1 CPD ¶531, GCR 103,256.
31. Vitro Servs., B-233040, 2/9/89, 89-1 CPD ¶136, GCR 102,856.
32. Techniarts Eng'g, B-234434, 6/7/89, 89-1 CPD ¶531, GCR 103,256.
33. Data Preparation, B-233569, 3/24/89, 89-1 CPD ¶300, GCR 103,020.

34. The Cadmus Group Inc., B-241372.3, 9/25/91, 91-2 CPD ¶271, GCR 105,879.
35. Mounts Eng'g, 65 Comp. Gen. 476 (1986), 86-1 CPD ¶358; Syscon Servs., Inc., B-235647, 9/21/89, 89-2 CPD ¶258.
36. Unisys Corp., B-232634, 1/25/89, 89-1 CPD ¶75.

CHAPTER 12

Evaluating Past Performance

Chapter 3 addressed the concept of using past performance as an evaluation factor. This chapter discusses how past performance should be evaluated and some of the associated problems.

FACTORS THAT AFFECT THE EVALUATION OF PAST PERFORMANCE

As noted in Chapter 3, past performance is one indicator of an offeror's ability to successfully perform a contract and its importance depends on the circumstances of the procurement. Chapter 3 also identified some of the more common areas to be considered in the evaluation of past performance, noting that the past performance evaluation criteria used should be tailored for the specific procurement. These common areas are:

- Conformance to specifications and standards of good workmanship
- Adherence to delivery and administrative schedules
- Record of forecasting and containing costs
- History of reasonable and cooperative behavior and commitment to customer satisfaction
- Other specific areas of concern.

In the context of the specific past performance areas specified for evaluation in the RFP, the following should be considered when evaluating an offeror's past performance:

- Impact on prospective performance;
- Extent of government's responsibility;

- Offeror's overall work record;
- Relevance of past performance information;
- New firms; and
- Contract type.

Impact on Prospective Performance

When evaluating an offeror's past performance, you should assess the extent to which the offeror's past performance is likely to affect its performance on the prospective contract. A demonstrable relationship should exist between the offeror's past performance and the prospective performance, particularly if there is adverse past performance information. For example, assume the past poor performance occurred in a corporate division that would not be involved in the prospective contract. If so, the past problems should not be counted against the offeror unless it can be demonstrated that the problems originated at the corporate level and thus, unless corrected, would be likely to adversely affect the prospective effort.

The use of unrelated deficient past performance to reject or significantly downgrade an offeror is not reasonable. Do not use the evaluation of past performance as a means to punish an offeror for past performance problems. Poor past performance should only be considered with respect to the risk that such problems will recur and adversely affect performance on your contract.

When evaluating past performance, assess the nature and severity of past problems and the effectiveness of any corrective action taken by the offeror in terms of the prospective performance. Use the proposal preparation instructions to require offerors to identify any past problems in referenced contracts and the corrective action taken. If the offeror fails to identify such problems and the corrective action taken, you are justified in assuming that the problems have not been corrected. If the past problems have not been corrected, determine if they are likely to recur and if they will adversely affect the chance of successful performance. If the problems have been successfully corrected or are unlikely to recur, the past problems are not germane to the prospective contract.

FAR 15.306(b)(1)(i) states that communications shall be held with offerors whose past performance information is a determining factor preventing them from being placed in the competitive range where the offeror has not had a prior opportunity to respond to such information. If it is decided that an offeror is to be included in the competitive range despite some adverse past performance information, this information should be identified as a discussion question to be addressed during discussions.

If an offeror fails to provide information on past problems and associated corrective action, or fails to respond to questions about such problems, you may determine that the problems are not corrected and evaluate the offeror's past performance accordingly, as shown in Example 12.1.

Example 12.1—If an offeror fails to respond to questions about past problems, you may assume the problems have not been corrected[1]

In this case, the protester was delinquent on two contracts and, in response to direct discussion questions, did not submit any evidence to explain the delinquencies. The protester challenged the evaluation of its past performance. The Comptroller General denied the protest.

Given the agency's discussion letter, which clearly placed Smith on notice that the firm needed to furnish additional evidence to improve its past performance rating, and Smith's failure to respond—in any fashion—to the agency's past performance concerns, we think the agency reasonably found Smith's proposal marginally acceptable under the past performance factor.

You should be careful, however, about what you evaluate as poor past performance. A contractor's exercise of its rights in contract administration, even where it annoys the government, should not be evaluated as poor performance, as noted in Example 12.2.

Example 12.2—Filing of contract claims is not poor performance[2]

While the claims apparently had no impact here, we agree with the protester that, absent some evidence of abuse of the process, agencies should not lower a firm's past performance evaluation based solely on its having filed claims. Contract claims, like bid protests, constitute remedies established by statute and regulation, and firms should not be prejudiced in competing for other contracts because of their reasonable pursuit of such remedies in the past.

This would encompass more than the taking of formal contractual actions. Disagreements with the government about contract administration, such as contract interpretation, do not constitute poor past performance, unless they are determined to be frivolous or deliberately misleading.

Government's Responsibility

One of the more difficult evaluation areas is determining the extent to which government actions contributed to an offeror's deficient performance. Government actions, such as faulty specifications, late delivery of government-furnished property (GFP), delivery of faulty GFP, failure to provide timely testing or other approvals, and numerous contract changes can contribute to cost overruns and late deliveries. When faced with an allegation of deficient performance, the contractor will often blame the government, and the government will usually deny any responsibility. Resolving these issues is not easy, nevertheless, the extent of government involvement should be resolved before any decisions are made. It is not reasonable to penalize a contractor for problems resulting from, or significantly affected, by government actions.

The best way to deal with this is to permit offerors to comment on adverse comments made in response to past performance queries by the contracting agency. With offeror rebuttals in hand, the evaluators are better prepared to resolve the issues.

Offeror's Overall Work Record

Examine the offeror's overall work record to determine whether past performance deficiencies are usual or unusual in terms of the offeror's performance record. You may evaluate an offeror's performance on the preponderance of its past efforts on the same or similar contracts where you cannot document a relationship between specific contracts and the prospective contract. If the preponderance of an offeror's past efforts is deficient, it should be treated as an unacceptable risk factor and evaluated as such.

Relevance of Available Past Performance Information

Consider the relevancy of the past performance information used in the evaluation. Generally, information on past performance should not be more than three years old, unless it can be shown that it is still relevant to the current effort. Relevance encompasses more than just similar work, but also the presence of the same management or technical personnel, the use of the same technology or methodology, or other similarities between the past effort and the current effort. If you cannot make a connection between the past effort and the current effort, the past performance information is not relevant.

New Firms

The evaluation of past performance must provide for newly formed firms that lack a history of relevant past performance. FAR 15.305(a)(2)(iv) states that firms without a past performance record or for whom past performance information is not available may not be evaluated favorably or unfavorably on past performance. In effect, you are to give such a firm a neutral rating, which, in theory, does not affect its competitive position.

When trying to ensure that new firms get a chance to compete in procurements using past performance as an evaluation factor, the evaluation scheme and its application must be examined closely to ensure fairness for all offerors. The use of neutral ratings can cause problems where past performance is, or becomes, the determinant factor in the evaluation. What happens when the award turns on a tradeoff between price and past performance, as can happen if the proposals are determined to be technically equal? This can make things difficult, as shown in Example 12.3.

Example 12.3—Using past performance to evaluate new firms—making price/past performance tradeoffs[3]

Award was made to a higher-priced proposal with a good performance record over a lower-priced proposal with no performance history. The unsuccessful offeror protested that the contracting officer did not make a proper price/past performance tradeoff. The Comptroller General sustained the protest.

In a recent case involving DLA's use of ABVM scoring, we concluded that the use of a neutral rating approach to avoid penalizing a vendor without prior experience does not preclude a determination to award to a higher-priced firm with a good past performance record over a lower priced vendor with a neutral past performance rating. Indeed, such a determination is inherent in the concept of best value. In Phillips,[4] the contracting officer's determination to select a higher priced vendor with an excellent ABVM score, rather than a new supplier with a neutral rating, was reasonable where the record in that case showed that the agency had backorders for the item and timely delivery was critical. Nonetheless, we expressed concern that the vendor without a performance history not be disqualified for award merely because it lacked a performance history; we pointed out that such an approach would be inconsistent with the FAR and the DLA ABVM clause. As DLA recognized in that case, FAR

15.305(a)(2) provides that in the case of an offeror without a record of relevant past performance or for whom information on past performance is not available, the offeror may not be evaluated favorably or unfavorably on past performance.[5] *The ABVM clause states that lack of performance history is not grounds for disqualification for award.*

There is nothing in the record to show that the contracting officer performed a comparative assessment of the vendors. The contracting officer merely checked a box on a form indicating that National was not selected because its 999.9 ABVM score was based on insufficient information and therefore, was not a true indicator of its capabilities. Nor is there any indication that the contracting officer performed a tradeoff that considered the significant price premium in ordering from Tara, or that the contracting officer considered in her decision that National quoted a significantly shorter delivery time and confirmed that the metal sheets were in stock. Unlike in Phillips, there is no indication that the item was in backlog or high demand status or that timely delivery was critical and worth the price premium to avoid the risk of using a vendor with no performance history. We conclude that the contracting officer failed to make a meaningful best value determination consistent with the SPA to justify paying a price premium to Tara. As a result, DLA's decision was tantamount to rejecting National's quotation based on its lack of performance history, which is inconsistent with 41 U.S.C. sect. 405(j)(2), FAR 15.305(a)(2), and the clauses which implement the ABVM program, as discussed in the Phillips decision.

In this example, a protest of an award to a higher-priced proposal that argued that the price/past performance tradeoff was not made properly was sustained because the contracting officer failed to make a price/past performance tradeoff that showed the award was worth the price premium—this had the effect of rejecting the protester because it lacked any performance history. It should be noted that in the Phillips case, referenced in the example, the decision was just the opposite—award to the higher-priced offeror with an excellent performance history over a lower-priced offeror with no performance history, was justified because of the need for timely delivery. The difference was in the price/past performance tradeoff.

When all other evaluation factors are equal, past performance is moot when a higher-priced offeror with an excellent past performance history competes with a lower-priced offeror with no past performance history. Unless a price/past performance tradeoff shows that timely and effective contract performance must be assured to meet the government's needs and that this assurance, based on past performance history, is worth the price premium to be paid, award would have to be made based on price.

Where a procurement may involve firms with no past performance records and you want to avoid the problems that occurred in Example 12.3, you may broaden the evaluation to include the experience of a firm's technical and management personnel in the past performance evaluation. This may present problems, however, if your findings are negative. Downgrading an offeror under the past performance factor solely because some of its proposed key personnel were involved with a past failed contract might be difficult to justify without some evidence that the subject personnel were responsible for the problems. To presume particular individuals are responsible for past problems requires some definitive evidence. There are many reasons why a contract goes bad, and they may be beyond the control of the responsible contractor personnel. It should be noted, however, that the presence of such individuals, depending on the circumstances, could be determined to be a performance risk and be evaluated as such.

You may also consider the performance of other companies when they are team members, affiliates, or significant subcontractors, as shown in Example 12.4.

Example 12.4—When should one company's past performance be attributed to another?[6]

We have stated that in determining whether one company's performance should be attributed to another, an agency must consider the nature and extent of the relationship between the two companies—in particular, whether the workforce, management, facilities, or other resources of one may affect contract performance of the other. In this regard, while it would be inappropriate to consider a company's performance record where that record does not bear on the likelihood of successful performance by the offeror, it would be appropriate to consider a company's performance record where it will be involved in the contract effort or where it shares management with the offeror. See NAHB Research CTR. and Fluor Daniel.[7] In these decisions, the proposals clearly showed that the affiliate or other company had meaningful involvement in the performance of the contract. Here the awardee's proposal does not establish this fact.

Thus, a newly formed firm may not have a past performance history of its own but still can have a performance history through other companies that will be significantly involved in the contract performance. It would be beneficial to explain this in the RFP's description of how past performance will be evaluated. Otherwise this information might not be provided in an offeror's proposal.

Example 12.4 dealt with the past performance of associated companies. Example 12.5 deals specifically with evaluating the past performance of subcontractors.

Example 12.5—Evaluating the past performance of subcontractors[8]

Can subcontractors be listed as past performance references? Here is what the Comptroller General said.

With regard to its claims regarding Porton's work on two of the contracts Battelle is essentially arguing that the only entity that may properly list a prior contract for purposes of past performance evaluation is the concern that actually performed the work relevant to that covered in the solicitation. We disagree. The general rule is that the prime contractor under a government contract is responsible for the performance of its subcontractors.[9] Further, subcontractors and joint venturers perform various portions of contracts and accordingly may obtain experience useful in predicting success in future contract performance. George A. and Peter A. Palivos[10] (experience of a proposed subcontractor may be considered in determining whether an offeror meets a past performance requirement in a solicitation).[11] Where an offeror was involved as a subcon-

tractor or joint venture in performing work under a prior contract similar to work to be included under the instant contract, such experience may properly be considered in assessing that offeror's past performance.[12]

So, a proposed subcontractor's past performance can be considered; and, if the offeror gained pertinent experience as a subcontractor, that past performance may also be considered.

You may decide not to use past performance as an evaluation factor at all, where you anticipate that the participation of a significant number of new firms will make the evaluation of past performance inappropriate. Or, if after receipt of the proposals, you find that the evaluation of past performance will not result in a level playing field because of the participation of new firms, you could amend the RFP to delete past performance from the evaluation criteria. At that point the offerors have already submitted their technical proposals and the deletion of past performance would not result in a requirement for revised proposals.

Contract Type

The types of previous contracts held by an offeror can affect the assessment of past performance, particularly the assessment of the implications of past performance problems.

Fixed-Price Contracts

Under fixed-price contracts, agencies usually assess past performance on the basis of *timely delivery and adherence to the contract requirements*. These are objective criteria and are not difficult to evaluate, except where there have been a number of contract changes. Contract changes often adversely affect timely delivery and adherence to the requirements, especially where the changes are significant. The impact of such changes is difficult to assess unless these issues have been documented at the time the contract was changed. Nevertheless, such problems should be considered when evaluating an offeror's past fixed-price contracts.

Other Than Fixed-Price Contracts

Under cost-reimbursement, time-and-materials, and labor-hour contracts performed on the basis of best efforts, past performance is more difficult to assess objectively. *Overruns,* for example, can be caused by the fact that the required effort—not fully defined at the time of contracting—proved to require greater effort than anticipated by either the government or the contractor. Since the contractor is committed only to applying its best efforts, it may not be fair to rule the overrun as poor performance. *Delivery times* often slip in such contracts as the requirement is redefined during contract performance. These redefinitions may or may not be supported by official contract modification of the delivery dates. *Adherence to contract requirements* in such contracts is often difficult to determine since in many instances, the requirements are not fully defined at the time of contracting.

If you use past performance as a significant evaluation factor, you must conduct a careful analysis of an offeror's past performance and document the findings. As noted earlier, numerous factors can affect a contractor's performance. These are not always fully or fairly recorded and there can be honest differences of opinion as to the significance of particular performance problems.

EVALUATING PAST PERFORMANCE

Evaluating past performance involves: (1) checking references, (2) using information close at hand, (3) using personal knowledge, (4) permitting offerors to rebut initial adverse findings, and (5) avoiding problems.

Checking References

Checking the past performance references provided by offerors is time-consuming. You can facilitate this process by limiting the number of references offerors may provide or simply by not contacting all references. Will you get in trouble if you fail to contact all of the references? Well, that depends on the circumstances, as shown in Example 12.6.

Example 12.6—Must all past performance references be checked?[13]

The Comptroller General has consistently ruled that there is no requirement that an agency contact all of the references provided by an offeror.

The protester objects to the agency's inability to contact the two other references. The agency, however, is only required to make a reasonable effort to contact the references, and it is not objectionable to evaluate an offeror's past performance on less than the maximum possible number of references the agency could have received. See IGIT, Inc.[14] (although agencies are required to evaluate the past performance of all offerors on the same basis, there is no general requirement that an agency contact all of an offeror's references, or contact the same number of references for each offeror).

While there is no *requirement* that all references be contacted, an allegation of poor past performance is a sore point with contractors and if an offeror feels that it was not treated fairly in the past performance evaluation, a protest is likely. The RFP should establish a maximum number of references to be provided. This number should be whatever number you think can be checked efficiently, but a good faith effort should be made to contact all of the references provided. Setting a minimum number is not a good idea for the following reasons: (1) This could cause a problem for a new firm with limited experience, and (2) Offerors might submit more references than the minimum set forth.

Evaluating past performance for a comparative assessment ordinarily requires more information than that required when evaluating past performance in terms of responsibility (responsibility determinations center on objective areas such as late deliveries, a failure to deliver, and a failure to meet contract requirements). Generally, the procedure for checking references involves sending questionnaires to agencies that had previously contracted with the offeror. Example 12.7 addresses what happens when the questionnaires are not returned.

Example 12.7—What happens when past performance questionnaires are not returned?[15]

The RFP required offerors to identify past contracts for review, but not to provide general information about their performance of the contracts, as the agency would obtain this information directly from the references. The awardee referenced three prior DOE contracts, and all of the references returned the past performance questionnaires. The protester referenced two DOE contracts and one from another agency. When none of the protester's references returned the past performance questionnaires, the protester was awarded a neutral past performance rating (this was provided for in the RFP). The evaluation panel later converted the neutral rating to a score of 8 out of 10 possible points.

Despite ADC's arguments to the contrary, there is no legal requirement that all past performance references be included in a valid review of past performance.[16] *For our Office to sustain a protest challenging the failure to obtain or consider a reference's assessment of past performance, a protester must show unusual factual circumstances that convert the failure to a significant inequity for the protester.*[17] *. . . In short, without a showing that the DOE evaluators here should have been aware of the assessments that would have been received, and without some other showing that an agency's evaluation was unreasonable, we deny this protest ground.*

It should be noted that in this decision, the Comptroller General suggested that (1) DOE should reconsider its prohibition on offerors providing information on past performance, and (2) DOE consider measures to require DOE components to comply with the FAR 42.1503(c) requirement to answer past performance inquiries when asked to do so.

The case presented in Example 12.7 is unusual in that DOE refused to allow offerors to comment on their past performance. One of the best indications of a problem is when the offeror and the responding agency differ significantly in their assessment of the offeror's past performance. In these situations, the responding agency should be queried again to validate its initial response. In this case, DOE deprived itself of this information. The result was a protest and, although the agency won, it still had to devote time and resources to respond to the protest.

If the RFP calls for references to be provided, offerors tend to think that all of the references will be checked. If you do not check all of the references, particularly if it turns out that you only checked the bad ones, there is likely to be a protest that you did not treat the offeror fairly. As noted above, protests are disruptive, regardless of the outcome.

As noted in Chapter 3, offerors should be told to show how the referenced contracts relate to the current effort, to identify any problems with the referenced contracts and how these problems were corrected, and to otherwise indicate how well they performed. This information is directly relevant to the evaluation of past performance.

Using Information Close At Hand

You should not become complacent by the fact that you are not required to check all references, particularly if there is other information "close at hand," as shown in Example 12.8.

Example 12.8—You must consider past performance information "close at hand"[18]

While agencies generally need not evaluate all past performance references or those not reflected in the proposals, our Office has recognized that in certain limited circumstances an agency evaluating an offeror's past performance has an obligation (as opposed to the discretion) to consider "outside information" bearing on an offeror's past performance.[19] Where we have charged an agency with responsibility for considering such outside information, the record has demonstrated that the information in question was "simply to close at hand to require offerors to shoulder the inequities that spring from an agency's failure to obtain, and consider, the information.[20] See GTS *Duratck, Inc.*[21] *(agency should have considered offeror's past performance of a prior contract where the contract discussed in the offeror's past performance proposal was so relevant as to have served as the basis for the government estimate for the subject solicitation, and the contracting officer's technical representative for the contract was a member of the technical evaluation team for the subject solicitation); G. Marine Diesel*[22] *(contracting officer that was personally aware of the awardee's continuing difficulties in performing a contract for services related to the subject solicitation, and considered the performance difficulties relevant to the extent that the contracting officer determined not to exercise the options in the contract awarded under the subject solicitation, erred in not considering the awardee's performance difficulties when determining whether the contract under the subject solicitation had been properly awarded); G. Marine Diesel; Phillyship*[23] *(agency should have considered awardee's prior experience under a directly relevant contract where the contract was referenced in the awardee's proposal and the agency personnel were familiar with the awardee's performance). However, the "close at hand" information in these cases generally concerned contracts for the same services with the same procuring activity, or at least information personally known to the evaluators.*[24]

An agency cannot overlook past performance information that is close at hand. Close at hand refers to information that is, or should be, known to the contracting officer or the evaluators. If an offeror has performed contracts for the agency in the recent past (and this can be easily checked), such contracts should be reviewed to determine if they can provide pertinent past performance information. While an agency can, at its discretion, query outside sources about an offeror's past performance, it is obligated to review information close at hand.

Example 12.9 illustrates the problems that arise when a contracting officer fails to consider performance information readily at hand simply because administrative procedures were not followed.

Example 12.9—Price/past performance tradeoff and the use of information "close at hand"[25]

A Veteran's Administration (VA) RFP stated that award was to be made to the technically acceptable proposal determined to be most advantageous to the government based on price and past performance. Award was made to an offeror with an excellent past performance rating and the lowest price. The award was protested on the grounds of an unreasonable past performance evaluation. The protester argued that the awardee did not have the direct experience required to earn an excellent past performance rating.

In preparing a response to the protest, the contracting officer reevaluated the awardee's past performance and discovered that the protester was right; the awardee did not have any direct experience. The contracting officer took corrective action, giving the awardee a neutral past performance rating.

During the reevaluation of the protester's past performance, the contracting officer identified two VA contract references directly applicable to the solicitation. She only considered one of them, however, because the individual responsible for responding to the other past performance questionnaire failed to complete and return the questionnaire.

The contracting officer then compared the protester's good rating with the awardee's neutral rating and decided that both proposals were essentially equal in past performance. Since the awardee offered the lowest price, the contracting officer concluded that the initial award was proper. The protester argued that its past performance evaluation was improperly conducted because the contracting officer did not consider both references. The Comptroller General agreed.

Where an RFP identifies past performance and price as the evaluation factors and indicates that an offeror with a better past performance record than that of another offeror can expect a higher past performance rating, proposals must be evaluated on that basis. The selection official, however, has the discretion to decide the appropriate tradeoff between past performance and price in determining which proposal represents the best value to the government.[26] *Such a tradeoff is not precluded under an evaluation scheme specifying a "neutral" rating for vendors with no past performance record.*[27]

Our disagreement with the agency springs from its overly mechanical application of its procedures for evaluating past performance. While the VA is correct in its view that there is no legal requirement that all past performance references be included in a valid review of past performance,[28] some information is simply too close at hand to require offerors to shoulder the inequities that spring from an agency's failure to obtain, and consider, the information.[29]

Here, the record shows that IBSI's proposal clearly identified a recent contract involving the same agency, the same services, and the same contracting officer, and asked that its performance of this contract be considered as part of its evaluation, as the solicitation anticipated and required. The record shows that the contracting officer was aware of IBSI's performance of this contract and had termed it "exemplary" in a letter to the SBA written barely 4 months before the award decision here. Under these circumstances, we conclude that the agency unreasonably failed to consider IBSI's performance on its earlier contract simply because an individual in the agency did not complete the assessment required. See G. Marine Diesel; Phillyship[30] (protest sustained where the Navy elected not to consider unsatisfactory past performance of awardee involving similar services and the same command because awardee did not include the controversial contract on its list of references for the past performance review).

In this case, the Comptroller General found that had the agency considered the second referenced contract, which the contracting officer had termed as "exemplary" performance, the contracting officer might not have found the two offerors essentially equal with respect to past performance and the tradeoff between price and past performance might have had a different result. The Comptroller General recommended that the agency redo the evaluation properly.

Using Personal Knowledge

As Examples 12.8 and 12.9 illustrate, there is no excuse for ignoring information close at hand—in fact, you would do well to explore the possibility of close at hand information with the evaluators and within your procuring agency. Close at hand information is often simply the personal knowledge of personnel involved in the evaluation process. Can an evaluator use his or her own personal knowledge about an offeror when evaluating past performance? The answer is yes—under certain circumstances—as shown in Example 12.10.

Example 12.10—Evaluator's personal knowledge may be used[31]

A protester maintained that its proposal was improperly downgraded under past performance based on the undocumented personal knowledge of the evaluators. This allegation was based on narrative comments contained in the evaluation score sheets for two of the three evaluators, which stated "info provided was responsive, but personal experience resulted in lower score." The Comptroller General did not agree with the protester.

An evaluator's personal knowledge of an offeror may properly be considered in a past performance evaluation.[32] *More specifically, where the solicitation provides for references to be used in the evaluation, as here, the agency may consider the unsatisfactory past performance of an offeror under a recent contract with the agency, thus, in effect, furnishing its own reference.*[33] *In an evaluation which takes into account the agency's own knowledge of offerors, the fundamental requirement that evaluation judgments be documented in sufficient detail to show that they are reasonable and not arbitrary still must be met.*

Based on these numerous documented complaints about Omega's past performance, which were the basis of the personal knowledge of two of the evaluators, and which are undisputed by the protester, we have no basis to question the downgrading of Omega's proposal under past performance.

Evaluators may use their personal knowledge or agency records to evaluate past performance, but this must be documented sufficiently to show the origin of the information and the basis for the findings. An evaluator cannot, however, assume something based on third party knowledge, that is, other people said this firm performed poorly on some other contracts. Likewise, past performance evaluations cannot be based solely on a firm's reputation, that is, this is a successful company, so it must be a good performer. You can use personal knowledge only when it is firsthand and it can be documented.

An agency may base an evaluation of past performance on its reasonable perception of inadequate prior performance, regardless of whether the offeror disputes the agency's interpretation of the facts. If this is the case, the evaluators may downgrade the offeror's proposal and the offeror could be eliminated from the competitive range, as shown in Example 12.11.

Example 12.11—An agency's perception of poor past performance prevails when supported by sufficient evidence[34]

The evaluators concluded that an offeror had a series of performance problems under prior contracts. The offeror was excluded from the competitive range and protested that the past performance evaluation was unfair. The Comptroller General did not agree.

An agency's evaluation of past performance may be based upon the procuring agency's reasonable perception of inadequate prior performance, regardless of whether the contractor disputes the agency's interpretation of the facts.[35] This record affords us no basis upon which to object to the Navy's conclusion regarding QFI/Hampton Roads's past performance—that it produced some items of poor quality under prior contracts and could not, or would not, manufacture certain items which are the subject of this solicitation. While QFI offers explanations and interpretations of the record that provide a more favorable picture of its performance history than drawn by the agency, this does not alter the fact that there was sufficient evidence for the agency to conclude that the firm had a series of performance problems under its prior contracts.

We also conclude that QFI's proposal was reasonably excluded from the competitive range. Under the solicitation, past performance was considered significantly more important than price and the agency was permitted to award to other than the lowest-priced offeror. Under this evaluation scheme, which placed paramount importance on past performance, it was a reasonable exercise of the agency's discretion to decide that a firm with an exceptional performance history (based on very favorable references and no deficiency reports) and a relatively low price would be the only firm with a reasonable chance for award when all other offerors had significantly higher prices and/or less attractive performance histories. This is particularly true since the agency's assessment of Tri-Way's past performance as exceptional is unchallenged. Since the agency reasonably concluded that QFI had no reasonable chance for award, the exclusion of its proposal from the competitive range is not legally objectionable.[36]

The protester, citing our decisions holding that agencies have the discretion to eliminate from the competitive range proposals which do not include information required by the solicitation,[37] *suggests that agencies are required to eliminate such proposals from the competitive range. We disagree. The fact that an agency may eliminate a proposal from the competitive range for failure to include within the proposal information required by the solicitation does not mean the agency would be acting improperly if it included the proposal in the competitive range.*[38]

Do not let the evaluation of past performance become a mechanical process—simply checking the boxes on a questionnaire or adding up scores. A respondent's report on past performance can be subjective and sometimes self-serving. Checking more than one or two references will provide a broader picture of an offeror's ability to perform. There is, of course, a practical limit on the number of references that can be effectively checked during the evaluation process. If you have multiple offerors with multiple references, the past performance evaluation is going to bog down and adversely affect the efficiency of the evaluation process. One solution is to set a limit on the number of references in relation to the expected number of offerors, but you should allow at least three references per offeror.

The RFP should indicate that you reserve the right to check less than the total number of references provided. After all, how many positive references do you need to check? You should, however, pay more attention to adverse past performance information than to reports of good performance. The adverse reports will affect an offeror to a greater degree than the positive reports, and you need to ensure the validity of the adverse reports.

As noted above, an agency's report on an offeror's past performance can be subjective and sometimes self-serving. You can level the playing field, however, by providing offerors an opportunity to rebut adverse past performance reports, whether they originate from the reference provided or are from other sources. Although time-consuming, allowing such rebuttals is preferable to dealing with a protest.

Permitting Offerors to Rebut Initial Adverse Findings

Offerors are reluctant to accept a determination that they are poor performers. Likewise, government officials may be reluctant to admit to another government agency that its actions contributed to an offeror's poor performance. A finding of poor past performance can easily degenerate into a dispute over facts and result in a protest that the offeror has not been treated fairly.

When the use of past performance as an evaluation factor first became popular, and protests mounted, the Comptroller General ruled that when adverse past performance information was received from a reference that the offeror had provided in its proposal, the government had no obligation to permit the offeror to comment on the adverse information. The Comptroller General viewed such information as historical in nature and the protester would be unlikely to be able to make a significant contribution to its interpretation.[39]

While poor past performance is indeed a historical matter and cannot be changed, the cause of the poor performance is subject to interpretation. Even a late delivery, which is a factual matter, can be interpreted as excusable under certain circumstances. To assume that a poor performance report is not subject to interpretation is to assume that all government reports are objective and correct—hardly a valid assumption these days.

An agency's comments on past performance often reflect the respondent's subjective judgment and may even be in error. For example, while discussing the background in a decision,[40] the Comptroller General revealed that the contracting officer had asked an offeror about comments made by another agency that indicated the offeror's technical performance was considered inadequate. In response, the offeror produced a letter of commendation from the contracting agency's project manager on its performance under the contract in question, in which the project manager praised the offeror's performance as outstanding and tacitly admitted that the government was responsible for the alleged problems. Had the offeror been denied an opportunity to respond to the adverse comments, the record would have shown that the offeror had performed poorly on a contract that it actually performed in an outstanding manner.

Generally, it is not a good idea to refuse an offeror the opportunity to rebut adverse past performance reports found during the initial evaluation. This is recognized, in part, in FAR 15.306(b)(4), which states that communications (before the establishment of the competitive range) shall address past performance information to which the offeror has not previously had an opportunity to comment.

The problem with this FAR reference is that it could be interpreted to mean that the contracting officer does not have to address adverse information from references provided by the offeror (particularly if the RFP has requested that offerors comment on any performance problems involved in the referenced contracts), since the offeror has already had a chance to comment on such problems in its proposal. This assumes, however, that all contractors are informed of any performance problems found during the course of a contract—because FAR 42.1503 requires that contractors be so informed. This is not a safe assumption.

It would be a good idea to allow offerors, whose past performance evaluation would be the primary reason for their exclusion from the competitive range, to rebut any adverse information received even if, theoretically, they have already had a chance to comment on the problems. This would not be that difficult to do and might help avoid an unnecessary protest. However, when offered the opportunity to respond, the offeror is responsible for providing a successful explanation of the poor past performance. If the offeror fails to do this, you are not required to pursue the matter further, as shown in Example 12.12.

Example 12.12—Offeror must successfully rebut adverse past performance information[41]

An award was made to the offeror with the lowest performance risk because the technical and management ratings were equal and the lower performance risk offset the relatively small difference in price.

The protester listed three contracts to support its performance record. For two of the contracts, the past performance reports indicated good performance but there were no specific strong points to report. The other contract was with an Army installation, and that installation replied with a negative report.

After receiving the negative performance report, the contracting agency permitted the protester to submit a rebuttal. The protester responded, but only with general allegations of corrective action. The protester failed to provide specific information about the nature of the deficiencies or their resolution. The contracting agency contacted the Army installation three more times in an attempt to reconcile the differences between its report and the protester's response. The Army installation's replies did not bring up any significant new information, and the protester was not advised of these contacts.

The protester argued that its proposal was not fairly evaluated because it was not informed of these additional contacts and permitted to comment on what the Army installation had said. The Comptroller General did not agree.

While Dragon offers general denials of the statements made by Fort Bragg contracting officials, as well as explanations and interpretations of the record that provide a more favorable picture of Dragon's activities than drawn by the Army, this does not alter the fact that there was sufficient evidence for the Army to conclude that the firm had a series of performance problems under the Fort Bragg contract. An agency's evaluation of past performance may be based upon the procuring agency's reasonable perception of inadequate prior performance, even where the contractor disputes the agency's interpretation of the facts. [42]

In this case the contracting agency went out of its way to ensure a fair evaluation, as evidenced by the fact that after the initial negative response, the agency contacted the Army installation three more times in an attempt to reconcile its negative report with the response by the protester. The Army installation did not change its position, so the evaluators were faced with one negative performance report and two positive reports. In light of the negative report (and no information from the protester indicating that the problems were resolved), the agency could not reasonably rate the performance as low risk, but the two positive reports (one on a current contract) precluded a rating of high risk. A rating of moderate risk was the only reasonable choice. With technical and management equal and a minimal price difference, award was properly made on the basis of lowest performance risk.

The real problem in this case is that when given the opportunity to rebut the initial negative findings, the offeror failed to fully respond. If the offeror fails to respond appropriately, you are not required to pursue the matter further.

It is the offeror's responsibility to fully support its proposal. When derogatory comments are made about past performance, the offeror must completely rebut these comments with proof (not self-serving generalized statements). The offeror must show that the past problems were not really problems, that they were beyond the offeror's control, or that they were corrected. If the problems have been corrected, the offeror must explain exactly what corrective action was taken and how such action resolved the problem so that it would not recur. If the offeror fails to do this in its initial response (either through communications before the establishment of the competitive range or discussions after establishment of the competitive range), the government has no choice but to consider the problem unresolved and likely to recur.

Avoiding Problems

There is no sure way to avoid problems when evaluating an offeror's past performance. Offerors are not likely to simply accept a report of poor past performance if this is the primary factor in their exclusion from the competitive range or failure to receive the award. The following, however, may help minimize problems with offerors when evaluating past performance.

1. The RFP should warn offerors that they must address instances of poor performance in referenced contracts and explain how these problems were resolved. Indicate that a failure to satisfactorily explain past performance problems will have an adverse affect on the evaluation of past performance.
2. Past performance problems identified during the initial evaluation, both those concerning referenced contracts and those identified by other sources, should be revealed to the offeror. The offeror should be afforded the opportunity to rebut adverse information before the establishment of the competitive range.
3. Past performance problems not resolved before establishment of the competitive range should be treated as significant weaknesses and addressed during discussions.
4. It is not necessary to open another round of discussions to address past performance problems first identified during discussions. You should advise offerors to address such issues in their final proposal revisions.
5. If offerors do not satisfactorily explain how past performance problems were resolved in their final proposal revisions, you should consider the problems to be unresolved and likely to recur.
6. Do not reopen discussions to address past performance problems first revealed in an offeror's final proposal revision. The receipt of final proposal revisions marks the end of discussions. Reopening discussions after receipt

of the final proposal revisions is done only in extreme circumstances to avoid making an improper award.

EVALUATING PAST PERFORMANCE IS NOT EASY

Evaluating past performance in a competitive environment is not easy. In a comparative assessment, the informational requirements encompass both negative and positive information and both must be well documented. Positive information (proposal strong points) is usually easier to obtain and is as important as negative information, particularly when making tradeoffs between past performance and other factors. Negative information is harder to deal with because it must be supported by greater detail. A comparative assessment requires sufficient information to enable evaluators to compare one proposal to another to determine the most highly rated proposals for inclusion in the competitive range and later to determine which proposal offers the beat value to the government.

While the current emphasis on the use of past performance as an evaluation factor was introduced as a way to make acquisition more efficient and effective, in fact, it often has become a bureaucratic problem spawning more paperwork and effort than it is worth. Complicated questionnaires, the need to resolve differing opinions, and the scoring or grading of offerors' past performance have made this process more difficult than was originally envisioned.

These are growing pains, however, and over time, contracting personnel and contractors will learn how to focus on those things that are worthwhile and efficient and to ignore the rest. Eventually, the evaluation of past performance will realize its goal—that of focusing contractor's attention on providing effective performance and permitting the government to select out those contractors who fail to provide effective performance.

References

1. Smith of Galeton Gloves, Inc., B-271686, 7/24/96, GCR 109,568.
2. Amclyde Engineered Products Co., Inc., B-282271; B-282271.2, 6/21/99, 99-2 CPD ¶5, n.5.
3. National Aerospace Group Inc., B-281958, 5/10/99.
4. Phillips Indus., Inc., B-280645, 9/17/98, 98-2 CPD ¶74 at 5.
5. 41 U.S.C. sect 405(j)(2) (1994).
6. Universal Building Maintenance, Inc., B-282456, 7/15/99.
7. NAHB Research Ctr., Inc., B-278876.2, 5/4/98, 98-1 CPD ¶150 at 4; Fluor Daniel, Inc., B-262501; B-262501.2, 11/21/95, 95-2 CPD ¶241 at 12.
8. Battelle Memorial Institute, B-278673, 2/27/98.
9. Neal R. Gross & Co., Inc., B-275066, 1/17/97, 97-1 CPD ¶30 at 4.
10. George A. and Peter A. Palivos, B-245878.2; B-245878.3, 3/16/92, 92-1 CPD ¶286 at 10.
11. See also Commercial BLDG Serv., B-237865.2; B-237865.3, 5/16/90, 90-1 CPD ¶473 at 6.
12. Phillips Nat'l, Inc., B-253875, 11/1/93, 93-2 CPD ¶252 at 6.
13. Universal Building Maintenance, Inc., B-282456, 7/15/99, fn 2.
14. IGIT, Inc., B-275299.2, 6/23/97, 97-2 CPD ¶7 at 6.
15. Advanced Data Concepts, Inc., B-277801.4, 6/1/98, GCR 110,318.
16. Dragon Servs., Inc., B-255354, 2/25/94, 94-1 CPD ¶151 at 8; Questech Inc., B-236028, 11/1/89, 89-2 CPD ¶407 at 3.
17. International Bus. Sys., Inc., B-275554, 3/3/97, 97-1 CPD ¶114 at 5, GCR 109,877.
18. TRW, Inc., B-282162; B-282162.2, 6/9/99.
19. International Bus. Sys., Inc., B-275554, 3/3/97, 97-1 CPD ¶114 at 5, GCR 109,877.
20. Id.

21. GTS Duratck, Inc., B-280511.2; B-280511.3, 10/19/98, 98-2 CPD ¶130 at 14.
22. G. Marine Diesel, B-231619.3, 8/3/89, 89-2 CPD ¶101 at 4-6.
23. G. Marine Diesel; Phillyship, B-232619; B-232619.2, 1/27/89, 89-1 CPD ¶90 at 4-5.
24. Morrison Knidsen Corp., B-280261, 9/9/98, 98-2 CPD ¶63 at 5-6.
25. International Bus. Sys., Inc., B-275554, 3/3/97, 97-1 CPD ¶114 at 5, GCR 109,877.
26. Excalibur Sys. Inc., B-272017, 7/12/96, 96-2 CPD ¶13 at 3.
27. Engineering and Computation Inc., B-275180.2, 1/29/97, 97-1 CPD ¶47 at 4-5; Excalibur Sys. Inc., supra.
28. Dragon Servs., Inc., B-255354, 2/25/94, 94-1 CPD ¶151 at 8; Questech Inc., B-236028, 11/1/89,

89-2 CPD ¶407 at 3.

29. G. Marine Diesel, 68 Comp. Gen. 577 (1989), 89-2 CPD ¶101 at 5-6; New Hampshire-Vermont Health Serv., 57 Comp. Gen. 347 (1978), 78-1 CPD ¶202 at 12-13; Continental Maritime of San Diego, Inc., B-249858.2; B-249858.3, 2/11/93, 93-1 CPD ¶230 at 6-8; G. Marine Diesel; Phillyship, B-232619; B-232619.2, 1/27/89, 89-1 CPD ¶90 at 4-5; Inlingua Schools of Languages, B-229784, 4/5/88, 88-1 CPD ¶340 at 5.
30. G. Marine Diesel; Phillyship, supra.
31. Omega World Travel, Inc., B-271262.2, 7/25/96, GCR 109,579.
32. TRESP Assoc., Inc.; Advanced Data Concepts, Inc., B-258322.5; B-258322.6, 3/9/95, 96-1 CPD ¶8.
33. G. Marine Diesel; Phillyship, B-232619; B-232619.2, 1/27/89, 89-1 CPD ¶90.
34. Quality Fabricators, Inc., B-271431; B-271431.3, 6/25/96, GCR 109,553.
35. Otto Einhaupl, B-241553 et al., 2/20/91, 91-1 CPD ¶192.
36. Counter Technology Inc., B-260853, 7/20/95, 95-2 CPD ¶39; Engineering & Computation Inc., B-258728, 1/31/95, 95-1 CPD ¶155.
37. Panasonic Communications & Sys. Co., B-239917, 10/10/90, 90-2 CPD ¶279.
38. Intermagnetics Gen. Corp.—Recon., 73 Comp. Gen. 333 (1994), 94-2 CPD ¶119.

39. Centrex Construction Co., Inc., B-238777, 6/14/90, GCR 104,470.
40. Columbia Research Corp., B-247073; B-247073.2, 4/23/92, GCR 106,570.
41. Dragon Services, Inc., B-255354, 2/25/94, 94-1 CPD ¶151, GCR 108,099.
42. Pannesma Co. Ltd., B-251688, 4/19/93, 93-1 CPD ¶333; Firm Otto Einhaupl, B-241533 et al., 2/20/91, 91-1 CPD ¶192.

CHAPTER 13

Other Problems in Evaluation

Chapter 11 addressed the process to be followed in the initial evaluation. Chapter 12 discussed the evaluation of past performance. This chapter deals with some of the other problems encountered in the initial evaluation.

Government personnel, as well as contractor personnel preparing proposals, need to be aware of problems others have encountered in proposal evaluations in order to avoid making the same mistakes. Two important areas are understanding the offeror's responsibilities when preparing and submitting a proposal and the government's responsibilities with respect to the evaluation process. Another common problem area is the evaluation of key personnel and staffing. These and other problems are demonstrated in the examples that follow.

OFFEROR RESPONSIBILITIES

The offeror has a number of responsibilities during the evaluation process.

Offeror Is Responsible for Submitting an Adequate Proposal

As noted in Chapter 10, an offeror is responsible for submitting an adequate proposal, that is, one that meets all RFP requirements and clearly demonstrates that the offeror can successfully perform the contract. An offeror who fails to submit an adequate proposal runs the risk of proposal rejection, as shown in Example 13.1.

Example 13.1—Offeror is responsible for submitting an adequate proposal[1]

We find that the agency reasonably evaluated Quality's proposal under this factor. From our review of the record it appears that not only did Quality's proposal fail to include an emergency disaster plan but that the two pages that Quality submitted for this factor were lacking in detail. The offeror has the burden of submitting an adequate proposal,[2] and on this record we see no basis for faulting the agency for not realizing that Quality's revised proposal was missing a page [the proposal pages were not numbered] or for not evaluating the proposal higher than it did under this factor.

The agency reasonably determined that Elcon's detailed eight-page management proposal was superior to the nonspecific three-page management proposal submitted by Quality. Contrary to the protester's assertions, an offeror's blanket offer of compliance is not an adequate substitute for detailed and complete technical information in a proposal establishing what the firm proposes will meet the government's needs.[3] An agency may downgrade a proposal for lack of detail pertaining to the requirements of the RFP, or consider a more detailed proposal superior.[4]

Further, the provision of the RFP that encourages offerors to structure their proposals in a "concise and specific" manner cannot be read to obviate the clearly expressed requirements to submit specified information with the proposal.[5] Based on our review of the record, we find that the agency reasonably concluded that Elcon's management plan was superior to Quality's management plan, in part because Elcon's management plan was significantly more detailed.

Here the protester not only failed to provide a required document, but also failed to provide sufficient detail in what it did submit. It is the offeror's responsibility to submit a proposal that adequately meets the RFP requirements. A blanket offer of compliance does not adequately substitute for detailed and complete technical information establishing that what the firm proposes will meet the government's needs. In cases like this, an agency may downgrade a proposal for the lack of detail pertaining to the RFP requirements and consider a more detailed proposal superior.

Evaluations Are Restricted to What Is in the Proposal Itself

With the exception of past performance and corporate experience, an evaluator may evaluate only that which is set forth in the proposal itself. An evaluator may not substitute his or her own opinion as to whether an offeror can meet a particular RFP requirement. If an offeror fails to show in its proposal that it can meet a particular RFP requirement, this must be evaluated as a deficiency or significant weakness, even if, based on the offeror's reputation or the evaluator's own experience with the offeror, the evaluator thinks the offeror could meet the requirement. The Comptroller General states this rather succinctly in Example 13.2.

Example 13.2—Evaluations are restricted to what is in the proposal itself[6]

In a negotiated procurement, an offeror must demonstrate within the four corners of its proposal that it will perform the required work in accordance with the terms and conditions set forth in the solicitation.[7]

Offeror Must Provide All Required Information

An offeror must provide all required information or risk having its proposal downgraded or rejected, as shown in Example 13.3.

Example 13.3—Offeror must provide all required information[8]

Where, as here, the solicitation specifically directs offerors to demonstrate their capabilities in their technical proposals, an offeror disregards any specific requirements at its peril.[9] *In the absence of specific information demonstrating compliance with the RFP requirements, the agency reasonably downgraded the protester's proposal under technical approach.*

Offeror Must Question Inconsistent Solicitation Provisions

It is the offeror's responsibility to review the RFP completely and to question any inconsistencies. Questions or protests regarding the RFP contents must be made before the time set for the receipt of proposals. Protests submitted after this time are untimely and will not be considered, as shown in Example 13.4.

Example 13.4—Offeror must question obviously inconsistent solicitation provisions before the time set for the receipt of proposals[10]

As stated above, Section M of the RFP clearly stated that the agency reserved the right to make award based on initial proposals without discussions. At the same time, Section L incorporated the standard clause regarding discussions with offerors. We think an offeror reasonably should have realized prior to the date set for receipt of initial proposals that the RFP contained two provisions which directly contradicted each other since this conflict was apparent on the face of the solicitation. In such situations, protesters do not have the option of simply making unilateral assumptions regarding the meaning of conflicting or patently ambiguous provisions in a solicitation and then expect relief when the agency does not act in the manner the protester assumed; rather, the patent impropriety in this solicitation had to be challenged prior to closing.[11]

Given the lack of a timely objection to the award methodology relied upon by the agency in making the award, we conclude that this award was consistent with the RFP as reasonably interpreted by the agency (that is, the boldfaced provisions of Section M controlled).

Unfortunately, this is not an unusual mistake. RFPs are often issued with conflicting provisions, particularly where some provisions or clauses are incorporated by reference and only the title is set forth in the RFP. It is the government's responsibility to review an RFP before it is issued to ensure that there are no inconsistencies between the SOW, the clauses that set forth the terms and conditions of the contract, the solicitation provisions that govern how proposals are to be submitted, and, particularly, the contents of Sections M and L. Inconsistencies in the RFP can result in a protest.

Offerors are also responsible for reviewing the RFP in the same manner, before the closing date. The offeror's responsibility governs. This is necessary to prevent offerors from taking advantage of the government's mistakes to gain an unwarranted advantage. It should also be noted that it is to the offeror's advantage to question inconsistent RFP contents in a timely manner. If this problem had been questioned properly and the agency failed to take corrective action, the responsibility would have passed back to the government.

Offeror Cannot Expect the Government to Search Out Omitted Information

As noted earlier, the offeror is responsible for submitting a complete proposal. The government is not obligated to search out information for qualifications that an offeror has omitted from its proposal. Offerors who assume that the government will fill in the blanks left by the offeror do so at their own risk, as shown in Example 13.5.

Example 13.5—Government not required to search out information omitted from proposal[12]

While EBA acknowledges that its submission did not expressly advise the agency as to which, if any, of the projects had been performed using metric measurement, EBA maintains that the agency should have been able to verify on its own that some of the projects had been performed in metric. However, offerors are responsible for preparing adequately written proposals,[13] and agencies are not obligated to search out information or qualifications that an offeror may have omitted from its proposal.[14] EBA's complaints regarding the agency's assessment of its experience with metric measurement falsely assumes the agency was required to seek and obtain information regarding EBA's qualifications beyond that provided by EBA.

As stated in Examples 13.2 and 13.3, it is the offeror's responsibility to respond to all RFP requirements, and if the offeror doesn't, the offeror must bear the consequences. It is not the government's responsibility to help complete an offeror's proposal.

Offeror Cannot Simply Parrot the Wording of the SOW

An offeror who simply parrots the wording of the SOW has failed to meet the requirement that it provide sufficient information to evaluate the proposal. If the offeror provides no other supporting information, it has failed to provide the specificity needed or the insights necessary to determine if it understands the RFP requirements and can meet them. The evaluators already know what is in the SOW; they need to determine what the offeror knows. Such proposals cannot be fully evaluated and should be rejected, as shown in Example 13.6.

Example 13.6—Watch for offeror who simply parrots back the wording of the SOW[15]

BOP reports that Bannum's proposals were excluded because they did not contain acceptable evidence of Bannum's right to use its proposed performance facilities and because they parroted the SOW requirements to such an extent that the agency could not discern Bannum's technical or management approach or understanding of the contract requirements. BOP states that the protester basically submitted the same technical proposal in all three procurements, even though the solicitations had different estimated requirements, different performance locations, and different penal purposes as between the solicited community corrections center and the comprehensive sanction centers. BOP also cites specific informational omissions in the protester's proposals, such as Bannum's failure to mention performance problems in prior BOP contracts, Bannum's omission of required documentation on its proposed food service subcontractors, and Bannum's submission of unacceptable evidence of its right to use the proposed facilities.

The offeror has the burden of submitting an adequately written proposal, and an offeror's mere disagreement with the agency's judgment concerning the adequacy of its proposal is not sufficient to establish that the agency acted improperly.[16]

We agree with BOP that Bannum's proposals basically repeat substantial portions of the SOW nearly verbatim and, as such, do not evidence whether the protester independently understands the requirements applicable to each solicitation. For example, where the SOW requires that "one operable washer and dryer for each sixteen residents shall be provided in-house or through a community establishment within one mile of the facility," the protester's proposal states, "Bannum will provide one operable washer and one operable dryer on the premises for every sixteen residents or through a community establishment within one mile of the facility," Despite the RFP's admonishment of the possible consequences of such mimicry, the protester's proposals rely so heavily upon repetition and provides so little specificity that it is not apparent, for example, whether Bannum has ever seen its proposed facilities or investigated any services or resources within the communities to be served. Such repetition of the SOW requirements allowed for little or no insight as to Bannum's approach to performing the contract work, such as the methods Bannum will use to monitor and discipline residents; the content of any training or educational courses it might offer; and the penal and rehabilitation goals that will instruct its approach to the contract work. In sum, Bannum's proposals simply do not present an independent technical and management approach for the agency to evaluate and were properly rejected as technically unacceptable.

The SOW states *what* work is to be done—the offeror's proposal must describe *how* the work will be done. It is permissible for an offeror to repeat the wording of the SOW, but only if it then goes on to describe how those requirements will be implemented. Proposals that fail to do this should be rejected.

GOVERNMENT RESPONSIBILITIES

The government also has a number of responsibilities during the evaluation process.

Government Must Follow the Published Evaluation Criteria

The government is required to tell offerors how proposals will be evaluated. Once this information is published in the RFP, the government does not have the discretion to change how the proposals will be evaluated unless all offerors are informed of the changes and permitted to revise their proposals accordingly, as shown in Example 13.7.

Example 13.7—Government must follow RFP's evaluation criteria[17]

American Lawn alleges that, contrary to the stated best value plan, the Navy awarded this contract on a lowest-price, technically acceptable basis. Although the RFP stated that the technical and price proposals were of equal importance and that this was a best value procurement, the Navy did not consider in its selection decision, the higher-rated, higher-priced BAFOs, such as the protester as "exceptional" rated BAFO. The agency did not conduct a price/technical tradeoff analysis, but rather awarded the contract on the basis of the lowest-priced, technically acceptable BAFO and did not inform offerors of this changed evaluation scheme. Agencies do not have the discretion to announce in the solicitation that they will use one evaluation plan and then follow another without informing all offerors of any significant changes in the evaluation scheme.[18] *Thus the agency improperly departed from the stated best value evaluation plan and we sustain the protest on this basis.*[19]

[and in a footnote] *Where the RFP provides for the assessment of price in order to evaluate an offeror as understanding the solicitation requirement, the agency must consider it in evaluating proposals.*[20]

The government must follow the published evaluation criteria; however, the government may deviate from an internal agency evaluation plan or any other agency instructions that have not been published in the RFP, as shown in Example 13.8.

Example 13.8—Failure to follow internal agency instruction does not provide a basis for protest[21]

Concerning the protester's arguments about the SSP, a contracting agency's failure to follow an SSP does not provide a basis for questioning the validity of an award selection because the SSP is an internal agency instruction, and as such, does not give outside parties any rights.[22]

It should be noted that internal agency instructions, such as a source selection plan, are written with the intent that they be followed. Any deviations from internal agency instructions should be documented with an explanation as to why the deviation was necessary. The Comptroller General's ruling protects you from disgruntled offerors, but not from agency management.

Government Offerors Must Provide a Common Basis for Submission of Proposals

It is a fundamental rule of competitive procurement that all offerors must be provided a common basis for the submission of proposals. An agency may not relax a mandatory RFP requirement for one offeror and not provide other offerors the same opportunity through an amendment to the solicitation, as shown in Example 13.9.

Example 13.9—Agency may not relax RFP requirement for one offeror and not provide other offerors the same opportunity[23]

Generally, our Office will question an agency's evaluation of proposals only if the evaluation lacks a reasonable basis or is inconsistent with the RFP's stated evaluation criteria.[24] *We find that the Corps's evaluation of GI's offer was not consistent with the RFP's stated scheme because GI did not satisfy the RFP's minimum expertise/experience requirement. We also find that the RFP overstated the Corps's actual needs regarding the type of expertise/experience that was necessary.*

It is a fundamental rule of competitive procurement that all offerors be provided a common basis for submission of proposals.[25] *When an agency relaxes its requirements, either before or after receipt of proposals, it must issue a written amendment to notify all offerors of the changed requirements.*[26] *We will sustain a protest where an agency, without issuing a written amendment, relaxes an RFP specification to a protester's possible prejudice (e.g., where the protester would have altered its proposal to its competitive advantage had it been given the opportunity to respond to the altered requirements).*[27]

As stated above, to justify accepting GI's offer the contracting officer relies on the proposal preparation instructions statement that alternative solutions to meet the government's requirements would be considered and on the evaluation scheme statement that the contracting officer could accept a proposal meeting the government's true needs that might not otherwise conform with all RFP requirements. It is not clear exactly what government requirements might be encompassed by the former, or what true needs by the latter, but in our view neither provision properly can be the basis for waiving a specific requirement that was identified in the RFP as a "Required Minimum Qualification" and which companies entering the competition expressly were advised was not waivable. That is, given the clear reference in the RFP to the need for TAMMIS experience and the unequivocal confirmation of the requirement at the preproposal conference—"similar software and approach" would not be considered acceptable—we think the agency's reliance on the two RFP provisions in issue to justify waiving the TAMMIS expertise/experience requirements for the awardee is misplaced.

In short, in awarding the contract to GI on the basis of its having expertise/experience with a similar software system, the agency improperly relaxed or waived the terms of the RFP without amending the RFP to notify all offerors of the changed requirement, to the likely prejudice of CNA. In this regard, CNA has submitted two affidavits to show that it would have sought competitive bids from several software vendors and probably would have been able to offer the Corps a lower price if it knew that other than TAMMIS expertise and experience was acceptable.[28] *Accordingly we sustain CNA's protest on this basis.*

An agency cannot sidestep Comptroller General rulings by writing something in the RFP such as, "the contracting officer could accept a proposal meeting the government's true needs that might not otherwise conform with all RFP requirements." This does not even make sense. The government should know what its true needs are and include them in the SOW, and, if the true needs are not known (and this is possible), this information should be provided for in the RFP by indicating that alternatives are permitted and any mandatory requirements deleted. Sliding in obscure solicitation provisions to cover yourself will not survive a protest.

Government Estimates Must Be Reasonably Accurate

When an agency solicits on the basis of estimated quantities, the estimates must be reasonably accurate. If the estimates are not reasonably accurate and the inaccuracies could make a difference in the competitive standings of offerors, or affect the best value determination, a proper award cannot be made and the procurement is fatally flawed, as shown in Example 13.10.

Example 13.10—Government estimates must be reasonably accurate[29]

Where the proposal of pricing discounts is not expressly prohibited by the RFP, there is nothing improper in an agency's decision to accept a contractor's offer to discount certain charges,[30] however, the offered discounts should be taken into account in the evaluation only if the condition on which the discount is based likely will be met.[31] Moreover, when the government solicits offers on the basis of estimated quantities to be offered over a given period, the estimates must be compiled from the best information available; while they need not be absolutely correct, the estimates must be a reasonably accurate representation of the agency's anticipated needs.[32] An award decision is not proper if the estimates misrepresented the government's needs such that the inaccurate estimates likely made a difference in the relative competitive positions of firms participating in the procurement,[33] or skewed the determination of which offer would result in the lowest cost to the government in terms of actual performance.[34]

Estimates, by their nature, are not absolutes, but they can be reasonably accurate if based on reliable data. The problem with estimates in solicitations is that offerors rely on them when developing their proposals. Inaccurate estimates affect more than just discounts; they affect all aspects of an offeror's proposal, including resource allocation and pricing. When dealing with estimates, you should ensure that they are as accurate as possible and if the accuracy of the estimates is uncertain, this should be indicated in the solicitation.

Government Must Consider the Effect the Evaluation Scheme Will Have on Newly Formed Firms

The contracting officer decides what evaluation factors will be used and how proposals will be evaluated. Generally, an agency evaluates the corporate experience of a new business based on the experience of its principal officers, or parent company, but, as noted in Example 13.11, an agency is not obligated to do so in every case.

Example 13.11—Unusual evaluation schemes may adversely affect a newly formed company[35]

We find the evaluation of MPI's experience was reasonable. While an agency may, in appropriate circumstances, evaluate the corporate experience of a new business by reference to the experience of its principal officers, or parent company, an agency is not obligated to do so in every case.[36] *Here, the solicitation clearly indicated that the Army considered a firm's experience to be different from its employees' individual experience. The RFP described the technical experience to be evaluated under the technical experience subfactor as "that specific experience related to the functional areas, and includes direct experience of personnel, the company, or business entity, and of any proposed subcontractors." In contrast, the solicitation included under the management factor separate evaluation subfactors for related management and contract experience and for qualifications of key personnel, and instructed offerors in responding to the related management and contract experience subfactor to "[d]escribe the company's background pertinent to performance of large service contracts during the past five years, especially contracts similar to this solicitation, and relate that experience to the requirements of the contract." Although the RFP stated that both corporate and personnel experience were to be evaluated under the technical experience subfactor, it only requested information concerning corporate experience under the related management and contract experience subfactor of the management factor and provided a separate personnel qualification subfactor under the management factor. Thus, we believe that the RFP contemplated a separate evaluation of corporate and personnel experience. In these circumstances, we see no basis to question the agency's refusal to consider the experience of MPI's key personnel as a substitute for its lack of corporate experience, and the subsequent downgrading of its proposal under the technical experience and related management and contract experience subfactors.*[37]

The agency evaluated the proposals properly in this case. It should be noted, however, that the Comptroller General reviewed the record as it stood, not the reasoning that went into it. Thus the agency got what it asked for—which may not have been what it wanted, Did the agency fail to consider the implications of evaluating corporate experience and personnel experience separately with respect to its effect on a newly formed firm? Or was the evaluation scheme developed as it was to ensure that newly formed firms could not compete? In any event, evaluation schemes should be reviewed to determine how they might affect newly formed firms, particularly with respect to corporate experience.

Evaluators May Use Personal Experience When Evaluating an Offeror's Prior Experience

Example 13.2 showed that evaluators are restricted to evaluating only what is set forth in the proposal. This applies to all factors except past performance and corporate experience. To evaluate these factors, evaluators must contact other sources to verify the offeror's statements about its past performance and corporate experience. In addition to reviewing other sources, evaluators may use their own personal experience, if it is pertinent to the evaluation, as shown in Example 13.12. For similar examples dealing with past performance, see Chapter 12, Examples 12.8 through 12.11. It should be noted that the concepts expressed in the

Chapter 12 examples would also apply to the evaluation of corporate experience.

Example 13.12—Evaluators may use their own personal experience when evaluating corporate experience[38]

Nevertheless, the TEP Chairman testified that during the evaluation he specifically noticed that the IRS headquarters complex was among the projects listed by Safeguard and acknowledged that he was personally aware that the building possessed significant ADP space that was maintained by Safeguard.[39] He also testified that he believed that he is specifically precluded from taking into account this personal knowledge in an evaluation.[40] However, an agency may properly use information known by its own evaluators, as with any other reference, to aid in the evaluation of proposals, including evaluating offeror experience, and may not simply ignore personally known information about an offeror's prior experience merely because it was not mentioned in the proposal.[41]

Care should be exercised in this area. Evaluators may use their personal knowledge about prior experience and past performance (these are historical facts). Evaluators may not, however, read something into a technical proposal that was not put there by the offeror simply because they have personal knowledge of how the offeror does business.

For example, if an offeror failed to provide certain information required by the RFP, or failed to address a technical issue, an evaluator may not simply assume that the offeror would perform properly in these areas because the evaluator is familiar with the offeror's performance on other contracts or because the offeror has a good reputation. If a requirement is left out of the technical proposal, this can only be evaluated as a deficiency or significant weakness; it cannot be ignored or assumed to be acceptable.

It should also be noted that the Comptroller General is talking about personal knowledge in the first-person sense. If an evaluator was personally involved with a contract performed by an offeror, whether referenced by the offeror or not, this information may be used to evaluate corporate experience or past performance—if fully documented. If an evaluator merely "heard" about an offeror's problems (or successes), this information may not be used in the evaluation. The evaluator may, however, contact the person who did have the firsthand information and obtain the information, but it must be in writing.

Contracting officers should brief evaluators on their use of personal knowledge before the start of the evaluation process.

RFP Must State the Relative Importance of the Cost/Price Factor

The RFP must state the importance of the cost/price factor in relation to all other evaluation factors. This was a requirement before the FAR 15 rewrite [15.605(d)(1)] and still is a requirement [15.304(e)]. Nevertheless, the FAR wording—to the effect that the RFP must state whether the technical factors are more important, equally important, or less important than the cost/price factor—is sometimes overlooked, often in cost-reimbursement contracts where cost is an unweighted evaluation factor (see the discussion in Chapter 5). As shown in Example 13.13, a failure to explain the relative importance of the cost factor will result in the technical and cost factors being considered as equal in importance—something that may not be intended.

Example 13.13—RFP must state the relative importance of cost/price with respect to the technical evaluation factors.[42]

The RFP did not identify the relative weight assigned to the cost factor. Where a solicitation fails to explicitly state the relative weight of cost in the evaluation scheme, it must be presumed that cost and technical considerations will be accorded equal weight and importance in the evaluation.[43]

When using cost as an unweighted evaluation factor, it is suggested that you use words in Section M to the following effect: "Cost is an unweighted evaluation factor. While the technical factors are significantly more important than cost, the relative importance of cost will increase as the technical proposals are evaluated as roughly equal and cost could become the determinative factor." This wording will satisfy the FAR requirement that the relative importance of cost be described. It also puts offerors on notice that even though cost is unweighted, it could become the determinative factor—something offerors should consider when pricing their proposals.

KEY PERSONNEL AND STAFFING

Evaluators need to be aware of the problems involved in the evaluation of key personnel and staffing. Two of the problems were addressed in Chapter 4 (see Example 4.4—Offer flexibility when listing experience or educational requirements, and Example 4.5—Offeror should propose personnel who can reasonably be expected to perform the work). The following examples demonstrate some of the other problems that evaluators may encounter in this area.

Bait and Switch Tactics

One of the problems often encountered is where an unsuccessful offeror alleges that the awardee used "bait and switch" tactics to win a contract. The Comptroller General defines bait and switch tactics in Example 13.14.

Example 13.14—Definition of bait and switch tactics[44]

"Bait and switch" refers to an offeror's misrepresentation in its proposal of the personnel it expects to use during contract performance. To demonstrate that a bait and switch has occurred, a protester must demonstrate not only that personnel other than those proposed are performing the services (i.e., that a switch has occurred), but also that the awardee represented in its proposal that it would rely on certain specified personnel in performing the services, that the agency relied on this representation in evaluating the proposal, and that it was foreseeable that the individuals named in the proposal would not in fact be available to perform the contract work.[45]

Problems with bait and switch tactics usually surface after award through a protest by an unsuccessful offeror. Evaluators, however, should be alert to the potential for such a problem. The characteristics of a bait and switch are:

1. The offeror represented in its proposal that it would rely on specified personnel in performing the services (the bait). These personnel are usually highly qualified and certain to be viewed favorably by the evaluators.
2. The agency relied on this representation in evaluating the proposal. This is an important factor, as shown in Example 13.15.
3. It is determined that personnel, other than those named, are actually performing the services (the switch). However, a change in the named personnel does not necessarily mean that a bait and switch has occurred (see the first paragraph of Example 13.16).
4. It was, or should have been, foreseeable by the offeror that the individuals named in the proposal would not, in fact, be available to perform the contract work. If, before submission of its final proposal revision, an offeror knows, or should have known, that named personnel would not be available, the offeror must provide the names and qualifications of substitute personnel in its final proposal revision. See the second paragraph of Example 13.16.

You can minimize the use of bait and switch tactics. In the proposal preparation instructions, offerors should be required to submit a letter of commitment from each of the named key personnel not currently employed full-time by the offeror. This letter should authorize the offeror to use the individual's name and resume in the proposal and agree to work under the contract in the event of award. The instructions should state that without such a letter, the named individual cannot be evaluated as available for performance under the contract. This requirement should be rigorously enforced.

You can also minimize problems relating to the availability of key personnel by expending extra effort at the end of discussions. When discussions are completed, the contracting officer, in writing, must request the submission of final proposal revisions. In addition to the required statements (see Chapter 16), the contracting officer should ask offerors if the key personnel commitments are still valid. The letter should inform the offerors that if some of the named personnel are no longer available, the offeror must provide the names and qualifications of substitute personnel in its final proposal revision. There is no regulatory requirement to do this—the offeror is responsible for keeping personnel commitments up to date—but it might help to remind offerors of this responsibility and avoid later problems.

Example 13.15—What happens if an agency does not rely on a bait and switch tactic?[46]

Apache also argues that LSI engaged in an improper "bait and switch" concerning its proposed subcontractors. To establish an improper "bait and switch," a protester must generally show that the firm in question either knowingly or negligently made a misrepresentation regarding resources that it did not expect to furnish during contract performance, that the misrepresentation was relied upon by the agency in the evaluation, and that this had a material impact on the evaluation results.[47] Here the agency did not evaluate offerors' proposed subcontractors. Accordingly, the agency did not rely on LSI's (or any other offerors') representations concerning its proposed subcontractors, and its subcontractors did not have a material impact on the evaluation results. There thus is no basis for a finding of a "bait and switch."

A key characteristic for an improper bait and switch (whether related to key personnel or some other area) is that the government relied on the misrepresentation in its evaluation and that this affected the evaluation results. In this case the government did not rely on what might have been a misrepresentation, so there was no problem.

Offerors are required to submit the names of key personnel in good faith and with the consent of the named individuals. Circumstances beyond an offeror's control do occur, however, and may make named individuals unavailable. A failure to provide the originally named individuals is not necessarily an improper bait and switch, as shown in Example 13.16 (see also Chapter 4, Example 4.5).

Example 13.16—A change in named personnel does not always mean that a bait and switch has occurred[48]

Offeror "bait and switch" practices, whereby an offeror proposes the use of personnel that it does not expect to actually use during contract performance, have an adverse effect on the integrity of the competitive procurement system and generally provides a basis for proposal rejection.[49] This does not mean that an offeror must use the personnel it proposed or risk losing the contract for which it is competing in every case. For example, where the offeror provides firm letters of commitment and the names were submitted in good faith with the consent of the respective individuals (that is, the offeror is not proposing personnel it has no intention of providing), the fact that the offeror, after award, provides substitute personnel does not make the award improper.[50]

Conversely, however, an offeror has a responsibility to propose persons who it reasonably may expect will be available for contract performance. In two recent cases, we have interpreted this obligation to require an offeror to confirm the continued availability of the personnel it proposes in certain circumstances. In Mantech Field Engineering,[51] the protest was sustained where the awardee failed to confirm the availability of one proposed key employee whose intention to accept employment with the awardee was questionable, and six other proposed employees whose resumes were received over 6 months before they were included in awardee's proposal. In CBIS Federal,[52] the protest was sustained where awardee lacked a letter of commitment as required by the RFP for one proposed key employee and unreasonably assumed she was still available despite strong indication to the contrary, and failed to confirm continued availability of second proposed key employee whose letter of intent was signed 8 months previously.

Bait and switch involves an offeror's deliberate or negligent misrepresentation of the availability of specified resources. Example 13.17 shows how the Comptroller General views such misrepresentations.

Example 13.17—Misrepresentation of the availability of key personnel can result in proposal rejection or contract termination[53]

In our review of protests involving service contracts where the most qualified personnel are often those currently performing the services, we are mindful of the difficulty faced by a nonincumbent contractor in securing a qualified workforce sufficient to win the competition.[54] Nevertheless, an offeror's misrepresentation concerning personnel that materially influences an agency's consideration of its proposal generally provides a basis for proposal rejection or reevaluation of the award decision based on the faulty proposal. ManTech Advanced Sys Int'l.,[55] (misrepresentation of proposal commitments, reevaluation recommended); CBIS Fed.[56] (misrepresentation of personnel availability, reevaluation recommended); Ultra Tech[57] (misrepresentation of availability of key person and use of name in proposal without permission, termination recommended absent other agency findings); Informatics[58] (misrepresentation of results of a survey of the availability of incumbent's personnel, exclusion recommended).

Proposed Key Personnel Must Meet RFP Qualifications

Offerors must propose key personnel who meet the qualification requirements set forth in the RFP. Failure to do so can result in proposal rejection even if the offered price was low, as shown in Example 13.18.

Example 13.18—Offeror must propose qualified personnel[59]

In short, offerors had to propose staff which met RFP requirements, or risk rejection of their proposals as unacceptable. Based on our review of the record, the Center reasonably concluded that the key personnel proposed by United were unacceptable because they failed to meet the RFP requirements. On this basis alone—lack of personnel who meet educational or experience requirements—the agency reasonably could view the protester's proposal as unacceptable and exclude it from the competitive range, irrespective of its lower offered price.[60]

Key personnel requirements are material requirements. A proposal that fails to meet a material requirement cannot be accepted.

Offeror Must Demonstrate Personnel Qualifications in Sufficient Detail for Evaluation

It is the offeror's responsibility to demonstrate the experience of its proposed key personnel in sufficient detail for evaluation. An offeror who fails to show exactly how its personnel meet the RFP's stated qualifications risks the rejection of its proposal. Example 13.19 shows the extent of detail required.

Example 13.19—Offeror must present sufficient detail to demonstrate the experience of proposed key personnel[61]

ESI's proposal provided almost no detail showing that its personnel had more than minimal unit conversion experience. ESI argues that a chart included in its proposal showed the unit conversion experience of its team members. However, this chart does no more than list the team members, a project (presumably a conversion project), the place where the project was performed and the date it was performed. The chart provides no information as to the named individual's function during the project. Even where ESI did attempt to provide information regarding the experience of its key personnel in performing unit conversions, it did so without providing any detail and did not show that the employee had extensive experience. For example, the resume of one key team member provides simply "[a]s Director of (a government unit) he negotiated acquisition and modification contracts for four unit conversions," and "[h]e tracked conversion programs for modifying budget allocations from the National Guard Bureau;" the resume does not provide any information about specific duties under the program, which is the kind of detail the agency required to evaluate personnel experience. Accordingly, the agency had no basis to conclude that ESI's personnel had adequate experience.

Whether proposed key personnel actually had the requisite experience is immaterial if the offeror does not clearly demonstrate the experience in its proposal. The offeror must show how the experience of the proposed personnel relates to the work to be performed under the prospective contract. Generally, a lack of detail translates into a lack of specific experience.

The Government Determines the Minimum Qualifications of Key Personal

The government has the discretion to determine its minimum needs, particularly where the requirement relates to human safety or national defense. An agency is not required to compromise its minimum needs for the purpose of maximizing competition. The fact that an offeror has difficulty in finding qualified personnel does not mean that the requirements are unduly restrictive, as shown in Example 13.20.

Example 13.20—Government determines the minimum qualifications of key personnel[62]

The determination of a contracting agency's minimum needs and the best method for accommodating them are primarily matters within the agency's discretion.[63] This discretion extends to determining whether key personnel need to have experience with work of a specific nature to be performed under the solicitation.[64] Further, where a requirement relates to human safety or national defense, as here, an agency has the discretion to define solicitation requirements to achieve not just reasonable results, but the highest possible reliability and effectiveness.[65] Where a protester challenges such requirements as unduly restrictive, we will review the record to determine whether the restrictions imposed are reasonably related to the agency's minimum needs.[66]

SA-TECH has not shown that the work required does not involve substantial integration with other Naval Air elements; that the specific experience requirements will not further that aspect of performance; or that Naval Air procedures are generic in the sense that experience with any Navy or other military activity will suffice (as SA-TECH asserts). We thus conclude that the experience requirements are reasonable.

The fact that SA-TECH has had difficulty finding personnel who can meet the Navy's qualifications, while unfortunate, is not a basis for challenging requirements such as these, which are reasonably related to the agency's needs.[67] *The agency is not required to compromise its needs for the purposes of maximizing competition.*[68]

Evaluating Differing Staffing Approaches and Associated Proposal Risk

An agency is not required to assume the best case scenario and ignore the worst case scenario when evaluating the impact of proposed staffing levels. Further, an agency is not required to sacrifice what it has determined to be the staffing necessary to achieve satisfactory, low risk performance. Example 13.21 shows that a proposal may be considered at higher risk, where the staffing is deemed to be inadequate, than a proposal offering adequate staffing. It also shows that an agency may consider a deficiency in more than one area of technical evaluation where the deficiency affects the acceptability of a proposal in more than one way (i.e., lower rating under technical for inadequate staffing and higher proposal risk for the same staffing deficiency).

Example 13.21—Evaluating differing staffing approaches and associated proposal risk[69]

Using fewer employees to perform a contract is a legitimate strategy that will reduce the cost of performance. However, such an approach also reasonably can be expected to result in more situations where an employee may not be available immediately when a task arises. While Proteus would argue that a careful, skilled management can minimize (and maybe even eliminate altogether) these situations, the agency was not compelled to assume this best case scenario, and to ignore the worst case scenario. We think the moderate risk rating reasonably reflects the evaluator's legitimate concerns regarding the worst case scenario.[70]

There is no support for Proteus's assertion that Arcata's proposed staffing was excessive. Proteus's staffing level was below the government estimate, and was specifically determined to be sufficient for Arcata's proposed approach. Proteus has not attempted to show—by means, for example, of specific references to Arcata's proposal—that the agency's determination was flawed. Further, the Air Force was not required to use an objective standard—a specific staffing level—for determining proper staffing. Indeed, the mechanical application of a government staffing estimate to determine the acceptability of proposed manning is improper, since the approach fails to take into consideration such things as unique or innovative technical approaches.[71] *Here, the Air Force did precisely what it should have done—it assessed the adequacy of each offeror's proposed staffing in light of its technical approach, finding as to both Proteus and Arcata that their staffing was acceptable for their approaches.*

Risk was an evaluation factor and the record shows that the SSA specifically considered the difference between Proteus's and Arcata's proposals, and found that Proteus's low staffing, extensive cross utilization, and the use of management personnel to perform work level tasks posed a risk to contract scheduling and could potentially have a negative effect on performance in terms of lost missions, degraded pilot training, and budget adjustments. This problem with Proteus's proposal was properly considered and reasonably affected both Proteus's proposal risk rating and its color/adjectival technical merit rating. See JB Industries[72] *(protester's proposal properly assigned both a yellow/marginal adjectival rating and a high risk rating based on inadequate staffing). See also Greenbrier Indus., Inc.*[73] *(agencies may properly consider a deficiency in more than one area of technical evaluation where the deficiency affects the acceptability of a firm's proposal in more than one way). The SSA weighed this risk, together with the overall negative impact of the inadequate staffing on the technical proposal, against Proteus's lower cost and determined that lower risk and increased staff were in the government's best interest.*[74] *While cross utilization and other staffing reduction strategies are approaches to reducing the cost of performance, the agency was not required to sacrifice what it determined was the staffing necessary for satisfactory, low risk performance; the agency's conclusion was consistent with the evaluation scheme, under which technical considerations were most important.*

Do not overlook the Comptroller General's comment that "the mechanical application of a government staffing estimate to determine the acceptability of proposed manning is improper, since such an approach fails to take into consideration such things as unique or innovative approaches." Government staffing estimates can and should be used in staffing evaluations, to point out differences between the government and an offeror with respect to staffing. These differences then should be evaluated, giving due consideration to the relationship of the offeror's proposed staffing and its proposed technical approach. Do not assume that the government's staffing estimate is the only way to perform the contract requirements and automatically downgrade any proposal that fails to meet the government estimate.

EVALUATION RESULTS MUST BE REASONABLE

The results of the initial evaluation must be reasonable. In the event of a protest, the Comptroller General will review the record to ensure that the evaluation was reasonable and consistent with the evaluation criteria. The following two examples demonstrate what happens when the agency actions are not reasonable.

Example 13.22—Evaluation results must be reasonable[75]

An unsuccessful offeror protested its exclusion from the competitive range. After reviewing the protest, the Technical Evaluation Panel (TEP) chairman reevaluated the protester's proposal and lowered its score—to zero in several places. The Comptroller General found the chairman's actions to be unjustified.

In reviewing an agency's decision to exclude a proposal from the competitive range, we look first to the agency's evaluation of proposals to determine whether the evaluation had a reasonable basis.[76] *Although we will not independently determine the merits of a proposal, in reviewing the agency evaluation, we examine the record to ensure the evaluation was reasonable and consistent with the evaluation criteria.*[77] *Such judgments by their nature are often subjective; nonetheless, the exercise of these judgments in the evaluation of proposals must be reasonable and must bear a rational relationship to the announced criteria upon which competing offerors are to be selected.*[78]

While the IRS may have considered an on-site manager to be more desirable and might have properly lowered Safeguard's score in light of this concern, since the RFP did not require an on-site project manager and since Safeguard did meet the requirement to have an on-site management official with the appropriate authority and experience, we find that the IRS had no reasonable basis for scoring Safeguard's proposal with zero points for this subfactor.[79]

In sum, the IRS had no reasonable basis to award Safeguard's proposal zero points for the organizational plan subfactor.[80] *While the IRS may have a reasonable basis to award less than a perfect score for this subfactor, we find, based on our review of Safeguard's organizational plan and IRS's evaluation of the competitive range proposals, that Safeguard's proposal could have received as many as 8 points under a proper evaluation for this subfactor.*

While we cannot say Safeguard's initial rating was not warranted, we do not find the assignment of zero points in the post-protest reevaluation was justified; we note that this type problem is easily resolvable during discussions.[81]

There were a number of problems with the evaluation of Safeguard's proposal, all of which were related to the reevaluation of Safeguard's proposal after its protest was received. If the IRS had not reevaluated the proposal and lowered the scores, the protest results might have been different because the areas in question did have weaknesses, but not enough to justify a zero score.

Example 13.23—Comparative assessment of complexity cannot be superficial[82]

While contract size may be relevant to contract complexity,[83] *evaluating "complexity" of contract requirements based on size alone, without considering such other indicators of complexity may not yield a meaningful conclusion about an offeror's probability of future success. An increase in the amount of waste to be disposed of under a contract, for example, or the number of pick-up locations are factors to be considered, but it does not follow that the complexity of the requirement has increased merely because of increases under these factors. In other words, if a contractor that has successfully disposed of 200,000 or 600,000 pounds of specific waste—as PMT has done under two prior contracts—now must dispose of 2 million pounds of waste, it may simply have to make more pick-ups using the same procedures and similar resources. On the other hand, the contractor may have to do considerably more, such as develop new procedures for handling hazardous waste with which it has no experience, provide more trucks and drivers, and coordinate the additional resources committed to the effort. The point to be made on the record is that one cannot simply say that because of the size of the contract has increased, its complexity has also increased.*

There has been absolutely no showing on this record that what is primarily a two-location requirement is more complex than the one-location requirement PMT previously serviced. In this regard. the agency's evaluation did not identify any types of waste, handling procedures, staffing requirements, or quantity and management resources which could make this RFP work meaningfully more complex than that performed under the Tooele contract. In sum, on this record, we cannot say that an agency's reliance on the size and number of waste generation locations reflects a reasonable analysis of PMT's prior contracts and, in the absence of a meaningful distinction in the complexity of this work as compared to PMT's previous work, that the agency's evaluation of PMT's past performance as "marginal" is reasonably based.

Although the SSA discounted the number of waste generation locations in increasing Moheat's past performance rating, the record shows that the SSA did not similarly consider the immateriality of those locations to PMT's rating. To the contrary, PMT's lack of experience with multiple locations under a single contract was a specific concern stated by the SSA in his selection decision.

The SSA selected Moheat for award after determining that the evaluated difference in the firms' past performance justified a more than one million dollar (49 percent) price premium. This tradeoff decision, however, is based upon an inadequate evaluation of PMT's past performance. Until there is a proper assessment of PMT's past performance, the SSA cannot reasonably determine whether Moheat's past performance is worth the 49 percent price premium.

In this case, the SSA simply accepted the evaluation results without a careful review of the basis for the evaluation results. The SSA compounded the problem by treating the offerors differently with respect to the number of waste generation locations. The fact that the basic evaluation was superficial and not well thought was overlooked by everyone involved in the evaluation. The concept that the contract was more complex, because it was bigger, was accepted without much analysis. The Comptroller General pointed out what should have been considered and why an award could not be made on the stated basis.

INCUMBENCY DOES NOT NECESSARILY PROVIDE AN UNFAIR COMPETITIVE ADVANTAGE

It is said that an incumbent has a competitive advantage because of its experience and contractual relationship with the contracting agency. This may be true—if the incumbent has performed well—but it does not relieve the incumbent of its responsibility to submit an adequate proposal. Keep in mind that evaluators may evaluate only that which is set forth in an offeror's technical proposal.

It is also alleged, on occasion, that the incumbent has an unfair competitive advantage and therefore should not receive the award. Example 13.24 explicitly sets forth the Comptroller General's view on this subject.

Example 13.24—Incumbency does not necessarily provide an unfair competitive advantage[84]

The mere existence of a prior or current contractual relationship between a contracting agency and firm does not create an unfair competitive advantage,[85] nor is an agency required to compensate for every competitive advantage inherently gleaned by a potential offeror's prior performance of a particular requirement.[86] For example, an incumbent contractor's acquired technical expertise or firsthand knowledge of the costs related to a requirement's complexity are not generally considered to constitute unfair advantages the procuring agency must eliminate.[87]

There is no basis to object to an offeror's advantage unless it is created by improper preference or other unfair action by the procuring activity.[88] On the contrary, incumbent contractors with good performance records can offer real advantages to the government and proposed strengths flowing from a firm's prior experience are proper considerations in selecting an awardee.[89] Here, the record provides no indication of improper preference or other unfair action by the agency. Moreover, the agency took reasonable measures to provide all potential offerors with all of the legally disclosable relevant information flowing from the terminated predecessor task order. Under these circumstances, there is no basis to require the exclusion of Excel from the competition because of its proposed use of I-Net as a subcontractor.

There is no basis to object to an incumbent's perceived competitive advantage unless it is created by improper preference or other unfair action by the procuring agency. Any protest on these grounds would have to specifically establish which actions were improper and why—simple allegations will not suffice.

While the government is not required to eliminate or compensate for advantages inherent to an incumbent, ensuring that other offerors have any pertinent information that can be legally disclosed may help to avoid time-consuming protests.

REJECTING AN OFFEROR FOR IMPROPRIETIES

A contracting officer may protect the integrity of the competitive procurement system by disqualifying an offeror from a competition if the firm may have obtained an unfair competitive advantage. While the firm in Example 13.25 was not rejected, the Comptroller General provides a detailed discussion of when and why an offeror could be excluded for improper actions.

Example 13.25—Rejecting an offeror for improprieties[90]

An agency's decision to exclude an offeror from a competition in order to remedy a problem related to the integrity of a particular procurement requires a balancing of competing interests set forth in the Federal Acquisition Regulation (FAR). On one hand, contracting officers are granted wide latitude in their business judgments to safeguard the interests of the United States in its contractual relationships.[91] On the other hand, the same section of FAR requires contracting officers to ensure impartial, fair, and equitable treatment of all contractors.[92]

A contracting officer may protect the integrity of the competitive procurement system by disqualifying an offeror from a competition where the firm may have obtained an unfair competitive advantage, even if no actual impropriety can be shown, so long as the determination is based on facts and not mere innuendo or suspicion.[93] We will overturn such a determination only when it is shown to be unreasonable.[94]

In reviewing the reasonableness of an exclusion decision, we examine both the nature of the information to which the offeror had access,[95] and the conditions under which the access was gained.[96] For example, we consider whether the information at issue is cost-related,[97] whether the information was proprietary,[98] or whether the information is source selection sensitive.[99] We also consider whether the information was obtained through improper business conduct,[100] or through more innocuous means, such as a Freedom of Information Act (FOIA) request pursued through appropriate agency channels.[101]

The contracting officer concluded here that IGIT's possession of the government estimate gave it an apparent competitive advantage over the other offerors, and it was IGIT's possession of this estimate that formed the basis of the decision to exclude IGIT from the procurement. While the Army concedes that the lump-sum government estimate in this case was not marked to indicate its confidential nature, it argues that the information is not normally given to offerors, and that it clearly imparts a competitive advantage when available to only one offeror. We agree. Given the obvious competitive value of an agency's estimate of the cost to perform solicited work, we find reasonable the contracting officer's determination that steps were necessary to alleviate the competitive advantage to IGIT.[102] See Holmes &

Narver Servs., Inc./Morrison-Knudson Servs., a joint venture; Pan Am World Servs., Inc., (protest against an alleged competitive advantage was sustained where awardee had access to the independent government estimate, acquisition plan, and evaluation criteria). Based on our review of the record, however, we do not find reasonable the Army's conclusion that excluding IGIT from the competition was appropriate or necessary to remedy the advantage created by its possession of this information.

Looking first at IGIT's conduct in this matter, we cannot conclude that IGIT acted improperly in obtaining the solicitation register. Exclusion of an offeror is a more reasonable sanction if the offeror's conduct in obtaining a competitive advantage was improper. See Compliance Corp.[103] (exclusion based on "industrial espionage" involving an attempt to induce an employee of a competing offeror to sell proposal information); See NFK Eng'g, Inc.,[104] (exclusion based on the hiring of the contracting officer's representative between submission of initial proposals and receipt of best and final offers, and a subsequent significant drop in that offeror's final price). In contrast, when the record did not show a likelihood of an actual impropriety or conflict of interest, we have overturned an agency's decision to exclude an offeror from the competition.[105] Here, nothing in the record before us contradicts IGIT's explanation for its possession of this document—i.e., that it was taped on the door of the laundry facility during the summer of 1995, apparently to advise IGIT of the agency's decision to resolicit for laundry services rather than exercising the existing options. We, therefore, have no basis to reject IGIT's version of events.

In addition, while we agree with the Army and the intervenors that IGIT should have returned the document to the contracting officer, IGIT's responses to the Army's questions suggest that it simply did not recognize the competitive value of the lump-sum estimate. IGIT's apparent failure to recognize the sensitive nature of the lump-sum estimate contained on the solicitation register may be explained by the fact that the figure included is essentially IGIT's bid price for the existing contract. On the continuum between improper actions such as "industrial espionage" and the more innocuous filing of a FOIA request, we consider IGIT's failure to return the page from the solicitation register closer to the latter than the former.

Finally, in considering the appropriate remedy for alleviating an offeror's competitive advantage, in a case where there is little evidence of improper activity, we view exclusion as a severe remedy that is reasonable only when other, less drastic, remedies are not practicable, or are insufficient. For example, in a case where we sustained a protest on the ground that the awardee had a conflict of interest—specifically, the awardee employed a former government official with access to restricted information (including the government estimate) to help draft the proposal,—we expressly rejected the remedy of excluding the awardee from the competition and instead recommended releasing the restricted information to all offerors and calling for a new round of proposals.[106]

Here, as in Holmes & Narver, release of the government estimate to all offerors is the reasonable remedy for the competitive advantage accruing to IGIT. Although the agency and the interested parties argue that the release of the estimate will create an auction, there are several factors to suggest that any adverse effect from the release of the estimate will be minimal, and will be consistent with our prior decisions. In this regard, we note that the government estimate in this case is considerably less detailed than the one released in Holmes & Narver, where the estimate included cost calculations for each of 27 separate functions. In addition, the estimate here conveys essentially no more information to offerors than the release of the contract price when the previous award was made to IGIT via sealed bids. Since the prior price of these services is clearly public information, and the difference between the two figures is essentially de minimus, we see no serious damage to the integrity of the procurement system from the release of this estimate. Thus under the circumstances here, eliminating IGIT's competitive advantage while retaining IGIT as an offeror outweighs the government's interest in not appearing to conduct an auction.[107]

Care should be exercised in this area. An offeror can be disqualified from a competition if it has gained an unfair competitive advantage by obtaining sensitive procurement information through improper business conduct. Exclusion, however, is a severe action that should not be taken when the record does not show a likelihood of an actual impropriety or conflict of interest. The Comptroller General suggests seeking other solutions, including the release of the sensitive information where the information was not obtained improperly. The release of the sensitive information is recommended even if doing so would create the appearance of an auction.

References

1. Quality Elevator Co., Inc., B-271899, 8/28/96, GCR 109,622.
2. MAR Inc., B-246889, 4/14/92, 92-1 CPD ¶367.
3. Whittaker Elec. Sys., B-246732.2, 9/10/92, 92-2 CPD ¶151.
4. ICONCO/NATIONAL Joint Venture, B-240119, 10/16/90, 90-2 CPD ¶296.
5. TLC Sys., B-243220, 7/9/91, 91-2 CPD ¶37.
6. Corion Corp., B-265602; B-265602.2, 12/15/95, GCR 109,267.
7. A&W Maintenance Servs., Inc., B-258293; B-258293.2, 1/6/95, 95-1 CPD ¶8.
8. Air-Flo Cleaning Systems, B-259562.2, 1/18/96, GCR 109,293.
9. Laboratory Sys. Servs., Inc., B-256323, 6/10/94, 94-1 CPD ¶359.
10. Christie Constructors, Inc., B-271759; B-271759.2, 7/23/96, GCR 109,628.
11. Bid Protest Regulations, 4 C.F.R. 21.2(a)(1) (1996); Inland Marine Indus.; Inc., B-249914; B-249918, 12/24/92, 92-2 CPD ¶442.
12. EBA Ernest Bland Assocs., B-270496, 3/13/96, GCR 109,415.
13. Caldwell Consulting Assocs., B-242767; B-242767.2, 6/5/91, 91-1 CPD ¶530.
14. Sunbelt Properties, Inc., B-245729.3, 3/12/92, 92-1 CPD ¶278.
15. Bannum, Inc., B-271076; B-271117, 5/22/96, GCR 109,497.
16. Premier Cleaning Sys., Inc., B-255815, 4/6/94, 94-1 CPD ¶241.
17. American Lawn Service, Inc., B-267715, 12/20/95, GCR 109,276.
18. DynCorp, 71 Comp. Gen. 129 (1991), 91-2 CPD ¶575.
19. Colonial Storage CO.; Paxton Van Lines, Inc., B-253501.5 et al., 10/19/93, 93-2 CPD ¶234.
20. PHP Healthcare Corp., B-251933, 5/13/93, 93-1 CPD ¶381; Binghamton Simulator Co., Inc., B-244839, 11/5/91, 91-2 CPD ¶429.
21. Allied Signal, Inc., B-272990; B-272990.2, 9/19/96, GCR 109,653.

22. Johnson Controls World Servs., Inc., 72 Comp. Gen. 91 (1993), 93-1 CPD ¶72.
23. CNA Industrial Engineering, Inc., B-271034, 6/7/96, GCR 109,530.
24. DEA Corp., Ltd., B-257185, 9/6/94, 94-2 CPD ¶95.
25. Container Prods. Corp., B-255883, 4/13/94, 94-1 CPD ¶255.
26. Id.
27. Id.
28. Logitek, Inc.,—Recon., B-238773.2; B-238773.3, 11/19/90, 90-2 CPD ¶401.
29. K. Comstock, Inc. and Liebert Federal Systems Inc., B-261711.6, 12/14/95, GCR 109,282.
30. AAI Eng'g Support, Inc., B-257857, 11/16/94, 95-1 CPD ¶2.
31. 48 Comp. Gen. 257 (1968).
32. The Saxon Corp., B-232694 et al., 1/9/89, 89-1 CPD ¶17.
33. Nationwide Roofing & Sheet Metal Co., B-234222.2, 6/22/89, 89-1 CPD ¶588.
34. Comstock Communications, Inc., B-242474, 5/6/91, 91-1 CPD ¶438; Petchem Inc., B-233006, 2/8/89, 89-1 CPD ¶126.
35. Management Plus, Inc., B-265852, 12/29/95, GCR 109,287.
36. York Sts. Corp., B-237364, 2/9/90, 90-1 CPD ¶172; Allied Management of Texas, Inc., B-232736.2, 5/22/89, 89-1 CPD ¶485; see generally, Talon Corp., B-248086, 7/27/92, 92-2 CPD ¶55.
37. Precision Elevator, Inc., B-259375, 3/20/95, 95-1 CPD ¶152.
38. Safeguard Maintenance Co., B-260983.3, 10/13/95, GCR 109,638
39. Tr. at 131-132, 135-136.
40. Tr at 145.
41. G. Marine Diesel; Phillyship, B-232619; B-232619.2, 1/27/89, 89-1 CPD ¶90; Inlingua Schools of Languages, B-229784, 4/5/88, 88-1 CPD ¶340.
42. Ogden Support Services, Inc., B-270012.2, 3/19/96, fn 2, GCR 109,436.
43. Meridian Corp., B-246330.3, 7/19/93, 93-2 CPD ¶29.
44. TDS, Inc., B-261827.3, 2/1/96, GCR 109,408.
45. Free State Reporting, Inc., B-259650, 4/4/95, 95-1 CPD ¶199, GCR 108,891.

46. Apache Enterprises, Inc., B-278855.2, 7/30/98, GCR 110,387.
47. USATREX Int'l, B-275592.2, 3/6/97, 98-1 CPD ¶99 at 9-10.
48. Professional Safety Consultants Co., Inc., B-247331, 4/29/92, GCR 106,589.
49. Informatics, Inc., B-188566, 1/20/78, 78-1 CPD ¶53.
50. Informatic Gen., B-224182, 2/2/87, 87-1 CPD ¶105; Unisys Corp., B-242897, 6/18/91, 91-1 CPD ¶577.
51. Mantech Field Eng'g, B-245886.4, 3/27/92, GCR 106496.
52. CBIS Federal, B-245844.2, 3/27/92, 92-1 CPD ¶308 at 5, 13, GCR 106,495.
53. Aerospace Design & Fabrication, Inc., B-278896.2; B-278896.3; B-278896.4; B-278896.5, 5/4/98, GCR 110,299.
54. Mantech Advanced Sys., Int'l., B-255719.2, 5/11/94, 94-1 CPD ¶326 at 5; CBIS Fed., Inc., B-245844.2, 3/27/92, 92-1 CPD ¶308 at 5, 13.
55. Mantech Advanced Sys., Int'l., supra at 5.
56. CBIS Fed., Inc., supra at 6-7, 17.
57. Ultra Tech Corp., B-230309.6, 1/18/89, 89-1 CPD ¶42 at 15.
58. Informatics, Inc., B-188566, 1/20/78, 78-1 CPD ¶53 at 13.
59. United International Investigative Services, B-265650, 12/18/95, GCR 109,268.
60. Electronics Sys., USA, Inc., B-246110, 2/14/92, 92-1 CPD ¶190; Systematic Management Servs., Inc., B-250173, 1/14/93, 93-1 CPD ¶41
61. Engineering Sys. Consult., Inc., B-271619, 7/15/96, GCR 109,556.
62. Systems Applications & Technologies, Inc., B-270672, 4/8/96, GCR 109,439.
63. Tucson Mobilephone, Inc., B-250389, 1/29/93, 93-1 CPD ¶79, aff'd, B-250389.2, 6/21/93, 93-1 CPD ¶472.
64. Marine Transport Lines, Inc., B-224480.5, 7/27/87, 87-2 CPD ¶91.
65. Tucson Mobilephone, Inc., supra; Marine Transport Lines, Inc., supra.
66. Id.
67. Industrial Maintenance Servs., Inc., B-261671, et al., 10/3/95, 95-2 CPD ¶157.

68. Harbor Branch Oceanographic Inst., Inc., B-243417, 7/17/91, 91-2 CPD ¶67.
69. Proteus Corporation; United International Engineering, Inc., B-270094; B-270094.2, 2/8/96, GCR 109,425.
70. JB Indust., B-251118.2, 4/6/93, 93-1 CPD ¶297.
71. KCA Corp., B-255115, 2/9/94, 94-1 CPD ¶94.
72. JB Industies, supra.
73. Greenbrier Indus., Inc., B-252943, 8/11/93, 93-2 CPD ¶91.
74. JWK Int'l., B-256609.4, 9/1/94, 95-1 CPD ¶66.
75. Safeguard Maintenance Co., B-260983.3, 10/13/95, GCR 109,638.
76. Intown Properties, Inc., B-249036.3, 1/15/93, 93-1 CPD ¶45.
77. A.G. Personnel Leasing, Inc., B-238289, 4/24/90, 90-1 CPD ¶416.
78. NITCO, B-246185, 2/21/92, 92-1 CPD ¶212.
79. Gardiner, Kamya & Assocs., B-258915.2, 4/12/95, 95-1 CPD ¶193; J.M. Cashman, Inc, B-233773, 4/14/89, 89-1 CPD ¶380.
80. Gardiner, Kamya & Assocs., supra; J.M. Cashman, Inc., supra.
81. Caldwell Consulting Assoc., B-242767; B-242767.2, 6/5/91, 91-1 CPD ¶530.
82. PMT Services, Inc., B-270538.2, 4/1/96, GCR 109,639.
83. Chem-Servs. of Indiana, Inc., B253905, 10/28/93, 93-2 CPD ¶262.
84. Optimum Technology, Inc., B-266339.2, 4/16/96, GCR 109,443.
85. ETEK, Inc., B-234709, 7/11/89, 89-2 CPD ¶29.
86. Versar, Inc., B-254464.3, 2/16/94, 94-1 CPD ¶230.
87. Id., Delta Oaktree Prods., B-248903, 10/7/92, 92-2 CPD ¶230; Rolm Corp., B-214052, 9/11/84, 84-2, CPD ¶280.
88. Versar, Inc., supra; Delta Oaktree Prods., supra; Rolm Corp., supra.
89. Saberliner Corp., B-242023; B-242023.2, 3/25/91, 91-1 CPD ¶326; Benchmark Sec., Inc., B-247655.2, 2/4/93, 93-1 CPD ¶133.
90. IGIT, Inc., B-271823, 8/1/96, GCR 109,591.
91. FAR 1.602-2; Compliance Corp., B-239252, 8/15/90, 90-2 CPD ¶126, aff'd. B-239252.3, 11/28/90, 90-2 CPD ¶435.

92. FAR 1.602-2(b); KPMG Peat Marwick, B-251902.3, 11/8/93, 93-2 CPD ¶272, aff'd , Agency for Int'l Development Alternatives, Inc.,—Recon., B-251902.4; B-251902.5, 3/17/94, 94-1 CPD ¶201.
93. NKF Eng'g, Inc., V. U.S., 805 F.2d (Fed. Cir. 1986); Holmes & Narver Servs., Inc.,/Morrison-Knudson Servs., Inc., a joint venture; Pan Am World Servs. Inc., B-235906; B-235906.2, 10/26/89, 89-2 CPD ¶379, aff'd, Brown Assocs. Management Servs., Inc.,—Recon., B-235906.3, 3/16/90. 90-1 CPD ¶299; Laser Power Technologies, Inc., B-233369.2, 3/13/89, 89-1 CPD ¶267.
94. Defense Forecasts, Inc., 65 Comp. Gen. 87 (1985), 85-2 CPD ¶629; Ramcor Servs. Group, Inc., B-253714, 10/7/93, 93-2 CPD ¶213.
95. Textron Marine Sys., B-255580.3, 8/2/94, 94-2 CPD ¶63.
96. KPMG Peat Marwick, supra.
97. General Elec. Gov't Servs., Inc., B-245797.3, 9/23/92, 92-2 CPD ¶196.
98. KPMG Peat Marwick, supra.
99. Holmes & Narver Servs., Inc./Morrison-Knudson Servs,. a joint venture; Pan Am World Servs., Inc., supra.
100. Compliance Corp., supra.
101. KPMG Peat Marwick, supra.
102. Holmes & Narver Servs., Inc./Morrison-Knudson Servs,. a joint venture; Pan Am World Servs., Inc., supra.
103. Compliance Corp., supra.
104. NFK Eng'g., Inc., 65 Comp. Gen. 104 (1985), 85-2 CPD ¶638.
105. KPMG Peat Marwick, supra.
106. Holmes & Narver Servs., Inc./Morrison-Knudson Servs., a joint venture; Pan Am World Servs., Inc., supra.
107. KPMG Peat Marwick, supra.; Holmes & Narver Servs., Inc./ Morrison-Knudson Servs,. a joint venture; Pan Am World Servs., Inc., supra.

CHAPTER 14

Making Award without Discussions

The concept of making an award without discussions is not new, although there has been increased emphasis on it in the past few years. The idea behind this concept is that the government should have the right to make an immediate award *when there is nothing of significance to discuss* (see Example 14.1). It should be noted that when award is to be made without discussions, the award must, in fact, be made without any written or oral discussions with any offeror. When there are things to discuss, however, such as technical deficiencies or pricing problems, discussions must be conducted with all offerors, regardless of an intention to award without discussions (see Example 14.2).

OVERVIEW OF FAR COVERAGE

The FAR does not provide extensive coverage of making award without discussions even though it favors the concept by requiring (at FAR 15.209(a)) the use of provision FAR 15.215-1, Instructions to Offerors—Competitive Acquisition (Feb 2000), in all competitive acquisitions where the government intends to make award without discussions.

The pertinent parts of this provision are in paragraph f(4), which states the following: "The Government intends to evaluate proposals and award a contract without discussions with offerors (except clarifications as described in FAR 15.306(a))," and "The Government reserves the right to conduct discussions if the Contracting Officer later determines them to be necessary." Note that the provision announces an intent to award without discussions, but reserves the right to conduct discussions if they become necessary.

FAR 15.306(a), *Clarifications and Award Without Discussions*, states that clarifications are limited exchanges between the government and offerors that may occur when award without discussions is contemplated. It also states that offerors may be permitted to clarify certain aspects of proposals (such as the relevance of past performance information), to rebut adverse past performance information to which the offeror has not previously had an opportunity to respond, or to resolve minor or clerical errors. It further states that award without discussions may be made only if the government gives notice of this intent (i.e., uses FAR provision 52.215-1) and that if the government changes its mind and decides that discussions are necessary, the rationale for doing so must be documented in the contract file.

FAR 15.306(b), *Communications with Offerors Before Establishment of the Competitive Range*, states that such communications shall not be used to cure proposal deficiencies or material omissions, materially alter the technical or cost elements of the proposal, and/or otherwise revise the proposal. The requirements of 15.306(b) would apply to any clarifications permitted under 15.306(a), including any oral presentations (see Chapter 9) that may be conducted. In short, offerors may not be permitted to revise their proposals (except for the correction of minor or clerical errors) as a result of the clarifications if the award is to be made without discussions.

The provision at 52.215-1 is safe to use in any competitive procurement because it permits the government to change its mind if the initial evaluation or clarifications indicate that there are problems that can be resolved only through discussions. Such problems include pricing uncertainties, unresolved technical questions, or any other uncertainty that might cloud a determination as to which proposal offers the best value to the government. For example, you may find that there are pricing questions that must be addressed before you can make a comparative analysis of the offered prices or determine that an offeror's proposed price is fair and reasonable. You cannot make an award unless you are sure that the price is fair and reasonable.

If you find that there are unresolved technical questions, such as deficiencies that must be corrected or significant weaknesses in what would otherwise be one of the most highly rated offers, you must hold discussions to address these issues. To make an award without discussions to an offeror whose proposal contained deficiencies would be improper. If you try to correct the deficiencies after award, not only will it cost you more, but it could serve as the basis for protests from unsuccessful offerors on the grounds that had they been allowed to correct their proposal deficiencies, the award decision would have been different.

If you intend to hold discussions, in any event, use provision 52.215-1 with Alternate 1. The pertinent part of Alternate 1 states the following: "The Government intends to evaluate proposals and award a contract after conducting discussions with offerors whose proposals have been determined to be within the competitive range."

It should be noted that if you use Alternate 1, an award without discussions is precluded, regardless of the results of the initial evaluation. This should not be cause for concern, however, if you discover after the initial evaluation that there is very little to discuss. This situation can be handled through the letter that opens the discussions and provides the discussion questions, by stating that no further discussions will be held and requesting that responses to the discussion questions be provided in the offerors' final proposal revisions (see Chapter 16). The request for final proposal revisions satisfies the requirement for discussions.

PROBLEMS IN MAKING AWARD WITHOUT DISCUSSIONS

The following examples illustrate some of the problems that can arise when making award without discussions.

Example 14.1—If there is nothing to discuss, award without discussions[1]

Here, the Navy reasonably determined that BAV's proposal contained no deficiencies and was clearly technically superior to

SWM's and AMSEC's and that this superiority clearly outweighed SWM's and AMSEC's cost advantage. Furthermore, the record supports the SSA's conclusion that while SWM and AMSEC could improve their proposals to some extent there is no reasonable possibility that either protester could improve its proposal to the level of BAV's proposal, given BAV's innovative approach which the SSA properly determined should not be disclosed to the protesters through discussions. Thus, the agency reasonably had no doubt as to which offeror represented the best value to the government. Under these circumstances, the Navy could properly make award to BAV on the basis of initial proposals. Compare Information Spectrum[2] *(discussions were not necessary where the agency reasonably could determine which offeror represented the best value to the government) with The Jonathan Corp; Metro Mach. Corp.*[3] *(discussions are necessary where the agency could not reasonably determine which proposal represented the best value to the government given the significant discrepancy between the agency's cost realism estimate and the cost proposals received and the closeness of the competition).*[4]

In Example 14.1, the agency documented a rationale establishing that one proposal clearly represented the best value to the government. In such instances, an award without discussions is proper. What happens, however, when the agency fails to provide such a rationale?

Example 14.2—If there is something to discuss, hold discussions[5]

An unsuccessful offeror protested an award without discussions. The protester was rejected because it failed to provide a line drawing and photograph required by the RFP (another offeror, who had provided the line drawing, but not the photograph was found to be acceptable). The protester's proposal was otherwise acceptable and it was the lowest priced proposal. The Comptroller General sustained the protest.

Here, we find that Agriculture improperly made award on the basis of initial proposals without conducting discussions because Wetlands's low-priced proposal was acceptable but for its failure to provide a color photograph and line drawing of phlox, and this relatively minor deficiency (an informational defect) was easily correctable through discussions.

Given the apparent ease with which Wetlands's informational deficiency could have been corrected, we think that Wetlands had a reasonable chance of being selected for award, considering its low price. Here, the photograph and line drawing were required as part of the third most important evaluation factor. More importantly, Wetlands demonstrated its technical ability and knowledge and was technically acceptable apart from the failure to provide the required photograph and drawing. Accordingly the agency could not reasonably find that award to Biotec on the basis of initial proposals would necessarily result in the lowest overall cost to the government.[6]

In Example 14.2, the agency, in order to make a quick award, chose to reject the lowest-priced offeror on the basis of a minor informational deficiency. This left the offeror who did not have any deficiencies as the lowest-priced offeror. The agency should have realized that the protester's deficiency was relatively minor and easily corrected through discussions. Since the deficiency was correctable, and the proposal was otherwise acceptable, award without discussions was improper.

Award without discussions can be made only when there is nothing to discuss that will impact the award decision. The fact that a solicitation provides the government the right to make award without discussions does not mean that the government can exercise this right arbitrarily as shown in Example 14.3

Example 14.3—The right to award without discussions is not absolute[7]

Award was made without discussions despite substantial cost differences between the proposals and with the government estimate (which was not revealed to the offerors). A computer program evaluated the costs and it was programmed to approximately "split the difference" between the government's labor hour or material cost estimate and each offeror's proposed labor hour and material cost for each of the 100 work items in a sample work package. As a result, significant adjustments were made in each cost proposal (the use of this computer program was also successfully protested; see Example 6.8 in Chapter 6). The contracting officer determined that all offers were technically equal and made award, without discussions, to the offeror with the lowest evaluated cost.

The award was protested and the agency argued, essentially, that it had the right to award without discussions because it put a provision in the RFP that said it had such a right. The agency's argument did not sway the Comptroller General, and the protest was sustained.

Pursuant to the regulations which authorize award without discussions, a contracting officer has discretion to decide in a particular procurement whether or not to hold discussions.[8] *Nonetheless, that discretion is not unfettered. Rather, the decision that discussions are not necessary must be reasonably based on the particular circumstances of the procurement, including consideration of the proposals received and the basis for the selection decision. Where, as here, the government estimate is not revealed to offerors and proposals substantially deviate from that estimate, the contracting agency should consider the possibility that the proposals may, nevertheless, be advantageous to the government and conduct discussions with the offerors concerning the discrepancy.*[9]

Our review of the record shows that the cost analyst prepared written questions for each of the offerors concerning their cost proposals. While the preparation of discussion questions, in itself, does not require that discussions be conducted, many of the questions here were in areas of the cost evaluation which the protesters have questioned and would have generated answers which could have significantly changed the nature and extent of the cost adjustments made by the Navy and therefore could have changed the outcome of the procurement.

. . . we conclude that discussions were required because of the disparity between the estimates of the government and the offerors, and because of the agency's numerous questions concerning the cost proposals.

When the initial evaluation indicates that significant pricing differences exist between the proposals and the government estimate (i.e., there are still issues to discuss before a fair and reasonable price could be determined), an award without discussions is not proper and discussions are required before a proper award can be made.

There are, however, certain things, such as the clarification and correction of clerical errors, that can be addressed prior to making an award without discussions, as shown in Example 14.4.

Example 14.4—Clarifying and correcting clerical errors is permitted prior to an award without discussions[10]

The RFP provided for award without discussions, and all offerors were notified of the proposed award to the lowest-priced offeror. Prior to the actual award, however, Miranda's Landscaping complained that its price was actually lower than the price of the proposed awardee. Upon examination, this was found to be true. Miranda had made a clerical error in pricing one item twice. When this error was corrected, Miranda's proposal was the lowest-priced proposal and Miranda became the proposed awardee.

Tony's Landscaping, who would have otherwise received the award, protested that the agency should not have corrected the proposal pricing error as a clerical error, but was required to conduct discussions with the offerors and request final proposal revisions. The Comptroller General did not agree.

Pursuant to FAR 15.306(a)(2), agencies may have limited exchanges with an offeror for the purpose of clarifying "certain aspects of proposals (e.g., the relevance of an offeror's past performance information and adverse past performance information to which the offeror has not previously had an opportunity to respond) or to resolve minor or clerical errors." These limited exchanges do not constitute discussions, which would generally require the conduct of discussions with all offerors in the competitive range.[11]

In this case, the existence of the mistake—the proposed awardee's double pricing of the same work—and the price intended was clearly established from the RFP and the proposal itself; that is, the same prices for the same work appear in both places. The protester does not contend otherwise. Thus, we agree with the agency that the proposed awardee's pricing error was a clerical error that could be corrected without conducting discussions.[12] *We also note that Miranda's Landscaping could not obtain any advantage from pricing this work twice because the contractor will only be paid for this work based on the hours actually worked at the labor rates proposed. Under these circumstances, there is simply no basis on this record to object to the agency's clarification and correction of the proposed awardee's proposal.*

As noted in Example 14.4, FAR 15.306(a)(2) also permits the clarification of certain past performance problems prior to an award without discussions. As shown in Example 14.5, however, this is not always the case.

Example 14.5—If award is to be made without discussions, an agency is not required to communicate with an offeror who failed to provide adequate past performance information[13]

An RFP called for award to be made without discussions. The RFP also instructed that past performance and experience questionnaires, copies of which were included in the solicitation package, were to be completed by the references and submitted to the offeror in sealed envelopes. The offeror was to submit these sealed envelopes with its technical proposal.

U.S. Constructors (USC) listed its references, including a brief description of the project and work performed, but told the agency that it would have to check the references because government agencies will only give past performance ratings to another agency. Although not required to, the contracting officer attempted to contact the references. She was able to contact only one, which reported that USC's performance was poor.

As a result, USC, which had the lowest price, was ranked third of four proposals, and award was made to the offeror with the technically superior proposal. USC protested that it should have been afforded an opportunity to address its past performance history prior to the award. The Comptroller General did not agree.

Federal Acquisition Regulation (FAR) 15.306(a)(2), which addresses clarifications and award without discussions, states in relevant part that "[i]f award will be made without conducting discussions, offerors may be given the opportunity to clarify certain aspects of proposals (e.g., the relevance of an offeror's past performance information and adverse past performance information to which the offeror has not previously had an opportunity to respond)." Pursuant to this provision, a contracting officer has broad discretion to decide whether to communicate with a firm concerning its performance history. We will review the exercise of such discretion to ensure that it was reasonably based on the circumstances of the procurement.[14]

Applying this standard to the circumstances of this procurement, we believe the contracting officer reasonably exercised her discretion in deciding not to communicate with USC concerning its performance history. In this regard, USC does not dispute that it failed to comply with the RFP requirement to submit completed past performance reference questionnaires in its initial proposal. USC also does not dispute that the contracting officer did more than was required by the terms of the solicitation by calling each of the firm's listed references. The record shows that the contracting officer reached one reference, who reported poor schedule compliance and project management for USC; she left a message for another USC reference that went unanswered prior to award; and she was unable to reach the last reference because the phone number provided by USC for this individual was no longer a working number. On this record, we think that in the first instance, it was incumbent upon USC to comply with the RFP requirement to furnish completed past performance reference questionnaires in its initial proposal before it could credibly argue that it was entitled to communications regarding its performance history.

Where an offeror like USC fails to satisfy its burden to submit a proposal adequate for evaluation, and where the offeror is on notice that the agency intends to make award based on initial proposals without discussions, we have no basis to object to a contracting officer's decision not to communicate with the firm regarding its performance history.[15] *Moreover, since under the RFP the technical evaluation factors were more important than price, and USC's price was not so low as to be considered advantageous, and where two reasonably priced proposals remained in the competition, the contracting officer's decision not to communicate with USC during the evaluation concerning the firm's performance history was reasonable.*[16]

It should be noted here, that if discussions were to be held and a competitive range established, USC's proposal could have been rejected for a failure to meet a material RFP requirement—that of providing the past performance questionnaires.

It should also be noted that USC was misinformed with respect to the availability of past performance ratings. FAR 42.1503(b) states that "The completed evaluation shall not be released to other than Government personnel and the contractor whose performance is being evaluated . . . ."

FAR 15.306(a)(2) states that where award will be made without discussions, offerors may be given the opportunity to clarify adverse past performance information to which the offeror has not previously had an opportunity to respond. This is discretionary and is not a requirement, as shown in Example 14.6.

Example 14.6—If award is to be made without discussions, an agency is not required to permit an offeror to rebut adverse past performance information[17]

In an RFP for a construction contract, award was to be made without discussions to the offeror whose proposal represented the best value to the government. Best value was to be determined based on a price/past performance tradeoff in which past performance was significantly more important than price. Award was made to DiCicco Contracting Company, the third lowest priced offeror, whose past performance received the highest rating. DiCicco's price was about 5 percent higher than A.G. Cullen Construction, Inc., the lowest-priced offeror, and DiCicco's past performance was rated higher than Cullen in all past performance subfactors.

Cullen protested on several grounds, one of which was that it should have been given the opportunity to address the past performance information that the agency obtained from one of its references. The reference in question rated Cullen as marginal in four of the nine areas listed under the timely performance subfactor.

The Comptroller General denied the protest.

The Federal Acquisition Regulation (FAR) 15.306(a)(2), which addresses clarifications and award without discussions, states in relevant part that where, as here, an award will be made without conducting discussions, "offerors may be given the opportunity to clarify certain aspects of proposals (e.g., the relevance of an offeror's past performance information and adverse past performance information to which the offeror has not previously had an opportunity to respond) or to resolve minor or clerical errors." Pursuant to this provision, a contracting officer has broad discretion to decide whether to communicate with a firm concerning its performance history. We will review the exercise of such discretion to ensure that it was reasonably based on the particular circumstances of the procurement.[18]

With regard specifically to clarifications concerning adverse past performance information to which the offeror has not previously had an opportunity to respond, we think that, for the exercise of discretion to be reasonable, the contracting officer must give the offeror an opportunity to respond where there clearly is a reason to question the validity of the past performance information, for example, where there are obvious inconsistencies between a reference's narrative comments and the actual ratings the reference gives the offeror. In the absence of such a clear basis to question the past performance information, we think that, short of acting in bad faith, the contracting officer reasonably may decide not to ask for clarifications.

Applying this standard here, we think that the contracting officer reasonably exercised his discretion in deciding not to communicate with Cullen regarding the adverse past performance information received from one of Cullen's references. There is nothing on the face of the reference that would create concerns about its validity. Given the permissive language of FAR 15.306(a)(2), the fact that Cullen may wish to respond to the reference does not give rise to a requirement that the contracting officer give Cullen an opportunity to do so.

Care should be exercised in this area. This decision appears to say that adverse references should be accepted at face value unless there are obvious inconsistencies and therefore there is no need to permit offerors an opportunity to rebut an adverse reference if there are no such inconsistencies. There is more to this case than that simplistic response.

Cullen received an overall rating of very good/significant confidence (DiCicco's proposal was rated as exceptional/high confidence) based on its ratings of very good in three of the subfactors, and satisfactory in the remaining two subfactors, including the one area—timely performance—in which it received the negative reference at issue. Even if Cullen's rating had been improved in that one area to the highest possible rating—exceptional—Cullen would still have scores of very good and satisfactory in the other four areas and its proposal would not have improved enough to be in line for award.

The contracting officer had no reason to consider permitting Cullen to respond to a rating that, while not the highest rating, was certainly an acceptable rating. Had Cullen received ratings that would have put it clearly out of the running, the contracting officer might have had a reason to look at the ratings more closely, but Cullen's overall rating was clearly acceptable, just not as high as DiCicco's rating. Where award without discussions is contemplated, the contracting officer is not required to seek clarifications just to see if an otherwise acceptable proposal might be made more acceptable.

The FAR's use of "may" in FAR 15.306(a)(2) clearly leaves it to the contracting officer's discretion as to whether to permit clarifications (note that FAR 15.306(b)(1), regarding communications with offerors before establishment of the competitive range uses "shall" in similar circumstances), but the exercise of that discretion is not solely related to how well a past performance questionnaire is filled out. The effect of the adverse information on the offeror's competitive position, what other references have to say about the offeror's past performance, the kinds of problems cited in the adverse performance report, and their relationship to the proposed contract performance are other factors to consider when exercising the discretion permitted by the FAR in this situation.

References

1. Southwest Marine, Inc.; American Systems Engineering Corp., B-265865 .3; B-265865.4, 1/23/96, GCR 109,335.
2. Information Spectrum Inc., B-256609.3; B-256609.5, 9/1/94, 94-2 CPD ¶251.

3. The Jonathan Corp; Metro Mach. Corp., B-251698.3; B-251698.4, 5/17/93, 93-2 CPD ¶174.
4. See also TRW, Inc., B-254045.2, 1/10/94, 94-1 CPD ¶18.
5. Wetlands Research Assoc., Inc., B-246342, 3/2/92, 92-1 CPD ¶251, GCR 106,437.
6. Hartridge Equip., B-228303, 1/15/88, 88-1 CPD ¶39, aff'd B-228303.2, 5/24/88, 88-1 CPD ¶491, GCR 101,950 (agency could not properly reject a low offer, which did not provide the required first article price, and make award to a higher-priced offeror, on the basis of initial proposals without discussions); see also JGB Enters., B-225058, 3/13/87, 87-1 CPD ¶283, GCR 100,456; AMP Inc., B-239287, 8/16/90, 90-2 CPD ¶131, GCR 104,632.
7. The Jonathan Corp.; Metro Machine Corp., B-251698.3; B-251698.4, 5/17/93, GCR 107,849.
8. FAR 15.610(a)(4).
9. Kinton, Inc., 67 Comp. Gen. 226 (1988), 88-1 CPD 112.
10. Tony's Landscaping, Inc., B-283794, 11/23/99.
11. FAR 15.306(d); Joint Threat Servs., B-278168; B-278168.2, 1/5/98, 98-1 CPD ¶18 at 12.
12. Joint Threat Servs, supra at 12-13.
13. U.S. Constructors, Inc., B-282776, 7/21/99.
14. Rohmann Servs., Inc., B-280154.2, 11/16/98, 98-2 CPD ¶134 at 8-9.
15. Booz-Allen & Hamilton, Inc., B-275934.2, 5/29/97, 97-1 CPD ¶222 at 8.
16. Rohmann, supra, at 9.
17. A.G. Cullen Construction, Inc., B-284049.2, 2/22/00.
18. Rohmann Servs., Inc., B-280154.2, 11/16/98, 98-2 CPD ¶134 at 8-9.

CHAPTER 15

Establishing the Competitive Range

Once the initial evaluation is complete and each proposal has been scored and ranked, the contracting officer must establish a competitive range composed of those offerors with whom the government will conduct negotiations. This chapter discusses the changes in the competitive range process brought about by the FAR 15 rewrite, and how this process is now accomplished. Related problems and suggested solutions are also addressed.

FAR 15 REWRITE CHANGES

The FAR 15 rewrite made two particular changes that affected the competitive range process: one changed the definition of the competitive range, thereby changing how the competitive range is determined; and the other affected communications with offerors before the determination of the competitive range.

Changed Definition of Competitive Range

The old definition of the competitive range (FAR 15.609) stated that "the competitive range shall be determined on the basis of cost or price and other factors that were stated in the solicitation and shall include all proposals that have a reasonable chance of being selected for award. When there is doubt as to whether a proposal is to be in the competitive range, the proposal should be included."

The new definition (FAR 15.306(c)(1)) states that "based on the ratings of each proposal against all evaluation criteria, the contracting officer shall establish a competitive range comprised of all of the most highly rated proposals unless the range is further reduced for purposes of efficiency pursuant to paragraph (c)(2)," and at paragraph (c)(2), "the contracting officer may determine that the number of most highly rated proposals that might otherwise be included in the competitive range exceeds the number at which an efficient competition can be conducted. Provided the solicitation notifies offerors that the competitive range can be limited for purposes of efficiency, (see 52.215-1(f)(4)), the contracting officer may limit the number of proposals in the competitive range to the greatest number that will permit an efficient competition among the most highly rated proposals."

To track how the changed definition affected the competitive range determination, it is necessary to dissect the new definition:

Based on the ratings of each proposal against all evaluation criteria, the contracting officer shall establish a competitive range . . . This is not new. Agencies must evaluate all proposals, and if discussions are to be conducted, establish a competitive range based on the ratings and relative ranking of each proposal.

The second part, however, . . . *comprised of all of the most highly rated proposals* . . . is new. Here, the definition eliminates the concept of keeping marginal proposals (proposals evaluated as being susceptible to being made acceptable) in the competitive range. Not only will marginal proposals no longer be kept in the competitive range, but acceptable, lower rated proposals will also be eliminated, because now the competitive range will be composed of only those proposals evaluated as being the most highly rated.

The next part of the definition, *unless the range is further reduced for purposes of efficiency pursuant to paragraph (c)(2),* is also new. Reducing the competitive range for purposes of efficiency is a new concept and the FAR provides little guidance on what this means. Paragraph (c)(2) states that *the contracting officer may determine that the number of most highly rated proposals that might otherwise be included in the competitive range exceeds the number at which an efficient competition can be conducted.* This appears to be aimed at those very competitive procurements where the sheer number of otherwise acceptable proposals is likely to overwhelm the resources available to conduct evaluations and unduly increase the time necessary to conduct negotiations. This is most likely to happen in the acquisition of commercial items, but could also be found in the acquisition of services, where there are many qualified contractors competing for relatively few contracts.

The FAR provides no guidance on how to determine "the number at which an efficient competition can be conducted." Some practical guidance might include the following:

- Do not use the option to reduce the competitive range for purposes of efficiency if at all possible. Rejecting some of the more highly rated proposals for the purpose of efficiency is likely to result in protests.
- Efficiency does not mean administrative convenience. You must have a better reason than that. While a safe number might be three to five, numbers alone are not sufficient, you must still be able to justify how you made the cut.
- Before you consider limiting the number of proposals, you must first complete the evaluation and determine the most highly rated proposals—keep in mind that the competitive range must include the *greatest* number that will permit an efficient competition among the most highly rated proposals.
- Examine the most highly rated proposals to see if there is a logical breakpoint in the ranking that would justify dropping some of the lower rated proposals on the basis that, considering the relative scores, they have no reasonable chance of improving their proposals enough to be in line for award. You may have already used this rationale in initially rejecting proposals from the competitive range, but the rationale might apply again for efficiency purposes.
- Look at the extent of discussions required (efficiency relates to time); the number might be limited based on how

long the discussions will take. But be careful with this one, there must be more than time alone as a justification.
- Examine the differences (points to be discussed, or strong points that influenced the scoring) between the proposals; if there is a breakpoint here, this might justify a limitation.
- Look at the pricing; this might also provide a breakpoint if there appears to be a significant difference in the pricing.
- You must document your reasoning. Such documentation can make the difference between winning and losing a protest.

The last part of the definition, *Provided the solicitation notifies offerors that the competitive range can be limited for purposes of efficiency, (see 52.215-1(f)(4)), the contracting officer may limit the number of proposals in the competitive range to the greatest number that will permit an efficient competition among the most highly rated proposals,* clearly indicates that there must be a notification of the limitation option—but there is a problem. The referenced provision, FAR 52.215-1, Instructions to Offerors—Competitive Acquisition, is used in all competitive solicitations except those for commercial items. Solicitations for commercial items use FAR 52.212-1, Instructions to Offerors—Commercial Items, instead. The aforementioned problem is this—the provision at FAR 52.215-1 informs offerors that the competitive range may be limited for reasons of efficiency, as noted in the definition—the provision at FAR 52.212-1 does not. This problem is not difficult to solve if you are aware of the problem. If your solicitation is for commercial items, simply add a provision in Section L similar to that found in 15.215-1(f)(4). This will make the required notification.

The most significant change in the new definition is the restriction of the competitive range to only the most highly rated proposals. This restriction eliminates the need to carry marginal proposals into the discussions, which is a plus for both the government and contractors. Yet, while the new definition is designed to reduce the number of offerors in the competitive range, deciding which proposals are the most highly rated may become a problem. It should also be noted that the competitive range may only be limited to the "greatest" number that will permit an efficient competition among the most highly rated proposals.

The decision as to which proposals are to be kept in the competitive range cannot be arbitrary. To decide that only the three highest scored proposals will be included in the competitive range and automatically eliminate all others would be considered to be arbitrary, particularly if there is little difference between the fourth highest proposal and the third highest proposal. There must be a supportable rationale based on the written technical narratives, not just the scores, for the competitive range determination. This also applies, as noted earlier, when reducing the competitive range for purposes of efficiency.

Changes in Communications with Offerors

Prior to the FAR 15 rewrite, communications with offerors after receipt of proposals, but before establishment of the competitive range, were discouraged and limited to clarifications for the purpose of eliminating minor irregularities, informalities, or apparent clerical mistakes in proposals. Further, a clarification by an offeror was restricted to explanations or substantiations that did not revise or modify the offeror's proposal, except for the correction of an apparent clerical mistake. Over the years, despite Comptroller General guidance, both contractor and government personnel had continuing problems distinguishing between clarifications (which did not result in revised proposals) and discussions (which did). This confusion led to premature determinations of the competitive range and protests when what the contracting officer intended to be clarifications turned out to be discussions because the offeror was afforded an opportunity to revise its proposal.

The FAR 15 rewrite changed the definitions relating to communications with offerors. Communications are now called exchanges, except in relation to communications before establishment of the competitive range—where the terms are interchangeable. This chapter addresses communications with offerors before establishment of the competitive range. Chapter 14, Award Without Discussions, addressed exchanges with offerors where award will be made without discussions (these exchanges are called clarifications—the only place where the term *clarifications* now applies). Chapter 16, Conducting Negotiations, addresses exchanges with offerors after establishment of the competitive range. These exchanges are called discussions (which is not new).

FAR 15.306(b) refers to communications as exchanges between the government and offerors, after receipt of proposals, leading to the establishment of the competitive range. It limits such communications to (1) those offerors whose past performance is the determining factor preventing them from being placed in the competitive range, but restricts such communications to exchanges about adverse past performance information to which the offeror has not had a prior opportunity to respond, and (2) offerors whose exclusion from, or inclusion in, the competitive range is uncertain for other reasons.

Communications About Past Performance

The FAR *requires* communications regarding adverse past performance information where such information might disqualify an offeror from the competitive range and the offeror has not had a prior opportunity to respond to such information. This wording, however, may cause a certain amount of confusion. The FAR does not explicitly define "adverse," but for purposes of determining the competitive range it is clear that the past performance information must be so negative that the offeror might not be included in the competitive range. What about an offeror whose proposal will be included in the competitive range despite some negative past performance information? Do you address this information with the offeror?

As discussed in Chapter 12, it is good policy to permit offerors to rebut adverse past performance information because it provides insight as to the validity of the adverse information and it could be important to the overall evaluation of the offeror's proposal. However, to keep a proper balance between communications before establishment of the competitive range and discussions after establishment of the competitive range and to move the process efficiently, the following is suggested:

- Before establishment of the competitive range, conduct communications regarding adverse past performance information with only those offerors who might be disqualified from the competitive range because of the adverse information.
- For offerors to be included in the competitive range despite some adverse past performance information, identify the adverse information as a significant weakness to be addressed during discussions.

These actions will expedite the determination of the competitive range by reducing the extent of the communications before establishment of the competitive range, but ensure equity by providing the other offerors with the same opportunity to discuss adverse past performance information during discussions.

Communications for Other Reasons

You can conduct communications with other offerors whose inclusion in the competitive range is uncertain by addressing issues that must be explored to enhance government understanding or permit a reasonable interpretation of the proposal.

However, it should be noted that while the FAR *requires* communications regarding past performance, it does not require communications for other reasons. This can be a "tricky" area. While the FAR permits such communications to address ambiguities in the proposal or other concerns (e.g., perceived deficiencies, weaknesses, errors, omissions, or mistakes), it also states that "such communications shall not be used to cure proposal deficiencies or material omissions, materially alter the technical or cost elements of the proposal and/or otherwise revise the proposal. Such communications may be considered in rating proposals for the purpose of establishing the competitive range."

The FAR wording here is unfortunate. Communications about perceived deficiencies, weaknesses, errors, and omissions have the potential effect of bringing back the pre-FAR 15 rewrite problems of distinguishing between clarifications and discussions. While problems in these areas can be explained, generally they can be fixed only through a proposal revision—which is not allowed at this point. So why bring it up at all? What is the likelihood that deficiencies and weaknesses of a nature that makes inclusion in the competitive range uncertain could be "explained away" without the need for a proposal revision and the proposal would be among those most highly rated?

The FAR provides the contracting officer with an option of communicating about problems other than past performance; but such communications are not required. You would be well advised to forgo that option except in the most unusual of circumstances.

Summary of the Changes

The competitive range now consists of only the most highly rated proposals. If the number of highly rated proposals is too great, the contracting officer has the option of further limiting the competitive range for purposes of efficiency. This option should be exercised judiciously, and if used, the rationale for the limitation should be well documented.

If adverse past performance information might disqualify the offeror from the competitive range and the offeror has not had a prior opportunity to respond to such information, communications must be conducted with the offeror before the establishment of the competitive range. This is a requirement. Contracting officers also have the option of communicating with offerors whose inclusion in the competitive range is uncertain because of reasons other than past performance where such communications are deemed necessary to determine whether a proposal should be placed in the competitive range. This option should be exercised judiciously, and, if used, you must ensure that the offeror understands that while it is invited to make explanations, its proposal may not be revised in any manner whatsoever.

MAKING THE COMPETITIVE RANGE DETERMINATION

After completion of the initial evaluation, the contracting officer receives the initial evaluation report showing the rating, or score, of each proposal arrayed according to their relative standing or ranking. Documentation consisting of the individual technical narratives and scoring by each evaluator, the consensus narrative supporting the evaluation results, and the proposed discussion questions must accompany the evaluation report. These documents serve as the basis for the competitive range determination. Keep in mind that the competitive range determination is based on the supporting documentation, not the scores assigned, as shown in Example 15.1.

Example 15.1—Decisions are based on the supporting documentation, not the scores or ratings[1]

While adjectival ratings and point scores are useful as guides to decision-making, they generally are not controlling, but rather must be supported by documentation of the relative differences between proposals, their weaknesses and risks, and the basis and reasons for the selection decision.[2]

While the Comptroller General decision in Example 15.1 addressed the selection decision, the same reasoning applies to the determination of the competitive range. In the past, when doubtful proposals were to be included in the competitive range, competitive range decisions were often based primarily on the ratings and ranking of the proposals and adequate documentation was often lacking. This was not usually a problem, however, because the emphasis was on expanding the competitive range, and only the clearly unacceptable proposals were rejected. Even then, however, it was not permissible to use predetermined cut-off scores (a score of 65 is in, but a score of 64 is not) to determine the competitive range. Now, with the competitive range to include only the most highly rated proposals, the supporting documentation is even more important to enable the contracting officer to distinguish the most highly rated proposals from the other acceptable proposals.

While the definition of the competitive range has changed significantly, the process of making the competitive range determination remains pretty much the same. Determining the competitive range is basically a process of elimination. Proposals are rejected until all that is left are the most highly rated proposals. Those proposals comprise the competitive range.

Generally, the contracting officer first examines the ratings and rankings to find those proposals at the lowest end of the ranking. Then the evaluation narratives for those proposals are examined to determine why they were ranked so low. The contracting officer must reject those proposals that are so deficient that it would take major revisions, tantamount to a new proposal, to correct the problems, as shown in Example 15.2.

Example 15.2—Reject proposals requiring major revisions[3]

In reviewing challenges to the exclusion of a proposal from the competitive range, we will not reevaluate the proposal; rather, our review is limited to determining whether the evaluation was reasonable and consistent with the RFP's evaluation scheme.[4] Agencies properly may eliminate a proposal from the competitive range where the proposal would require major revision to become acceptable.[5]

This ruling is one of a number of long-standing and still applicable Comptroller General rulings stating that if meaningful discussions could not be conducted unless the offeror first submitted a substantially revised proposal, tantamount to a new proposal, the proposal must be rejected—because an offeror may not submit a new proposal after the time set for the receipt of proposals. In addition, a proposal that is seriously deficient is not likely to be among the most highly rated proposals. Therefore, seriously deficient proposals are the first to be rejected.

The contracting officer also examines the pricing to identify any proposals whose price is so far out of line with the other proposals that any significant price change would also require corresponding technical changes, tantamount to the submission of a new proposal. The reason for rejection here is not the out of line pricing, but the substantial technical changes that would be required if the pricing were to be changed.

The remaining proposals are considered to be technically acceptable, but the review is not yet complete. The lower rated technically acceptable proposals are now examined to identify those proposals that, when compared to other higher rated proposals, do not have a reasonable chance for award. These are those proposals that even with revisions, are not likely to be improved enough to be in reasonable competition with the other higher rated proposals, as shown in Examples 15.3 and 15.4.

Example 15.3—Reject otherwise acceptable proposals that have no chance of award when compared to other higher rated proposals #1[6]

The technical evaluation of a proposal is based on information submitted in it, and an offeror runs the risk of having its proposal downgraded and rejected if the proposal submitted is inadequately written.[7] Accordingly, to the extent that the protester is arguing that the evaluators did not understand the resumes and that the Navy could have resolved any questions in additional discussions, HSQ, like all offerors, was required to demonstrate the merits of its proposal within the four corners of the proposal and ran the risk of rejection if it failed to do so.[8]

The stated basis for the exclusion of HSQ's proposal was the agency's determination that, overall, it was not among the most highly rated offers being considered for award. An agency may properly determine whether to include a proposal within the competitive range by comparing the proposal evaluation scores and the proposal's relative standing. A proposal that is technically acceptable need not be included in the competitive range when, relative to other acceptable offers, it is determined to have no reasonable chance of being selected for award.[9] *We will not disturb a determination to exclude a proposal from the competitive range unless the record indicates the determination was unreasonable.*[10]

While the Comptroller General indicated that competitive range decisions can be made by comparing evaluation scores and relative ranking, this holds true only if written technical narratives support the scores, as shown in Example 15.1.

Example 15.4—Reject otherwise acceptable proposals that have no chance of award when compared to other higher rated proposals #2[11]

We do not read the revised language to require agencies to retain in the competitive range a proposal that is not among the most highly-rated ones or that the agency otherwise reasonably concludes has no realistic prospect of award.[12] *Here the record shows that while Matrix submitted an acceptable proposal, it was not included in the competitive range because the Matrix proposal did not address the capability criteria as well as the three competitive range offerors and, as a result, was not among the most highly rated proposals.*

The revised language referenced above is found at FAR 15.306(c)(1). Generally, the otherwise acceptable proposals to be eliminated are identified by examining the array of scores to find a breakpoint in the scoring that shows a significant difference between the higher rated and lower rated acceptable proposals. The evaluation narratives are then examined to determine why these proposals were scored lower than the others, and if the proposals could be improved enough through discussions to realistically be considered as one of the highest rated proposals. If the proposals could not be improved sufficiently, they are rejected.

Before the FAR 15 rewrite, the proposals still under consideration at this point would be considered to be within the competitive range. Even now, if all of the remaining proposals are ranked closely, and you are satisfied with the number of proposals left, you may consider them all as within the competitive range.

Scoring disparities, however, might still exist among the remaining proposals. You have a choice at this point—you may consider all of the remaining proposals to be within the competitive range or you may decide that further examination is required to determine the "most highly rated" of the remaining proposals. The first review of the "acceptable" proposals culled out those clearly out of the competition because of their ranking relative to the other, higher scored proposals. This review would examine the next echelon of lower ranked proposals and would require a re-examination of the evaluation narratives to determine if the deficiencies and weaknesses in any of these proposals might warrant rejection based on the fact that, even with revisions, they have no reasonable chance of receiving the award. If you do this, you must ensure that you fully document your rationale for rejection because protests are likely to result if you cannot convince the offerors that the rejections were soundly based.

You also have the option of limiting the number of the most highly rated proposals for reasons of efficiency by simply rejecting the lower rated proposals until you reach the "magic number" required for an efficient procurement. You must keep in mind, however, that the FAR states that the limited number shall be the *greatest number* that will permit an efficient competition among the most highly rated proposals. Frankly, if you cannot justify rejecting a proposal on the basis that it has no reasonable chance for award, you would be better off dealing with a larger than desired competitive range rather than arbitrarily rejecting otherwise acceptable proposals. Arbitrary actions generate protests and protest resolution, even if the government prevails, is likely to take longer than it would take to negotiate with a few extra offerors.

What happens if you complete the process of determining the competitive range and only one proposal is left? Are you in trouble? Not necessarily, according to the Comptroller General decision in Example 15.5.

Example 15.5—A competitive range of one is OK if no other proposal has a reasonable chance for award[13]

SDS seems to argue that, no matter how low its proposal's evaluation rating relative to Tiger's, the agency was required to retain its proposal in the competitive range since it was the second-highest rated. We find no merit in this argument, which is apparently based on the recent rewrite of Part 15 of Federal Acquisition Regulation (FAR) that changed the language governing competitive range determinations. The earlier language FAR 15.609(a) (June 1997), stated that the competitive range "shall include all proposals that have a reasonable chance of being selected for award" and that "[w]hen there is doubt as to whether a proposal is in the competitive range, the proposal should be included." The current language, which governs this procurement, states, "based on the ratings of each proposal against all evaluation criteria, the contracting officer shall establish a competitive range comprised of all of the most highly rated proposals, unless the range is further reduced for purposes of efficiency pursuant to paragraph (c)(2) of this section.[14] We do not read the revised language to require agencies to retain in the competitive range a proposal that the agency reasonably concludes has no realistic prospect of award, even if that proposal is, as here, the second highest-rated proposal.

The explanatory preamble published at the time the final version of the FAR Part 15 rewrite was issued to make clear that the intent of the revised language was to permit a competitive range more limited than under the prior "reasonable chance of being selected for award" standard. That preamble states that the drafters had elected to require contracting officers to retain in the competitive range "only" the most highly rated offers rather than include in that range the potentially broader range of proposals that could be viewed as having a reasonable chance of award.[15] Specifically, the preamble stated that the new language would ensure that offerors with little probability of success . . . are advised early on that their competitive position does not merit additional expense in a largely futile attempt to secure the contract."

Accordingly, we conclude that the Part 15 rewrite does not require that agencies retain in the competitive range a proposal that is determined to have no reasonable prospect of award simply to avoid a competitive range of one. We have long held that there is nothing inherently improper in a competitive range of one,[16] *and we do not view the Part 15 rewrite as effecting a change in that regard; conducting discussions and requesting BAFOs from an offeror with no reasonable chance of award would benefit neither the offeror nor the government. See 62 Fed. Reg. 51,226 (retaining marginal offers in the competitive range imposes additional and largely futile effort and cost on government and industry).*

The key here, of course, is to be able to clearly establish that the other proposals have no chance of award in any event. To do this your decisions must be fully documented and clearly show that the rejections were warranted.

Generally, proposals are rejected from the competitive range because (1) the offeror has failed to provide information required by the RFP, (2) informational deficiencies indicate that the offeror does not understand the requirements, and (3) the offeror has merely parroted back the language of the solicitation. In each of these instances, the lack of sufficient information inhibited the government's ability to determine that the proposals represented a reasonable chance of successful contract performance. It is the offeror's responsibility to submit an initial proposal that meets the requirements of the RFP and demonstrates an ability to successfully perform the contract. A failure to do this warrants proposal rejection, as shown in Example 15.6.

Example 15.6—Offeror is responsible for submitting an adequate proposal[17]

An offeror must submit an initial proposal that is adequately written and that affirmatively presents its merits, or run the risk of having its proposal rejected as technically unacceptable.[18] *Generally, offers that are technically unacceptable as submitted and would require major revisions to become acceptable are not required to be included in the competitive range.*[19] *Procuring agencies may reasonably find a proposal to be unacceptable based on the offeror's general statements that it will comply with those requirements rather than providing a sufficiently detailed explanation of how the requirements will be performed.*[20] *In reviewing whether a proposal was properly rejected as technically unacceptable for informational deficiencies, we examine the record to determine, among other things, whether the RFP called for detailed information and the nature of the informational deficiencies—for example, whether the deficiencies tend to show that the offeror did not understand what it would be required to do under the contract.*[21] *Although we will closely scrutinize an agency's decision, such as this one, which results in a competitive range of one, we will not disturb such a determination absent a clear showing that it was unreasonable.*[22]

Once the competitive range is established, the contracting officer opens discussions with those offerors in the competitive range. It should be noted, however, that the competitive range may be redetermined, if during the discussions, an offeror's response to discussion questions reveals that its proposal will not be corrected sufficiently and that the offeror no longer has a reasonable chance for award, as noted in Example 15.7.

Example 15.7—Competitive range may be redetermined during discussions[23]

The offeror has the burden of submitting an adequately written proposal and proposal revisions for the agency to evaluate. . . . If the agency's evaluation is reasonable, there is nothing improper in an agency's making more than one competitive range determination and dropping a firm from further consideration once it becomes evident that the offeror no longer has a reasonable chance of receiving the award.[24]

The fact that a proposal may be rejected after the establishment of the competitive range does not diminish the need to make a careful and fully documented determination of the competitive range. The concept of keeping a doubtful proposal (susceptible to being made acceptable) is no longer valid.

Cost, or price, must be considered in all evaluations, including the initial evaluation. At this point in the competition, however, pricing is still tentative, and often changes as a result of discussions. During the initial evaluation, cost analysis and cost realism analysis can be used to develop an "evaluated" price, but it would not be wise to reject a proposal in the initial evaluation because its evaluated price was too high, or too low, unless it can be shown that changes to the price would require corresponding changes to the technical approach, tantamount to the submission of a new proposal.

The key here is that there must be a mechanism for the evaluation of an offeror's pricing in the initial evaluation that will be reflected in an offeror's ranking and rating. It should be noted, however, that the results of cost analysis and cost realism analysis are most effectively applied after the final evaluation when tradeoffs can be made based on an offeror's final proposal revision. It should also be noted that a proposal that is technically unacceptable must be rejected regardless of the pricing (see Example 15.8).

One area in which the evaluation of pricing presents a challenge is in indefinite-delivery, indefinite-quantity service contracts where the work to be required can only be described in very general terms. It is difficult to calculate accurate pricing when the work to be done cannot be described.

One approach to the evaluation of pricing is to use historical information from past contracts of the same or similar nature to estimate the types and quantities of labor and materials that would be required, incorporate these estimates into the RFP, and require offerors to submit proposals based on these estimates for evaluation purposes. This permits the agency to see the effect, in the context of the historical ordering pattern, of offerors' differing cost elements, such as labor rates. One problem with basing the cost or price evaluation on estimated quantities of labor hours for each labor category is that it fails to take into account differences in offerors' technical approaches. This problem, however, could be resolved during discussions, assuming that the particular offeror's proposal is among the most highly rated.

Another approach is to use sample task orders (representative of the type of work to be done) to assess the probable cost of competing offerors in light of both the offerors' differing technical approaches and their labor rates. The problem here is the artificial nature of using hypothetical sample task orders to evaluate competing proposals.

Actually, these approaches could be combined to cover both pricing and technical understanding. Use the historical labor categories and estimated labor hours to fix the pricing and the sample task orders to see how the offerors would staff up for the technical aspects of the sample task (i.e., technical understanding).

In any event, cost or price must be considered in the initial evaluation and the establishment of the competitive range. The following two cases demonstrate what might happen if this is not done properly.

Example 15.8—Cost or price must be considered #1[25]

In a solicitation for the award of three to five indefinite-delivery, indefinite-quantity, cost reimbursement advisory and assistance support services contracts, cost was an unweighted evaluation factor to be evaluated for reasonableness and appropriateness of proposed rates.

An offeror excluded from the competitive range protested that the evaluation of its proposal was unreasonable, and therefore, the competitive range determination, which was based on that evaluation, was flawed.

There were a number of problems with the evaluation, and the protest was sustained. The following excerpt from the Comptroller General decision addresses the cost evaluation.

The likelihood that SCIENTECH would have been included in the competitive range is strengthened by the fact that the SEP failed to consider the offerors' relative costs when making the competitive range determination. While a technically acceptable proposal may be eliminated where it does not have a reasonable chance for award,[26] FAR 15.609(a) requires that the competitive range be determined on the basis of cost or price as well as other factors that were stated in the solicitation and that, when there is doubt as to whether a proposal has a reasonable chance of being selected for award, the proposal should be included in the competitive range. Cost or price must be considered as a factor; it is improper to exclude an offeror from the competitive range solely on the basis of technical considerations, unless the proposal is technically unacceptable.[27]

The failure to consider cost in competitive range and award decisions is improper. Agencies must consider cost to the government in evaluating competing proposals.[28] *Agencies have considerable discretion in determining the appropriate methods for taking cost into account; they do not have the discretion, however, not to consider cost at all, as happened here.*[29]

The record shows that cost/rate proposals were evaluated for reasonableness, but no comparison of the offerors' costs was made as part of the competitive range determination. This was apparently because the SEP was unable to develop most probable cost estimates for the competing proposals, since, as the SEP noted, the RFP did not include what the SEP referred to as "artificial methods" such as sample tasks or estimates of the quantities of labor hours to be ordered under each labor category.

As shown by the FAR reference quoted above, this decision was rendered before the FAR 15 rewrite. The requirement noted in the FAR reference has not changed; however, FAR 15,306(c), Competitive Range, states that agencies shall evaluate all proposals in accordance with 15.305(a), and 15.305(a)(1) requires the evaluation of cost or price.

This decision turned on the fact that costs were evaluated for reasonableness, but there was no comparative assessment of costs when making the competitive range decision—this was the fatal error.

Example 15.9—Cost or price must be considered #2[30]

In an RFP for fixed-price indefinite-quantity contracts for general repair and alteration services, the only pricing information that the RFP required for evaluation purposes was the offeror's mark-up rates, which were to include all contractor overhead, G&A costs, bonds, insurance, other indirect costs, profits, and other fees that the offeror will use on a "not to exceed" basis.

An offeror protested on the basis that it was defective because the RFP's evaluation scheme did not include evaluation of price or cost to the government.

The agency responded that the evaluation of the proposed mark-up rates was sufficient and the evaluation of price and other factors would take place when the individual delivery orders were completed.

The Comptroller General did not agree and sustained the protest.

Cost or price to the government must be included in every RFP as an evaluation factor, and agencies must consider cost or price to the government in evaluating competitive proposals.[31] *While it is up to the contracting agency to decide upon the appropriate method for evaluation of cost or price in each procurement, an agency must use an evaluation method that provides a basis for a reasonable assessment of the cost of performance under the competing proposals.*[32] *Here, we conclude that GSA's methodology provides no reasonable basis to compare the cost of the competing proposals.*

The agency correctly notes that there will be a price competition that will take into account the competing firms' differing number and mix of labor hours and material costs, whenever individual task orders are competed. That competition, however, will not include firms whose proposals are not selected for an "umbrella" contract in the competition at issue in this protest. The RFP anticipates that the agency will award only three umbrella contracts (one of which will be to an 8(a) firm), which will entitle only the firms holding those contracts to compete for the individual task orders. The statutory requirement that cost or price be considered in the evaluation and selection of proposals for award is not satisfied by the promise that cost or price will be considered later, during the award of individual task orders. Instead, the statutory requirement means that the agency cannot eliminate a proposal from consideration for award of an umbrella contract without taking into account the relative cost of that proposal to the government.[33]

The question presented here is whether GSA's consideration of the mark-up rate alone, without taking into account potential differences in offerors' labor rates, number of hours, mix of labor categories, and material costs, represents adequate consideration of a proposal's cost to the government, as the agency contends. We conclude that it does not.

Essentially, this case, a post-FAR 15 rewrite decision, repeats that cost or price must be considered in the initial evaluation. Generally, what is evaluated is the "evaluated" cost or price, rather than the proposed cost or price. The RFP should provide for a method of evaluating the estimated cost/price that will permit both the assessment of the reasonableness of the pricing and the comparison of the prices.

SUMMARY

The following should be considered when establishing the competitive range:

- A proposal is rejected if it is so technically inferior that meaningful discussions could not be conducted unless the offeror first submitted a substantially revised proposal, tantamount to a new proposal.
- A proposal is rejected if it is so out of line in price that it could be brought in line only by making technical changes that would substantially revise the proposal, making the revisions tantamount to the submission of a new proposal.
- A proposal is rejected, even if it is otherwise acceptable, if the offeror's low score, in comparison to the array of scores of other offerors, demonstrates that the proposal does not have a reasonable chance for award. These are what would otherwise be called marginal proposals.
- Since the competitive range will consist of only the most highly rated proposals, a final cut must be made among the remaining proposals to eliminate those proposals that are acceptable, but not the most highly rated.

Offerors whose proposals have been rejected from the competitive range must be promptly notified and afforded an opportunity for a pre-award debriefing. Chapter 20 addresses debriefings.

The FAR 15 rewrite made significant changes in the determination of the competitive range. Unfortunately, the rewrite was lacking in guidance and definition, ostensibly to provide contracting officer flexibility. Thus, the Comptroller General and the Federal courts are left the job of providing the needed guidance through their decisions on contractor protests. Unfortunately it will take a number of years for the cases to come up and even longer for the decisions to be translated into the FAR or other regulations.

In time, however, these changes will make the competitive process more efficient by allowing the government to eliminate proposals, based on the initial evaluation, that do not stand a reasonable chance of award. This benefits contractors because it saves offerors the time and expense of remaining in a competition when they do not have a reasonable chance for award. It also encourages offerors to make their best proposal first and not to wait until discussions to improve their technical proposals and pricing because (1) there may be no discussions at all, and (2) they could be eliminated from the competitive range if their proposals are not among the most highly rated.

References

1. Century Environmental Hygiene Inc., B-279378, 6/5/98, GCR 110,325.
2. Engineering and Computation Inc., B-261658, 10/16/95, 95-2 CPD ¶176 at 3.
3. Engineering Sys. Consult. Inc., B-271619, 7/15/96, GCR 109,556.
4. International Resources Corp., B-259992, Apr 14, 1995, 95-1 CPD ¶200.
5. W.N. Hunter & Assocs.; Cajar Defense Support Co., B-237259; B-237259.2, 1/12/90, 90-1 CPD ¶52.
6. HSQ Technology, B-279707, 7/9/98, GCR 110,349.

7. Research Analysis and Maintenance, Inc., B-242836.4, 10/29/91, 91-2 CPD ¶387 at 5.
8. Hornet Joint Venture, B-258430.2, 1/27/95, 95-1 CPD ¶55 at 7.
9. Coe-Truman Techs., Inc., B-257480, 9/12/94, 94-2 CPD ¶136 at 3.
10. Intown Properties, Inc., B-250392, 1/18/93, 93-1 CPD ¶73 at 3.
11. Matrix General, Inc., B-282192, 6/10/99.
12. SDS Petroleum Prods., Inc., B-280430, 9/1/98, 98-2 CPD ¶59 at 5, GCR 110,405.
13. SDS Petroleum Products, Inc., B-280430, 9/1/98, 98-2 CPD ¶59, GCR 110,405.
14. FAR 15.306(c)(1) (FAC 97-02).
15. 62 Fed. Reg. 51,224, 51,226 (1997).
16. Cobra Techs, Inc., B-272041; B-272041.2, 8/20/1996, 96-2 CPD ¶73 at 3.
17. Dynamic Marketing Services, Inc., B-279697, 7/13/98, GCR 110,418.
18. Defense Group, Inc., B-253795, 10/25/93, 94-1 CPD ¶196 at 5.
19. Engineering & Computation, Inc., B-258728, 1/31/95, 95-1 CPD ¶155 at 3.
20. Tri-Services, Inc., B-256196, 9/30/94, 94-2 CPD ¶121 at 4.
21. Engineering & Computation, Inc., B-258728, 1/31/95, 95-1 CPD ¶155 at 3.
22. Native Am. Consultants, Inc.; ACKCO, Inc., B-241531, 2/6/91, 91-1 CPD ¶129 at 5-6.
23. Applied Companies, B-279811, 7/24/98, GCR 110,388.
24. Este Medical Servs. Inc., B-261845.2, 9/29/95, 95-2 CPD ¶240 at 4.
25. SCIENTECH, Inc., B-277805.2, 1/20/98, 98-1 CPD ¶33.
26. Techniarts Eng'g, B-271509, 7/1/96, 96-2 CPD ¶1 at 3-4.
27. S&M Property Management, B-243051, 6/28/91, 91-1 CPD ¶615 at 4; HCA Gov't Servs., Inc., B-224434, 11/25/86, 86-2 CPD 611 at 3-4.
28. 41 U.S.C. sec. 253a(b)(1) (1994).
29. Health Servs., Int'l, Inc.; Apex Envt'l., Inc., B-247433; B-247433.2, 6/5/92, 92-1 CPD ¶493 at 4.

30. S.J. Thomas Co., Inc., B-283192, 10/20/99.
31. 41 U.S.C. sect. 253a(c)(1)(B) (1994); FAR 15-304(c)(1).
32. Health Servs., Int'l, Inc.; Apex Envt'l., Inc., B-247433; B-247433.2, 6/5/92, 92-1 CPD ¶493 at 4; KISS Eng'g Corp., B-221356, 5/2/86, 86-1 CPD ¶425 at 4.
33. SCIENTECH, Inc., B-277805.2, 1/20/98, 98-1 CPD ¶33 at 7.

CHAPTER 16

Conducting Negotiations

Negotiations are exchanges, in either a competitive or sole source environment, between the government and offerors, that are undertaken with the intent of allowing the offeror to revise its proposal.

The FAR 15 rewrite made significant changes in the wording of the FAR coverage of the conduct of negotiations, but made relatively few changes in how negotiations are to be conducted.

OVERVIEW OF CURRENT COVERAGE

When negotiations are conducted in a competitive acquisition, they take place after establishment of the competitive range and are called discussions [FAR 15.306(d)].

Discussions are tailored to each offeror's proposal, and should be conducted by the contracting officer with each offeror in the competitive range [15.306(d)(1)]. The primary objective of discussions is to maximize the government's ability to obtain best value, based on the requirement and the evaluation factors set forth in the solicitation [15.306(d)(2)].

The contracting officer shall indicate to, or discuss with, each offeror still being considered for award significant weaknesses, deficiencies, and other aspects of its proposal (e.g., cost, price, technical approach, past performance, terms and conditions) that could, in the opinion of the contracting officer, be altered or explained to enhance materially the proposal's potential for award. The scope and extent of discussions are a matter of the contracting officer's judgment [15.306(d)(3)].

In discussing other aspects of the proposal, the government may (if the RFP stated that evaluation credit would be given for technical solutions exceeding any mandatory minimums) negotiate with offerors for increased performance beyond the mandatory minimums, and if an offeror has exceeded any mandatory minimums (in ways not integral to the design) the government may suggest that the proposal would be more competitive if the excesses were removed and the offered price decreased [15.306(d)(3)].

If, after discussions have begun, an offeror is no longer considered to be among the most highly rated offerors being considered for award, that offeror may be eliminated from the competitive range whether or not all material aspects of the proposal have been discussed, or whether or not the offeror has been afforded an opportunity to submit a proposal revision [15.306(d)(4)]. If an offeror's proposal is eliminated or otherwise removed from the competitive range, no further revisions to that offeror's proposal shall be accepted or considered and the offeror shall be promptly so notified [15.307(a)]. The notification shall also state the basis for the rejection [15.503(a)] and how the offeror may request a debriefing before award [15.505].

Government personnel involved in the acquisition (Note: not just those involved in discussions) shall not engage in conduct that [15.306(e)] includes the following:

(1) Favors one offeror over another.
(2) Reveals an offeror's technical solution, including unique technology, innovative and unique uses of commercial items, or any other information that would compromise an offeror's intellectual property to another offeror.
(3) Reveals an offeror's price without that offeror's permission. However, the government may inform an offeror that its price is too high or too low, and reveal the results of the analysis supporting that conclusion. The government may also indicate to all offerors the cost or price that the government's price analysis, market research, and other reviews have identified as reasonable. It should be noted, however, that the release of

this information is discretionary; the contracting officer is not required to release such information.

(4) Reveals the names of individuals providing reference information about an offeror's past performance.

(5) Knowingly furnishes source selection information.

Proposal revisions are changes to proposals after discussions. The contracting officer may request or allow proposal revisions to clarify and document understandings reached during negotiations [15.307(b)]. At the conclusion of discussions, each offeror still in the competitive range shall be given an opportunity, in writing, to submit a final proposal revision. The letter request for final proposal revisions must establish a common cut-off date for receipt of the final proposal revisions and advise offerors that the final proposal revisions shall be in writing and that the government intends to make award without obtaining further revisions.

Terminology

The FAR 15 rewrite made some changes to avoid confusion in terminology:

1. *Clarifications* are limited exchanges, between the government and offerors, that may occur when award without discussions is contemplated. These exchanges may only be used to clarify certain aspects of a proposal or to resolve minor or clerical errors. The term *clarifications* applies *only* when award will be made without discussions, therefore, there can be no proposal revisions. [15.306(a)].
2. *Communications* are exchanges between the government and offerors, after receipt of proposals, leading to the establishment of the competitive range. These exchanges may not be used to materially alter or revise proposals [15.306(b)].
3. *Negotiations* are exchanges between the government and offerors that are undertaken with the intent of al-

lowing the offeror to revise its proposal. When negotiations are conducted in a competitive acquisition, they take place after establishment of the competitive range and are called *discussions* [FAR 15.306(d)].

In the past, these terms were used more or less interchangeably in the conduct of negotiations. This caused misunderstandings and protests, often with respect to when proposal revisions might be submitted. Now these terms and their relation to proposal revisions should be clear.

Bargaining

The FAR (before and after the FAR 15 rewrite) indicates that negotiations may include bargaining (persuasion, alteration of assumptions and positions, give-and-take) and may apply to price, schedule, technical requirements, type of contract, or other terms of a proposed contract [15.306(d)].

It should be noted that bargaining generally applies only to sole source situations—any change to a material condition of a proposed contract in a competitive environment would require notification to all other offerors and a formal amendment to the RFP [15.206(a) and (d)].

Negotiation strategies, bargaining positions, and other tactics generally do not apply when faced with a number of competing proposals. While discussions can, and often do, address details of an offeror's technical and pricing proposal, the requirement that the government not favor one offeror over another and that all offerors receive the same information precludes much of the flexibility that is found in sole source negotiations.

Proposal Revisions

The FAR 15 rewrite made a significant change when it specifically stated that the contracting officer may request or allow proposal revisions to clarify and document understandings reached during negotiations [15.307(b) and 15.001]. Before the FAR 15 rewrite, the FAR did not address this area and the Comptroller General ruled that offerors could submit proposal revisions at their discretion any time between the opening and closing of discussions. Problems arose when contracting officers only sought a clarification and did not request a proposal revision but the offeror submitted one anyway, often creating a need for further discussions (see Greenleaf Distribution Services[1] (every offeror within the competitive range has a right to change or modify its proposal, including price, for any reason whatsoever, so long as negotiations are still open)).

The FAR 15 rewrite appears to have corrected this problem by stating that offerors may submit proposal revisions during discussions *only* when requested or allowed by the contracting officer. This seems to preclude offerors from submitting proposal revisions at their own discretion, but this has yet to be considered by the Comptroller General.

Information Releases

FAR 15.413-1(a) had prohibited an agency from revealing any information contained in a proposal, the number of proposals received, and the identity of offerors. This FAR reference was deleted by the FAR 15 rewrite thus eliminating this wording. Essentially, these prohibitions are now found in the definition of source selection information (FAR 3-104-3), which includes "competitive range determinations that identify proposals that have a reasonable chance of being selected for award," and FAR 3-104-4 which prohibits the revelation of source selection information. So the prohibition in 15.413-1(a) has not been eliminated, just placed elsewhere in the FAR. Once proposals have been received, agencies cannot reveal any information about the proposals or the offerors to anyone outside the evaluation process.

CONDUCTING DISCUSSIONS

Discussions are usually opened by a letter from the contracting officer to each offeror that identifies the offeror's proposal problems and informs the offeror how the discussions will be conducted. Regardless of how the discussions will be conducted, offerors should be given a reasonable amount of time to respond. This time period provides each offeror with an opportunity to prepare its response to the contracting officer's letter.

Generally, face-to-face discussions are held at the contracting agency (minimizes the use of government travel funds). It is not unusual, however, for such discussions to be held at the offeror's facility, particularly if viewing the offeror's workplace would facilitate the government's understanding of the proposal. The place for discussion is at the contracting officer's discretion.

Discussions should be initiated as soon as practicable after the contracting officer receives the initial evaluation report. Once the competitive range is established, the contracting officer reviews the evaluation results and the discussion questions developed for each offeror still in the competition. The discussion questions developed by the evaluators in the initial evaluation provide the primary basis for discussions, but the contracting officer may add or delete discussion questions at his or her discretion.

One important thing to remember is that the evaluation results and proposed discussion questions must be fully documented. If the documentation is inadequate, the contracting officer must go back to the evaluators and request that they provide the proper documentation. To proceed with discussions with inadequate supporting documentation could be a fatal error in the event of a protest. You must correct such problems before discussions are opened.

Where the technical and pricing questions are not complex and it is anticipated that any questions can be easily resolved in the final proposal revision, the contracting office could opt for written discussions. In such instances, the contracting officer would indicate that offerors are required to respond to the letter opening discussions with their final proposal revisions by a specific date. It should be noted that this is not an award without discussions. The contracting officer's letter, sent to each offeror, constitutes a round of discussions. The letter should also indicate that no further discussions are contemplated, after receipt of the final proposal revisions.

Where it is not certain that all concerns can be resolved by a final proposal revision, the letter opening the discussions should indicate where, when, and how further discussions will be conducted. Keep in mind that each exchange with an offeror is a round of discussions, starting with the letter opening the discussions.

KINDS OF DISCUSSIONS

The type or duration of discussions with different offerors need not be equal. The FAR states that all offerors shall be treated fairly and impartially, but need not be treated the same [1.102-2(c)(3)]. Discussions may be conducted by telephone with one offeror, by letter with another, and face to face with a still another offeror. The type of discussion used depends on what is to be discussed. Not only can discussion types vary among offerors, but they can also vary with an individual offeror if multiple rounds of discussions are required. Since discussions are necessarily related solely to each offeror's proposal, the length of each discussion depends on what needs to be discussed and can be as long or short as required.

Face to Face

Generally face-to-face discussions are reserved for large, complex procurements in which there are many and varied issues to address. Face-to-face discussions are usually the most effective type of discussion because the government can react to the offeror's response on the spot and avoid misunderstandings that might otherwise be difficult to resolve. Face-to-face discussions can be lengthy, however, not only with respect to duration, but also with respect to scheduling. It is not recommended to have competing offerors sitting together in the same room, waiting their turn. Discussions should be scheduled so that the second offeror is due to arrive well after the first offeror has departed. Generally no more than two or three discussions can be conducted in one day and this can lengthen the overall time required to conduct discussions. In this instance, the contracting officer's letter opening discussions should indicate where and when the initial discussions will be held.

Telephonic

Telephonic discussions are next in terms of effectiveness. They are effective for noncontroversial and less complex issues where oral exchanges are necessary to help avoid misunderstandings, but the intimacy of face-to-face discussions is not necessary. Telephonic discussions may also be more efficient than face-to-face discussions because more can be conducted in one day. The contracting officer's letter opening discussions should indicate when the telephonic discussions will be held.

Letter

Discussions may also be conducted by letter. In letter discussions, each offeror must respond to the contracting officer's letter opening discussions with a written response (but not necessarily a proposal revision). This is appropriate when the issues to be addressed are simple, noncomplex, and not likely to generate misunderstandings. Although the contracting officer's letter opening discussions should indicate a deadline for receipt of the offeror's response, this is only an administrative requirement (to manage multiple discussions). The FAR states that such deadlines are only required for the final proposal revisions. Nevertheless, administrative timetables are often necessary to expedite offeror responses.

ROUNDS OF DISCUSSIONS

It has been an unwritten rule that while discussions need not be equal as to type or duration, each offeror must have an equal number of opportunities (discussion rounds) to discuss and revise its proposal before submission of the final proposal revisions (i.e., discuss with one, discuss with all). This may no longer apply due to a post FAR 15 rewrite Court of Federal Claims ruling, as shown in Example 16.1.

Example 16.1—Can the government conduct multiple rounds of discussions with, and receive multiple revised proposals from, one offeror but not the others.[2]

The plaintiff in this case was Miller-Holzwarth Inc. (MHI). The intervenor was Optex Systems Inc. (the awardee).

The Army opened discussions with MHI by a letter indicating that there were problems with MHI's past performance, specifically, scheduling. These problems were discussed and, without the need for a proposal revision, the Army raised MHI's past performance rating to the same as that of Optex.

The Army opened discussions with Optex indicating by letter that the Army found no weaknesses in its proposal, but that Optex's price was too high. Optex reduced its pricing but made the revision contingent on other awards. The Army informed Optex that the revisions were unacceptable because of the contingencies.

The Army then closed discussions, requesting best and final offers (BAFO). MHI submitted a BAFO with a slightly reduced price. Optex's BAFO removed all the contingencies from its revised proposal and reduced its price significantly.

Award was to be based on past performance and price, with past performance being more important. Both offerors' past performance was evaluated as equal, however, and award was made to Optex based on its lower price.

MHI contended that the Army violated FAR 15.306(e)(1) and the spirit of the 1997 revisions by conducting two rounds of price negotiations with intervenor (Optex), while conducting only one with MHI. MHI cited SmithKline and Paramax[3] (setting aside award because agency conducted another round of price discussions with one offeror after receiving BAFOs and not doing the same with protester) and contended that the Army's conduct violated the "fundamental principle of federal procurement that all offerors must be treated equally," and the more specific principle that "all offerors are entitled to an equal opportunity to revise their proposals." The Court did not agree.

FAR 1.102-2(c)(3) states that "[a]ll . . . prospective contractors shall be treated fairly and impartially but need not be treated the same." Plaintiff's proposition that the Army must conduct price negotiations with all offerors if it does so with any offeror that has submitted an unreasonably high price overlooks the import of this section. Pursuant to FAR 15.306(d)(3), the Army "shall . . . discuss with, each offeror still being considered for award, significant weaknesses, deficiencies, and other aspects of its proposal (such as cost, price, . . .) that could, in the opinion of the contracting officer, be altered or explained to enhance materially the proposal's potential for award." Nothing in this provision compels the Army to conduct negotiations with one offeror regarding a weakness perceived in another offeror's proposal. In the instant case, the Army determined that intervenor's proposal was weak in the area of price and that the plaintiff's proposal was weak in the area of past performance. Plaintiff's argument, insofar as it is grounded in notions of fundamental fairness, would be stronger if the Army had not afforded plaintiff the opportunity to enhance its proposal prior to the submission of BAFOs. Not only did the Army raise plaintiff's past-performance rating based on promises of future performance, but advised expressly plaintiff in the May 4, 1998 request for BAFOs that "[a]ny revision to your offer, including price, may be received prior to that time." These facts, when considered in conjunction with the pertinent FAR provision, support a finding that plaintiff was not subject to any unfairness resulting from the Army's price negotiations with intervenor.

The decisions of the Comptroller General on which plaintiff relies do not stand for the proposition that fair treatment among offerors requires that each be treated the same. The critical distinction between the instant matter and SmithKline[4] and Paramax[5], is that SmithKline and Paramax involve negotiations with one offeror not before, but after submission of BAFOs. Unlike the period prior to submission of final proposals during which the government is encouraged to engage in discussion with offerors for the purpose of addressing and revising weaknesses in each offer, FAR 15.307(b) states that "[r]equests for final proposal revisions shall advise offerors that the final proposal revisions shall be in writing and that the government intends to make award without obtaining further revisions." The Army did not conduct negotiations with intervenor or plaintiff after submission of BAFOs; therefore, the Army by its conduct did not violate FAR 15.307(b) or come within the restrictions imposed by these decisions.

Decisions of the Comptroller General that do closely parallel the facts of the instant case support intervenor's contention that the Army did not have a duty to discuss price with the plaintiff. In Applied Remote Technology Inc.[6]*, the Comptroller General stated that "an agency has no responsibility to inform an offeror that its price is too high unless the government has reason to think that the price is unreasonable." Similarly, in Talos Corp.*[7]*, the decision stated that "If an offeror's higher cost is not considered excessive . . . the higher cost is not a deficiency required to be pointed out during discussions." See OK's Cascade Co.*[8]*, (explaining the agency did not need to enter discussions with offeror that submits price considered reasonable). These decisions stand for the general proposition that reasonableness is the touchstone for initiating discussions with an offeror with respect to price.*

. . . The unfortunate reality confronting the plaintiff is that, if an agency initiates discussion with another offeror on price, regardless of the reasonableness of that price, a substantial likelihood exists that the price will be reduced. It appears that FAR, even in its current formulation, fails to appreciate the practical effect upon business judgment attendant to negotiations with respect to price that may not necessarily be present in negotiations on e.g., past performance or technical criteria. This area of concern notwithstanding, no basis is present in the record before the court to declare any provision of the FAR unlawful or to find the actions of the Army arbitrary or capricious.

The judge in this case pointed to FAR 1,102-2(c)(3) (promulgated as part of the FAR 15 rewrite), which states "all . . . prospective contractors shall be treated fairly and impartially but need not be treated the same," to justify the unequal number of discussions. In this case, the offerors had different proposal problems: MHI had past performance problems; Optex had pricing problems. The discussions addressed these problems. MHI was able to resolve its problems during discussions without the need to revise its proposal. Optex needed to revise its pricing as a result of the discussions, but its pricing revision was rejected because of included contingencies. In their final proposal revisions, both offerors changed their pricing: MHI made a minimal reduction; Optex not only substantially reduced its price but also removed the offending contingencies—and consequently received the award.

The court indicated that when opposing offerors have different proposal problems, it may be necessary to hold more rounds of discussions with one offeror to resolve the problems than with the other offeror—and this is permissable—as long as it happens before the final proposal revisions are submitted. After submission of the final proposal revisions, any discussions with one offeror would require that the other offerors also be permitted an opportunity to submit another final proposal revision.

This decision is probably not the last word with respect to the concept of "discuss with one, discuss with all." The fact that the discussions addressed different topics was important to this decision. But what happens when there are two competing offerors, both with staffing problems, and only one discussion is held with the first offeror, but several discussions are held with the second? Is the second offeror getting more information than the first? Will this better prepare the second offeror for its final proposal revision? Eventually a case like this will come up. Until then it is suggested that this decision not be used as an excuse to hold an uneven number of discussions without considering the questions just asked.

The FAR statement that "prospective contractors shall be treated fairly and impartially, but need not be treated the same" clearly applies to the fact that the discussions themselves do not have to be the same for each offeror, but where uneven numbers of discussions are contemplated it would be best to look at the first part of the statement "fairly and impartially" before relying on the last part.

OLD TERMS ARE NOT FORGOTTEN

The FAR 15 rewrite deleted some terms—technical leveling, technical transfusion, and auctioning—that were important to the conduct of negotiations. The Comptroller General first used these terms to describe negotiating activities that created situations that were not fair or equitable to all offerors. Over time, the procurement regulations incorporated these terms as prohibited activities. Now these terms have been deleted, probably to give contracting officers more flexibility in obtaining the best value—but the concepts that these terms represented still remain.

Technical Leveling

The FAR 15 rewrite deleted the term *technical leveling* (helping an offeror to bring its proposal up to the level of other proposals through successive rounds of discussions by pointing out weaknesses that remain in a proposal due to an offeror's lack of diligence, competence, or inventiveness, after having been given an opportunity to correct them). Does this mean that technical leveling is now permitted? The case in Example 16.2 would seem to say so—if not read carefully.

Example 16.2—Technical leveling[9]

After receiving the final proposal revisions, NASA reopened discussions and asked offerors to submit a second final proposal revision. Award was then made on the basis of best value. The unsuccessful offeror protested that during the second rounds of discussions, NASA improperly raised issues with FDC relating to its proposed staffing that NASA had already raised during the first round of discussions. The protester, Dynacs, maintained that it was improper to afford FDC a second opportunity to respond to its concerns and that, if FDC had not been given a second opportunity to correct the deficiencies, the deficiencies would have remained and Dynacs would have been entitled to the award. The Comptroller General disagreed and commented on the changes made by the FAR 15 rewrite.

Even if the protester is correct that NASA raised the same concerns in both *rounds of discussions (NASA disputes this), doing so was not improper. Solicitations issued after January 1, 1998, such as the one here, are governed by the Federal Acquisition Regulation (FAR), as amended by Federal Acquisition Circular (FAC) NO. 97-02. The FAR 15 rewrite included in this version of the regulation revised the provisions that apply when an agency is contracting using negotiated procedures, including those provisions governing exchanges with offerors after receipt of proposals as set forth in FAR 15.306. The prior version of the FAR contained provisions that could be read to limit the extent to which agencies conducted ongoing discussions with an offeror. For example, agencies were prohibited from engaging in technical leveling (helping an offeror to bring its proposal up to the level of another proposal through successive rounds of discussions, such as by pointing out weaknesses resulting from the offeror's lack of diligence, competence, or inventiveness in preparing its proposal).*[10] *Agencies were also cautioned against reopening discussions after receipt of best and final offers unless it was clear that the information already available was inadequate to reasonably justify contractor selection and award.*[11] *These restrictions were eliminated by the FAR 15 rewrite. The current FAR does not discourage agencies from resolving a given proposal weakness or deficiency by means of multiple rounds of discussions with rite offeror.*[12] *Indeed, we think that both the stated primary objective of discussions—to maximize the government's ability to obtain the best value, based on the requirements and evaluation factors set forth in the solicitation, FAR 15.306(d)(2)—and, more significantly, the definition of discussions—which includes bargaining, consisting of persuasion, alteration of assumptions and positions, and give and take, FAR 15.306(d)—arguably presuppose that there may be multiple discussions regarding an issue. Nothing in the regulation suggests that further discussions on an issue are impermissible simply because that may occur on separate occasions, over a period of time. We conclude that there was nothing improper in the agency's raising the same concerns in two rounds of discussions with FDC* [and in footnote 2 here].

2. We note that, even under the prior version of the FAR, a procuring agency properly could reopen discussions to discuss a previously raised item when the agency felt such action was necessary to resolve its concerns before making award.[13] *Here, it appears NASA's reason for reopening discussions on the same items—it believed it had not discussed, or adequately discussed, certain deficiencies—would meet this standard.*

The key to this decision lies in footnote 2 and in the next to the last sentences in the excerpt above, "Nothing in the regulation suggests that further discussions on an issue are impermissible simply because that may occur on separate occasions, over a period of time. We conclude that there was nothing improper in the agency's raising the same concerns in two rounds of discussions with FDC." Unfortunately, the discussion of the FAR 15 rewrite changes, while correct, is misleading.

The discussion of technical leveling in this decision is misleading because (1) the concept of technical leveling applies only where there are successive rounds of discussions (more than two) on the same subject, and that did not happen here, and (2) the wording of this decision gives the impression that because the term *technical leveling* has been deleted from the FAR, it is no longer impermissible. This is not so.

Comptroller General decisions prohibited technical leveling long before it was prohibited by the FAR. It is likely that the Comptroller General will maintain this position regardless of the FAR coverage, where the multiple rounds of discussions *create an unfair situation*.

Technical leveling is the process of deliberately repeating discussions of an offeror's proposal problems and how they might be corrected in order to improve that proposal and make it technically equal to other proposals, or inadvertently allowing this to happen through the way discussions are conducted. Where repeated discussions (more than two rounds of discussions) create an unfair competitive advantage for one offeror, the Comptroller General is likely to rule against the agency conducting the discussions. In this example the second round of discussions with FDC did not create an unfair situation.

Technical leveling is unfair on two levels: It is unfair to competing offerors because one offeror is being given more information than that provided to the other offerors; it is also unfair to the government, which through discussion of how a proposal problem might be corrected, is essentially assisting the offeror in improving its proposal. Thus the final proposal is partly the government's and partly the offeror's. The problem then is that there is no way to be sure that the offeror can actually perform in accordance with the revised proposal. In its desire to obtain the award and respond to the government's suggestions, an offeror may promise more than it can deliver.

Some technical leveling is bound to occur in competitive procurement, particularly where the simple identification of a problem is enough to reveal to an offeror how the proposal should be corrected. This is proper and is supposed to happen in meaningful discussions. It is the *repetitive discussions of* proposal problems with one offeror and how they might be corrected that creates an unfair situation and is improper.

Example 16.3 shows that multiple discussions with an offeror where proposal problems are more clearly identified does not constitute technical leveling.

Example 16.3—Multiple discussions do not necessarily translate to technical leveling[14]

Technical leveling occurs where an agency, through successive rounds of discussions, helps to bring a proposal up to the level of another proposal by pointing out weaknesses that remain in a proposal due to an offeror's lack of diligence, competence, or inventiveness after having been given an opportunity to correct them.[15] *In this regard, our Office has recognized the tension between the requirement for meaningful discussions with all responsible sources whose proposals are within the competitive range, and the admonitions in the FAR against technical leveling, technical transfusion, and auctions.*[16] *We have held that this is an area where agencies necessarily have considerable discretion,*[17] *and where an agency points out informational deficiencies in an offeror's proposal, this does not constitute technical leveling, because the agency's purpose is to ascertain what the offeror is proposing to furnish.*[18]

Although the first round of discussions generally addressed deficiencies in ITT's key personnel resumes, we think that the agency, on reopening, simply tailored its discussions to ITT's proposal by specifying the precise organizational and presentation shortcomings in the firm's resumes for purposes of obtaining from ITT amplification of the information previously provided.[19] *Requesting correction of such informational deficiencies does not constitute technical leveling.*

Technical leveling should not be a problem. You can avoid it by identifying deficiencies, weaknesses, and other proposal problems during discussions, but not discussing how they might be corrected or repeatedly asking the same questions until the offeror finally gets it right. This applies even where multiple discussions are necessary.

The term *technical leveling* may have been deleted from the FAR because there were many cases where contracting officers felt that providing too much information when describing proposal problems would constitute technical leveling, so they failed to adequately describe deficiencies and weaknesses. Trying to avoid the technical leveling problem caused another—contracting officers were not adequately informing offerors as to their proposal problems. Deleting the term may alleviate such problems, and as long as contracting officers remember that the concept of technical leveling has not gone away, we will not return to the early 1970s when the way discussions were conducted gave birth to the concept in the first place.

Discussions, whether in the initial round of discussions or in later rounds, must center on the problems found in each offeror's proposal. Do not permit the discussions to include comparisons between proposals, either directly or indirectly. This would be improper, as shown in Example 16.10 later in this chapter.

Technical Transfusion and Auctioning

The FAR 15 rewrite eliminated two other terms related to prohibited activities—*technical transfusions* (government disclosure of technical information pertaining to one offeror's proposal to another offeror that results in improvement of the other offeror's proposal) and *auctioning* (indicating to an offeror a cost or price that must be met to obtain further consideration or advising an offeror of its standing relative to another offeror). The terms may be gone but the activities related to those terms are still prohibited.

FAR 15.306(e)(2) addresses the limitations on exchanges after establishment of the competitive range and includes technical transfusion (but without using the term), by stating that revealing an offeror's technical solution, including unique technology, innovative and unique uses of commercial items, or any information that would compromise an offeror's intellectual property to another offeror, is a prohibited activity. Providing information from one proposal—usually from an unsuccessful proposal containing an idea or approach that the government likes—to another offeror, usually the otherwise unsuccessful offeror, to improve that proposal and take advantage of the idea or approach from the unsuccessful proposal, is not proper. The term "technical transfusion" may be gone but the concept is still in effect.

FAR 15.306(e)(3) prohibits revealing an offeror's price without that offeror's permission (this used to be called auctioning) and then goes on to explain that the government may tell an offeror that its price is considered to be too high or too low. What is new here is that now the government may reveal the analysis that supports that conclusion. In addition, the government may now tell offerors the cost or price that the government's price analysis, market research, and other reviews have identified as reasonable.

The authors of the FAR 15 rewrite may have felt that the use of these terms caused more problems than they helped. Nevertheless, such activities became prohibited activities because the Comptroller General ruled them so. Since these activities became prohibited by Comptroller General rulings before the FAR addressed them, the fact the FAR no longer addresses them, does not make them acceptable to the Comptroller General if an unfair situation is created.

WHAT MUST BE ADDRESSED DURING DISCUSSIONS

Certain areas must be addressed during discussions.

Discussions Must Identify Deficiencies and Significant Weaknesses

The contracting officer is required to tell offerors of those proposal problems (deficiencies, significant weaknesses, risks, etc.) that might adversely affect their opportunity for award. Identifying deficiencies is not usually a problem because these are areas of the proposal that are unacceptable. Identifying weaknesses is not as easy, because some weaknesses are significant and some are not. Example 16.4 points out the kinds of weaknesses that must be identified.

Example 16.4—Need only identify significant weaknesses[20]

We review the adequacy of discussions to ensure that agencies point out weaknesses that, unless corrected, would prevent an offeror from having a reasonable chance for award.[21] *An agency is not required to discuss every aspect of an offeror's proposal that receives less than the maximum score.*[22] *Neither is an agency required to advise an offeror of minor weaknesses that are not considered significant, even where the weaknesses subsequently become a determinative factor between two closely ranked proposals.*[23] *Contracting agencies have wide discretion in determining the nature and scope of discussions and their discretion will not be questioned unless it is clearly shown to be without a rational basis.*[24]

A significant weakness is a weakness that, unless corrected or clarified, is likely to affect the offeror's chance for award. Weaknesses that, based on the initial evaluation, do not appear to be significant enough to threaten the award need not be identified, even if they become more important later.

Given the current concept of including only those most highly rated proposals in the discussions, the determination of which weaknesses to discuss may become more difficult. There should be few, if any, deficiencies in a highly rated proposal; thus what weaknesses there are will take on greater significance as discriminators. Take a good look at the differences between the significant weaknesses and the minor weaknesses to ensure that they have been categorized properly. Prudence should be the by-word here. It will be easier to identify a weakness for discussion than it will be to explain to a protester why a weakness was not revealed. Even if you win the protest, you will have expended a significant amount of time and effort in responding to the protest.

Discussion Must be Meaningful

FAR 15.306(d)(1) states that the discussions must be tailored to each offeror's proposal and shall be conducted by the contracting officer with each offeror in the competitive range. This means that discussion must be:

- Meaningful—all significant issues that might affect award must be identified
- Equitable—fair to all, i.e., no offeror is favored over another
- Not misleading—misleading an offeror into responding in a manner that does not address agency concerns is not proper.

The area of meaningful discussions covers a variety of problems. Examples 16.5 through 16.10 address some of them.

Example 16.5—Agency not required to "spoon feed" an offeror as to each and every item that could be revised so as to improve its proposal.[25]

Du & Associates (D&A) was included in the competitive range initially. Oral discussions were held and written questions were provided to D&A. D&A submitted a revised proposal. The contracting officer redetermined the competitive range and rejected D&A as not being among the most highly rated proposals (based primarily on technical considerations). D&A requested a debriefing and then protested the award.

D&A argued that discussions were inadequate because the discussion questions were not specific enough to put them on notice of the perceived problems. The agency claimed that the questions were specific enough to lead the offeror to the areas of concern. The Comptroller General agreed with the agency.

Solicitations issued after January 1, such as this one, are governed by the revisions to Part 15 of the Federal Acquisition Regulation (FAR) contained in Federal Acquisition Circular (FAC) No. 97-02. The Part 15 rewrite revised the rules that apply when an agency is contracting using negotiated procedures, including those rules governing the exchanges with offerors after the receipt of proposals. Section 15.306(d)(3) includes guidance with respect to the conduct of discussions and states, in pertinent part, that:

"The contracting officer shall . . . indicate to, or discuss with, each offeror still being considered for award, significant weaknesses, deficiencies, and other aspects of its proposal . . . that could, in the opinion of the contracting officer, be altered or explained to enhance materially the proposal's potential for award. The scope and extent of discussions are a matter of contracting officer judgment."

We view the statutory and regulatory mandate for discussions with all competitive range offerors, which was not changed in the FAR Part 15 rewrite, as requiring that such discussions must be meaningful, equitable and not misleading.[26] *At issue here is whether the FAR Part 15 rewrite altered the rules governing the content of discussions in a way relevant to the outcome of this protest. We recognize that the FAR rewrite could be read to limit the discretion of the contracting officer by requiring discussion of all aspects of the proposal "that could, in the opinion of the contracting officer, be altered or explained to enhance materially the proposal's potential for award." We do not believe, however, that it was the intention of the rewrite to limit the contracting officer's discretion in this manner, cf SDS Petroleum Prods., Inc.*[27] *(intent of Part 15 rewrite was to give contracting officers discretion to establish a more limited competitive range than was permitted previously). Consequently, we do not view the rewrite as having changed the prior legal requirements governing discussions in a manner which affects this case.*[28] *The rule thus remains that, while an agency is required to conduct meaningful discussions leading an offeror into the areas of its proposal requiring amplification or revision, the agency is not required to "spoon-feed" an offeror as to each and every item that could be revised so as to improve its proposal.*[29] *This is especially the case where, as here, the RFP evaluation criteria and instructions to offerors on proposal preparation are detailed and clear with respect to the problem area.*

The FAR 15 rewrite did not change how meaningful discussions should be conducted. It is not necessary to describe proposal problems in such detail that the offeror could have no doubt as to their identity or nature. Proposal problems need only be described in a manner that would lead the offeror to the areas of the proposal that require amplification or correction (i.e., only significant problems likely to affect the award need be discussed). In contrast to Example 16.5, Example 16.6 addresses a situation where an offeror was not put on notice of a significant government concern.

Example 16.6—Discussions are not meaningful unless they lead the offeror to those problems that must be addressed for it to have a reasonable chance for award[30]

In this case the protester argued that discussions were not meaningful because it was not put on notice that the evaluators had concerns about its pricing methodology. The Comptroller General agreed.

ACS argues that the agency did not conduct meaningful discussion with the firm. In support of its argument, ACS points out that in its report to the CO, the TEP expressed concern that between the base and option years, ACS's proposal reflected an increase in price per account serviced, and that ACS has not adequately explained this increase. ACS maintains that since its price was of material concern to the TEP in its recommendation, and was also a concern expressed by the SSO, HUD should have given the firm an opportunity to address this during discussions.

The FAR requires that contracting officers discuss with each offeror being considered for award "significant weaknesses, deficiencies, and other aspects of its proposal . . . that could, in the opinion of the contracting officer, be altered or explained to enhance materially the proposal's potential for award."[31] The statutory and regulatory requirement for discussion with all competitive range offerors[32] means that such discussions must be meaningful, equitable, and not misleading.[33] Discussions cannot be meaningful unless they lead an offeror into those weaknesses, excesses or deficiencies of its proposal that must be addressed in order for it to have a reasonable change of being selected for award.[34]

While the record is not clear as to what impact ACS's pricing methodology had on the TEP's recommendation or on the SSO's selection decision, it is clear that, at a minimum, it was of sufficient concern for the evaluators to raise it in the TEP's report to the CO, and that the SSO agreed with the TEP's view that ACS has not adequately explained its pricing strategy. Despite this stated concern, however, there is no evidence in the record that HUD raised this issue during its discussions with ACS. We therefore agree with ACS that discussions with the firm regarding its price were not meaningful

As noted in Example 16.6, offerors must be put on notice of significant proposal problems. Despite the concerns expressed at all evaluation levels, the concerns about ACS's pricing were never addressed during discussion. That was a fatal error.

Example 16.7—Discussions, prior to the request for final proposal revisions—need not be equal[35]

Award was to be made to the lowest priced, technically acceptable offeror. Discussions were held. During the first round of discussions, two of the offerors were asked to clarify that their proposed staffing levels were sufficient to support the requirements of specific PWS paragraphs. The eventual awardee was asked to clarify the total staffing offered. The protester was advised that it failed to describe how a certain support task would be performed and that it misunderstood certain related staffing requirements.

The responses from these offerors indicated that they did not understand the staffing requirements. The agency then amended the RFP to provide the government's estimated staffing requirements (this had not been provided previously) and indicated that the government estimate should be used for guidance in their responses. This constituted a second round of discussions.

All but the protester increased their staffing levels to approximate the government estimate. The protester made some increases, but not enough to demonstrate it could perform to the government requirements. The government redetermined the competitive range and rejected the protester's proposal as being not technically acceptable.

The protester argued that the contracting agency conducted prejudicially unequal discussions by asking the offerors—but not the protester—questions related to the sufficiency of their proposed staffing levels during both rounds of discussions and asking the protester a similar question during the second round of discussions only. According to the protester, this made the discussion unequal, improper, and prejudicial. The Comptroller General did not agree.

The record shows, moreover, that the discussion item given to the most relevant offeror, the eventual awardee, at this time could not have put it on notice that its staffing levels were insufficient since it was only asked to clarify a discrepancy in its proposal. As a result, that offeror, MCA, was in exactly the same position as I.T.S. going into the second round of discussions. Most important, unlike the situation in National Medical Staffing, Inc.,[36] *the principal precedent relied upon by I.T.S., the agency did eventually put the protester on notice of the precise issue of concern, thereby mitigating any inequity that might have initially occurred.*

We simply do not agree with I.T.S. that two of the offerors here increased their staffing levels to approximate the government standard only because the second round discussion item somehow reinforced the first. It is clear that the key piece of information given to all of the offerors was the government standard. This point is reinforced by the fact that MCA, the awardee, was in the same position as I.T.S. and substantially increased its staffing based solely on the same second round of discussion item provided to I.T.S. As a result, we cannot conclude that the agency conducted prejudicially unequal discussions.

The Comptroller General denied the protest on the grounds that the discussions were not unequal because neither the protester nor the awardee was specifically told that its staffing was inadequate during the first round of discussions; therefore, they were on equal ground at the start of the second round of discussions. The key information, the government's own staffing estimate, was released to all offerors at the start of the second round of discussions. This put the protester and the awardee on an equal basis going into the second round of discussions, and therefore the discussions were not unequal or prejudicial to the protester. The situation in Example 16.7 is unlike that in Example 16.1 because all offerors were afforded the same number of discussions. In both cases, however, the key was that all offerors were on an equal footing at the time final proposal revisions were requested.

But what happens when on offeror has no technical problems, but the other offeror does? This situation is addressed in Example 16.8

Example 16.8—Discussions where there are no weaknesses or deficiencies[37]

KBM's proposal was found to contain no deficiencies or weaknesses and to offer a number of strengths under each of the evaluation factors. With respect to Milvets' marginally rated proposal, the TEP noted both strengths and weaknesses. Oral and written discussions were conducted with each competitive range offeror. Because no weaknesses or deficiencies were identified in KBM's initial technical proposal, discussions with KBM concerned only its price proposal. BATF conducted both technical and price discussions with Milvets.

Final proposal revisions were received and evaluated. KBM made no changes to its technical proposal in light of the agency's lack of technical discussions with the firm. Milvets made numerous changes in its technical proposal in response to each of the agency's identified concerns.

The SSEB concluded that, although the two proposals offered different strengths, the firm's final proposals were essentially equal technically and recommended to the SSA that award be made to Milvets, based upon that firm's substantially lower price.

KBM protested that the discussion were unequal because Milvets received technical discussion while KBM did not. The Comptroller General did not agree.

In negotiated procurements, contracting agencies generally must conduct discussions with all offerors whose proposals are within the competitive range.[38] *Although discussions must be meaningful, leading an offeror into the areas of its proposal requiring amplification or revision, the agency is not required to "spoon feed" an offeror as to each and every item that could be raised as to improve its proposal.*[39] *An agency has not satisfied its obligation to conduct meaningful discussions if it misleads an offeror or conducts prejudicially unequal discussions.*[40]

KBM also complains that BATF conducted unequal discussions because Milvets received technical discussions while KBM did not. Although an agency must treat offerors fairly and provide offerors with an equal opportunity in discussions to revise their proposals, discussions with each offeror need not be identical. Rather, a procuring agency should tailor its discussions to each offer since the need for clarifications or revisions will vary with the proposals.[41] *BATF satisfied that obligation here. The agency conducted technical discussions with Milvets because the firm's technical proposal contained a number of evaluated weaknesses. KBM's proposal, on the other hand, did not have any evaluated weaknesses or deficiencies, and therefore the agency found nothing in KBM's proposal that need to be clarified or revised during discussions.*

We have long recognized that evaluation ratings, be they adjectival, numerical, or color, are merely guides for intelligent decision-making in the procurement process.[42] *The more important consideration is whether the documented evaluation record and source selection decision reasonably assess the relative merits of the proposals in accordance with the stated evaluation criteria.*[43] *Here, the record shows that the relative merits of KBM's and Milvet's proposals were adequately and reasonably documented and considered. Specifically, as noted above, the strengths of each firm's proposal was identified in the agency's evaluation documents and weighted in the agency's cost/technical analysis; this includes the strengths that KBM asserts should have entitled it to a higher adjectival rating.*

As noted earlier, an agency is not required to discuss every aspect of an offeror's proposal. If the initial evaluation does not find deficiencies, weakness, or excesses that require amplification or correction in areas of the technical proposal, it is not necessary to address these areas, even if they are not rated as high as another proposal. Discussions are based on each offeror's proposal, not what is in other proposals.

However, there is another concern with respect to the conduct of discussions. That concern is that the discussions must not be misleading, i.e., the discussions must not mislead an offeror into responding in a manner that does not address agency concerns, as shown in Example 16.9.

Example 16.9—Discussions must not be misleading[44]

In a solicitation for drydocking facilities and repair services for ships homeported at the Mayport Naval Station in the Jacksonville, Florida area, the RFP provided the offerors could proposed for use, a government-furnished property, a Navy floating drydock or a contractor-furnished drydock. The proposed mooring location for the drydock must be within a 75-mile radius and a 90-minute commute of the Mayport Naval station. Metro machine proposed to use its own drydock, at a site to be leased from the Jacksonville Port Authority, but would perform any required production shop work at its facility in Norfolk, Virginia.

During discussions, Metro was asked how it proposed to mitigate the problems associated with the physical distance between Jacksonville and Norfolk. Metro responded to this question in its final proposal revision. However, the agency found Metro's final revised proposal to be unacceptable because the use of the Norfolk facility made the proposal technically unacceptable.

Metro protested, contending that the Navy conducted materially misleading discussions regarding Metro's proposal to perform production shop work in Norfolk. Metro complained that if the proposed use of the Norfolk facility would make its proposal technically unacceptable, why didn't the Navy say so, instead of asking Metro to explain how it proposed to mitigate the problems associated with the physical distance between Jacksonville and Norfolk. Asking the question gave the impression that the Norfolk facility might be acceptable—and this was misleading. The Comptroller General agreed.

It is a fundamental precept of negotiated procurement that discussions, when conducted, must be meaningful and must not prejudicially mislead offerors.[45] *Specifically, an agency may not mislead an offeror—through the framing of a discussion question or a response to a question—into responding in a manner that does not address the agency's concerns; misinform the offeror concerning a problem with its proposal; or misinform the offeror about the government's requirements.*[46] *More specifically, when an agency asks a general question indicating concern regarding a perceived weakness in an offeror's proposal, then subsequently rejects the proposal as technically unacceptable on the basis of this concern, a question which could not reasonably be construed as putting the offeror on notice of the agency's actual concern regarding the acceptability of its proposal does not constitute adequate discussions.*[47]

In any event, even if the agency had reasonably viewed the RFP as mandating the provision of production facilities within the geographical limitation applicable to the mooring location, it would have been misleading for the agency to suggest during discussions that Metro could propose actions to "mitigate the problems associated with the physical distance between Jacksonville and Norfolk." Rather, if the SSA's stated views regarding the RFP requirement for the production facilities to be located near Jacksonville were correct, that fact should have been communicated to Metro.

In short, the agency's discussions effectively communicated to Metro that its proposal to perform production shop work in Norfolk was acceptable, though in need of enhancements or modifications to mitigate problems associated with distance, when, in fact, only a proposal to perform the production shop work in the Jacksonville area would have been acceptable.

Under these circumstances, in order for the discussions to be meaningful, the agency was required to convey to Metro that its proposed approach to performing production shop work would have to be fundamentally altered—not merely explained or enhanced. Accordingly, on the record here, the agency failed to conduct meaningful discussions with Metro.

What happened here was that the TEPT chair who was responsible for preparing the discussion questions did not think the use of the Norfolk facility made Metro's proposal technically unacceptable, and asked Metro to explain how it would handle the distance problem.

The SSA, however, thought that the RFP required all work to be performed in the Jacksonville area, subject to the stated geographical/time limitations, and therefore rejected Metro's final revised proposal for not meeting the RFP's technical requirements. (As it turned out, the SSA's position was incorrect—the way the RFP was written, the geographical/time limitations applied only to where the drydock was moored.)

Apparently the SSA and the TEPT chair never discussed Metro's proposal and the SSA failed to check the discussion questions or monitor the subsequent face-to-face discussions because Metro was never told that the SSA viewed its proposal as technically unacceptable. This made the discussion question misleading and the discussion improper.

Example 16.10—Meaningful discussions must be related to offeror's own proposal deficiencies [48]

The noted concerns in no way reflected a finding of deficiencies in the RBS proposals. Rather the criticisms noted were identified primarily in connection with the evaluator's comparative assessment of the two proposals for purposes of choosing between the firms' respective technical approaches . . . Agencies are not required to—and in fact ordinarily should not—discuss elements of a competitor's technical approach that render it comparatively superior; such matters are not properly for discussions.[49]

Discussions must relate solely to the deficiencies, weaknesses, risks and other problems found in an offeror's proposal. Any reference, direct or indirect, that relates to the contents of another offeror's proposal is improper.

Pricing Factors

The discussion of pricing factors should not be overlooked simply because the procurement is competitive. Theoretically, competition establishes price reasonableness. This would apply, for instance, where award is to be made to the lowest priced technically acceptable offer. But what happens when the competition encompasses both pricing and technical factors? In such instances, cost realism analysis offers the best chance to determine what the government should realistically expect to pay for the proposed effort, the offeror's understanding of the work, and the offeror's ability to perform the work at the proposed price. Any problems identified as a result of the cost realism analysis should be addressed during discussions.

Pricing discussions should center on the validity and realism of proposed costs, homing in on the direct costs for doing the work plus associated overheads. The discussions should address cost items in relation to the technical proposal, such as cost figures related to the type and quality of personnel to be assigned and the estimated number of hours, or the type and quality of material or equipment to be used. The discussions might also address the pricing procedures to be used such as the structuring of overheads, indirect costs, the use of uncompensated overtime, and proposed travel.

Keep in mind, however, that the pricing discussions, like the technical discussions, must only entail questions about the perceived problems. Do not indicate what the pricing should be; the offeror must determine the pricing. Example 16.11 addresses what can, and cannot, be addressed with respect to pricing.

Example 16.11—Pricing discussions[50]

An agency may not inform an offeror of a cost it must meet to obtain further consideration of its relative price standing[51] and need not inform an offeror that its cost is too high unless the government has reason to think the cost is unreasonable.[52] Further, an agency has no duty to enter into price discussions with an offeror solely because its price is significantly higher than the prices proposed by other offerors. In fact, pursuant to FAR

15.610(e)(2), an agency is prohibited from informing an offeror that its price is high in relation to another offeror's, unless its price is unrealistic for what is offered.

The FAR 15 rewrite superseded the FAR reference cited above. The applicable citation now would be 15.306(e)(3), which simply states that an agency may not reveal an offeror's price without that offeror's permission.

The new citation also states that an agency may tell an offeror that its price is considered to be too high or too low for what it is offering and reveal the analysis supporting that conclusion. An agency may also, at its discretion, tell all offerors the cost or price that the government's price analysis, market research and other reviews have identified as reasonable (i.e., the independent government cost estimate). It should be noted, however, that this is all at the contracting officer's discretion. There is no requirement to reveal this information.

CLOSING DISCUSSIONS

The contracting officer controls all facets of the discussions. Discussions may be ended when all offerors in the competitive range have been informed of the significant problems in their proposals and they have had an opportunity to revise their proposals accordingly. This could be as soon as the offerors have had an opportunity to submit written responses to the letter opening the discussions or after a number of rounds of discussions.

FINAL PROPOSAL REVISIONS

Generally, after the first round of discussions, the contracting officer determines if the results of the discussions and any proposal revisions submitted indicate that additional rounds of discussions are required with one or more offerors. As noted earlier, FAR 15.307(b) provides that the contracting officer may request or allow proposal revisions to clarify and document understandings reached during negotiations (see Examples 16.1 and 16.6). For example, additional rounds may be required if discussion questions were not answered adequately, or a proposal revision introduced new problems. Additional discussion rounds may also be required when the responses to discussion questions indicate that the offerors did not understand the requirements and the RFP must be amended to clarify the government requirement—in this case additional discussions would be conducted with all offerors still in the competitive range (see Example 16.6).

Evaluation of Proposal Revisions

The evaluation of proposal revisions submitted during discussions is part of the discussion process rather than the evaluation process. It is not necessary for the original evaluation team to convene to review the revisions. Generally, the contracting officer or individual evaluators with the requisite expertise, rather than the entire evaluation team, evaluate such proposal revisions.

If the results of the discussions indicate that a proposal is no longer considered among the most highly rated (whether the offeror was permitted to submit a proposal revision or not), the contracting officer may reject the proposal on the basis that the proposal has no reasonable chance of award. In essence, the contracting officer is redetermining the competitive range.

How Discussions Are Closed

Discussions are closed by a written request to each offeror still in the competitive range for the submission of its final proposal revision. This request must establish a common cut-off date for the receipt of final proposal revisions and advise offerors that the final proposal revisions must be in writing and that award will be made without obtaining further revisions. It should be noted here that the FAR 15 rewrite changed the term *best and final offer* to *final proposal revision.* The rewrite also simplified the language but made no substantive changes to the coverage [15.307(b)].

While not required by the FAR, the letter requesting final proposal revisions should remind offerors, that they must fully substantiate any changes made in their final proposal revision because they will have no further opportunity to explain themselves. This is particularly important with respect to providing supporting information for changes in pricing or in the technical approach, such as changes in proposed staffing levels or key personnel. The government is not required to reopen discussions to address problems first introduced in a final proposal revision (see Chapter 17, Example 17.3).

The decision to reopen discussions after receipt of the final proposal revisions is largely within the discretion of the contracting officer. The reopening of discussions sometimes becomes necessary to correct agency errors or to otherwise ensure that the discussions are equitable (see Chapter 17, Example 17.4). When discussions are reopened, they are reopened with all offerors still in the competitive range. It is not necessary to actually hold discussions with all offerors but each must be provided the opportunity to submit another final proposal revision (which in itself is a discussion round).

Once all discussions are completed, all offerors still in the competitive range are requested to submit their final proposal revisions. The next step is the final evaluation (see Chapter 17).

NEGOTIATING UNDER THE SIMPLIFIED ACQUISITION PROCEDURES

This book is primarily directed at *contracts*, acquisitions over $100,000 or acquisitions for commercial items in excess of $5,000,000. Simplified acquisition procedures apply generally to procurements of $100,000 or less, although these procedures may be used for commercial acquisitions up to $5,000,000. The simplified acquisition procedures involve a considerable number of acquisitions and the FAR coverage is a little less than clear about how these procurements should be evaluated, negotiated, and documented. A short discussion of this area is in order.

The following references apply:

13.003(g)

(1) May use any appropriate combination of the procedures in FAR parts 13, 14, 15, 35, or 36 for contracts up to $100,000.

(2) For commercial items up to $5,000,000 may use any appropriate combination of Parts 12, 13, 14, and 15.

(3) Must promote competition to maximum extent practicable.

13.106-1

(1) When soliciting quotations and offers the contracting officer shall notify potential quoters/offerors the basis on which award will be made (price alone or price and other factors, e.g., past performance and quality).

(2) Contracting officers are encouraged to use best value.

(3) Solicitations are not required to state the relative importance assigned to each evaluation factor and subfactor, nor are they required to include subfactors.

13.106-2

(1) Contracting officer has broad discretion in fashioning suitable evaluation procedures.
The procedures described in FAR Parts 14 and 15 are not mandatory. At the contracting officer's discretion, one or more, but not necessarily all, of the evaluation procedures of Parts 14 and 15 may be used.

(2) If using price and other factors, ensure that quotations or offers can be evaluated in an efficient and minimally burdensome fashion. Formal evaluation plans, establishing a competitive range, conducting discussions, and scoring quotations or offers are not required. Contracting officers may conduct comparative evaluations of offers. Evaluation of other factors, such as past performance, may be based on information such as the contracting officer's knowledge of and previous experience with the supply or service being acquired, customer surveys, or other reasonable basis.

13.106-3

(1) Before making award the contracting officer shall document that the proposed price is fair and reasonable.

(2) Documentation must be kept to the minimum, however, if award is based on other than price-related factors, additional statements supporting the award decision must be kept.

13.501(b)

For commercial item acquisitions, the contract file shall include:

(1) A brief written description of the procedures used in awarding the contract; including the fact that the test procedures in FAR Subpart 13.5 were used.
(2) The number of offers received.
(3) An explanation, tailored to the size and complexity of the acquisition of the basis for the contract award.
(4) Any required sole source justification and approval.

So, with respect to the FAR Part 15 negotiation procedures, FAR Part 13 seems to say that you can select among the Part 15 procedures, using only those procedures deemed suitable. However, this is not necessarily so, according to the U.S. Court of Federal Claims, as shown in Example 16.12.

Example 16.12—Agency must clearly indicate that simplified acquisition procedures are being used #1[53]

This case involved an acquisition of commercial items in which the government accepted final proposal revisions to a proposal that was not technically acceptable, but did not accept revisions from other offerors. In addition, the government's actions occurred after the deadline for revised proposals. The protester argued that the discussions that led to these revisions were improper.

The government belatedly claimed that the procurement was conducted under FAR Part 13 and that the protester's argument that the discussions conducted were improper was inapplicable. The court did not agree.

An agency must, as a matter of fundamental fairness, inform offerors in the solicitation whether it is involving the subpart 13.5 test program and using simplified acquisition procedures - even though there is no such express requirement in the FAR.

Further, when a contracting officer opts to hold discussions under a FAR Part 13 *procurement, the contracting officer must comply with the FAR Part 15.307(b) requirement that all offerors still in the competitive range at the conclusion of discussions be given the opportunity to submit a final proposal revision.*

The court also noted that the procurement used FAR Part 15 procedures such as the following:

- Identifying the solicitation as a RFP
- Identifying the technical evaluation factors and weights in the solicitation
- Conducting discussions with the offerors in the competitive range
- Requesting written proposal revisions to be submitted by a common cut-off date
- Providing postaward debriefings.

The Court said that none of these actions were necessary if simplified acquisition procedures were used. The Court also pointed out that the record failed to contain the documentation required by 13.501(b) and therefore the government claim that FAR 13 applied was an "afterthought" and not the government's original intention.

In relation to the use of FAR 15 procedures, the Court indicated that once the request for proposal revisions has been issued at the end of discussions, an agency generally may not engage in further discussions with any offerors.

Moreover, the discussions with one offeror after the issuance of a request for final proposal revisions that enable it to make its proposal technically acceptable, as was the case here, are prohibited.

The government claimed the challenged discussions were "clarifications." The Court said clarifications are exchanges conducted in procurements where discussions are not expected to be held. The term has no application to exchanges that occur after discussions have been conducted with offerors.

In Example 16.12, it appears that the agency did not make it clear initially that simplified acquisition procedures were being used and did not document the file in accordance with the Part 13 requirements for commercial item acquisitions. Because it was not clear that the simplified acquisition procedures were being used, the Part 15 rules applied. This is consistent with a Comptroller General ruling, as shown in Example 16.13.

Example 16.13—Agency must clearly indicate that simplified acquisition procedures are being used #2[54]

An agency procured commercial items under Part 13.5 test procedures. It issued a Request for Quotations clearly stating that procurement was a commercial item acquisition and included the FAR clauses required for commercial item solicitations. Two responses were technically acceptable. The agency discussed certain features of the lowest-priced quote, allowed the quoter to submit a revised quotation, and made award to that quoter. The agency did not offer the other quoter an opportunity to revise its quote, and the offeror protested that this was not permitted under FAR Part 15.

GAO denied the protest.

Where, as here, simplified acquisition procedures are used, contracting agencies are to use innovative approaches to the maximum extent practicable in order to award a contract in the manner that is most suitable, efficient, and economical in the circumstances of each acquisition.

GAO also said that FAR Part 13 states that the evaluation procedures of FAR Part 15 are not mandatory and do not require the development of an evaluation plan, a competitive range, or formal discussions.

Examples 16.12 and 16.13 seem to indicate that if the solicitation indicates that simplified acquisition procedures will be used, an agency may use whatever approach it so chooses. However, even under the relaxed Part 13 procedures, an agency must evaluate and award in accordance with the procedures established in the solicitation, as shown in Example 16.14.

Example 16.14—Must evaluate in accordance with the terms of the solicitation[55]

An RFP for custodial services contemplated the use of commercial item procedures and the use of simplified acquisition procedures as authorized by FAR Subpart 13.5. The RFP called for written technical proposals to address past performance, types of equipment, and organizational structure and described the standards to be met. The RFP also called for oral presentations to address quality control and plan of operation. Offerors were to submit a price proposal with the technical proposal. Award would be made to the responsible firm whose proposal was considered to be most advantageous to the government, technical factors and price, when combined, being considered equal in value.

After a postaward debriefing, UMBI protested that the contracting officer performed an inadequate price/technical tradeoff when it awarded at a price 22 percent above that proposed by UMBI. UMBI argued that the record showed that the contracting officer basically adopted, without explanation, the evaluation board's recommendation based on the higher total point score for technical factors given to the awardee. UMBI pointed out that the evaluators and the contracting officer did not identify any deficiencies in its proposal, or state why the awardee's proposal was considered more advantageous and worth the price premium.

The agency argued that it performed a proper price/technical tradeoff. It pointed out that the acquisition was conducted under simplified acquisition procedures that do not require a formal source selection process or the detailed documentation required under FAR Part 15. It argued that "the contracting officer, through the technical panel, carefully applied the various criteria for award and arrived at a well reasoned well documented conclusion as to the offeror that presented the best value."

The Comptroller General did not agree with the agency.

Simplified acquisition procedures are designed to, among other things, reduce administrative expenses, promote efficiency and economy in contracting, and avoid unnecessary burdens for agencies and contractors.[56] *Although the procedures for simplified acquisitions do not require detailed justifications supporting a best value determination, the FAR requires that the contracting officer evaluate proposals "on the basis established in the solicitation" and support "the award decision if other than price-related factors were considered in selecting the supplier."*[57] *Thus, even when using simplified acquisition procedures, an agency must conduct the procurement consistent with a concern for fair and equitable competition and must evaluate proposals in accordance with the terms of the solicitation.*[58] *In reviewing protests against an allegedly improper simplified acquisition evaluation and selection decision, we examine the record to determine whether the agency met this standard and exercised its discretion reasonably.*[59]

In addition, as applicable here, there are several FAR provisions governing commercial item acquisitions that require the agency to explain and document its award decision. Under FAR Subpart 12.6, Streamlined Procedures for Evaluation and Solicitation for Commercial Items, which the agency recognizes is applicable here, the contracting officer is to "[s]elect the offer that is most advantageous to the Government," and to [f]ully document the rationale for selection of the successful offeror including discussion of any trade-offs considered."[60] *Also, under the test program for commercial items, the agency is required to include in the contract file "[a]n explanation, tailored to the size and complexity of the acquisition, of the basis for the contract award decision."*[61] *Here, we conclude that the selection decision was flawed because the contracting officer made no qualitative comparison of the technical differences between the proposals to determine whether the awardee's technical superiority justified the price premium. Further, the award decision was not adequately supported and documented.*

The contemporaneous record shows that the contracting officer's selection decision consisted of her signing off on the evaluation panel's recommendation. There is no evidence in the record that the contracting officer actually considered whether the relative differences in the proposals, as reflected by the point scores, represented any meaningful qualitative differences that warranted the payment of a price premium to the awardee. In fact, the contracting officer states that she basically disregarded the protester's low price because its proposal was not among the top four technically rated proposals based on points. The tradeoff was limited to the top four technically rated firms. Here, the record clearly shows that the award decision was based on point scores, and that the contracting officer "ratified" the evaluation panel's recommendation without any consideration of the protester's proposal.

If award is to be made on the basis other than price alone, even when using simplified acquisition procedures, the award decision must be fully documented and be consistent with the evaluation and award criteria set forth in the solicitation.

FAR 13.003(g) indicates that simplified acquisition procedures may combine the procedures of other FAR Parts. FAR 13.106-1 states that solicitations are not required to state the relative importance assigned to evaluation factors, and FAR 13.106-2 states that one or more, but not necessarily all, of the evaluation procedures of Parts 14 and 15 may be used and formal evaluation plans, competitive range determinations, scoring and discussions are not required. These references notwithstanding, procurements using simplified acquisition procedures must be conducted consistent with a concern for fair and equitable competition, and proposals must be evaluated in accordance with the terms of the solicitation.

It should be clear from the problems shown in Examples 16.12 and 16.14 that the FAR coverage is creating problems. While the indecisive coverage is designed to enhance contracting officer flexibility and promote efficiency and economy, it also leaves the contracting officer hanging where it says you can use some of this and some of that, but not all of anything. Eventually, after enough decisions have been made like those in the examples, more explicit direction will be provided. In the meantime, the important thing to remember is that (1) you must evaluate and award in accordance with the terms of the solicitation, and (2) if award is to be made on factors other than price, the award rationale must be documented well enough to show the validity of the award decision.

SOLE SOURCE NEGOTIATIONS

While this book deals primarily with competitive procurement, a few words about sole source negotiation are in order.

FAR 15.002(a) indicates that when contracting in a sole source environment, the RFP should be tailored to remove unnecessary information and requirements such as evaluation criteria and voluminous proposal preparation instructions. This would seem logical, except for one thing—even a sole source proposal must be evaluated. The fact that the solicitation is sole source does not guarantee that an award will be made if it turns out that the sole source does not understand the requirement, has proposed unacceptable terms and conditions, or has proposed an unacceptable price.

What is the difference between a sole source solicitation and a competitive solicitation? Some clauses and provisions certainly, but what about Sections L and M? Section M could probably be eliminated from a sole source solicitation because any problems with the proposal could be handled in discussions. Section L, however, particularly the proposal preparation instructions, is needed to ensure that the proposal addresses those areas of interest to the government. If you want to be able to evaluate a proposal, it is important that you tell the offeror what you want to see in the proposal. Therefore, FAR notwithstanding, it is suggested that proposal preparation instructions be used to ensure receipt of a proposal that contains the required information.

FAR 15.306(d) states that negotiations may include bargaining such as persuasion, alteration of assumptions and positions, and give-and-take, and may apply to price, schedule, technical requirements, type of contract, or other terms of a proposed contract. While bargaining generally does not apply to competitive procurements, it does apply to sole source negotiations. Since only one party was involved, any facet of the procurement, including the requirement itself, is subject to negotiation.

It is not intended here, to address the art of negotiation, that is, how to establish negotiation positions, do fact finding, establishing strategies, etc. Another book would be needed to address that topic. The point is, in the context of this book, that the only real restraints on sole source negotiations are the amount of funding available and that bargaining does not include any changes in the requirements that might open the procurement to competition. Any changes made as a result of bargaining must be within the envelope of the sole source justification.

Often when negotiating sole source, you do so because the contractor knows more about the requirement than you do.

The concept of incorporating all or part of the contractor's proposal by reference is more amenable to sole source procurement than competitive procurement. When doing so, it is important to ensure that the contractor does not include something, in that part of its proposal that is to be incorporated by reference, that is not to the government's advantage. This should be one of the focal points in the negotiation. There is nothing wrong with requiring the contractor to rewrite those parts of its proposal until the contractor "gets it right." In fact, it would be a mistake not to do so.

Likewise, when negotiating sole source, technical leveling should be the rule—you want to be sure that the contractor is proposing to do what you want done. If you do not have a complete meeting of the minds before award, fixing the problems later will be expensive.

Another point to remember is that even though you are negotiating sole source, the government is still in charge. You can be sure that the contractor wants the contract as much as you do—even more perhaps, because the jobs of the contractor personnel involved may depend on getting the contract.

It is the government's responsibility to be fair. A fair and reasonable price is one that is fair and reasonable for both parties. You should ensure that the contract price will provide the contractor with a reasonable profit. If you put the contractor's "back to the wall" on pricing, you are likely to have a problem contract as the contractor tries to "get well" through contract changes or corner cutting.

References

1. Greenleaf Distribution Servs., Inc., B-221335, 4/30/86, 86-1 CPD ¶422.
2. Miller-Holzwarth Inc. vs. United States No. 98-576C (Fed. Cl. Jan 6, 1999).
3. SmithKline Beecham Pharms., N.A. 93-2 CPD ¶79 at 4; Paramax Sys. Corp.; CAE-Link Corp., 93-2 CPD ¶282 at 6.
4. 93-2 CPD ¶79.

5. 93-2 CPD ¶282.
6. 93-1 CPD ¶58 at 2.
7. 98-2 CPD ¶30 at 11.
8. 94-2 CPD ¶154 at 8.
9. Dynacs Engineering Co. Inc., B-284234; B-284234.2; B-284234.3, 3/17/00.
10. FAR 15.610(d) (June 1997); Professional Servs. Group, Inc., B-274289, 12/19/96,97-1 CPD ¶54 at 5.
11. FAR 15.61l(c) (June 1997).
12. FAR 15.306; Spectrum Science & Software, Inc., B-282373, 6/22/99, 99-1 CPD ¶ 114 at 4.
13. Telos Corp., B-279493.3, 7/27/98, 98-2 CPD ¶30 at 9-11; Prospective Computer Analysts, Inc., B-275262.2, 2/24/97, 97-2 CPD ¶22 at 3-5.
14. Telos Corporation, B-279493.3, 7/27/98, GCR 110,365.
15. FAR 15.610(d)(June 1997); Battelle Mem'l Inst., B-259571.3, 12/8195, 95-2 CPD ¶284 at 5.
16. Matrix Int'l Logistics, Inc., B-249285.2, 12/30/92, 92-2 CPD ¶452 at 5.
17. *id.*
18. CBIS Fed. Inc., B-245844.2, 3127/92, 92-1 CPD ¶308 at 11-12.
19. Planning Sys, Inc., B-246170.4, 12/29/92, 92-2 CPD ¶445 at 7.
20. Technical & Administrative Services, Corp., B-279828, 7/27/98, GCR 110,423.
21. Brown & Root, Inc, and Perini Corp. a joint venture, B-270505.2, 9/12/96, CPD ¶ 143 at 6.
22. DAE Corp., B-259866; B-259866.2, 5/8/95, 95-2 CPD ¶ 13 at 4-5.
23. Brown & Root, Inc, and Perini Corp. a joint venture.
24. PRB Assocs., Inc., B-277994; B-277994.2, 12/18/97, 98-1 CPD ¶ 13 at 5-6.
25. Du & Assocs., Inc., B-280283.3, 12/22/98, 98-2 CPD ¶ 156 at 7.
26. See 41 U.S.C. sec. 253(d)(1)(A) (1994); FAR 15.306(d)(1).
27. SDS Petroleum Prods., Inc., B-280430, 9/18/98, 98-2 CPD ¶ 59 at 5.
28. See MCR Fed., Inc., B-280969, 12/4/98, 98-2 CPD para. __ at 10-11.

29. See Applied Cos., B-279811, 7/24/98, 98-2 CPD ¶ 52 at 8.
30. ACS Government Solutions Group, Inc., B-282098; B-282098.2; B-282098.3, 6/2/99.
31. FAR 15.306(d)(3).
32. 41 U.S.C. sect. 253b (d)(1)(A) (1994); FAR 15.306(d)(I).
33. Du & Assocs., Inc., B-280281.3, 12/22/98, 98-2 CPD ¶ 156 at 7.
34. Eldyne, Inc., B-250158 et. al., 1/14/93, 93-1 CPD ¶ 430 at 6, recon denied, Department of the Navy – Recon., B-250158.4, 5/28/93, 93-1 CPD ¶ 422.
35. I.T.SD. Corp., B-280431, 9/29/98.
36. National Medical Staffing, Inc., B-259402; B-259402.2, 3/24/95. CPD ¶ 163.
37. KBM Group Inc., B-281919; B-281919.2, 5/3/99.
38. FAR 15.306(d)(1).
39. Du & Assocs., Inc., B-280281.3, 12/22/98, 98-2 CPD ¶ 156 at 7-8.
40. Biospherics Inc., B-279278, 1/14/98, 98-1 CPD ¶ 161 at 6.
41. FAR 15.306(d)(1); The Pragma Corp., B-255236 et. al., 2/18/94, 94-1 CPD ¶ 124 at 9.
42. Grey Advertising Inc., B-184825, 5/14/76, 76-1 CPD ¶ 325 at 9.
43. Southwest Marine Inc.; American Sys Eng'g Corp., B-265865.3; B-265865.4, 1/23/96, 96-1 CPD ¶ 56 at 10-11.
44. Metro Machine Corp., B-281872; B-281872.2; B-281872.3; B-281872.4, 4/22/99.
45. STS Techs., B-254425.2, 9/14/94, 94-2 CPD ¶ 125 at 6; Ranor, Inc., B-255904, 4/14/99, 94-1 CPD ¶ 258 at 4.
46. Price Waterhouse, B-254492.2, 2/16/94, 94-1 CPD ¶ 168 at 11; DTH Management Group, B-252879.2; B-252879.3, 10/15/93, 93-2 CPD ¶ 227 at 4.
47. Data Preparation, Inc., B-233569, 3/24/89, 89-1 CPD 300 at 5-6.
48. Research for Better Schools, B-270774.3, 6/17/96, GCR 109,576.
49. Bioqual, Inc., B-259732.2; B-259732.3, 5/15/95, 95-1 CPD ¶243.
50. Blue Cross Blue Shield of Texas, Inc., B-261316.4, 11/9/95, 95-2 CPD ¶248 at 6-7, GCR 110,445, fn8.

51. Innovative Training Sys., B-251225.3, 10/19/93, 93-2 CPD ¶232.
52. Price Waterhouse, 65 Comp. Gen. 205 (1986), 86-1 CPD ¶54; Applied Remote Technology, Inc., B-250275, 1/22/93, 93-1 CPD ¶58; Warren Elec. Constr. Corp., B-236173.4; B-236173.5, 7/16/90, 90-2 CPD ¶34.
53. Dubrinsky vs. U.S. Fed. Cl. No. 98-884C, 3/31/99.
54. United Marine International LLC, B-281512, 2/22/99.
55. Universal Building Maintenance, Inc., B-282456, 7/15/99.
56. FAR 13.002.
57. FAR 13.106-2(a)(2) and 13.106-3(b)(3)(ii).
58. National Aerospace Group Inc., B-281958, 5/10/99; Sawtooth Enters., Inc., B-281218, 12/7/98, 98-2 CPD ¶139 at 3.
59. Sawtooth Enters., Inc., supra.
60. FAR 12.602(c).
61. FAR 13.501(b)(3).

CHAPTER 17

Conducting the Final Evaluation

The final evaluation is conducted after discussions are completed and the final proposal revisions are received. The purpose of the final evaluation is to assess the impact of the proposal revisions on each proposal and to determine which proposal offers the best value to the government. This is an evaluation of the final version of the proposal; it includes the original proposal, any revisions made during discussions, and any revisions that first appear in the final proposal revision. The final evaluation is conducted in accordance with the same evaluation criteria used in the initial evaluation.

WHO EVALUATES

The original evaluation team may or may not be convened to conduct the final evaluation. As long as the RFP does not require that the same evaluators conduct the final evaluation (and it should not), these individuals do not have to be used. Generally, in formal source selection (for major acquisitions), the same evaluation organization is used throughout the evaluation process. In informal source selection, use of the original evaluation team often depends on the complexity of the final evaluation. Generally, the evaluation team leader is used throughout the process, but even this is not mandatory, as shown in Example 17.1.

Example 17.1—Use of all original evaluators is not required in the final evaluation[1]

In this case, the protester argued that it was treated unfairly during the final evaluation because all of the original evaluators were not used. The Comptroller General did not agree.

*Our Office has recognized that all of the original evaluators need not rescore revised proposals. As we stated in Ray F. Weston Inc.,[2] "Weston challenges the manner in which the revised proposals were evaluated since only two members of the TEP conducted the reevaluation rather than reconvening the entire TEP as required by the RFP." However, the RFP stated that "the revised proposal will be reevaluated and scored in accordance with the solicitation evaluation criteria." This does not require the entire TEP to reevaluate the revised proposals and our Office has recognized that all of the original evaluators need not rescore the revised proposals.[3] Here, the RFQ stated that initial quotations would be evaluated by a "team of government personnel" and that the "initial evaluation of proposals may be revised in light of ***[final offers]." We do not consider that these RFQ statements were breached in the final evaluation of proposals."*

In this case, the Comptroller General relied on the wording of the solicitation document to support the decision. It should be noted, however, that there is no requirement to use the entire evaluation team, or even any of the original evaluators, *unless* the solicitation document says they must be used.

CHECK FOR DEVIATIONS FROM THE STATED REQUIREMENTS

The final evaluation is more than just a review of revisions. You must ensure that the final proposal addresses all contractual requirements. Each proposal must be evaluated as a whole. During the discussion process and resulting revisions, things promised in the initial proposal may have been changed or deleted. Whether these alterations were intentional or inadvertent, award is made on the final proposal, as written.

If you accept changes that deviate from the stated requirements, you are deviating from the requirements of the RFP and must first amend the RFP and give the other offerors an opportunity to similarly revise their proposals, as shown in Example 17.2.

Example 17.2—Deviations from RFP requirements cannot be accepted unless the RFP is amended to permit the other offerors the same opportunity[4]

It is a fundamental rule of competitive procurements that all offerors be provided a common basis for submission of proposals.[5] When an agency relaxes its requirements, either before or after receipt of proposals, it must issue a written amendment to notify all offerors of the changed requirements.[6] Accordingly our Office will sustain a protest where an agency, without issuing a written amendment, relaxes an RFP specification that may prejudice the protester, e.g., where the protester would have altered its proposal to its competitive advantage had it been given the opportunity to respond to the altered requirements.[7]

It is the contracting officer's responsibility to make sure that the proposal selected for award meets all RFP requirements. To do this, each proposal must be evaluated in its entirety, as revised, and strict adherence to the stated requirements is required.

ENSURE ALL DISCUSSION QUESTIONS HAVE BEEN ADDRESSED

Discussion questions that the offeror has failed to answer or has answered inadequately should be so noted. Determine whether this failure constitutes a deficiency or a weakness. If it constitutes a deficiency, consider the failure to be an unsatisfactory response and an uncorrectable problem (it cannot be corrected because there are no further discussions after the submission of the final proposal revisions).

Even if you think the problem could be corrected, the response must still be evaluated as unsatisfactory because to do otherwise would be unfair to the other offerors. If one offeror receives a favorable rating for an unsatisfactory response because of your expectations rather than the substance of its proposal, you would, in effect, be granting that offeror a waiver of an RFP requirement that was not provided to the others.

Generally, you should not make an award to an offeror whose final proposal contains deficiencies. Weaknesses, however, may be accepted but should be so noted. If that offeror receives the award, the file should be flagged to put the contract administrators on notice of potential contract problems.

ENSURE ALL FINAL PROPOSAL REVISIONS ARE FULLY SUBSTANTIATED

All technical and pricing changes must be fully substantiated.

Technical Changes

Any changes an offeror makes for the first time in its final proposal revision are final. Such revisions can change an otherwise acceptable proposal to an unacceptable proposal that must be rejected. Generally, such proposals are rejected only if the changes are not fully explained and cast doubt on the offeror's ability to perform as required. The contracting agency is under no obligation to reopen discussions to address deficiencies that first appear in the final proposal revision, as shown in Example 17.3.

Example 17.3—Offerors must take responsibility for changes made in final proposal revisions[8]

FBS submitted with its BAFO a revised equipment list that reflected various changes in product quality and quantity from its earlier equipment list (the Air Force did not require the submission of this list in the BAFO). The list did not include two mandatory pieces of equipment that had been in FBS's earlier submission. The Air Force rejected the BAFO as technically unacceptable and FBS protested on the grounds that the original list still applied. The Comptroller General did not agree.

In a negotiated procurement, an offeror must affirmatively demonstrate that its proposal will meet the government's needs where required by the solicitation.[9] *Where, as here, a solicitation requires offerors to furnish information necessary to establish compliance with the specifications, an agency may reasonably find a proposal that fails to include such information technically unacceptable.*[10]

FBS argues that its BAFO equipment list did not need to incorporate or to restate its earlier offers of the teleconferencing system or the galvanized steel conduits because its prior written clarifications bound it to provide these features. We disagree. A BAFO may revise or supersede any aspect of a prior proposal, provided that the offeror is willing to take the risk that the changes may render a previously acceptable proposal unacceptable.[11] *See also Dynalectron Corp.; Lockheed Elecs. Co., Inc.,*[12] *(agency could reasonably interpret salary information in BAFO cost proposal as superseding salary information in initial technical proposal). By including an equipment list in its BAFO that failed to mention certain features offered in a prior proposal, we believe that FBS created, at the very least, an ambiguity as to whether its BAFO had retained or withdrawn the required teleconferencing system and galvanized steel conduits.*

In our view, the protester's failure to reference these features in its revised BAFO equipment list provided a reasonable basis for the rejection of its proposal as unacceptable, as these features were clearly related to the proposal's acceptability. FBS assumed the risk that revisions to its BAFO might raise questions about whether its system satisfied the contract requirements which might result in a determination of technical unacceptability, since an agency is not obligated to reopen discussions so that an offeror may remedy defects introduced into a previously acceptable proposal.[13]

The offeror is responsible for ensuring that all final proposal revision changes are fully substantiated and that the changes do not make its proposal unacceptable. The mistake FBS made was to submit what appeared to be a new and revised equipment list rather than clearly indicating that certain changes had been made in its originally submitted equipment list.

Reopening discussions because of problems related to the final proposal revisions is done only when necessary to correct agency errors or otherwise ensure that the award is valid and represents the best value to the government, as shown in Example 17.4.

Example 17.4—Discussions may be reopened to correct agency mistakes or to otherwise ensure that the discussions are equitable[14]

An agency reopened discussions and called for a second round of best and final offers because it had failed to advise an offeror (the eventual awardee) during the first round of discussions of a deficiency in its proposal that rendered it unacceptable. The unsuccessful offerors protested that it was improper for the agency to reopen the discussions. The Comptroller General did not agree.

In order for discussions to be meaningful, an agency must lead offerors into areas of their proposals which require correction or amplification.[15] *Pursuant to this requirement, the agency concluded that it had an obligation to identify the deficiency existing in Travel Centre's proposal, and that its failure to do so would render either its subsequent award to Travel Centre or its subsequent rejection of Travel Centre's proposal vulnerable to a legal challenge. We see nothing unreasonable in the agency's ultimate decision to remedy its earlier oversight through a second round of discussions and a request for BAFOs.*[16]

Generally agencies do not reopen discussions after the submission of final proposal revisions except to correct agency errors discovered during the final proposal evaluation. If necessary, however, discussions may be reopened even after award,, as shown in Example 17.5.

Example 17.5—Reopening discussions to take corrective action while a protest is pending is permissible[17]

Unsuccessful offerors for a solicitation involving multiple awards challenged the technical and price evaluations of several of the ten awardees. After evaluating the protests, the agency determined that the solicitation's price evaluation scheme was unworkable and effectively prevented the agency from accurately determining best value in making multiple awards. The agency took corrective action in response to the protests, including rescinding awarded contracts, amending the solicitation, reopening negotiations, and requesting a second round of best and final offers, notwithstanding the disclosure of limited information from awardees' proposals.

The contractors whose awards were rescinded protested this action. They argued that more limited corrective action, or none at all, would be more appropriate. The Comptroller General did not agree.

Contracting officials have broad discretion to take corrective action where the agency determines that such action is necessary to ensure fair and impartial competition.[18] *It is not necessary for an agency to conclude that the protest is certain to be sustained before it may take corrective action; where the agency has reasonable concern that there were errors in the procurement, even if the protest could be denied, we view it as within the agency's discretion to take corrective action.*[19] *An agency may amend a solicitation and request and evaluate a second round of BAFOs where the record shows that the agency made the decision to take this action in good faith, without the specific intent of changing a particular offeror's technical ranking or avoiding an award to a particular offeror.*[20] *We will not object to an agency's proposed corrective action where the agency concludes that the award, because of the perceived flaws in the procurement process, was not necessarily made on a basis most advantageous to the government, so long as the corrective action taken is appropriate to remedy the impropriety.*[21]

[And in footnote 3] In taking corrective action on the improper awards, the agency correctly concluded that it could not simply request the offeror to remove the qualification, thereby changing its price, without engaging in discussions with that offeror. If negotiations are reopened with that offeror, they must be reopened with all offerors in the competitive range.[22]

Pricing Changes

It is not unusual for offerors to make pricing changes in their final proposal submissions that may or may not be related to specific technical changes. In any event, offerors must fully substantiate any pricing changes because the original cost or price analysis, cost realism analysis, and cost/technical tradeoff (see Chapter 18) may have to be revised. An offeror's failure to fully substantiate pricing changes could make it impossible to evaluate the relationship between the offeror's proposed cost and promised performance. If the lack of substantiation precludes a valid evaluation, you may ignore the change and use the information previously submitted as the basis for the final evaluation. Such an action, however, is likely to draw a protest, so do this only when you can fully justify your actions through contemporaneous documentation.

Offerors take a chance when they make pricing changes in the BAFO. Examples 17.6 through 17.8 (all taken from the same case) illustrate the problems that can occur when offerors make changes in their final proposal revisions that affect the pricing.

Example 17.6—Pricing changes: Unsupported personnel changes[23]

The protester argued that the cost realism adjustment made in its proposal was unreasonable because the agency "reassigned" some of the contractor's personnel to cost centers other than those proposed in its BAFO revision. The Comptroller General did not agree.

Contrary to the protester's arguments, Purvis's BAFO does not explain or justify the reallocation of personnel between the cost centers. Nor does the BAFO address how Purvis intends to satisfy the required design and development of test equipment contract tasks without the reassigned senior engineers or technicians. It is an offeror's obligation, when introducing changes in its BAFO, to demonstrate how its revised offer will satisfy the government's requirements since the agency is not required to reopen discussions to afford an offeror an opportunity to demonstrate compliance. See Loral Elecs. Sys.[24] (insufficiently explained cost center revisions in BAFO justified down-grading of BAFO from initial proposal rating).

The record reasonably shows that Purvis's unsupported shifting of personnel in its BAFO was merely intended to reduce proposed costs, a reduction that the Navy reasonably determined may not be realized in actual performance of the contract. Accordingly, we think the agency reasonably adjusted Purvis's proposed BAFO costs by placing the reassigned high salaried personnel in the cost center where they were originally proposed.

When an offeror fails to support a BAFO revision that changes costs, such as switching higher-priced personnel from the highest overhead cost center to the lowest overhead cost center, you may properly adjust costs back to original proposal when reviewing the cost realism analysis in the final evaluation.

Example 17.7—Pricing changes: Unsupported reduction of overhead[25]

The protester argued that the cost realism adjustments made in its proposal were unreasonable because the agency used its fiscal year 1991 indirect cost rates in lieu of the rates proposed in its BAFO revision. The Comptroller General did not agree.

We think the agency reasonably concluded that Purvis's projections of its future business and overhead expenses were too speculative to support the proposed indirect cost rates, particularly in light of the historical data that showed Purvis's indirect cost rates had been steadily increasing since its 1987 fiscal year (this might reflect its declining business). Even though NUSC expressed its concerns about the proposed rates to Purvis during discussions, Purvis lowered its overhead still further in its BAFO, and did so without adequate justification. Under the circumstances, NUSC could reasonably rely upon the prior year's rates as the best information available to the agency to determine the indirect cost rates that it could reasonably be required to pay under the contract.[26]

You may use actual indirect cost rates from a prior fiscal year when reviewing the cost realism analysis where the offeror proposes a significantly lower rate (much lower than historical rate) in a final proposal revision that is based on speculative projections of future business and unexplained overhead reductions.

Example 17.8—Pricing changes: Unsupported site rates and escalation rates[27]

The protester argued that the cost realism adjustments made in its proposal were unreasonable because the agency made adjustments to the subcontractor's overhead and labor escalation rates proposed in the protestor's BAFO revision. The Comptroller General denied the protest.

The record also supports the agency's adjustment of Purvis's subcontractor's overhead. Purvis's subcontractor, for the first time in its BAFO and without explanation, lowered its proposed overhead rates by changing its proposed place of performance from "on-site" to "off-site." Since the RFP required all performance to be on the contractor's site, NUSC used the overhead rate associated with the subcontractor's on-site performance. Purvis now argues that its subcontractor's intended off-site performance was to be at Purvis's facility. Since this was not explained in Purvis's BAFO, we think the agency reasonably assumed that the subcontractor improperly intended to perform at a facility that was not on the contractor's site and disregarded the unsubstantiated reduction in overhead associated with is change.

Regarding NUSC's adjustments to the subcontractor's labor escalation rate, the record shows that during discussions NUSC questioned the subcontractor's offer of a substantially lower escalation rate than that established by the Office of the Assistant Secretary of the Navy (Shipbuilding and Logistics) (ASN(S&L)). While Purvis's subcontractor responded that its proposed labor escalation rate reflected its actual escalation of salaries for 13 months, it provided historical data for just three labor categories that the subcontractor intended to use in performing the contract. The agency found that the information provided was too limited in time and scope to demonstrate the reasonableness of its lower proposed escalation. Given that the offerors and other subcontractors—all who must perform the required services in the New London, Connecticut, labor market area—utilized the same rate as the ASN (S&L) rate and in the absence of more adequately documented support for the subcontractor's proposed labor escalation rate, we think the agency reasonably adjusted Purvis's costs to reflect the ASN (S&L) rate.[28]

When reviewing the cost realism analysis in the final evaluation, the use of the on-site overhead rate is permissible, when performance is to be on-site, regardless of a proposed "off-site" rate in a final proposal revision if use of the off-site rate is not explained. Agency labor escalation rate guidelines may be used when the offeror lowers the rate in its final proposal revision and fails to fully support the rate used.

It is in your best interest to ensure the receipt of acceptable proposals. You can minimize or avoid the problems noted in Examples 17.6 through 17.8 by warning offerors in the letter requesting final proposal revisions that any technical or pricing revisions made in the final proposal revision must be fully substantiated and must clearly indicate the parts of the initial proposal that have been changed and the parts that are still in effect.

MAKE COMPARISONS BETWEEN PROPOSALS

The final evaluation largely determines which offeror should receive the award. This evaluation cannot be done without comparing the relative strengths and weaknesses of the competing proposals. The comparisons, however, should not be made until after the final evaluation has established the acceptability of the individual proposals.

The comparisons should identify the significant technical and pricing differences between the competing proposals and assess the significance of these differences on the source selection decision. The assessment of proposal differences forms the basis for the cost/technical tradeoff determination (see Chapter 18).

REACH A CONSENSUS ON THE OVERALL EVALUATION

After evaluating the individual final proposal revisions, the evaluators should meet to reach a consensus on the final evaluation, as they did in the initial evaluation. The consensus discussions should involve not only the individual evaluations but also the comparisons between the proposals and any other factors that would be of significance to the final source selection decision. Consensus discussions ensure that all proposals are fully evaluated and scored and ranked properly in the order of their relative value.

When reading a consensus, the evaluators should identify any remaining deficiencies and weaknesses, discuss the significant differences between the proposals, and assess the impact of these differences on the relative acceptability of the proposals.

DEVELOP A RATIONALE FOR THE AWARD RECOMMENDATION

The final evaluation usually includes an award recommendation, unless the evaluators are specifically directed not to do so. An award recommendation should include a rationale for the selection of the otherwise successful offeror that the source selection authority can use for the official source selection determination. This rationale may include, as appropriate, a cost/technical tradeoff determination (see Chapter 18).

DOCUMENT THE RESULTS OF THE FINAL EVALUATION

As with the initial evaluation, the results of the final evaluation must be fully documented. The documentation provides the primary basis for the source selection decision. A lack of sufficient documentation can negate an award as in the case in Example 17.9.

Example 17.9—Documenting the final evaluation for a source selection decision[29]

Biospherics challenged the agency's evaluation of its proposal, contending that its proposal should have been rated technically superior to LAI's (the awardee) proposal. Biospherics further challenged the agency's decision to award a contract to LAI as a technically superior offeror.

In reviewing protests against allegedly improper evaluations, it is not our role to reevaluate proposals. Rather our Office examines the record to determine whether the agency's judgment was reasonable and in accord with the RFP's stated evaluation criteria.[30] *In order for us to review an agency's selection determination, an agency must have adequate documentation to support that decision.*[31] *While adjectival ratings and point scores are useful as guides to decision-making, they generally are not controlling, but rather, must be supported by documentation of the relative differences between proposals, their weaknesses and risks, and the basis and reasons for the selection decision.*[32]

Here the record is devoid of any documentation of the agency's evaluation of final revised proposals. There is no indication of an analysis of the revised proposals, no information in the record regarding proposal strengths and weaknesses after discussions, and no discussion as to why the strengths and weaknesses from the initial evaluation remained the same. In the absence of such documentation, we are unable to determine the reasonableness of the agency's evaluation upon which the selection of LAI for award was made.

In sum, the evaluation and source selection record furnished to our Office—numerical scores and a blanket determination of acceptability, no post-discussion narratives, and the source selection memorandum which contains no explanation of how the revised proposals affected the initial evaluation—is insufficient for our Office to determine the reasonableness of the agency's evaluation of proposals and the reasonableness of the agency's selection decision.[33]

DEVELOP THE FINAL EVALUATION REPORT

The final evaluation report documents the impact of the final proposal revisions on the overall evaluation of each proposal and the effect of the revisions on the relative standing of the offerors. It reflects the consensus reached by the evaluators on the scoring and ranking of each proposal and documents the rationale for each finding. As noted earlier, this document serves as the primary basis for the source selection decision.

The final evaluation report should contain the following:

- A summary of the findings of the initial evaluation, including the rating and ranking of the initial proposals
- A discussion of the revisions made to each proposal and the impact of the revisions on the acceptability of the proposal
- Identification of the significant technical and pricing differences between the proposals and their impact on the acceptability of the proposals, including any cost/technical tradeoffs
- The final scoring and ranking of the proposals
- An award recommendation, as required. The award recommendation should include the rationale supporting the recommendation.

Differences of opinion that cannot be resolved should be included as a minority report to ensure that the source selection official has a complete record of the evaluation findings.

HOW TO FIX A BROKEN EVALUATION

This chapter cannot end without an illustration of what can go wrong in the evaluation process and what can be done to correct the problems. Example 17.10 is a classic case.

Example 17.10—How to fix a broken evaluation[34]

An agency issued a solicitation for a cost-plus-fixed fee contract for logistical management and support services for specific conferences. It received ten proposals in May. The evaluation was completed in June. Award was made in late January. The incumbent contractor, an unsuccessful offeror, protested. The following is the chronology of the events leading up to the award.

June

The evaluation panel reported that the incumbent had submitted a perfect proposal with no weaknesses and was given a score of 100 points. One other offeror (not the awardee) was marginally acceptable at 66.75 points, and the remaining offerors (including the awardee) were technically unacceptable.

This evaluation concerned the contracting officer who expected the scoring to be closer because (1) several of the offerors had successfully performed similar work for the agency, (2) several of the offerors had received technical scores in the high 80s and 90s in recent competitive procurements, and (3) it seemed unlikely that such qualified offerors would submit such markedly inferior proposals.

The contracting officer suspected bias and examined the evaluation worksheets. She found that the evaluators' score sheets contained numerous blank spaces, too many general statements, and too few specific statements and did not sufficiently justify the range of low scores.

July

The contracting officer instructed the evaluation panel as to how to document their evaluation and directed them to reevaluate the proposals and more adequately explain the scoring.

August

The panel resubmitted its evaluation. This time it reported the incumbent's proposal at 93.66, with certain weaknesses. The panel made almost no change in its evaluation of the other proposals. The contracting officer concluded that the panel's findings were not responsive to her request for reevaluation because of the lack of adequate documentation of the problems with the other proposals.

September

The contracting officer dismissed the evaluation panel and convened a new panel that was specifically instructed how to adequately document the strengths and weaknesses of each proposal.

October

The new panel evaluated the incumbent's proposal at 88.3 points, another at 63 points, the awardee at 60 points and the rest ranging from 58.6 to 31 points. This time, however, the evaluation was fully documented and the contracting officer used the reported technical weaknesses as the basis for discussions.

November

Discussions were concluded and BAFOs received and evaluated. The evaluation panel concluded that the incumbent's response did not add to or detract from its initial proposal, so its score remained at 88.3 points. The score of the second-ranked proposal also remained the same, at 63 points. The awardee had revised its proposal and improved its score to 85 points, however, the evaluation panel did find that its proposed staff time was too low and should be increased.

The two highest ranked offerors were the incumbent at 88.3 technical points with a cost estimate of $323,988, and the awardee at 85 technical points with a cost estimate of $241,144.

December

The contracting officer wanted to award to the awardee, but decided to ask it to revise its BAFO to add more staff time. The awardee submitted a revised BAFO but refused to substantially change its staffing estimate, adding less than $1,000 to cover extra part-time conference personnel.

About this time, the incumbent protested the evaluation of the proposals (apparently alerted by a leak from the agency that it was not going to get the award). In reviewing the protest, the contracting officer realized that asking one offeror to revise its BAFO without reopening the BAFO discussions for all offerors was an error and informed the awardee that the revised BAFO would not be considered. The awardee acknowledged this and stated that its original BAFO would stand.

January

By now the contracting officer had decided to reopen discussions with both the incumbent and the awardee and permit revised BAFOs from each. She then received a second letter from the incumbent supplementing the incumbent's initial protest. Based on the detailed information in that letter, the contracting officer concluded that the incumbent must have received inside agency information. Due to the extent of the improper disclosures to the incumbent, the contracting officer had no confidence that the competitors could compete on an equal basis if discussions were reopened.

The contracting officer therefore made award to the awardee on the basis of the original BAFOs, concluding that the technical proposals were roughly equal and awarding on the basis of low price. The incumbent protested to the Comptroller General. The Comptroller General concurred with the contracting officer's actions and denied the incumbent's protest.

With respect to the first evaluation, the Comptroller General issued the following ruling.

We recognize that the contracting officer has broad discretion concerning the amount of detail she would deem necessary to (1) advise unsuccessful offerors why they were excluded from the competitive range, and (2) conduct meaningful discussions with offerors selected for the competitive range. While technical evaluators may know which proposals are the best and why, their views are worthless unless they are effectively communicated to the contracting officer. Here, the contracting officer knew from personal experience with at least three non-incumbent vendors that they could do the work and the contracting officer reasonably, in our view, was alerted that all three could not have submitted poor quality proposals. With that knowledge and knowing that our Office carefully scrutinizes visibly narrow competitive ranges, we can understand why the contracting officer rejected the first evaluation because the panel's explanation of the scoring was incomplete, too general in part, and lacking specific reasons for the assigned scores. We cannot conclude that her action was unreasonable or outside her broad discretion in this area.

With respect to the second evaluation by the first evaluation panel, the Comptroller General issued the following ruling:

We note that the contracting officer gave the panel explicit instructions as to what details she needed and the panel had a lengthy memo describing the format in which the report should be. From the contracting officer's perspective the panel took about one month to merely reformat the first report without being responsive to the contracting officer. In our view, the second scoring by the first panel did not add enough to effectively respond to the contracting officer's request. Faced with this second inadequate report, the contracting officer effectively had the following options: (1) give the panel one more chance; (2) do it herself without technical advice; or (3) convene a new panel that may be better able to communicate its views to the contracting officer. We have no basis to object to the rejection of the first two options as unacceptable in favor of the third option.

With respect to the third evaluation (by another evaluation panel), the Comptroller General issued the following ruling:

While only one member of the second panel was as familiar with the incumbent's work as the members of the first panel were, the members of the second panel were able, in the contracting officer's view, to successfully articulate the reasons for the scores assigned to the technical proposals and to state the perceived strengths and weakness of the proposals. See University of New Orleans[35] *(composition of technical evaluation panels is within the procuring agency's discretion) and Ads Audio Visual Productions*[36] *(protester has the burden of showing that evaluators are not qualified). The record contains no evidence to suggest that the members of the second panel were not qualified or that the agency abused its broad discretion in the composition of the second panel. Further, we note that there are substantive differences between the first and second panel's reports and we cannot conclude that the contracting officer abused her discretion by accepting the report of the second panel.*

Example 17.10 illustrates the problems that can occur with an evaluation and how long it can take to fix a broken procurement. If evaluators are not properly briefed before the initial evaluation, they can produce faulty and useless evaluations. When evaluators are biased, and this can happen where one of the competitors is a trusted incumbent, the results of their work cannot be used. Proper preparation and orientation of the evaluators before the initial evaluation might help avoid these problems.

Example 17.10 also illustrates what the contracting officer, or other source selection official, can do in such cases. The contracting officer may give the panel one more chance; fire the original panel and convene a new panel; or ignore the evaluation findings and make a unilateral source selection decision without technical assistance.

Typically, when the evaluation results are inadequate, a briefing on the proper evaluation and documentation procedures followed by a reevaluation will serve to fix the problem. Convening a new panel is usually done only where the evaluators cannot overcome their bias for a particular offeror and conduct the evaluation properly. Unilateral source selection decisions are not that uncommon; they usually happen, however, when the evaluation is conducted properly but the source selection official does not agree with the evaluation results (see Chapter 19).

References

1. Logistical Systems Inc., B-196254, 6/24/80, 80-1 CPD ¶442.
2. Ray F. Weston Inc., B-197866, B-197949, 5/14/80, 80-1 CPD ¶340.
3. Checchi and Co., B-187982, 4/4/77, 77-1 CPD ¶232; Columbia Research Corp., B-193154, 5/15/79, 79-1 CPD ¶353.
4. IRT Corp., B-246991, 4/22/92, 92-1 CPD ¶378, GCR 106,563.
5. ATT&T Coms., 65 Comp. Gen. 412 (1986), 86-1 CPD ¶247.
6. FAR 15.606.
7. Federal Computer Corp., B-239432, 8/29/90, 90-2 CPD ¶175, GCR 104,676.
8. Federal Business Systems, Inc., B-246514, 3/13/92, 92-1 CPD ¶283, GCR 106,470.
9. Electronic Comms., Inc., 55 Comp. Gen. 636 (1976), 76-1 CPD ¶15; Intertec Aviation, B-239672.4, 4/4/91, 91-1 CPD ¶348, GCR 105,355.
10. Inter-Contental Equip., Inc., B-224244, 2/5/87, 87-1 CPD ¶122, GCR 100,306.
11. Control Data and KET Inc., 60 Comp. Gen. 548 (1981), 81-1 CPD ¶531; Electronic Coms., Inc., 55 Comp.Gen. 636 (1976), 76-1 CPD ¶15.
12. Dynalectron Corp.; Lockheed Elecs. Co., Inc., 54 Comp. Gen. 1009 (1975), 75-1 CPD ¶341.
13. RCA Serv. Co., B-219643, 11/8/85, 85-2 CPD ¶563.
14. Dube Travel Agency & Tours Inc.; Garber Travel, B-270438; B-270438.2, 3/6/96, GCR 109,402.
15. FAR 15.610; Stone & Webster Eng'g Corp., B-255286.2, 4/12/94, 94-1 CPD ¶306.
16. Systems & Defense Servs., Int'l., B-254254.2, 2/9/94, 94-1 CPD ¶91; HLJ Management Group, Inc., B-225843.3, 10/20/88, 88-2 CPD ¶375, aff'd B-254254.2, 2/9/94, 94-1 CPD ¶97.

17. Patriot Contract Servs, LLC.; Keystone Shipping Servs, Inc.; MTL Ship Management; V-Ships Marine Ltd., B-278276.11; B-278276.12; B-278276.13; B-278276.14, 9/22/98, GCR 110,408.
18. Rockville Mailing Servs., Inc., B-270161.2, 4/10/96, 96-1 CPD ¶184 at 4; Oshkosh Truck Corp.; Idaho Norland Corp., B-237058.2; B-237058.3, 2/14/90, 90-1 CPD ¶274 at 4.
19. Main Bldg. Maintenance, Inc., B-279191.3, 8/5/98, 98-2 CPD ¶ at 3.
20. PRC, Inc., B-233561.8; B-233561.9, 9/29/92, 92-2 CPD ¶215 at 3-4; Burns & Roe Servs. Corp., B-248394, 8/25/92, 92-2 CPD ¶124 at 5; Unisys Corp., B-230019.2, 7/12/88, 88-2 CPD ¶35 at 5.
21. Rockville Mailing Servs., Inc., supra.
22. SmithKline Beecham Pharmaceuticals, N.A., B-252226.2, 8/4/93, 93-2 CPD ¶79 at 4.
23. Purvis Systems Inc., B-245761; B-245761.2, 1/31/92, 92-1 CPD ¶132, GCR 106,328.
24. Loral Elecs. Sys., B-224540, 2/10/87, 87-1 CPD ¶143, GCR 100,334.
25. Purvis Systems Inc., B-245761; B-245761.2, 1/31/92, 92-1 CPD ¶132, GCR 106,328.
26. Marine Designs, B-221897, 5/29/86, 86-1 CPD ¶502.
27. Purvis Systems Inc., B-245761; B-245761.2, 1/31/92, 92-1 CPD ¶132, GCR 106,328.
28. Raytheon Servs. Co.; Informatics Info., Sys. Co., Inc., 59 Comp. Gen. 316 (1980), 80-1 CPD ¶214.
29. Biospherics Inc., B-278508.4; B-278508.5; B-278508.6, 10/6/98, GCR 110,428.
30. Engineering and Computation, Inc., B-261658, 10/16/95, 95-2 CPD ¶176 at 2-3.
31. Arco Management of Washington D.C., Inc., B-248653, 9/11/92, 92-2 CPD ¶173 at 3.
32. Century Envtl. Hygiene, Inc., B-179378, 6/5/98, 98-1 CPD ¶164 at 4; Engineering & Computation, Inc., B-261658, 10/16/95, 95-2 CPD ¶176 at 3.
33. Labat-Anderson Inc., B-246071; B-246071.2, 2/18/92, 92-1 CPD ¶193 at 5-8.

34. CSR Inc., B-205776, 9/20/82, 82-2 CPD ¶237.
35. University of New Orleans, B-184194, 5/26/78, 78-1 CPD ¶401.
36. Ads Audio Visual Productions, B-190760, 3/15/78, 78-1 CPD ¶206.

CHAPTER 18

Best Value Procurements and Cost/Technical Tradeoffs

The concepts of best value and the use of functional statements of work are not new, but the emphasis placed on them is. The current emphasis is likely to generate additional regulatory and perhaps statutory coverage of this subject directed to more clearly defining the key to making a best value procurement—the cost/technical tradeoff.

BEST VALUE PROCUREMENT

Best value is a relatively new term for an old concept—that the government will award a contract to the responsible offeror whose offer, conforming to the solicitation, will be the *most advantageous* to the government, cost or price and other factors considered. Under both the *best value* and *most advantageous* concepts, the government procures its requirements on the basis of the best overall value to the government (best combination of quality and price) rather than on the basis of the acceptable offer (meets the minimum requirements) with the lowest price.

Negotiated procurements may still be made on the basis of the technically acceptable offer with the lowest price where the best value to the government does not require technical quality above a stated minimum. In such cases, discussions are limited to establishing that offerors have submitted technically acceptable proposals and then price is the primary consideration. Cost/technical tradeoffs are not made in these procurements.

AWARDING ON THE BASIS OF QUALITY

The concept of awarding on the basis of quality (such as technical excellence, past performance, management capability, prior experience, personnel requirements, and compliance with solicitation requirements) rather than simply the low price is not new, as illustrated by Example 18.1.

Example 18.1—Awarding on the basis of quality, rather than just low price[1]

The following was extracted from the Comptroller General's 1976 Grey Advertising decision where, quoting from the 1975 Tracor Jitco decision,[2] the Comptroller General stated:

Uniformly, we have agreed with the exercise of the administrative discretion involved—in the absence of a clear showing that the exercised discretion was not rationally founded—as to whether a given technical point spread between competitive-range offerors showed that the higher-scored proposal was technically superior. On a finding that technical superiority was shown by the point spread and accompanying technical narrative, we have upheld awards to concerns submitting superior proposals, although the awards were made at costs higher than those proposed in technically inferior proposals.[3] Similarly, on a finding that the point score and technical narrative did not indicate superiority in the higher-ranked proposal, we have upheld awards to offerors submitting less costly, albeit lower-scored technical proposals.[4] This reflects our view that the procuring agency's evaluation of proposed costs and technical approaches are entitled to great weight since the agencies are in the best position to determine realism of costs and corresponding technical approaches.[5] Our practice of deferring to the agency involved in cost/technical trade-off judgments has been followed even when the agency official ultimately responsible for selecting the successful contractor disagreed with an assessment of technical superiority made by a working level committee.[6] Our review of the subject award, therefore, is limited to deciding whether the record reasonably supports a conclusion that the award was rationally founded.[7]

The Comptroller General sees little difference between the terms "best value" and "most advantageous." In a 1992 protest, in which the protester attempted to differentiate between the "best value" and "most advantageous" concepts, the Comptroller General stated ". . . *we fail to see generally any significant difference between the "most advantageous" standard and the "best value" standard."* The Grey Advertising/Tracor Jitco decision is still cited in Comptroller General decisions.[8]

Relationship to Functional Statements of Work

The 1991 Defense Appropriations Act made the first official use of the term *best value,* although the term has been used unofficially for years. The term fits nicely with the current concept of using performance or functional statements of work in preference to the use of design-oriented statements of work.

A design-oriented statement of work specifies exactly *how* the work under the contract is to be performed and applies equally to all offerors. Each offeror must submit a technical proposal demonstrating how it meets the minimum requirements. Deviations from these requirements are not normally permitted. Since all offerors are proposing to perform the same effort, price is usually the primary consideration for award. Design-oriented statements of work are appropriate only if your requirement demands that the work be performed in a particular manner *and* it can be done under a fixed-price contract.

Functional (or performance) statements of work describe the government's needs in terms of *what* is to be accomplished but do not detail how the work is to be accomplished.[9] Each offeror must submit a technical proposal that describes how it will accomplish the work. The proposals are then evaluated based on the RFP's stated evaluation criteria. These criteria are designed to enable the government to determine the relative worth of the offeror's technical approach, understanding of the requirement, expertise, past experience, and any other criteria that demonstrate the offeror's ability to successfully perform the contract. The government makes award based on the most advantageous combination (best value) of technical and cost or price considerations.

A functional statement of work is appropriate for services, requirements that may be accomplished successfully in a number of different ways, or when a pricing arrangement other than fixed-price is contemplated. The government prefers to use a functional statement of work because its use encourages creativity and innovation in the offeror's proposals and enables the government to benefit from state-of-the-art developments.

Functional statements of work also enable the government to focus on the quality of the effort proposed and to award contracts accordingly. This usually involves making a tradeoff between cost and technical (noncost) factors to determine which offer is most advantageous to the government, or as it is now called, the best value.

COST/TECHNICAL TRADEOFFS

In the FAR 15 rewrite, the term *tradeoff* was adopted, but without the "cost/technical" descriptor. This was probably done because there are other tradeoffs that might be appropriate during the source selection process, for example, "past performance/pricing" tradeoffs. For purposes of this book, the term "cost/technical tradeoff" encompasses all tradeoffs made during the source selection process. FAR 15.101-1 states that a tradeoff process (i.e., cost/technical tradeoff) is appropriate when it may be in the government's best interest to consider award to other than the lowest priced offeror or other than the highest technically rated offeror.

The FAR did not address the cost/technical tradeoff process before the FAR 15 rewrite, but the Comptroller General used it extensively when describing what must be done to justify and document a source selection decision, as shown in Example 18.2.

Example 18.2—Cost/technical tradeoffs[10]

Generally, the government is not required to make an award to a technically acceptable firm offering the lowest price under an

RFP unless the RFP specifies that price will be the determinative factor. Here, the RFP award criteria did not require award to the low-priced offeror. It, in fact, expressly advised that the contract would not necessarily be awarded to the low-priced offeror, that technical consideration would be involved, and that these technical concerns were more important than price. Thus, under the RFP, the agency was required to take both technical considerations and price into account, and make an appropriate judgment as to whether one offeror was technically superior to another and if so whether that superiority was worth any price premium involved. In other words, the RFP required the agency to make a cost/technical tradeoff.[11]

When the RFP states that award is to be made to the acceptable offeror with the lowest evaluated price, the source selection decision is relatively simple. When award is to be based on other criteria, however, such as "technical superiority," and price is not determinative, the source selection decision becomes more complicated. The cost/technical tradeoff determination is the synthesis of the evaluation process.

The term *cost/technical tradeoff* refers to the assessment of the relative value of the cost and technical differences between proposals and their impact on the award decision. The process is a value assessment rather than an analysis of what the cost or price is likely to be. The cost/technical tradeoff focuses on the differences between the proposals still competing for award and attempts to measure the value or worth to the government of those differences. The source selection official uses this information to determine if award to the high-technical, higher-priced proposal is worth the price premium to be paid over award to a lower-priced and lower-technically rated proposal. Conversely, a cost/technical tradeoff may also be used (where the technical factors are more important than price) to justify award to other than the highest rated technical proposal.

A cost/technical tradeoff is not done until all other evaluation activity is finished. The evaluation personnel assigned to the final evaluation or the source selection official or in some circumstances, both, perform this assessment. If the evaluation team performs the assessment, it is the last evaluation activity before development of the final evaluation report. If the source selection official performs the assessment, it is the first activity in making the source selection decision. If the source selection official does not agree with the recommendations of the evaluators, the source selection official may ignore the evaluator's recommendations, but in such instances, the source selection official must make an independent cost/technical tradeoff determination to support the source selection decision (see Chapter 19).

It should be noted that during the initial evaluation, the evaluators may conduct a limited cost/technical tradeoff when comparing proposals for ranking purposes and determining which proposals are the most highly rated. The cost/technical tradeoff addressed in this chapter is conducted to determine which proposal offers the best value and should be selected for award.

Making Cost/Technical Tradeoffs

The cost/technical tradeoff relates to the award decision; therefore, it is the responsibility of the source selection official. The technical evaluators may be charged with developing a cost/technical tradeoff, but the acceptance or rejection of the cost/technical tradeoff rationale is the source selection official's personal responsibility.

Cost/technical tradeoffs are based on the evaluated cost or price, not the proposed cost or price. Evaluated costs and prices are developed from pricing adjustments made as a result of cost or price analysis and the assessment of cost realism. These pricing adjustments provide a more accurate assessment of the likely costs and form a better basis for the cost/technical tradeoff than the unadjusted proposed pricing. This is particularly true where the requirements cannot be well defined and it is necessary to use a cost-reimbursement type contract, as shown in Example 18.3.

Example 18.3—Tradeoffs are based on the evaluated costs, not the proposed costs[12]

Although the agency states in its report that its trade-off was based on a comparison of BAFO costs, the record shows that the trade-off in fact was based on the firms' evaluated costs. It would be improper to award a cost reimbursement contract based only on a comparison of proposed costs.[13]

In a cost-reimbursement contract, the proposed costs are not binding; therefore, the evaluated costs are considered a better assessment of the likely, actual costs and more appropriate for use in a tradeoff decision. Fortunately for the agency, the Comptroller General recognized that the agency misstated the basis for its tradeoff decision.

Cost or price must always be considered in an award decision, but award to the lowest cost/price is required only when so stated in the RFP. Therefore, a determination must be made as to the extent to which the evaluated cost or price will affect the award decision. Evaluate the proposed cost or price for reasonableness, realism, and risk, and make those adjustments necessary to bring the proposed pricing to what the effort will most likely cost (the evaluated cost/price). Then assess the cost and technical considerations (i.e., make a cost/technical tradeoff), to determine which proposal presents the best value.

Assess the technical differences first, then the pricing differences. Identify the significant discriminators (differences) between the proposals by comparing their strengths, weaknesses, and risks. Look for areas of differences that are important to the agency's mission or program objectives or that will have an impact (positive or negative) on agency operations, such as operational effectiveness, productivity, or delivery.

It should be noted that technical differences are initially identified by the differences in the technical scores assigned. While technical scores are useful as guides for intelligent decision-making, do not place too much reliance on them. Technical scores provide guidance only and are not to be used as a determining factor in the cost/technical tradeoff. As the Comptroller General stated in its Grey Advertising decision, *". . . evaluation ratings, be they adjectival, numerical, or color, are merely guides for intelligent decision-making in the procurement process."*[14]

Whether a given point spread between two competing proposals indicates a significant superiority of one proposal over another depends on the facts and circumstances of each procurement (i.e., based on the technical evaluation narratives) and a considered judgment of the significance of the technical differences. The tradeoff determination must assess technical differences in terms of contract performance and what it would cost to take advantage of the differences. In other words, the source selection official must first determine if the scoring differences actually represent technical differences in terms of contract performance and then determine if the superior proposal (when priced higher than the lowest-priced acceptable proposal) is worth the price premium to be paid.

Despite scoring differences, evaluators may determine that the proposals are roughly equal in terms of contract performance. For example, it not unusual for evaluators to score an incumbent's proposal high based more on what the incumbent has done in the past than on what the incumbent is actually proposing to do. If the source selection official feels this is the case, the technical differences may be discounted when making the cost/technical tradeoff determination. Technical differences may also be discounted if the source selection official simply does not agree with the evaluator's findings. The documentation of the tradeoff determination, however, must fully support any such changes.

Where cost is assigned evaluation points along with other technical factors, the fact that a proposal receives the highest number of evaluation points does not in itself justify acceptance of the highest rated proposal without regard to estimated cost to the government. Even where the RFP evaluation factors indicate that award should be made to that offeror with the highest point score, before you award to the highest priced, technically superior offeror rather than a lower priced, technically acceptable offeror, you must justify such award in light of the cost/price premium to be paid. Conversely, if you want to award to a lower priced proposal that is not the technically superior proposal, you must justify this decision on the basis that award to the high technical proposal is not worth the cost or price premium to be paid. In either case, a cost/technical tradeoff must support the decision.

Keep the cost/technical tradeoff as simple as possible. While it is possible to develop complicated formulas to measure the value of specific points of difference, the reliance on formulas as a substitute for individual analysis can be misleading, particularly where differing approaches or methodologies are involved. As the General Services Board of Contract Appeals (GSBCA) pointed out, *"There is no formulaic methodology for conducting a best value determination; what matters is that award is consistent with the terms of the solicitation and that any price premium is justified by specific technical enhancements."*[15]

Documenting Cost/Technical Tradeoffs

FAR 15.612(d)(2) required agencies to document their selection decisions to show the relative differences between proposals, their weaknesses and risks, and the basis and reasons for the selection decision. The results of the initial and final evaluations and the cost/technical tradeoff determination would provide the necessary documentation. The following text in the FAR 15 rewrite replaced this coverage:

- FAR 15.305(a) states that the relative strengths, deficiencies, significant weaknesses, and risks supporting proposal evaluation shall be documented in the contract file.
- FAR 15.305(a)(3) states that when tradeoffs are performed, the source selection records shall include an as-

sessment of each offeror's ability to accomplish the technical requirements and a summary, matrix, or quantitative ranking, along with appropriate supporting narrative, of each technical proposal using the evaluation factors.

- FAR 15.308 states that the source selection decision shall be documented, and the documentation shall include the rationale for any business judgments and tradeoffs made or relied on by the source selection official, including benefits associated with additional costs. Although the rationale for the source selection decision must be documented, that documentation need not quantify the tradeoffs that led to the decision.

The FAR 15 rewrite did not significantly change the old FAR coverage; it just spread it around. One change that could be significant, however, is that the source selection documentation need not quantify the tradeoffs that led to the decision, that is, the decision need not be justified based on numbers or a mathematical formula. This will give the source selection official some flexibility in documenting the source selection decision.

Documentation of the cost/technical tradeoff is important because it provides a basis for the source selection decision, as shown in Example 18.4.

Example 18.4—Tradeoff documentation must support the selection decision[16]

Cost/technical tradeoffs may be made in selecting an awardee subject only to the test of rationality and consistency with the established evaluation factors.[17] *Accordingly, we will object to a tradeoff where a reasonable basis is not evident from the record.*[18]

In the ruling above, the Comptroller General indicated that the record must support the cost/technical tradeoff decision, that is, something in writing must support the decision made. The most effective way to handle this is to ensure that the source selection decision is supported by a document that discusses the cost/technical tradeoff and shows the reasons the particular decision was made. This is not difficult if the initial and final evaluations have been adequately documented and the source selection official agrees with the evaluators.

Documenting the cost/technical tradeoff becomes more difficult when the source selection official does not agree with the evaluators and awards to some other offeror. In the event of a protest, the evaluation record will not support the selection decision, and the source selection official will bear the entire responsibility to justify the award. If the source selection official does not document his or her decision properly, it will be difficult to justify the source selection decision, as shown in Example 18.5.

Example 18.5—Source selection decision must be fully documented[19]

The technical evaluation panel (TEP) recommended award to the high-technical, higher-priced offeror. The contracting officer, however, decided that while the recommended awardee had a better technical proposal, it was not so superior as to warrant the price premium to be paid. The contracting officer then found that there was no significant technical difference between the proposals and made award to the low-technical, lower priced offeror. The high-technical offeror protested. The Comptroller General reviewed the evaluation record and sustained the protest.

Where there is inadequate supporting rationale in the record for a decision to make an award to a lower priced offeror with a lower technical ranking notwithstanding a solicitation's emphasis on technical factors, we cannot conclude that the agency has a reasonable basis for its decision.[20]

The record here fails to establish how the contracting officer's selection decision was consistent with the RFP's evaluation scheme, which stated that technical merit was considered more important than price. The evaluation documents show that the TEP considered D&D's proposal superior to G&O's, while the contracting officer believed that D&D had submitted "a better proposal" than G&O. The contracting officer did not provide—and in responding to D&D's protest still has not provided—a cogent rationale in support of his determination that D&D's superior rating was not worth its 20% higher price, given the RFP's emphasis on technical factors.

The decision document also did not discuss any of the differences between D&D's and G&O's proposals, or otherwise offer any support for the contracting officer's ultimate conclusion that D&D's proposal, while superior to G&O's, was not "substantially" superior such that warranted payment of a higher price. This unsupported semantical distinction is refuted by the evaluation documents which explain why the TEP considered D&D's proposal "significantly better" than G&O's. The contracting officer did not adequately explain why he discounted the TEP's conclusion as to the significance of the technical differences, and, in particular, did not address the outstanding deficiencies in G&O's proposal.

In sum, the contracting officer may have converted the selection basis from the one described in the solicitation, which emphasized technical superiority, to one in which award would go to the acceptable, low priced proposal.

Although the source selection official is not bound by the evaluation results, and may ignore the evaluation recommendations, the decision to do so must be justified and fully documented. The problem in Example 18.5 was that the contracting officer failed to fully document his cost/technical tradeoff decision when he disagreed with the evaluation findings. Had he done so, by addressing each of the differences between the proposals in a manner that clearly demonstrated that the differences were not actually significant with respect to contract performance, the results of this protest might have been different.

When ruling on protests, the Comptroller General examines the entire procurement record, including the initial and final evaluation documentation, the source selection statement or determination, including any tradeoffs made, and the report generated by the agency in response to the protest. This documentation must clearly support the award decision. The cost/technical tradeoff determination is a key document in this review process. If your documentation is inadequate, you may find yourself on the wrong end of a protest decision.

The documentation supporting a cost/technical tradeoff decision should be objectively reviewed and corrected, as appropriate, before the award decision becomes official. The documentation must do the following:

- Specifically identify the factors that demonstrate the greater worth of the selected proposal and show how this was determined. (Do not make unsupported generalizations.)
- Provide a comparison of the significant differences between the proposals, assessing their technical and pricing strengths, weaknesses, and risks in terms of their relative worth.
- Clearly indicate which proposal offers the best value and why the other offerors could not perform the contract as effectively as the selected offeror.

Using Mathematical Formulas in Cost/Technical Tradeoffs

Standard evaluation formulas, such as those set forth in Chapter 6, may be used in the final evaluation and cost/technical tradeoffs, but you are not required to publish their use in the RFP. If you publish the formulas in the RFP you are committing yourself to the mathematical results. You will gain significant flexibility in the evaluation and cost/technical tradeoffs if you do not indicate that you will be using a specific formula. You may still use the formula to display the rating and ranking of offerors, but you are not committed to using the results in your decision-making.

If you publish a mathematical formula in the RFP, the offerors will expect, and rightly so, that you will use the formula results as indicated. If your cost/technical tradeoff determination indicates an award result different from the formula results, a protest is likely to result and your explanation becomes more difficult. Mathematical formulas should not be used as the primary basis for an award decision. The cost/technical tradeoff must be fully documented and simple reliance on the numbers generated by a mathematical formula does not adequately support decision-making. You must base your decision primarily on your analysis of the evaluator's written technical narratives and the evaluation panel's evaluation report. These documents describe the strengths and weaknesses of the proposals and provide a basis for determination of the relative significance of the technical and cost factors.

One of the mathematical techniques used to display the best value is the "cost or price per technical point." This technique purports to show the relative value of each proposal, thus allowing the source selection official to select the best value. While a permissible technique, it must be used carefully. In Example 18.6 the Comptroller General links a cost per technical point breakdown to a best value analysis.

Example 18.6—Cost per technical point/best value[21]

The record shows that a contract price/cost analyst prepared for the contracting officer a "cost per technical point" breakdown, or a "best value" analysis, and a ranking of offerors on that basis, with the awardee ranked first with a value of $109.65 per technical point and the protester third, with a value of $119.58 per technical point. In selecting Holmes & Narver for award, the contracting officer determined that the awardee had "submitted the technically acceptable proposal offering the best value to the government." While the RFP did not specifically provide for the numerical scoring of both price and technical factors into a combined score, the fact remains that the solicitation emphasized technical excellence and consideration of cost. The record contains no evidence that the agency considered the protester's proposal to be technically equal to the awardee's proposal, so that price alone would have become the primary basis for selection. To the extent the protester argues that scoring of price increased its weight in the selection decision, its use benefited, rather than harmed the protester, which was the lowest cost offeror.

The Comptroller General found that the agency had properly conducted a cost/technical tradeoff; the protester's technical score was significantly lower than the awardee's technical score, and cost was considered through the best value analysis. The Comptroller General did not, however, comment directly on the use of the cost per technical point breakdown, other than to indicate that this was not much different from the methods used to determine the "most advantageous" proposal.

The following is a simplified example of the use of cost or price per technical point.

Figure 18.1—Cost Per Technical Point Example

Procurement is for a cost-reimbursement contract and technical considerations are paramount.

Technical	*Evaluated*	*Cost per*	
Offeror	*Points*	*Cost (1)*	*Technical Point (2)*
A	92	$1,520,000	$16,522
B	89	$1,150,000	$12,921
C	75	$ 890,000	$11,867

(1) Use the evaluated cost (what you think, after cost analysis and cost realism analysis, that the effort should cost) rather than the offeror's proposed price. This type of analysis is valid only after receipt of the final proposal revisions, because proposed costs can change significantly as a result of the discussions.
(2) Divide the evaluated cost by the technical points to get the cost per technical point.

This technique is useful in displaying the relative value of competing proposals but should not be used as the primary support for a selection decision. The problem with using cost or price per technical point as a decision-maker, or even as a significant factor in the decision-making, should be obvious from Figure 18.1.

Offeror C's proposal would seem to represent the best value because its cost per technical point is the lowest. However, since technical considerations are paramount and Offeror C has the lowest technical score, its status as the best value is clearly in question. This could be a case of "you get what you pay for," and an award decision should not be made without first examining the significance of the technical differences between the proposals and the relative value of the technical and pricing differences.

Another problem with this concept is that the numbers can mask differences between the proposals. The best value proposal, on a cost per technical point basis, may contain technical or pricing weaknesses that belie its real value. Even though you use "evaluated" pricing figures in the calculations, a technically weak proposal increases the potential for cost overruns that cannot be accurately estimated by cost analysis and an assessment of cost realism. Such problems can best be found by a subjective assessment of the individual proposals and the differences between the proposals, including an assessment of proposal risk.

Use Mathematical Calculations Only as Support for the Cost/ Technical Tradeoff

Evaluation formulas and cost per technical point breakouts are useful in displaying the relative ranking of the proposals and quantifying their differences, but the award decision must be made based on a valid cost/technical tradeoff.

The cost per technical point example in Figure 18.1 presents three different award scenarios, each of which must be validated by a cost/technical tradeoff determination:

- *Award to Offeror A as the high-technical offeror.*
  The RFP makes technical considerations paramount, but you cannot ignore the lower evaluated cost of Offeror C's technically acceptable proposal. To justify an award to Offeror A, you must assess the value of the 17-point technical difference against the $630,000 difference in cost. This assessment is based not on numbers (the point score differences), but on your judgment concerning the significance of the differences.

In this case, the cost/technical tradeoff must establish that the technical superiority of Offeror A's proposal is worth the cost premium to be paid and explain why. The documentation to support this decision must identify the technical and pricing differences and show that Offeror A's proposal offers technical advantages significant enough to warrant the payment of an additional $630,000.

- *Award to Offeror C, as the lowest-priced offeror.*
  Even though the RFP makes technical considerations paramount, award to Offeror C is possible if, through a cost/technical tradeoff, you can determine (1) that the proposals are roughly equal technically, despite the differences in technical scores, and (2) that award to the high-technical offeror is not worth the price premium to be paid.

  While unlikely, justifying an award to Offeror C is possible, particularly if Offeror A is the incumbent and it is determined that the higher score of Offeror A reflects the evaluators' greater "comfort" with the incumbent contractor, rather than actual technical superiority.

  If you can establish that the scoring of Offeror A reflects other than actual technical superiority, you could find that, despite the scoring, the proposals are roughly equal technically. This would permit you to make an award based on the lower price. Your decision and its rationale must, of course, be fully documented.
- *Award to Offeror B, as best value offeror.*
  Depending on the results of the cost/technical tradeoff, it is possible to find that Offeror B's proposal is most advantageous to the government. To do this you would have to establish that the technical superiority of Offeror B's proposal outweighed the cost savings represented by Offeror C's proposal and that the cost premium to be paid for award to Offeror A is not worth the relatively small technical advantage of Offeror A's proposal.

  Given the closeness of the technical scores between Offerors A and B, Offeror B's price advantage over Offeror A, and the technical superiority of Offeror B over

Offeror C, which may be worth paying for, award to Offeror B is a definite possibility.

Any of the above scenarios are possible depending on the results of the cost/technical tradeoff. The numbers generated by the cost per technical point calculations (or any other scoring scenario) serve only to display the differences between the proposals. It is the cost/technical tradeoff rationale that gives meaning to the numbers and creates the basis for the source selection decision.

Do not make your award decision and then develop a cost/technical tradeoff to support it. This may lead you to overlook factors that do not support your initial decision, but that, when examined closely, turn out to be determinative. Try to conduct the cost/technical tradeoff without preconceived preferences and let the results speak for themselves, keeping in mind that your interpretation of the results must be reasonable and in accordance with the RFP's evaluation scheme.

You may use mathematical formulas, and other numerical techniques, as guides to your decision-making, but do not attempt to substitute "objective" numbers for what should be a fully documented, subjective determination.

References

1. Grey Advertising, Inc., B-184825, 5/14/76, 76-1 CPD ¶325.
2. Tracor Jitco, Inc., 54 Comp. Gen. 896 (1975).
3. 52 Comp. Gen. 358 (1972); B-171696, 7/20/71; B-170633, 5/3/71.
4. 52 Comp. Gen. 686 (1973).
5. Raytheon Company, 54 Comp. Gen. 169 (1974); 50 Comp. Gen. 390 (1970).
6. B-173137(1), 10/8/71.
7. Vinnell Corp., B-180557, 10/8/74.
8. S-V Company, A Joint Venture, B-248566; B-248566.3, 8/27/92, 92-2 CPD ¶131, GCR 106,865.

9. This includes the Performance Work Statements for Performance Based Service Contracts (PBSC).
10. Kenneth L. Latham, B-245137, 12/18/91, 91-2 CPD ¶559, GCR 106,160.
11. Encon Management Inc., B-234679, 6/23/89, 89-1 CPD ¶595, GCR 103,308.
12. Resource Consultants, Inc., B-245312.2, 3/23/92, 92-1 CPD ¶301, GCR 106,488, Footnote 1.
13. Joule Tech. Corp., B-192125, 5/21/79, 79-1 CPD ¶364.
14. Grey Advertising Inc., B-184825, 5/14/76, 76-1 CPD ¶325 at 9.
15. Grumman Data Systems Corp., vs. Department of the Air Force, GSBCA, No. 11939-P, 11/20/92, redacted 1/13/93, released in entirety 3/22/94.
16. Kenneth L. Latham, B-245137, 12/18/91, 91-2 CPD ¶559, GCR 106,160.
17. Maytag Aircraft Corp., B-237068.3, 4/26/90, 90-1 CPD ¶430, GCR 104,334.
18. Avanco Int'l, Inc., B-241007.2, 3/13/91, 91-1 CPD ¶276, GCR 105,284.
19. Dewberry & Davis, B-247116, 5/5/92, 92-1 CPD ¶421, GCR 106,603.
20. Hattal & Assoc., 70 Comp. Gen. 632 (1991), 91-2 CPD ¶90, GCR 105,697; PharmChem Labs., supra.
21. S-V Company, A Joint Venture, B-248566; B-248566.3, 9/27/92, 92-2 CPD ¶131, GCR 106,865.

Chapter 19

Making the Source Selection Decision

Source selection is the last step of the preaward evaluation process. The source selection official makes the selection decision. This is a separate and additional action, taken after all other evaluation actions are completed. Once the final evaluation is complete, the source selection official uses the final evaluation report, its supporting documentation and the evaluator's recommendations, and, as appropriate, a cost/technical tradeoff as the primary basis for the source selection decision.

SOURCE SELECTION RESPONSIBILITY

The source selection official is given significant discretion in weighing the significance of the relationship between technical scores and cost differentials and making the source selection decision. This helps ensure that the government gets the greatest value for its money. With this discretion, however, comes responsibility. The source selection official is responsible for exercising his or her discretion reasonably and within the bounds of the stated evaluation criterion.

The source selection official does not suddenly appear unannounced and make an award pronouncement. Generally, source selection concerns relate to matters that should be decided well before the source selection decision is made. The source selection official is, or should be, involved in the entire evaluation process from start to finish. Except for formal source selection, the source selection official is usually the contracting officer. Decisions made early in the process will have a direct effect on the source selection official's ability to make a reasonable source selection decision. It is, therefore, in the source selection official's best interests to make sure that the evaluation process is carried out properly and adequately documented.

FAR 15.303 requires the source selection authority (whether the contracting officer or another appointed official) to be involved in the procurement from the very beginning of the acquisition, before the RFP is released. Example 13.23, in Chapter 13, illustrates what happens when "nobody is paying attention." In that example the contracting officer downgraded an offeror's past performance (the primary evaluation factor) because the offeror had not previously performed a contract of similar "complexity" as the contemplated contract. Complexity was determined solely on the size of the contract (amount of waste to be disposed of) without considering any other indicators of complexity. The source selection authority (SSA) accepted the evaluation results without a careful review of the basis for the evaluation. Little consideration was given to the fact that "bigger" and "more complex" are not necessarily the same. This matter should have been addressed in the RFP's planning stages when past performance evaluation should have been discussed. It should also have been addressed by the SSA when making the past performance/price tradeoff. Early involvement by the source selection official can prevent later problems.

Erroneous Advice

Decisions by the source selection official must be reasonable, and must not be arbitrary. The source selection official bears the sole responsibility for his or her decisions, even when following the advice of experts. If a decision is reasonably made, based on the advice provided, but it turns out that the advice was erroneous, the decision is not reasonable, as shown in Example 19.1.

Example 19.1—Source selection official is ultimately responsible for making correct decision[1]

The Comptroller General found that an agency had conducted its cost realism analysis improperly. The agency requested reconsideration of the decision sustaining the protest against contract award. It argued that the award should stand because the contracting officer had no reason to know at the time of award that DCAA's preaward advice (which the contracting officer relied on) was incorrect. The Comptroller General denied the request for reconsideration because no new information was presented, but went on to discuss the responsibilities of the source selection authority.

In any event, we disagree with the apparent belief of DSS-W and AMS that a contracting officer's cost realism determination will be deemed reasonable, although based on incorrect information, where the incorrect information was provided to the contracting officer by experts outside the procuring agency—e.g., DCAA—and the contracting officer has no reason to know that the advice was erroneous. A contracting officer's cost realism determination may not reasonably be based upon erroneous audit advice, even where the procuring agency is unaware at the time of the determination that the audit information is incorrect.

[And in a footnote here] *We note that this same rule applies to other judgments of contracting officers. See Fiber-Lam,*[2] *(contracting officer may not automatically rely upon information provided by transportation rate specialists that results in improper or unreasonable evaluations of offered prices). In this regard, the courts and board of contract appeals have imputed audit information to contracting officers. See United States v. Hanna Nickel Smelting Co.*[3] *(knowledge of contractor's accounting practices imputed to agency), and E-Systems, Inc.,*[4] *(knowledge of contractor's pooling and allocation of material costs, known to DCAA, was imputed to the contracting officer). Similarly, a contracting officer is not insulated from responsibility for erroneous advice provided by experts within the procuring agency, i.e., a price analyst or a technical evaluator.* [End Footnote]

While a contracting officer may ordinarily rely on DCAA in performing a cost realism analysis rather than perform all aspects himself,[5] *this does not mean that a contracting officer is thereby insulated from a responsibility for error.*[6] *A contracting officer's judgment concerning the realism of an offeror's proposed costs must be reasonably based and not arbitrary.*[7] *Where this judgment is founded upon incorrect information, it will not be deemed reasonable.*[8]

This decision makes sense. The source selection official has the final decision-making responsibility and the decisions made must be right. An erroneous decision by the source selection official, even made in good faith, is still erroneous. An offeror should not be made to suffer because the government made a mistake.

This responsibility also extends to situations where the record does not support the reported evaluation results and the source selection official does not look beyond the reports provided, as shown in Example 19.2.

Example 19.2—Source selection decision is not proper when based on a flawed evaluation[9]

After a debriefing, an unsuccessful offeror protested that its proposal had not been properly evaluated. After examining the record, the Comptroller General agreed.

Where an agency chooses between a higher-priced, higher-rated proposal and a lower-priced, lower-rated proposal, we will review the agency's source selection decision to determine whether it is consistent with the stated evaluation criteria and whether the agency's price/technical tradeoff is reasonable.[10] A source selection decision based on inconsistent or inaccurate information concerning the technical evaluation or the relative merits of the offeror's technical proposals is not reasonable.[11]

Here, the source selection of LBM for award was flawed because the SSA was provided information that contained uncorrected errors concerning New Breed's ratings, failed to accurately represent LBM's past performance record, and provided conclusions about the two proposals' technical differences that were inconsistent with the evaluation record and the offerors' proposals.

In this case, the Source Selection Board (SSB) required the Technical Evaluation Board (TEB) to correct problems in its evaluation. The TEB resubmitted its revised report, but apparently without any supporting documentation. The SSB accepted the revised TEB evaluation without independently evaluating the proposals or reviewing any supporting documentation. The SSB then passed these findings to the SSA with an award recommendation. The SSA accepted the reports without reviewing any of the supporting documentation. Unfortunately, the initial evaluation was not done properly and these mistakes were passed on unnoticed, because no adequate review was performed.

Despite the fact that the TEB failed to do its job properly, as did the SSB—by not reviewing the evaluation's supporting documentation—the responsibility rests with the SSA to ensure that the source selection decision is proper.

Disagreements With Evaluators

The evaluators and others involved in the evaluation process provide support, but the final decision rests with the source selection official. Examples 19.3 through 19.5 address what happens when the source selection official and the evaluators do not agree.

Example 19.3—The source selection official is not bound by evaluator's recommendations #1[12]

After the technical proposals were found to be substantially equal and award was based on the lowest price, an unsuccessful offeror protested the reasonableness of the proposal evaluation. The protester noted that several evaluations were conducted before discussions and argued that this reflected bias and contracting officials' improper influence on the technical evaluators.

Actually, the evaluation process involved five evaluations. The first three evaluations came about because of a conflict between the technical evaluators and the contracting personnel about how to describe and score the relative merits of the proposals. The technical evaluators believed the protester's proposal was technically superior, but the contracting personnel were not persuaded by the documentation submitted and considered the proposals substantially equal in technical merit.

The contracting officer found the first evaluation unacceptable, briefed the evaluators on how to do their job properly, and directed a reevaluation. The documentation of the second evaluation, however, was no better than the first. The contracting officer then replaced the chief technical evaluator and directed a third evaluation. This evaluation was acceptable.

The final two evaluations were conducted after receipt of BAFOs. The technical evaluators conducted one of the post-BAFO evaluations while the contracting officer conducted her own evaluation.

During this process and after submission of BAFOs, the contracting personnel and the technical evaluators held numerous discussions concerning how the evaluation should be conducted and documented. Both post-BAFO evaluations found that the proposals were substantially equal, although the contracting officer's evaluation scored the protester's proposal slightly lower. Award, therefore, was made on the basis of price and the unsuccessful offeror protested. The Comptroller General denied the protest and commented on the differences of opinion between evaluators and the contracting officer.

In reviewing an agency's selection decision, we will examine the underlying evaluation to ensure that it was reasonable and consistent with the stated evaluation criteria.[13] *It is important to recognize in a case like this one that the selection official is not bound by the recommendation of lower-level evaluators.*[14] *In determining whether the award decision was proper, it is the ultimate evaluation by the agency, which is governed by the tests of rationality and consistency with the RFP evaluation criteria, not the assessment by working-level evaluators that will be primarily considered.*

Moreover, we find no evidence of bias or other impropriety in the evaluation process. The fact that contracting officials reviewed the findings of the technical evaluators and discussed their feelings with them does not itself indicate bias, since it is the contracting officials that bear ultimate responsibility for the procurement.[15] *Neither is bias indicated by the fact that there were multiple evaluations; subsequent evaluations at the behest of contracting officials are appropriate to correct errors, misconceptions or inconsistency with evaluation criteria.*[16] *In short, the record does not support the conclusion that the actions of the contracting personnel, the multiple evaluations, and the rescoring of proposals were motivated by bias or other improper considerations. It only shows that the finding of essential technical equality as between the proposals of MACA and Verify was both rational and consistent with the evaluation criteria.*

In Example 19.3, the evaluators initially failed to conduct and document the evaluation properly. The documentation did not convince the contracting officer that the protester's proposal was technically superior. When faced with unacceptable evaluation results, a contracting officer has three options: (1) require a reevaluation, (2) convene a new evaluation group to conduct another evaluation, or (3) ignore the evaluation results and conduct an independent evaluation (see Example 18.10). In this case, the contracting officer took all three actions.

The contracting officer's final option is to ignore the evaluator's recommendations and make an independent evaluation and source selection. While having the authority to do this, the contracting officer must fully justify and document the rationale for the source selection. This is difficult to do if the evaluators have failed to adequately document the evaluation process. In Example 19.3, the contracting officer conducted her own evaluation of the BAFOs, even as the evaluators were doing the same. Both evaluations came to the same conclusion—the proposals were substantially equal technically. The award decision, however, was based on the contracting officer's evaluation.

When faced with an evaluation that has not been conducted or documented properly, briefing the evaluators on the evaluation requirements and requesting a reevaluation is the most effective corrective action. It should be noted that most evaluation problems stem from evaluator's misconceptions of their responsibilities and the documentation requirements rather than from a bias or other impropriety.

It should also be noted, however, that a reevaluation is required only when the evaluation has not been done, or documented, properly. A reevaluation should not be required if the source selection official simply disagrees with the results. If the source selection official disagrees with the evaluation results and wants to award to an offeror other than the one recommended by the evaluators, the source selection official must conduct an independent evaluation and document a rationale that supports his or her source selection decision. If the evaluators have done their work properly, it would not be reasonable for the source selection official to direct continued reevaluations until the evaluators provide a recommendation he or she favors.

In Example 19.4, the evaluation was done properly, but the source selection official did not agree with the results.

Example 19.4—The source selection official is not bound by evaluator's recommendations #2[17]

An offeror responded to ten different solicitations for the same services, to be performed in ten different geographical locations. One evaluation panel evaluated six proposals and by a second evaluation panel evaluated the other four proposals. The contracting officer did not agree with the scoring of the second panel and rescored those proposals downward. The offeror protested the rescoring but the Comptroller General denied the protest.

Nor do we find that the record supports a conclusion that the contracting officer acted improperly in adjusting Pro-Mark's quality control scores downward in the four instances in which he corrected the ratings made by the substitute evaluation panel under RFP Nos. 169, 171, 172, and 174. Contracting officers are not bound by recommendations from technical evaluators and they may reevaluate proposals and downscore them if necessary.[18] *As with any technical evaluations, contracting officers' decisions in this regard will be reviewed to ensure that they are reasonable and consistent with the stated evaluation criteria and the fact that a protester or an evaluator may disagree with a contracting officer's conclusions does not itself render his evaluation unreasonable.*

Example 19.4 shows that evaluators make recommendations, but the source selection official makes decisions. The source selection official is responsible for assessing the evaluation results and determining whether to accept the recommendations made. The source selection official is not bound by the evaluation results but must be able to document that the source selection decision was reasonable and consistent with the stated evaluation criteria.

Example 19.5—The source selection official is not bound by evaluator's recommendations #3[19]

EBA challenged the source selection official's determination to award to SaLUT notwithstanding the recommendation of the evaluators. EBA argued that the evaluation panel was better qualified to make its recommendation for the award and the source selection official failed to justify his award decision. The Comptroller General did not agree.

Source selection officials in negotiated procurements are not bound by the recommendations or evaluation judgments of lower-level evaluators, even though the working level evaluators may normally be expected to have the technical expertise required for such evaluations.[20] Thus, SSOs have broad discretion in determining the manner and extent to which they will make use of the technical and cost evaluation results, and their technical judgments are governed only by the tests of rationality and consistency with the stated evaluation criteria.[21]

In Example 19.5, the source selection official was faced with a divided evaluation panel that could not reach a consensus and, the source selection official felt, had made some errors in its considerations. So he made his own evaluation and documented his decision, to which the Comptroller General concurred.

In formal source selection, where there are multiple levels of evaluation, the different evaluation groups sometimes cannot agree. In such cases, it is the source selection official's responsibility to make the final decision, as shown in Example 19.6.

Example 19.6—The source selection official makes the final decision[22]

The source selection evaluation board (SSEB) and the source selection advisory council (SSAC) disagreed on the evaluation of staffing. The SSA agreed with the SSAC's findings and made the award accordingly. The award was protested on the grounds that the SSEB's views should have prevailed. The Comptroller General denied the protest.

In the evaluation of proposals, neither the selection official nor upper-level evaluators are bound by the recommendations of lower-level evaluators, and as a general rule, our Office will defer to the higher-level officials' judgment even when those officials disagree with an assessment made by a working level evaluation board or individuals who normally might be expected to have the technical expertise required for such evaluations.[23] *The final evaluation itself is to be governed by the tests of rationality and consistency with the RFP evaluation factors. In determining whether a particular evaluation conclusion is rational, we do not make an independent determination of a proposal's merit: we will, however, examine the record before us and determine whether the judgment exercised by the evaluators was fair and reasonable.*[24]

It is the job of the source selection official and upper-level officials to review the evaluation findings and, when necessary, change them—as long as the changes demonstrate the use of good judgment and are in accordance with the evaluation criteria set forth in the RFP.

Disagreements with Higher Authority

The source selection official is considered to be the final authority concerning the source selection. But nothing is really final in government and there is always someone with greater authority, as illustrated by Example 19.7.

Example 19.7—The source selection official makes the final decision, unless overruled by higher authority[25]

Although the contracting officer agreed with the evaluation results and the award recommendation, the agency's director did not. He reevaluated the proposals and directed award to an offeror other than the lowest-priced offeror, who had been recommended for award by the evaluators. An offeror protested, contending that the agency director lacked the authority to change the evaluation results. The Comptroller General denied the protest.

While it may be true that in most procurements, the contracting officer ultimately makes the award decision, the contracting officer derives the power to bind the government from the general grant of contracting authority to the agency head.[26] *Here 20 U.S.C. 1221e(1) (1982) authorizes the Director to conduct educational research to carry out NIE's objectives of improving education in the United States. Further, 20 U.S.C. 1221e(f)(1) vests authority in the Director to, among other things, enter into contracts to carry out NIE's functions.*

We do not agree with Bank Street's contention that the Director may only exercise his contracting authority when the "standard contracting procedures have not been properly followed." Rather, as NIE's ultimate contracting authority, the Director has the discretion to exercise his contracting authority whenever he thinks that it will further NIE's statutory objectives.[27] *Thus we have no basis to object to the Director's participation in the selection process.*

The selection official, here the Director, is not bound by the recommendation of the evaluators, and as a general rule our Office will defer to such an official's judgment even when that official disagrees with an assessment of technical superiority made by a working level evaluation board or individuals who normally may be expected to have the technical expertise required for such evaluations.[28] *The selection decision, and the manner in which such official uses the results of the technical and cost evaluations and the extent, if any, to which one is sacrificed for the other are governed only by the tests of rationality and the consistency with established evaluation factors.*[29]

In Example 19.7, the agency head overruled the contracting officer's source selection decision and the Comptroller General agreed that he had the authority to do so. So where does it end? Example 19.8 demonstrates how high the source selection authority can go.

Example 19.8—In government, hierarchy rules[30]

After the SSA made an award decision in a formal source selection, the Under Secretary of the Military Service requested a briefing regarding the SSA's selection decision. After a detailed briefing and study of the related documentation, the

Under Secretary "vacated" the SSA's selection decision and directed award to another offeror. The original selectee protested on the grounds that the Under Secretary did not have the authority to vacate the SSA's decision, since the SSA was the official in charge of selecting the contractor under the formal source selection procedures contained in the FAR. The Comptroller General denied the protest.

It is clear that the Under Secretary had the authority to make the source selection under this RFP. In this regard, we have consistently held that the authority of agency supervisory or secretarial level officials to direct and supervise agency functions of lower echelon agency components necessarily encompasses procurement operations, including the evaluation of proposals and the award of contracts.[31] *That is, such officials are authorized to review source selections decisions, reverse or vacate those decisions and make their own reasonable source selection decisions in accordance with the RFP evaluation criteria. Although SATO distinguishes Grey Advertising as permitting a supervisory agency official to vacate a source selection decision only where his review is provided for under agency regulations, in both Bank Street and AFL-CIO Appalachian Council no such regulations are cited; the supervisory and management responsibility of the higher officials in those cases permitted them to intervene in the source selection process.*

[And in a footnote] *Contrary to sato's assertion, FAR 15.612 does not preclude higher agency officials from exercising such authority nor is there any implied contract under this RFP that any particular individual will make the source selection. Indeed, the RFP here does not mention who the SSA is, much less require the Army to use any particular SSA; it only requires that evaluation and selection be consistent with the RFP's stated evaluation criteria.*

The Comptroller General based its reasoning on the fact that by statute, the Office of the Secretary, which included the Under Secretary, had the sole responsibility for seven designated functions, including acquisition.[32] In addition, the Under Secretary in question was designated as the "Acquisition Executive," responsible for "conducting" the acquisition function. The Comptroller General ruled that the authority to review, vacate, or make source selection decisions is inherent in the function of an Acquisition Executive.

Someone higher in the chain of command who has the same or greater contracting authority may overturn a source selection decision. Contracting authority is vested in the head of each executive agency and passed down to the contracting officer (or other selection official). You should note, however, that it is against the law for someone lacking the requisite contracting authority to attempt to influence the decision of a contracting officer or other source selection official.

DOCUMENTING SOURCE SELECTION DECISIONS

With respect to the source selection decision, FAR 15.308 says that "the source selection authority's (SSA) decision shall be based on a comparative assessment of proposals against all source selection criteria in the solicitation. While the SSA may use reports and analyses prepared by others, the source selection decision shall represent the SSA's independent judgment. The source selection decision shall be documented, and the documentation shall include the rationale for any business judgments and tradeoffs made or relied on by the SSA, including benefits associated with additional costs."

The last sentence in the previous paragraph took the place of the following pre-FAR 15 rewrite coverage of source selection documentation requirements: "The source selection authority shall prepare supporting documentation for the selection decision that shows the relative differences among proposals and their strengths, weaknesses, and risks in terms of the evaluation factors. The supporting documentation shall also include the basis and reasons for the source selection decision." While these words have been superseded, this does not mean they are no longer valid. The source selection documentation must clearly support the source selection decision.

All source selection decisions must be fully documented in the contract file. In the event of a protest, the Comptroller General will examine the record to see if the cost/technical tradeoff and source selection decisions are fully documented. If the record does not support the decisions made, the government is likely to lose the protest.

When examining the record, the Comptroller General places more weight on contemporaneous documentation generated at the time of the source selection decision than on documentation developed in response to a protest as shown in Example 19.9.

Example 19.9—Contemporaneous documentation is accorded greater weight[33]

When arguing about what information the Comptroller General should consider in resolving its protest, ITT cited the Boeing Sikorsky Aircraft decision[34] as barring consideration of any material other than the Selection Statement itself. The Comptroller General did not agree with ITT and explained the Boeing decision as follows.

Our decision in Boeing *involved an agency's post-protest hypothetical cost/technical tradeoff presented to demonstrate a lack of prejudice from any alleged agency errors. Prejudice to the protester is critical to our decision making, since our Office will not sustain a protest unless the protester demonstrates a reasonable possibility of prejudice, that is, unless the protester demonstrates that, but for the agency's actions, it would have had a substantial chance of receiving the award.*[35] *In responding to Boeing's challenges to the propriety of the technical and cost evaluations, the agency answered that even if Boeing were to prevail on its protest grounds it still would not be awarded the contract because of the awardee's superior management evaluation. In this regard, the agency submitted a new cost/technical tradeoff analysis prepared during the pendency of the protest which assumes the validity of many of Boeing's allegations, but concluded that the award decision would not change.*[36]

In deciding what weight to accord the agency's reevaluation, our Office held that "[w]hile we must consider the entire record, . . . we accord greater weight to contemporaneous source selection materials rather than judgments, such as the source selection officials' reevaluation here, made in response to protest contentions."[37] *We further reasoned that the "lesser weight that we accord these post-protest documents reflects the concern that, because they constitute reevaluations and redeterminations prepared in the heat of an adversarial process, they may not represent the fair and considered judgment of the agency, which is a prerequisite of a rational evaluation and source selection process."*[38]

A counterpoint to Boeing *is our decision in* NWT, Inc.; PharmChem Labs Inc.[39] *where we distinguished post-protest reevaluation and redetermination from memorialization of contemporaneous analysis. In NWT; PharChem, we stated that "[p]ost-protest explanations that provide a detailed rationale for contemporaneous conclusions, as is the case here, simply fill in previously unrecorded details, and will generally be considered in our review of the rationality of selection decisions, so long as those explanations are credible and consistent with the contemporaneous record.*[40]

To show a lack of prejudice from alleged agency errors, the government must have contemporaneous documentation of the differences between the proposals and an analysis of these differences to support a contention that a protester would not have received award under any circumstances. The *NWT; PharmChem* decision cited above allowed post-protest explanations only to the extent that they were credible and consistent with the contemporaneous record. So, post-protest explanations that support what is already in the record and simply provide more detail will be considered, but post-protest explanations or analyses that present new information will be accorded lesser weight, if considered at all. The bottom line is that the source selection decision must be fully documented at the time it is made. The source selection official should review this documentation to ensure that the documentation will sustain the government's position, before making the award.

The supporting documentation for the source selection decision is, therefore, in addition to the documentation of the evaluation process even where the source selection official agrees with the evaluation results. The source selection documentation is necessary to substantiate the reasonableness of the source selection decision. This is important because the source selection official could face a number of different scenarios:

1. *The source selection official agrees with the evaluator's recommendations, and the evaluation has been adequately documented.* In this instance, the source selection documentation should indicate agreement with the evaluation results and summarize the evaluation findings. Note, however, that the source selection official cannot simply say "I agree with the evaluation findings." The source selection documentation must meet the requirements of FAR 15.308, as noted in the opening paragraph of this section.
2. *The source selection official agrees with the evaluator's recommendations, but the evaluation has been inadequately documented.* Here, the source selection official must brief the evaluators on the specific documentation requirements and require a reevaluation. This is necessary because where the supporting documentation is inadequate, it will be difficult to establish that there was a reasonable basis for the selection decision, should it be questioned in a protest.

   When responding to a protest, the agency must substantiate each argument and rebut every allegation by the other party. Arguments and rebuttals must be supported by the record (preferably) or by a written statement submitted in response to the protest. The party that fails to address a point made by the other party is very likely to lose that point. It is difficult to successfully respond to a protest if the evaluation is poorly documented.
3. *The source selection official disagrees with the evaluator's recommendations, even though the evaluation has been adequately documented.* If the source selection official disagrees with the evaluator's findings, the source selection official must develop and document an independent cost/technical tradeoff and source selection decision.

   This documentation should specifically identify and discuss the areas in which the source selection official and the evaluators disagree and demonstrate why the source selection official came to a conclusion different from that of the evaluators. The source selection official must document the differences between the offerors and provide an interpretation of the significance of these differences in the cost/technical tradeoff and selection decision. The strengths, weaknesses, and relative risks of the proposals in line for award must be addressed, as well as the basis and reasons for the selection decision.

4. *The source selection official disagrees with the evaluator's recommendations, and the evaluation has been inadequately documented.* As noted earlier, the source selection official may ignore the evaluation results and develop and document his or her own cost/technical tradeoff and source selection decision, but this is difficult to do if the basic evaluation documentation is inadequate. In this instance the source selection official should direct a reevaluation to ensure that the evaluator's findings are adequately documented before deciding to make an independent evaluation and selection decision that is contrary to the evaluator's recommendations.

The source selection decision is largely driven by how the evaluators conduct and document the evaluation process. The best way to prepare to ensure the validity of the source selection decision is to make sure that the evaluation process is done properly.

This chapter could not close without showing a classic case of a muddled source selection decision. While this is a pre-FAR 15 rewrite case, the rewrite has not changed any of the applicable factors.

Example 19.10—How not to make a source selection decision[41]

This procurement was for a Time and Materials (T&M) contract to provide disaster relief assistance. The RFP stated that technical merit would be more important than price in the award decision, but noted that price could become the deciding factor if proposals were found to be technically equal.

Three BAFOs were received, but the competition was primarily between the high-technical, higher-priced offer (Dewberry & Davis) and the low-technical, lowest-priced offeror (Greenhorne & O'Mara). The other offeror had effectively priced itself out of the competition. The final TEP report recommended award to Dewberry & Davis, but the contracting officer decided to award to Greenehorne & O'Mara. A protest resulted.

To support his decision, the contracting officer executed a negotiation memorandum stating "[n]otwithstanding the panel's preference for the higher rated technical company (Dewberry & Davis), Federal Acquisition Regulations are too firmly embedded in the philosophy and practice of the "low bidder" and "minimal needs of the government" to make any other rational choice in this matter beside the firm of Greenehorne & O'Mara.

"As iterated by the technical evaluation panel in their report, all three offerors were deemed to be "acceptable." It should be noted that even though Dewberry & Davis has a substantially higher technical score, this does not impact the competition. As evidenced by the panel's comments, they feel Dewberry & Davis is the most qualified (and preferred from a program standpoint) of the three offerors, and Greenehorne & O'Mara is the least preferred and on the low end of the acceptable spectrum. However, the panel was neither willing to deem Greenehorne & O'Mara as "unacceptable," nor make a case of technical superiority for Dewberry & Davis. The situation at hand is a perfect example of the old adage of "the government drives Chevrolets, not Cadillacs." It is evident that the government's minimal needs in this situation can be met by Greenehorne & O'Mara at a substantially lower cost than the services proposed by Dewberry & Davis."

In essence, the contracting officer determined that the protester had a better technical proposal, but not a superior one, and concluded that there were no significant technical differences between the proposals. Therefore the award was made based on price. The Comptroller General did not agree.

In a negotiated procurement, contracting officers have broad discretion in determining the manner and extent to which they will make use of technical and cost evaluation results.[42] *However, they do not have the discretion to announce in the solicitation that they will use one evaluation plan, and then follow another; once offerors are informed of the criteria against which their proposals will be evaluated, the agency must adhere to those criteria in making its award decision or inform all offerors of any significant changes made in the evaluation scheme.*[43]

Of course, a contracting agency properly may find that a significant difference in technical scores does not represent a corresponding difference in technical merit and make award based on cost; the propriety of such a selection turns on whether the contracting agency's judgment of the significance of that difference was reasonable in light of the RFP evaluation scheme.[44] *Where cost is secondary to technical considerations under the RFP evaluation scheme, as here, selection of a lower priced proposal over a higher technical score requires adequate justification, i.e., some showing the agency reasonably concluded that, notwithstanding the point differential between the two proposals, they were essentially equal.*[45] *The Federal Acquisition Regulation (FAR) requires agencies to document their selection decisions to show the relative differences between proposals, their weaknesses and risks, and the basis and reasons for the selection decision.*[46] *Where there is inadequate supporting rationale in the record for a decision to make award to a lower priced offeror with a lower technical ranking notwithstanding a solicitation's emphasis on technical factors, we cannot conclude that the agency has a reasonable basis for its decision.*[47]

The record here fails to establish how the contracting officer's selection decision was consistent with the RFP's evaluation scheme, which stated that technical merit was considered more important than price. The evaluation documents show that the TEP considered D&D's proposal superior to G&O's while the contracting officer believed that D&D had submitted "a better proposal" than G&O. The contracting officer did not provide—and in responding to D&D's protest still has not provided—a cogent rationale in support of his determination that D&D's superior rating was not worth its 20 percent higher price, given the RFP's emphasis on technical factors.

The contracting officer's selection decision did not refer at all to the RFP's technical evaluation criteria. In fact, as discussed above, the decision document expressly discounted the need for technical superiority based on a perceived FAR preference for award to the "low bidder" based on the "minimal needs of the government." This perception of the FAR caused the contracting officer to focus on G&O's low cost instead of on D&D's technical superiority in reaching his award decision, contrary to the RFP's emphasis on technical merit over cost, as well as the FAR 15.612(d) requirement that award decisions be based on the factors stated in the RFP. See John Snow Public Health Group[48] (agency improperly based selection decision on preference for "Chevrolet" instead of "Cadillac" proposal when solicitation emphasized technical factors).

The decision document also did not discuss any of the differences between D&D's and G&O's proposals, or otherwise offer any support for the contracting officer's ultimate conclusion that D&D's proposal, while superior to G&O's, was not "substantially" superior such that it warranted payment of a higher price. This unsupported semantical distinction is refuted by the evaluation documents which explain why the TEP considered D&D's proposal "significantly better" than G&O's. The contracting officer did not adequately explain why he discounted the TEP's conclusion as to the significance of the technical differences, and, in particular, did not address the outstanding deficiencies in G&O's proposal. For example, the contracting officer did not address the TEP's view that G&O's managers lacked the proper experience, and that "considerable time and effort, which equates to money," would be required to complete assigned tasks. Obviously, this finding by the TEP potentially had a dual impact in the evaluation since it brought G&O's relative technical capability into question as well as raising the possibility that G&O's cost of performance ultimately may increase due to this deficiency.

In sum, the contracting officer may have converted the selection basis from the one described in the solicitation, which emphasized technical superiority, to one in which award would go to the acceptable, low priced proposal. At a minimum, the contracting officer's selection memorandum does not explain his conclusion that D&D's proposal was not so superior to G&O's as to warrant payment of a price premium. While both proposals earned an adjectival rating of acceptable, the approximately 25 percent differential between D&D's and G&O's numerical scores appears to be based on substantial differences in the quality of the two technical proposals. While there was a $21 million price difference between the two proposals, the record does not show what effect this difference would have had in a proper technical/cost tradeoff.

[And in a footnote] *FEMA's counsel argues that the difference between the two firms' technical scores was primarily due to D&D's incumbency advantage, and agencies may discount incumbency advantages in making award decisions. However, there are no references to an incumbency advantage in the decision document and evaluation documents. The record does not support the assertion that D&D's incumbency advantage was a factor in the decision.*[49]

There is an interesting sidebar to this case. After writing his decision memorandum, but before announcing the award, the contracting officer asked a supervisor of one of the TEP members to explain the wide disparity between the technical scores (the protester received 98.9 points and the awardee received 74.3 points). The supervisor said that D&D should receive award only if its superiority was "significant" and indicated that he did not consider D&D's proposal significantly superior. The contracting officer then "conceptually rescored" D&D's proposal, determined that it was a better, but not a superior, proposal, and concluded that because there was no significant technical differences between the proposals, award could be based on price alone.

If the contracting officer lacked confidence in the evaluation results, he should have consulted with the TEP members, not a third party with second-hand information. If, after such a consultation, the contracting officer still lacked confidence in the evaluation results, he could have directed a reevaluation or convened a new panel to redo the evaluation. At the very least, the contracting officer should have conducted a cost/technical tradeoff to support the award decision. Unilaterally rescoring the proposals is a last resort action that, while permissible, should be done only after all else has failed to generate a proper evaluation. Documenting his decision on the concept of "low bidder" and "minimum needs of the government" (concepts which were out of date well before this case was decided) without regard for the stated RFP requirements was a fatal error.

Dewberry & Davis was the incumbent contractor, and as FEMA's legal counsel belatedly pointed out, an incumbency advantage could have accounted for the difference in the technical scoring. If this were the case, however, the correct action would have been to convene a new panel rather than make a "conceptual rescoring" that had no support whatsoever.

Example 19.10 illustrates what should not be done when making a source selection decision. Keep in mind that unsuccessful offerors have a right to be debriefed. If you want to avoid a protest, ensure that your decisions are fully supported by the appropriate documentation.

References

1. American Management Systems, Inc.; Department of the Army—Reconsideration, B-241569.2; B-241569.3, 5/21/91.
2. Fiber-Lam, B-237716.2, 4/3/90, 90-1 CPD ¶351, GCR 104,256.
3. United States v. Hanna Nickel Smelting Co. 253 F. Supp. 784 (D. Ore. 1966); aff'd on other grounds, 400 F. 2d 944 (9th Cir. 1968).
4. E-Systems, Inc., ASBCA No. 18877, 2/23/76, 76-1 BCA 11,797.
5. NKF Eng'g; Stanley Assoc, B-232143; B-232143.2, 11/21/88, 88-2 CPD ¶497, GCR 102,578.
6. FAR 15.805-1 states that the contracting officer exercises sole responsibility for the final pricing decision. Also see PAI Inc., 67 Comp. Gen. 516 (1988), 88-2 CPD ¶36, GCR 102,115.
7. Grey Advertising, 55 CG 1111 (1976), 76-1 CPD ¶325.
8. Vinnel Corp., B-180557, 10/8/74, 74-2 CPD ¶190.
9. New Breed Leasing Corp., B-259328, 3/24/95, GCR 109,627.
10. Central Texas College, 71 Comp. Gen. 164 (1992), 92-1 CPD ¶121.
11. SDA, Inc., B-248528.2, 4/14/93, 93-1 CPD ¶320.
12. Verify, Inc., B-244401.2, 1/24/92, 92-1 CPD ¶107, GCR 106,296.
13. Contel Federal Sys., B-243624.2, 10/10/91, 91-2 CPD ¶325, GCR 105,928.
14. Wyle Laboratories, Inc.; Latecoere Int'l Inc., 69 Comp. Gen. 648 (1990), 90-2 CPD ¶107, GCR 104,608.
15. Latecoere Int'l Inc., Advisory Opinion, B-239113.3, 1/15/92, 92-1 CPD ¶70, GCR 106,260.
16. L&E Assocs., Inc., B-224448, 11/17/86, 86-2 CPD ¶568.
17. Pro-Mark, Inc., B-247248 through B-247258, 5/18/92, 92-1 CPD ¶448, GCR 106,638.

18. Bank Street College of Education 63 Comp. Gen. 393 (1984), 84-1 CPD ¶607.
19. EBA Engineering, Inc., B-275818, 3/31/97.
20. Grey Advertising, Inc., 55 Comp. Gen. 1111, 1120 (1976), 76-1 CPD ¶325 at 11; Calspan Corp., B-258441, 1/19/95, 95-1 CPD ¶28; Benchmark Sec., Inc., B-247655.2, 2/4/93, 93-1 CPD ¶133.
21. Grey Advertising, Inc., supra; Calspan Corp., supra.
22. Burnside-Ott Aviation Training Center, Inc., B-233113, 2/15/89, GCR 102,879.
23. Bank Street College of Education 63 Comp. Gen. 393 (1984), 84-1 CPD ¶607.
24. Cadillac Gage Co., B-209102, 7/15/83, 83-2 CPD ¶96.
25. Bank Street College of Education, B-213209, 6/8/84, 84-1 CPD ¶607.
26. 41 U.S.C. 251 et seq. (1976).
27. See Grey Advertising, Inc., 55 Comp. Gen. 1111 (1976), 76-1 CPD ¶325 (agency official's authority to direct and supervise all agency functions necessarily encompasses the procurement operations, including the evaluation of proposals and the award of contracts of lower echelon components).
28. Boone, Young & Assoc., Inc., B-199540.3, 11/16/1982, 82-2 CPD ¶443.
29. Grey Advertising, Inc., 55 Comp. Gen. 1111 (1976), 76-1 CPD ¶325; BDM Corp., B-211129, 8/23/83, 83-2 CPD ¶234.
30. Scheduled Airlines Traffic Offices, B-229883, 3/29/88, GCR 101,779.
31. Bank Street College of Education, 63 Comp. Gen. 394 (1984), 84-1 CPD ¶607; Grey Advertising, Inc., 55 Comp. Gen. 1111 (1976), 76-1 CPD ¶325; AFL-CIO Appalachian Council, Inc., B-216878, 4/12/85, 85-1 CPD ¶419.
32. The Goldwater-Nichols Department of Defense Reorganization Act of 1986, P.L. 99-433.
33. ITT Federal Services International Corp., B-283307; B-283307.2, 11/3/99.
34. Boeing Sikorsky Aircraft Support, B-277263; B-277263.2, 9/29/97, 97-2 CPD ¶91.
35. McDonald-Bradley, B-270126, 2/8/96, 96-1 CPD ¶54 at 3; Statistica, Inc. v. Christopher, 102 F,3d 1577, 1581 (Fed. Cir, 1996).

36. Boeing Sikorsky Aircraft Support, supra at 14.
37. Id at 15.
38. Id.
39. NWT, Inc.; PharmChem Labs Inc., B-280988; B-280988.2, 12/17/98, 98-2 CPD ¶158.
40. Id. at 16.
41. Dewberry & Davis, B-247116, 5/5/92, GCR 106,603.
42. TRW, Inc., 68 Comp. Gen. 511 (1989), 89-1 CPD ¶584.
43. Greenebaum and Rose Assocs., B-227807, 8/31/87, 87-2 CPD ¶212.
44. Dayton T. Brown, Inc., B-229664, 3/30/88, 88-1 CPD ¶321; PharmChem Laboratories, Inc., B-244385, 10/8/91, 91-2 CPD ¶317.
45. PharmChem Laboratories, Inc., supra; DynCorp, B-245289; B-245289.2, 12/23/91, 71 Comp. Gen. 129, 91-2 CPD ¶575.
46. FAR 15.612(d)(2). This reference has been replaced by FAR 15.308, with different wording, but the documentation requirements are essentially the same.
47. Hattal & Assocs., 70 Comp. Gen. 632 (1991), 91-2 CPD ¶90; PharmChem Laboratories, Inc., supra.
48. John Snow Public Health Group, Inc., 59 Comp. Gen. 498 (1980), 80-1 CPD ¶366.
49. See generally DynCorp, B-245289; B-245289.2, supra.

CHAPTER 20

Debriefing Unsuccessful Offerors

Debriefing is the last step in the evaluation/award process. Technically, debriefing is not part of the process because it usually takes place after award, but since the debriefing is primarily based on the documentation resulting from the evaluation process, it is appropriate to include it here.

The purpose of debriefing is twofold: (1) to assure offerors that their proposals were evaluated fairly, and (2) to help offerors to better understand the evaluation process in the hope that they will be able to use this information to improve proposals that they may submit in the future.

PREAWARD DEBRIEFINGS

Preaward debriefings are subject to a number of regulations.

Prompt Notification of Exclusion from the Competitive Range

Contracting officers must notify offerors promptly in writing when their proposals are excluded from the competitive range or otherwise eliminated from the competition. The notice must state the basis for the determination and that a proposal revision will not be considered. This applies to those proposals excluded when the competitive range is initially established and to any proposals later excluded by a redetermination of the competitive range during discussions.

Prompt Response

Offerors must request a preaward debriefing, in writing, within three days of receiving the notification of exclusion from the competitive range. As an alternative, offerors may request that the preaward debriefing be delayed until after award so that they may receive all the information provided in a postaward debriefing.

An offeror is entitled to only one debriefing per proposal, however, so once the offeror receives the preaward notification, it must request either a preaward debriefing or a delayed debriefing. If the offeror does not respond, the contracting officer is not required to provide a debriefing. It should be noted, however, that this is at the contracting officer's discretion. The FAR does not prohibit the granting of a late request for a debriefing, but the rule of only one debriefing does apply. It should also be noted that the government may refuse the request for preaward debriefing if, for compelling reasons, it is not in the best interests of the government to provide a prompt debriefing. In such instances, the government must provide a debriefing no later than the time it provides postaward debriefings.

Provided as Soon as Practicable

The contracting officer must provide the preaward debriefing as soon as practicable. The FAR sets no particular time for this debriefing, but generally it should be provided within a week of receipt of the offeror's debriefing request. Debriefings may be done orally, in writing, or by any other method at the discretion of the contracting officer. If done face-to-face, the contracting officer should conduct the debriefing, with the evaluators present to provide support. The contract file must include a summary of each preaward debriefing.

What Must Be Disclosed

At a minimum, the preaward debriefing must include the agency's evaluation of the significant elements in the offeror's proposal and a summary of the rationale for eliminating the offeror from the competition. The debriefers must also provide reasonable responses to relevant questions about whether the evaluation procedures were conducted properly. It should be noted that preaward debriefings provide far less information than postaward debriefings.

What Must Not Be Disclosed

Preaward debriefings must not disclose the number or identity of the other offerors, what they proposed, how they were evaluated with respect to specific evaluation factors, or how they were ranked in comparison to other offerors. These prohibitions are necessary because the competition is still ongoing. Also, when addressing the rationale for the proposal's elimination from the competitive range, debriefers cannot disclose the names of individuals providing reference information about an offeror's past performance.

POSTAWARD DEBRIEFINGS

Postaward debriefings are also subject to a number of requirements.

Prompt Notification of Award

Within three days after contract award, the contracting officer must notify all unsuccessful offerors (except those who had received a preaward notification) that award has been made. This notification must include the following:

- The number of offerors solicited and the number of proposals received
- The name and address of each offeror receiving an award
- The items, quantities, and any stated unit prices of each award (unless the number of items would make this impractical, then only the total contract price need be furnished)
- In general terms, the reasons why the offeror's proposal was not accepted.

The contracting officer may also provide this information to offerors who had received a preaward notification of exclusion and had requested a delayed debriefing.

Prompt Response

Offerors must request a postaward debriefing, in writing, within three days of receiving the award notification. An offeror who fails to submit a timely postaward debriefing request is not entitled to a debriefing. Untimely requests, however, may be accommodated at the contracting officer's discretion. It should be noted, however, that the granting of an untimely request or the provision of a delayed debriefing does not affect the timeliness of any protest filed subsequent to the debriefing.

Provided as Soon as Practicable

To the maximum extent practicable, the contracting officer should provide the postaward debriefing within five days of receiving an offeror's written request for a debriefing. This time period also applies to those offerors who requested a postaward debriefing in lieu of a preaward debriefing and those offerors whose preaward debriefing was delayed for government purposes. Debriefings may be conducted orally, in writing, or by any other method at the discretion of the contracting officer. If conducted face-to-face, the contracting officer should conduct the debriefing, with the evaluators present to provide support. The contract file must contain a summary of each postaward debriefing.

What Must Be Disclosed

Generally, postaward debriefings are limited to a discussion of each offeror's own proposal. The debriefing is based primarily on the documentation developed during the evaluation process, such as the written technical narratives that discuss the weaknesses and deficiencies in each proposal and revisions made as a result of discussions. FAR 15.506(d) requires that the postaward debriefing include the following information:

- The agency's evaluation of the significant weaknesses or deficiencies in the offeror's proposal
- The overall evaluated cost or price (including unit prices) and technical rating of the awardee and the offeror being debriefed
- The overall rankings of all offerors
- A summary of the rationale for award
- In the case of commercial items, the make and model of the item being provided by the successful offeror
- Reasonable responses to relevant questions about whether the source selection procedures contained in the solicitation, applicable regulations, and other applicable authorities were followed.

What you can or cannot tell offerors in debriefings also depends on each agency's own published guidance; generally, however, if the information can be released under the Freedom Of Information Act, it can be discussed in a debriefing. With respect to the offeror being debriefed, debriefing information could include the color/adjectival ratings, proposal risk assessment, performance risk assessment, the calculations related to cost realism adjustments and cost/technical tradeoffs, the offeror's past performance information (but not the names of individuals providing the information), and problems with the proposal format and contents, if any of these were a factor in the evaluation results.

What Must Not Be Disclosed

Do not conduct the debriefing on the basis of comparisons between the proposal being debriefed and other proposals. Except for the general details noted above, debriefers should limit the debriefing to the particular offeror's proposal. FAR 15.506(e) states that there are certain things you cannot tell the offeror being debriefed, such as information protected by the Privacy Act or exempt from release under the Freedom of Information Act, including other offeror's trade secrets, privileged or confidential manufacturing processes and techniques, and commercial and financial information that is privileged or confidential including cost breakdowns, profit, indirect cost rates, and similar information (this includes those of the successful offeror). And, as noted earlier, the FAR prohibits the release of the names of individuals providing reference information about an offeror's past performance.

In addition to the above, the debriefing should not include the following information:

- Any information on other offerors, other than their overall ranking. In particular, do not make point-by-point comparisons of the debriefed offeror's proposal with any other proposals, including the awardee's proposal.
- Government competition or negotiation-sensitive information (such as cost estimates) if this information might adversely affect other ongoing procurements.
- Evaluation and analysis worksheets or the identity of individual evaluators or advisors who filled them out.
- Information that is not relevant. Relevant information is information that tends to explain the rationale for the decision as related to the proposal of the offeror being debriefed. Information that does not support the decision with respect to the unsuccessful proposal should not be released.
- Classified information, unless offeror has the appropriate clearance.

As with the rest of the evaluation process, each debriefing should be documented. The documentation should indicate the information provided, the questions asked, and the responses provided. Information provided at debriefings is often used as the basis for protests; it is important, therefore, that you have contemporaneous documentation of what was discussed.

APPENDIX

Listing of Examples

CHAPTER 1—DEVELOPING AN EVALUATION PLAN

1.1 Internal agency instructions do not give rights to outside parties
Lear Siegler Services, Inc., B-280834; B-280834.2, 11/25/98, GCR 110,471.

1.2 Using a combination assessment
Lithos Restoration, Ltd., B-247003, 4/22/92, 92-1 CPD ¶379, GCR 106,564.

1.3 Ensure that evaluation procedures used are consistent with published procedures
Trijicon Inc., B-244546, 10/25/91, 71 Comp. Gen. 41 (1991), 91-2 CPD ¶375, GCR 105,981.

1.4 Evaluation scheme published in RFP takes precedence over internal agency evaluation plan
Technical Support Services, Inc., B-279665, B-279665.2, 7/8/98, GCR 110,370.

1.5 You must show the relative importance of evaluation factors, but not all of the details
Ebasco Constructors, Inc., et al., B-244406 et al., 10/16/91, 91-2 CPD 341, GCR 105,940.

CHAPTER 2—ESTABLISHING EVALUATION FACTORS

2.1 Evaluate only what you identify as an evaluation factor in the RFP
Envirosol, Inc., B-254223, 12/2/93, GCR 107,960.

2.2 Include all significant subfactors in the RFP
Devres Inc., B-224017; 12/8/86; 86-2 CPD 652, GCR 100,119.

2.3 Unstated subfactors clearly related to primary factor need not be revealed
Management Systems Designers, Inc.; Information Technology & Applications Corporation; Epoch Engineering Inc., B-244383.4; B-244383.5; B-244383.6, 12/6/91, GCR 106,116.

2.4 Government is not required to reveal its staffing estimate in RFP
Aerostat Services Partnership, B-244939.2, 1/15/92, 92-1 CPD 71, GCR 106,261.

2.5 Explain in the RFP what you mean by corporate experience
Keeson, Inc.; Ingram Demolition Inc., B-245625; B-245655, 1/24/92, 92-1 CPD 108, GCR 106,297.

2.6 Definition of corporate experience particularly important for evaluating small or new firms
General Offshore Corp., B-246824, 4/1/92, 92-1 CPD 335, GCR 106,523.

CHAPTER 3—USING PAST PERFORMANCE AS AN EVALUATION FACTOR

No Examples

CHAPTER 4—OTHER CONSIDERATIONS IN SELECTING EVALUATION FACTORS

4.1 Use cost/price realism analysis on a fixed-price proposal only when necessary as a measure of the offeror's understanding of the requirement
RMS Information Systems Inc., B-280521.3, 10/21/98, GCR 110,447.

4.2 Government may allow bidder time to cure responsibility problems #1
New Life Group, Inc., B-247080.2, 5/22/92, 92-1 CPD 463, GCR 106,650

4.3 Government may allow bidder time to cure responsibility problems #2
Base-Operation-Management-Service Inc., B-218223, 2/26/85, 85-1 CPD ¶242.

4.4 Findings of nonresponsibility must be reviewed by the SBA
F&H Manufacturing Corp., B-244997, 12/6/91, 91-2 CPD ¶520, GCR 106,118.

4.5 Responsibility factors evaluated on a pass/fail basis rather than by comparative assessment are subject to SBA review
Modern Sanitation Systems, Corp., B-245469, 1/2/92, 92-1 CPD ¶9, GCR 106,205.

4.6 Offer flexibility when listing experience or educational requirements
Dynamic Isolation Systems, Inc., B-247047, 4/28/92, 92-1 CPD ¶399, GCR 106,587.

4.7 Offeror must propose key personnel who can reasonably be expected to perform the work
CBIS Federal Inc., B-245844.2, 3/27/92, 92-1 CPD ¶308, GCR 106,495.

4.8 Proposal risk can be evaluated even if not stated as an evaluation factor #1
Quantum Research, Inc., B-242020, 3/21/91, GCR 105,316.

4.9 Proposal risk can be evaluated even if not stated as an evaluation factor #2
Herley Industries, Inc., B-251792.2, 4/16/93, GCR 107,508.

4.10 Security clearance requirements may be an evaluation factor
G.S. Link and Assoc., B-229604; B-229606, 1/25/88, GCR 101,535.

CHAPTER 5—EXPRESSING THE RELATIVE IMPORTANCE OF EVALUATION FACTORS

5.1 Expressing the relative importance of technical evaluation factors
BDM Services Co., B-180245, 5/9/74, 74-1 CPD 237.

5.2 Protester's disagreement with agency does not establish that evaluation was unreasonable
Battelle Memorial Institute, B-278673, 2/27/98, GCR 110,270.

5.3 If the relative importance of the cost/price factor is not stated, it is equal to the technical factors
Logicon RDA, B-252031.4, 9/20/93, GCR 107,854.

5.4 Application of cost/technical formula where technical is 70 percent and cost is 30 percent

5.5 Application of cost/technical formula where technical is 60 percent and cost is 40 percent

5.6 Application of the cost/technical formula where prices are generally in line with one another

CHAPTER 6—SCORING PLANS

6.1 Deviations from internal agency instructions, such as a scoring plan, do not provide a basis for protests
Ralph G. Moore & Assocs., B-270686; B-270686.2, 2/28/96, GCR 109,398.

6.2 Evaluators must use a common scoring plan
____

6.3 Scoring plans are only guides #1
RCA Service Co., B-208871, 8/22/83, 83-2 CPD 221.

6.4 Scoring plans are only guides #2
Century Environmental Hygiene Inc., B-279378, 6/5/98, GCR 110,325.

6.5 Any sensible scoring plan is acceptable #1
Peterson Builders, Inc., B-244614, 11/1/91, 91-2 CPD ¶419, GCR 106,022.

6.6 Any sensible scoring plan is acceptable #2
Cardinal Scientific Inc., B-270309, 2/12/96, GCR 109,388.

6.7 Never use predetermined cutoff scores
Moxon, Inc./SRC Division, B-179160, 3/13/74, 74-1 CPD ¶134.

6.8 Objectively assess the applicability of evaluation software before using it
The Jonathan Corp.; Metro Machine Corp., B-251698.3; B-251698.4, 5/17/93, GCR 107,849.

6.9 Proposal risk is an inherent evaluation factor #1
Communications International, Inc., B-246076, 2/18/92, 92-1 CPD ¶194, GCR 106,383.

6.10 Proposal risk is an inherent evaluation factor #2
Herley Industries, Inc., B-251792.2, 4/16/93, GCR 107,508.

6.11 Agencies need not disclose price scoring formulas
Heimann Systems Inc., B-272182, 9/9/96, GCR 109,652.

CHAPTER 7—PROPOSAL PREPARATION INSTRUCTIONS

7.1 Offerors must adhere to page and format limitations
Infotec Development, Inc., B-238980, 7/20/90, 90-2 CPD ¶58, 104,561.

CHAPTER 8—REVIEWING WHAT HAS BEEN DONE

8.1 Evaluation results must be fully documented
Biospheres Inc., B-278508.4; B-278508.5; B-278508.6, 10/6/98, GCR 110,428.

8.2 Offerors must be provided with a common basis for the submission and evaluation of proposals
Pasco Realty, B-245705, 1/8/92, 92-1 CPD ¶39, GCR 106,229.

8.3 Select and word evaluation factors carefully
H.J. Group Ventures, Inc., B-246139, 2/19/92, 92-1 CPD ¶203, GCR 106,410.

8.4 Conflicts between the SOW, evaluation criteria, and RFP provisions may lead to protests
Glen Industrial Communications, Inc., B-248223, 5/19/92, 92-1 CPD ¶453, GCR 106,641.

CHAPTER 9—ORAL PRESENTATIONS

9.1 Do not get carried away with the use of oral presentations
Kalpath Technologies; Computer & Hi-Tech Mgt., Inc., B-283137.3; B-283137.4; B-283137.5; B-283137,6, 12/30/99.

CHAPTER 10—PREPARING FOR THE EVALUATION

10.1 Presumptions—past experience
Dynamic Isolation Systems, Inc., B-247047, 4/28/92, 92-1 CPD ¶399, GCR 106,587.

10.2 Presumptions—incumbency #1
All Star Maintenance, Inc., B-244143, 9/26/91, 91-2 CPD ¶294, CCH 105,882, f 5.

10.3 Presumptions—incumbency #2
National Credit Union Admin.; Schreiner, Legge & Co.— Recon., B-244680.2; B-244680.3, 4/1/92, 92-1 CPD ¶329, GCR 106,517.

10.4 Presumptions—lack of detail
InterAmerican Research Associates, Inc., B-253698.2, 11/19/93, GCR 107,943.

10.5 Offerors are responsible for submitting adequate proposals
Sunbelt Properties, Inc., B-245729.3, 3/12/92, 92-1 CPD ¶278, GCR 106,466.

10.6 Comptroller General bases decisions on the evaluation documentation
Dynamic Isolation Systems, Inc., B-247047, 4/28/92, 92-1 CPD ¶399, GCR 106,587.

10.7 Evaluation documentation must be complete #1
Son's Quality Food Co., B-244528.2, 11/4/91, 91-2 CPD ¶424, GCR 106,028.

10.8 Evaluation documentation must be complete #2
DNL Properties, Inc.; Crawford/Edgewood Managers, Inc.; Pearl Properties, B-253614.2; B-253614.3; B-253614.5; B-253734, 10/12/93, GCR 107,953.

10.9 Evaluation results cannot be supported without contemporaneous documentation or other explanation
U.S. Defense Systems Inc., B-245563, 1/17/92, GCR 110,280.

10.10 Agency explanations can overcome a lack of contemporaneous evaluation documentation
Bannum, Inc., B-271075; B-271076; B-271117, 5/22/96, GCR 109,497

CHAPTER 11—CONDUCTING THE INITIAL EVALUATION

11.1 Cost or price must be evaluated
SCIENTECH, Inc., B-277805.2, 1/20/98, GCR 110,190.

11.2 Proposal strong points can be used to determine the competitive range
Curry Construction Co., Inc., B-254355, 12/13/93, GCR 107,991.

11.3 You must document your cost realism analysis
Spectrum Sciences & Software, Inc., B-243792, 8/14/91, 91-2 CPD ¶147, GCR 105,761.

11.4 Do not substitute a mechanical formula or standard adjustment for an independent analysis
Bendix Field Engineering Corp., B-246236, 2/25/92, 92-1 CPD ¶227, GCR 106,416.

11.5 Normalization pitfalls—Adjustments to account for the use of uncompensated overtime
General Research Corp., B-241569, 2/19/91, GCR 105,198.

11.6 Normalization pitfalls—Adjustments to labor rates
Health Services Int'l, Inc.; Apex Environmental, Inc., B-247433, 6/5/92, 92-1 CPD ¶493, GCR 106,679.

11.7 Normalization pitfalls—Faulty calculations
Health Services Int'l, Inc.; Apex Environmental, Inc., B-247433, 6/5/92, 92-1 CPD ¶493, GCR 106,679.

11.8 Normalization pitfalls—Adjustments to labor escalation costs
General Research Corp., Inc., B-241569, 2/19/91, GCR 105,198.

11.9 Normalization pitfalls—Adjustments to labor union costs
Bendix Field Engineering Corp., B-246236, 2/25/92, 92-1 CPD ¶27, GCR 106,416.

11.10 Normalization pitfalls—Adjustments to travel costs
Bendix Field Engineering Corp., B-246236, 2/25/92, 92-1 CPD ¶27, GCR 106,416.

11.11 Normalization pitfalls—Adjustments to proposed fees
Bendix Field Engineering Corp., B-246236, 2/25/92, 92-1 CPD ¶27, GCR 106,416.

11.12 Word discussion questions to elicit clear, specific answers
ITT Electron Technology Division, B-242289, 4/18/91, GCR 105,388.

11.13 Reaching evaluation consensus
The Cadmus Group Inc., B-241372.3, 9/25/91, 91-2 CPD ¶271, GCR 105,879.

CHAPTER 12—EVALUATING PAST PERFORMANCE

12.1 If an offeror fails to respond to questions about past problems, you may assume the problems have not been corrected
Smith of Galeton Gloves, Inc., B-271686, 7/24/96, GCR 109,568.

12.2 Filing of contract claims is not poor performance
Amclyde Engineered Products Co., Inc., B-282271; B-282271.2, 6/21/99, 99-2 CPD ¶5, n.5.

12.3 Using past performance to evaluate new firms—making price/past performance tradeoffs
National Aerospace Group Inc., B-281958, 5/10/99.

12.4 When should one company's past performance be attributed to another?
Universal Building Maintenance, Inc., B-282456, 7/15/99.

12.5 Evaluating the past performance of subcontractors
Battelle Memorial Institute, B-278673, 2/27/98.

12.6 Must all past performance references be checked?
Universal Building Maintenance, Inc., B-282456, 7/15/99, fn 2.

12.7 What happens when past performance questionnaires are not returned?
Advanced Data Concepts, Inc., B-277801.4, 6/1/98, GCR 110,318.

12.8 You must consider past performance information "close at hand"
TRW, Inc., B-282162; B-282162.2, 6/9/99.

12.9 Price/past performance tradeoff and the use of information "close at hand"
International Bus. Sys., Inc., B-275554, 3/3/97, 97-1 CPD ¶114 at 5, GCR 109,877.

12.10 Evaluator's personal knowledge may be used
Omega World Travel, Inc., B-271262.2, 7/25/96, GCR 109,579.

12.11 An agency's perception of poor past performance prevails when supported by sufficient evidence
Quality Fabricators, Inc., B-271431; B-271431.3, 6/25/96, GCR 109,553.

12.12 Offeror must successfully rebut adverse past performance information
Dragon Services, Inc., B-255354, 2/25/94, 94-1 CPD ¶151, GCR 108,099.

CHAPTER 13—OTHER PROBLEMS IN EVALUATION

13.1 Offeror is responsible for submitting an adequate proposal
Quality Elevator Co., Inc., B-271899, 8/28/96,GCR 109,622.

13.2 Evaluations are restricted to what is in proposal itself
Corion Corp., B-265602; B-265602.2, 12/15/95, GCR 109,267.

13.3 Offeror must provide all required information
Air-Flo Cleaning Systems, B-259562.2, 1/18/96, GCR 109,293.

13.4 Offeror must question obviously inconsistent solicitation provisions before time set for the receipt of proposals
Christie Constructors, Inc., B-271759; B-271759.2, 7/23/96, GCR 109,628.

13.5 Government not required to search out formation omitted from proposal
EBA Ernest Bland Assocs., B-270496, 3/13/96, GCR 109,415.

13.6 Watch for offeror who simply parrots back the wording of SOW
Bannum, Inc., B-271076; B-271117, 5/22/96, GCR 109,497.

13.7 Government must follow RFP's evaluation criteria
American Lawn Service, Inc., B-267715, 12/20/95, GCR 109,276.

13.8 Failure to follow internal agency instruction does not provide a basis for protest
Allied Signal, Inc., B-272990; B-272990.2, 9/19/96, GCR 109,653.

13.9 Agency may not relax RFP requirement for one offeror and not provide other offerors the same opportunity
CNA Industrial Engineering, Inc., B-271034, 6/7/96, GCR 109,530.

13.10 Government estimates must be reasonably accurate
K. Comstock, Inc., and Liebert Federal Systems Inc., B-261711.6, 12/14/95, GCR 109,282.

13.11 Unusual evaluation schemes may adversely affect a newly formed company
Management Plus, Inc., B-265852, 12/29/95, GCR 109,287.

13.12 Evaluators may use their own personal experience when evaluating corporate experience
Safeguard Maintenance Co., B-260983.3, 10/13/95, GCR 109,638.

13.13 RFP must state the relative importance of cost/price with respect to the technical evaluation factors
Ogden Support Services, Inc., B-270012.2, 3/19/96, fn. 2, GCR 109,436.

13.14 Definition of bait and switch tactics
TDS, Inc., B-261827.3, 2/1/96, GCR 109,408.

13.15 What happens if an agency does not rely on a bait and switch tactic?
Apache Enterprises, Inc., B-278855.2, 7/30/98, GCR 110,387.

13.16 A change in named personnel does not always mean that a bait and switch has occurred
Professional Safety Consultants Co., Inc., B-247331, 4/29/92, GCR 106,589.

13.17 Misrepresentation of the availability of key personnel can result in proposal rejection or contract termination
Aerospace Design & Fabrication, Inc., B-278896.2; B-278896.3; B-278896.4; B-278896.5, 5/4/98, GCR 110,299.

13.18 Offeror must propose qualified personnel
United International Investigative Services, B-265650, 12/18/95, GCR 109,268.

13.19 Offeror must present sufficient detail to demonstrate the experience of proposed key personnel
Engineering Sys. Consult., Inc., B-271619, 7/15/96, GCR 109,556.

13.20 Government determines the minimum qualifications of key personnel
Systems Applications & Technologies, Inc., B-270672, 4/8/96, GCR 109,439.

13.21 Evaluating differing staff approaches and associated proposal risk
Proteus Corporation; United International Engineering, Inc., B-270094; B-270094.2, 2/8/96, GCR 109,425.

13.22 Evaluation results must be reasonable
Safeguard Maintenance Co., B-260983.3, 10/13/95, GCR 109,638.

13.23 Comparative assessment of complexity cannot be superficial
PMT Services, Inc., B-270538.2, 4/1/96, GCR 109,639.

13.24 Incumbency does not necessarily provide an unfair competitive advantage
Optimum Technology, Inc., B-266339.2, 4/16/96, GCR 109,443.

13.25 Rejecting an offeror for improprieties
IGIT, Inc., B-271823, 8/1/96, GCR 109,591.

CHAPTER 14—MAKING AWARD WITHOUT DISCUSSIONS

14.1 If there is nothing to discuss, award without discussions
Southwest Marine, Inc.; American Systems Engineering Corp., B-265865 .3; B-265865.4, 1/23/96, GCR 109,335.

14.2 If there is something to discuss, hold discussions
Wetlands Research Assoc., Inc., B-246342, 3/2/92, 92-1 CPD ¶251, GCR 106,437.

14.3 The right to award without discussions is not absolute
The Jonathan Corp.; Metro Machine Corp., B-251698.3; B-251698.4, 5/17/93, GCR 107,849.

14.4 Clarifying and correcting clerical errors is permitted prior to an award without discussions
Tony's Landscaping, Inc., B-283794, 11/23/99.

14.5 If award is to be made without discussions, an agency is not required to communicate with an offeror who failed to provide adequate past performance information
U.S. Constructors, Inc., B-282776, 7/21/99.

14.6 If award is to be made without discussions, an agency is not required to permit an offeror to rebut adverse past performance information
A.G. Cullen Construction, Inc., B-284049.2, 2/22/00.

CHAPTER 15—ESTABLISHING THE COMPETITIVE RANGE

15.1 Decisions are based on the supporting documentation, not the scores or ratings
Century Environmental Hygiene Inc., B-279378, 6/5/98, GCR 110,325.

15.2 Reject proposals requiring major revisions
Engineering Sys. Consult. Inc., B-271619, 7/15/96, GCR 109,556.

15.3 Reject otherwise acceptable proposals that have no chance of award when compared to other higher rated proposals #1
HSQ Technology, B-279707, 7/9/98, GCR 110,349.

15.4 Reject otherwise acceptable proposals that have no chance of award when compared to other higher rated proposals #2
Matrix General, Inc., B-282192, 6/10/99.

15.5 A competitive range of one is OK if no other proposal has a reasonable chance for award
SDS Petroleum Products, Inc., B-280430, 9/1/98, 98-2 CPD ¶59, GCR 110,405.

15.6 Offeror is responsible for submitting an adequate proposal
Dynamic Marketing Services, Inc., B-279697, 7/13/98, GCR 110,418.

15.7 Competitive range may be redetermined during discussions
Applied Companies, B-279811, 7/24/98, GCR 110,388.

15.8 Cost or price must be considered #1
SCIENTECH, Inc., B-277805.2, 1/20/98, 98-1 CPD ¶33.

15.9 Cost or price must be considered #2
S.J. Thomas Co., Inc., B-283192, 10/20/99.

CHAPTER 16—CONDUCTING NEGOTIATIONS

16.1 Can the government conduct multiple rounds of discussions with, and receive multiple revised proposals from, one offeror but not the others?
Miller-Holzwarth Inc. Vs United States No.98-576C (Fed. Cl. Jan 6, 1999).

16.2 Technical leveling
Dynacs Engineering Co. Inc., B-284234; B-284234.2; B-284234.3, 3/17/00.

16.3 Multiple discussions do not necessarily translate to technical leveling
TELOS Corporation, B-279493.3, 7/27/98, GCR 110,365.

16.4 Need only identify significant weaknesses
Technical & Administrative Services Corp., B279828, 7/24/98, GCR 110,423.

16.5 Agency not required to "spoon feed" an offeror as to each and every item that could be revised so as to improve its proposal
Du & Assocs., Inc., B-280283.3, 12/22/98, 98-2 CPD ¶156 at 7.

16.6 Discussions are not meaningful unless they lead the offeror to those problems that must be addressed for it to have a reasonable chance for award
ACS Government Solutions Group Inc., B-282098; B-282098.2, B-282098.3, 6/2/99.

16.7 Discussions, prior to the request for final proposal revisions—need not be equal
I.T.S. Corp., B-280431, 9/29/98.

16.8 Discussions where there are no weaknesses or deficiencies
KBM Group Inc., B-281919; B-281919.2, 5/3/99.

16.9 Discussions must not be misleading
Metro Machine Corp., B-281872; B-281872.2; B-281872.3; B-281872.4, 4/22/99.

16.10 Meaningful discussions must be related to offeror's own proposal deficiencies
Research for Better Schools, B-270774.3, 6/17/96, GCR 109,576.

16.11 Pricing discussions
Blue Cross Blue Shield of Texas, Inc., B-261316.4, 11/9/95, 95-2 CPD ¶248 at 6-7, GCR 110,445, fn8.

16.12 Agency must clearly indicate that simplified acquisition procedures are being used #1
Dubrinsky Vs. U.S. Fed. Cl. No. 98-884C, 3/31/99.

16.13 Agency must clearly indicate that simplified acquisition procedures are being used #2
United Marine International LLC, B-281512, 2/22/99.

16.14 Must evaluate in accordance with the terms of the solicitation
Universal Building Maintenance, Inc., B-282456, 7/15/99.

CHAPTER 17—CONDUCTING THE FINAL EVALUATION

17.1 Use of all original evaluators is not required in the final evaluation
Logistical Systems Inc., B-196254, 6/24/80, 80-1 CPD ¶442.

17.2 Deviations from RFP requirements cannot be accepted unless the RFP is amended to permit the other offerors the same opportunity
IRT Corp., B-246991, 4/22/92, 92-1 CPD ¶378, GCR 106,563.

17.3 Offerors must take responsibility for changes made in final proposal revisions
Federal Business Systems, Inc., B-246514, 3/13/92, 92-1 CPD ¶283, GCR 106,470.

17.4 Discussions may be reopened to correct agency mistakes or to otherwise ensure that the discussions are equitable
Dube Travel Agency & Tours Inc.; Garber Travel, B-270438; B-270438.2, 3/6/96, GCR 109,402.

17.5 Reopening discussions to take corrective action while a protest is pending is permissible
Patriot Contract Servs., LLC.; Keystone Shipping Servs, Inc.; MTL Ship Management; V-Ships Marine Ltd., B-278276.11; B-278276.12; B-278276.13; B-278276.14, 9/22/98, GCR 110,408.

17.6 Pricing changes: Unsupported personnel changes
Purvis Systems Inc., B-245761; B-245761.2, 1/31/92, 92-1 CPD ¶132, GCR 106,328.

17.7 Pricing changes: Unsupported reduction of overhead
Purvis Systems Inc., B-245761; B-245761.2, 1/31/92, 92-1 CPD ¶132, GCR 106,328.

17.8 Pricing changes: Unsupported site rates and escalation rates
Purvis Systems Inc., B-245761; B-245761.2, 1/31/92, 92-1 CPD ¶132, GCR 106,328.

17.9 Documenting the final evaluation for a source selection decision
Biospherics Inc., B-278508.4; B-278508.5; B-278508.6, 10/6/98, GCR 110,428.

17.10 How to fix a broken evaluation
CSR Inc., B-205776, 9/20/82, 82-2 CPD ¶237.

CHAPTER 18—BEST VALUE PROCUREMENTS AND COST/TECHNICAL TRADEOFFS

18.1 Awarding on the basis of quality, rather than just low price
Grey Advertising, Inc., B-184825, 5/14/76, 76-1 CPD ¶325.

18.2 Cost/technical tradeoffs
Kenneth L. Latham, B-245137, 12/18/91, 91-2 CPD ¶559, GCR 106,160.

18.3 Tradeoffs are based on the evaluated costs, not the proposed costs
Resource Consultants, Inc., B-245312.2, 3/23/92, 92-1 CPD ¶301, GCR 106,488, Fn 1.

18.4 Tradeoff documentation must support the selection decision
Kenneth L. Latham, B-245137, 12/18/91, 91-2 CPD ¶559, GCR 106,160.

18.5 Source selection decision must be fully documented
Dewberry & Davis, B-247116, 5/5/92, 92-1 CPD ¶421, GCR 106,603.

18.6 Cost per technical point/best value
S-V Company, A Joint Venture, B-248566; B-248566.3, 9/27/92, 92-2 CPD ¶131, GCR 106,865.

CHAPTER 19—MAKING THE SOURCE SELECTION DECISION

19.1 Source selection authority is ultimately responsible for making correct decision
American Management Systems, Inc; Department of the Army—Reconsideration, B-241569.2; B-241569.3, 5/21/91.

19.2 Source selection decision is not proper when based on a flawed evaluation
New Breed Leasing Corp., B-259328, 3/24/95, GCR 109,627.

19.3 The source selection official is not bound by evaluator's recommendations #1
Verify, Inc., B-244401.2, 1/24/92, 92-1 CPD ¶107, GCR 106,296.

19.4 The source selection authority is not bound by evaluator's recommendations #2
Pro-Mark, Inc., B-247248 through B-247258, 5/18/92, 92-1 CPD ¶448, GCR 106,638.

19.5 The source selection official is not bound by evaluator's recommendations #3
EBA Engineering, Inc., B-275818, 3/31/97.

19.6 The Source selection authority makes the final decision
Burnside-Ott Aviation Training Center, Inc., B-233113, 2/15/89, GCR 102,879.

19.7 The source selection authority makes the final decision, unless overruled by higher authority
Bank Street College of Education, B-213209, 6/8/84, 84-1 CPD ¶607.

19.8 In government, hierarchy rules
Scheduled Airlines Traffic Offices, B-229883, 3/29/88, GCR 101,779

19.9 Contemporaneous documentation is accorded greater weight
ITT Federal Services International Corp., B-283307; B-283307.2, 11/3/99

19.10 How not to make a source selection decision
Dewberry & Davis, B-247116, 5/5/92, GCR 106,603

CHAPTER 20—DEBRIEFING UNSUCCESSFUL OFFERORS

No Examples